THE DAIRY BOOK OF HOME COOKERY

By Sonia Allison

Published by Wolfe Publishing Ltd.
10 Earlham Street, London WC2
for the Dairy Industry.

The author would like to
thank the following for
their co-operation in
supplying accessories
for use in the photographs:

LIBERTY & CO. LTD.,
SELFRIDGES LTD.,
THE WORCESTER ROYAL PORCELAIN CO. LTD.,
J. & A. ØSTMO.,
HARVEY NICHOLS & CO. LTD.,
HEAL & SON LTD.,
HABITAT DESIGNS LTD.,
ENGLISH ELECTRIC CO. LTD.,
THE CRAFTS CENTRE OF GREAT BRITAIN

Photography by ROBERT GIBB

Filmset by Photoset Ltd., London

Contents

INTRODUCTION   Page 4
  Milk   4
  Cream   4
  Yogurt   5
  Soured (or Cultured) Cream   5
  Butter   5
  Cheese   6
  Oven Temperatures   7
  Weights & Measures   7
  General Food Care   7
  Herbs & Spices   9
MILK & YOUR DIET   10
APPETISERS   11
  Dips & Dunks   14
SOUPS & SOUP GARNISHES   18
STUFFINGS   25
PASTRY   28
SAUCES   31
  Savoury Sauces   31
  Savoury Butter Sauces   38
  Barbecue Sauces   39
  Sweet Sauces   39
MARINADES & SAVOURY
                 BUTTERS   43
  Marinades   43
  Savoury Butters   44
HORS-D'ŒUVRES   46
FISH   53
SHELLFISH   61
  Crabs   61
  Lobsters   61
  Scallops   62
  Mussels   62
  Oysters   63
  Scampi & Prawns   64
LAMB   65
BEEF   69
PORK   74
VEAL   79
OFFAL   82
CHICKEN   86
DUCKLING & GOOSE   90
TURKEY   93

GAME   96
VEGETABLES   101
SALADS   114
  Side Salads   115
  Main Course Salads   118
SALAD DRESSINGS   122
MERINGUES   128
BATTERS   131
  Sweet Pancakes   131
  Savoury Pancakes   133
  Savoury Batter Puddings   136
  Sweet Batter Puddings   136
  Coating & Fritter Batters   137
SCONE MIXTURES   139
BISCUITS   143
LARGE & SMALL CAKES   149
FILLINGS & FROSTINGS   161
YEAST RECIPES   165
COLD PUDDINGS   172
HOT PUDDINGS   185
FROZEN DESSERTS   196
DISHES FROM ABROAD   203
SANDWICHES & SANDWICH
                 FILLINGS   208
  Basic Sandwiches   208
  Danish-Style Open Sandwiches   212
  Toasted Sandwiches   214
  Club Sandwiches   215
LUNCH & SUPPER DISHES   216
VEGETARIAN DISHES   221
CONFECTIONERY   225
HOT & COLD DRINKS   229
  Cold Drinks   229
  Hot Drinks   233
PRESERVES   236
SOUFFLÉS   239
  Cold Sweet Soufflés   239
  Hot Sweet Soufflés   241
  Hot Savoury Soufflés   242
OMELETTES   243
  Savoury Omelettes   243
  Sweet Omelettes   246
INDEX   247

Introduction

MILK

Milk is one of today's finest bargain buys. Its versatility enables it to be taken in so many attractive forms that it can appeal to everyone, whatever age, sex or condition. For expectant and nursing mothers, infants and children, milk is essential for nourishment and sound growth. It provides teenagers with vital energy and aids healthy mental and physical development. Adults find it revitalising and refreshing. For invalids and the aged, milk is easily digested and a convenient way of taking nourishment.

Milk tempts, pleases and satisfies. To drink, cook and bake with it is a good habit for better living.

GRADES OF MILK

All milk produced in Britain today is tuberculin-tested.

UNTREATED

This is raw milk which has not undergone any form of heat treatment.

UNTREATED FARM BOTTLED

This is raw milk which must be bottled at the farm where it is produced. It may be from any breed of cow, provided the stock conditions on the farm comply with Government regulations and the producer holds a licence to use the special designation 'Untreated'.

PASTEURISED

This is milk which has been subjected to heat treatment which destroys harmful bacteria and prolongs its keeping qualities.

HOMOGENISED

This is pasteurised milk, processed to break up the globules of butterfat evenly throughout the milk.

STERILISED

This is homogenised milk which has been heat treated in the bottle and vacuum-sealed. This extends the keeping quality of the milk. Unopened, it will keep fresh for at least a week.

ULTRA HEAT TREATED (UHT)

This long-keeping milk is homogenised milk which is raised to an ultra-high temperature. This milk will keep for several months.

CHANNEL ISLANDS AND SOUTH DEVON

Milk from Jersey, Guernsey and South Devon breeds of cow — with a minimum butterfat content of 4%.

LEGAL STANDARDS

Ordinary milk must have a minimum of 3% butterfat and 8.5% solids not fat. Milk sold as Channel Islands, Jersey, Guernsey or South Devon must contain not less than 4% butterfat.

CARE OF MILK

Ask the milkman to leave it in a shady place away from direct sunlight and avoid leaving it on the doorstep for too long.

If you find the birds are helping themselves, invest in some discs which fit over the bottle tops. When you bring milk indoors, either put it straight into the refrigerator or stand it in a basin or bowl of water, covering it with a clean cloth with its corners dipping into the water. Evaporation of the water keeps the milk cool and fresh.

Never mix new milk with old. And never pour milk into anything but a spotlessly-clean container.

BOILING MILK

If milk must be boiled, then do it quickly, stirring all the time, and cool it immediately. Prolonged heating of milk will not only affect it nutritionally, but will also cause the lactose (milk sugar) to caramelise, giving the milk a cooked flavour. As milk boils over with surprising rapidity, never leave a saucepan of heating milk unwatched.

CREAM

Cream is a delicious food which can be used in a wide variety of sweet and savoury dishes. It is easily digested and contains not only butterfat but also protein, milk sugar, minerals and vitamins. Cream is exceptionally rich in energy-giving calories.

TYPES OF CREAM

DOUBLE

This must, by law, have a butterfat content of not less than 48%. If desired, double cream can be whipped. When whipping, add one tablespoon milk. This lowers the butterfat content and minimises any risk of overwhipping.

SINGLE

This must, by law, have a minimum butterfat content of not less than 18%. It is generally used as pouring or coffee cream and will not whip.

CLOTTED

This usually contains 50% to 60% butterfat, although the legal minimum requirement is 48%.

LONG-KEEPING

This type of cream is heat treated and has a keeping quality longer than that of fresh cream but shorter than that of sterilised cream. Single cream, double cream and clotted cream may all be treated in this way.

ULTRA HEAT TREATED (UHT)

This cream is ultra heat treated and has a long shelf-life.

STERILISED CREAM

This cream must, by law, have a minimum butterfat content of 23%. It is sterilised with its container to kill all the bacteria and will keep indefinitely. It has a different flavour from fresh cream and will not whip.

CARE OF CREAM

Cream should always be kept cool, clean and covered and away from bright light and strong sunshine. Fresh pasteurised cream will keep three to four days in summer and up to one week in winter if refrigerated. Sterilised, long-keeping and UHT cream will keep for long periods without refrigeration, provided the containers remain unopened. All types of cream must be treated as fresh once the container is opened.

WHIPPING CREAM

Everything must be really cold before cream is whipped – bowl, whisk and the cream itself.
Cream should be whipped quickly until a matt surface appears – then slowly to avoid over-whipping and making it buttery.

YOGURT

Yogurt is a delightful way of taking milk. Slightly acidic in taste, it is refreshingly stimulating and very versatile. It is available natural, in a wide variety of flavours and with pieces of fruit added. Yogurt teams well with sweet and savoury dishes, it is particularly delicious with breakfast cereals, stewed and canned fruit, in summer drinks and with freshly-made buttered scones and jam. When added to soups, sauces, stews and casseroles, or poured over white fish before baking, Yogurt not only enhances the flavour of the dish but also adds to the nutritional value.
When cooking with Yogurt care should be taken not to heat it too vigorously as it might acquire a curdled appearance, although this does not affect the taste.

HOME-MADE SOFT YOGURT

1 pint Pasteurised, Sterilised, Channel Island or South Devon Milk
1 carton (5 oz.) natural yogurt

1. Warm milk to blood heat (about 98°F.). **2.** Remove from heat. **3.** Gently whisk in Yogurt with wire whisk or fork. **4.** Transfer to bowl or basin and cover with plate. **5.** Leave in warm place for 8 to 12 hours or until set. **6.** If cold Yogurt is preferred, refrigerate after it has set. **Approximately 1¼ pints.**

● *As an alternative to the carton of natural yogurt, yogurt culture (which can be bought from some dairy companies, chemists and health food shops) may be used.*

FOR FIRMER YOGURT

Use Ultra Heat Treated (UHT) Milk.

FOR FRUIT YOGURT

Stir small pieces of fresh, canned or frozen and thawed fruit into Yogurt after it has set.

SOURED (OR CULTURED) CREAM

Soured cream has a piquant and refreshing taste, combined with a smooth texture. This enhances the flavour and creaminess of many made-up dishes. It is delicious with raw or cooked fruit, meat, fish and vegetable dishes, soups, stews and sauces. Salad dressings made up with soured cream are ideal for use in the cold buffet.

BUTTER

Butter has a unique and luxurious flavour and a tremendous versatility of usage. It has always been the foundation of French *haute cuisine*. In ordinary, everyday cooking and baking and as a spread on bread, toast, crumpets, muffins, buns, biscuits and scones, it has no rival.

THE VALUE OF BUTTER

Butter is an energy and protective food usually containing rather more than 80% butterfat. It also contains vitamins A and D (the amount varying with the season) and small amounts of protein, milk sugar and minerals.

CARE OF BUTTER

Butter should be kept cool, covered and away from foods with strong flavours or smells. It is, like milk, affected by light and should be stored in a dark place.

CHEESE

There are many varieties of cheese produced in England and Wales and although they are all made from cows' milk, they are, nevertheless, all different in flavour and texture. This is due to slight variations in the manufacturing processes, developed regionally over hundreds of years, and to soil differences which affect the food which the cows eat.

VARIETIES OF CHEESE

ENGLISH CHEDDAR

Cheddar, the most popular English cheese, is famed for its unique 'nutty' flavour which becomes deeper as the cheese matures. With its close creamy texture it is used in a wide variety of ways.

CHESHIRE

Cheshire is a mellow, open-textured and crumbly cheese. Its keen tangy flavour is said to be due to the salty soil in Cheshire. Red and white Cheshire both have the same flavour and are delicious for 'elevenses' with fruit, cake or biscuits. Blue Cheshire has a rich flavour and is very rare.

DERBY

This is a pale honey-coloured cheese with a close smooth texture and soft mild flavour. Derby is well suited for interesting flavour combinations such as cheese and pineapple, or for use in a salad garnished with sprigs of mint or parsley.

SAGE DERBY

This is Derby cheese flavoured with sage leaves.

DOUBLE GLOUCESTER

Double Gloucester is a rich straw colour. It has a smooth velvet texture and a full but mellow flavour. Delicious with bread, butter and a pint of ale, or with fresh fruit salad and cream.

LEICESTER

This is a mild orange-coloured cheese with a soft flaky texture. It is especially recommended as a dessert cheese.

CAERPHILLY

Caerphilly is creamy-white with a mild flavour and semi-smooth texture. It is a great favourite with children and excels with celery and thin slices of bread and butter.

LANCASHIRE

Although Lancashire cheese has a mild flavour when young, it develops a full and rather pungent flavour as it matures. Its texture makes it ideal for crumbling over soups and hot-pots and it is renowned for its toasting qualities. A sage Lancashire is also available.

WENSLEYDALE

Wensleydale is pale parchment in colour with a subtle and unique honeyed after-taste ideal with apple pie. Blue Wensleydale is occasionally made.

BLUE STILTON

Blue Stilton — the 'king of cheeses' — has a close texture intermingled with blue veins which give it its special rich flavour and appearance.

WHITE STILTON

This is a younger version of the Blue Stilton and is milder in flavour, chalky white in colour and crumbly in texture.

COTTAGE CHEESE

This is a creamy, acid curd cheese with a distinctive, delicate flavour. It is made from pasteurised, fat-free milk inoculated with a special curd to develop texture and flavour. It also contains added cream and salt. Cottage cheese is a particularly valuable source of protein and riboflavin (vitamin B_2). It is easily digested and is especially useful in the feeding of babies, invalids and old people. It should always be stored in a cool place.

CHEESE AS A FOOD

As all well-known English cheeses are made from whole milk, they are rich in protein, fat, calcium, riboflavin and vitamins A and D and contain approximately 120 calories per ounce.

CARE OF CHEESE

English cheese will stay fresh and moist if wrapped in a polythene bag or aluminium foil and then stored in a cool larder or refrigerator. In the latter case it should be brought to room temperature before serving. This takes about half an hour.

OVEN TEMPERATURES

225°F.	240°F./115.6°C.	Gas No. $\frac{1}{4}$	Very
250°F.	265°F./129.5°C.	Gas No. $\frac{1}{2}$	cool
275°F.	290°F./143.3°C.	Gas No. 1	Cool
300°F.	310°F./154.5°C.	Gas No. 2	
325°F.	335°F./168.3°C.	Gas No. 3	Moderate
350°F.	355°F./179.5°C.	Gas No. 4	
375°F.	380°F./192.7°C.	Gas No. 5	Fairly
400°F.	400°F./204.5°C.	Gas No. 6	hot
425°F.	425°F./218.3°C.	Gas No. 7	Hot
450°F.	445°F./229.5°C.	Gas No. 8	
475°F.	470°F./243.3°C.	Gas No. 9	Very hot

The above temperature chart is a guide only. To be absolutely safe, always refer to your own cooker instruction book. The second column shows the nearest temperature equivalent to the Gas Numbers but, for ease of setting, it is more usual to give electric temperature in units of 25°F. (see first column). Although the cooking position in oven is given in the recipes, it is again advisable to check with your own instruction book. Cookers vary according to where the gas burners or electric elements have been placed: for this reason the temperature in different parts of the oven (top, centre or bottom) is not standard.

The following are all approximately 1 ounce:

2 level tablespoons — Flour, custard powder, cornflour and other powdery starches.

1 level teacup — Cereals (such as cornflakes).

2 level tablespoons — Semolina.

1 level tablespoon — Rice.

5 level tablespoons — Breadcrumbs (fresh).

3 level tablespoons — Breadcrumbs (dry).

4 level tablespoons — Grated cheese (fairly dry).

1 level tablespoon — Granulated, caster and brown sugar.

3 level tablespoons — Icing sugar (sifted).

2 level tablespoons — Desiccated coconut.

1 level tablespoon — Syrup, honey, treacle and jam.

2 level tablespoons — Ground almonds, hazelnuts and walnuts.

2 level tablespoons — Dried fruits (currants, sultanas and raisins.)

2 level tablespoons — Cocoa powder

When spoon measures are mentioned in recipes, these refer to ordinary household spoons.
In most recipes, level spoon measures have been recommended. This is because a level measure is more accurate and reliable than a rounded or heaped measure.

WEIGHTS & MEASURES

LIQUID MEASURES

20 fluid ounces — 1 pint

10 fluid ounces — $\frac{1}{2}$ pint

5 fluid ounces — $\frac{1}{4}$ pint (or 1 gill)

8 tablespoons of liquid equals 5 fluid ounces or $\frac{1}{4}$ pint

1 breakfast cup of liquid equals approximately $\frac{1}{2}$ pint

1 tea cup of liquid equals approximately 6 fluid ounces.

SPOON MEASURES

2 teaspoons equal 1 dessertspoon

2 dessertspoons equal 1 tablespoon

GENERAL FOOD CARE

DAIRY PRODUCTS

Always keep milk, cream, yogurt, cheese and butter in a cool pantry or larder or in the special compartments provided in the refrigerator. Make sure they are in clean, covered containers and well away from strong-smelling foods. This is important because uncovered dairy products easily pick up strong taints.

FROZEN FOODS

Be guided by star markings on packets of frozen food and on the freezing compartment of your refrigerator. One star indicates that the frozen food will keep 1 week; two stars 1 month; three stars 3 months. If the refrigerator is an older model and has no star markings, do not keep frozen food longer than a few days. Once frozen food has thawed, do not attempt to re-freeze it and never try to freeze your own foods unless you have a proper domestic deep freeze.

MEAT AND OFFAL

Unwrap bought meat, stand it on a piece of aluminium foil or waxed paper and put it straight into the coldest part of the refrigerator. Never seal raw meat in airtight containers or cover it tightly with foil or polythene; the meat will keep fresher if cold air from the refrigerator or larder gets to it directly. Protect raw meat in a pantry or larder with a loose covering of thin muslin, and once again, do not wrap it closely or seal it in containers. Most raw meat can be kept two or three days in the refrigerator or very cold pantry or larder, but minced raw meat, pork, veal, sausages and offal should be cooked within 24 hours.

All frozen meat must be allowed to thaw completely before use, and meat from the refrigerator should be allowed to reach room temperature before it is either roasted, grilled or fried.

Before cooked meat is put into the refrigerator or larder, it should be foil-wrapped or placed in either polythene bags or plastic containers with lids. This helps to keep the meat fresh-tasting and moist and prevents dryness. Cooked meat should be eaten within two days.

POULTRY

Even if kept in the refrigerator, it is advisable to cook whole fresh chickens within 36 hours of purchase and chicken joints within 24 hours of purchase. Poultry should otherwise be treated exactly as meat and offal.

FISH

Fresh fish bought from the fishmonger should be stiff with shimmering scales, reddish gills, bulging eyes and a natural covering of slime. The skin of flat fish should be wrinkle-free and the spots bright. Fish should be put into the coldest part of the refrigerator or larder straight away and, if possible, cooked and eaten within 24 hours. Like meat, it should not be tightly covered.

Once frozen fish has thawed, it must be treated in exactly the same way as fresh fish.

EGGS

Eggs should not be stored near strong-smelling foods as they easily pick up odours. For freshness, they should be kept in a refrigerator, cold pantry or larder, their rounded ends uppermost. Cold eggs should be allowed to reach room temperature before being used, while new-laid eggs should not be used on the day of laying, but kept for 2 or 3 days.

VEGETABLES

The fresher the better. But sprouts, shredded cabbage, cauliflower, spinach, spring greens, parsley and salad greens will keep crisp and fresh for about a week if put into polythene bags or airtight plastic containers and stored in a refrigerator or cold larder. Root vegetables shrivel quickly in the warm and should therefore be kept in a cool, dry and dark place. Plastic bags do help keep root vegetables fresh, but they must not be sealed or the vegetables will begin to rot. Tomatoes and cucumbers keep best in the least cold part of the refrigerator or larder.

FRUIT

Apples, bananas, fresh pineapples, melons, pears and citrus fruits should be kept in a dry cool and airy pantry or larder. Grapes, gooseberries, rhubarb and fresh apricots and peaches keep best in the least cold part of the refrigerator, as do soft berry fruits, which should be spread out onto plates and used within 8 to 12 hours. A sprinkle of lemon juice will prevent sliced bananas, apples and pears from turning brown.

CANNED GOODS

These will keep more or less indefinitely in a dry cupboard, provided they are rust-free and undented. However, despite their long shelf life, it is advisable to use canned goods within 18 months of purchase.

DRY GOODS

Flour should be used within two months of purchase and dried fruits within three months. Baking powder, provided the tin or jar is tightly closed, will remain active for about six months. Bicarbonate of soda has a shorter life and should be used within two months. Cocoa should not be kept longer then six months and nor should cornflour, tapioca, sago, barley and rice. Cereals should be used within a month of purchase and ground coffee should be bought a little at a time and used within a week. White sugar will keep several months in a dry, dark place but icing and brown sugar tend to harden on standing and should be used fairly soon after purchase. Packets of dried convenience foods should be stored exactly as directed by the manufacturer.

HERBS & SPICES

As interest in herbs and spices grows and their use in cooking is becoming more widespread, the following guide may be found useful.

HERBS

BASIL
This mild and fragrant herb teams well with all tomato dishes, and also with mushrooms, cheese and eggs.

BAY LEAVES
Mild and distinctive, bay leaves are used in pickling, stews, sauces and gravies, meat and poultry casseroles and some vegetable dishes. They are often part of a 'bouquet garni' (or bag of mixed herbs).

CHIVES
Grass-like in appearance, chives are a much milder version of the onion and have little or no after taste. Excellent with all foods but particularly delicious with cottage cheese, omelettes and scrambled eggs. Snipped chives make a colourful and attractive garnish.

MARJORAM
A delicate herb with a very distinctive flavour. It goes well with practically all foods but particularly with poultry, veal and lamb, fish and egg dishes, and for adding to carrots, peas, spinach and tomatoes while they are cooking.

MINT
This is used for mint sauce, which teams so admirably with lamb, and as a flavouring for potatoes and peas. A little chopped mint is excellent in poultry stuffing.

ROSEMARY
This has quite a pungent flavour and should be used fairly sparingly. Particularly good with poultry, lamb and mutton it can also be added to pea, chicken and spinach soup and to salad dressings.

PARSLEY
Probably the best known and most widely-used herb of all, parsley makes a most attractive garnish and improves the flavour of any dish to which it is added.

SAGE
Another popular herb, sage is strong and aromatic and is used mainly in pork dishes and in stuffings for duck and goose.

TARRAGON
This is a bitter-sweet herb that is both aromatic and distinctive. Particularly good in certain sauces and with poultry, fish and shell fish dishes.

THYME
This is a strong-flavoured herb recommended for mutton and pork dishes and for adding — sparingly — to cream and cottage cheese. Small amounts are good in omelettes, salads and stuffings.

SPICES

ALLSPICE
This is a dried berry of a West Indian shrub. Whole, it is used to add flavour to boiled meats, pot roasts and poached fresh water fish. When ground, it can be added to gravies, cakes and Christmas puddings.

CINNAMON
This is the bark of a type of laurel which grows in the Far East. It can either be rolled (cinnamon sticks) or powdered. It has a sweet, fragrant and distinctive flavour and can be added to hot drinks and punches, apple dishes, cakes, buns, biscuits, puddings and curries.

CLOVES
These are the dried and unopened buds of a type of myrtle with a strong and distinctive flavour. They should be used sparingly. Traditionally used with stewed apples, they also improve the flavour of stewed pears, pickles, curries and boiled meats.

MACE
This is the golden outer husk of the nutmeg and is available in blade or ground form. It has an exotic and subtle flavour, milder than nutmeg. Blades of mace are used in some soups and sauces and also for pickling. Ground mace is especially good with veal and beef.

NUTMEG
Another popular spice from the Far East and Caribbean, nutmeg is the seed of a pulpy fruit. Apart from its use in milk puddings, nutmeg gives a flavour lift to poultry, egg dishes and egg nogs, creamed potatoes and parsnips, cakes, biscuits, buns and puddings.

PAPRIKA
This is a mild, bright red pepper made from dried ground capsicums. It adds piquancy and colour to meat, fish and vegetable dishes and makes an ideal garnish for soups and pale-coloured savoury dishes of all descriptions.

Milk and Your Diet BY A HARLEY STREET SPECIALIST

Growth and fitness depend on a proper balance of the different components in our food. The body needs daily protein to form new tissue, and to maintain the continuous processes of repair and replacement. It needs energy to sustain activity, supplied by sugars and fats in the right proportion. Besides these main requirements, the body must be fed regularly with small amounts of a large number of different vitamins and minerals which have a specialist role. Each is concerned with a vital function, such as the formation of bone and blood or the proper function of essential organs, and lack of any single one can lead to ill health and disease within a short time. Certain of these vitamins and minerals are found only in a small range of foods, so that an individual shortage can easily occur. Finally everyone must drink enough fluid every day; preferably three or four pints.

The exceptional value of milk and its products lies in the wealth of essential food materials that are contained, and the readiness with which these can be digested and absorbed in to the body. Milk is one of the most complete foods known. One pint of milk supplies about three-quarters of the calcium, about one-fifth of the protein, two fifths of the Vitamin B $_2$ (Riboflavin) and about one-eighth of the Calories required daily by a moderately active man.

One of the most important constituents of milk is first-class protein. Milk alone builds up the muscle and tissue of every baby during its early months when growth is more rapid than at any other time of life, whilst five pints contains enough protein to meet all the needs of a full-grown adult.

It is also brimful of energy both as instant sugar and protective fat, in forms which most people find easy to digest. This is why a quick glass of milk is so valuable when there is no time to stop for a meal at the usual times.

Besides the fulfilment of these basic needs, milk supplies most vitamins and minerals. It is the richest source of calcium and phosphorus, essential for the growth and strength of bones and teeth, and contains large amounts of vitamins A and B. Children who received a regular daily supply at school were found to grow taller, stronger and brighter, and the introduction of Government schemes for cheap milk in schools has played a major part in raising the general standard of child health. The well-balanced diet requires further foods rich in vitamin C and iron, such as fresh fruit and vegetables.

The amount of milk and its products consumed daily by the average person in any country is an index of that country's overall standard of living.

To ensure optimal health, the average person should drink at least one pint as a beverage each day, with a product such as cheese or yogurt with at least one meal.

The nutritional value of milk and its products make these the essential basis of the diet at all ages both in health and sickness.

In health, special diets are required for two main reasons: to provide energy or to lose weight.

People who undertake heavy manual work or athletes who take a great deal of excercise may require to double their intake of Calories in a balanced form that will not overload their digestive system. Milk will supply approximately 380 Calories from each pint, and this energy is even more concentrated in butter, cream and cheese. Children over the age of twelve need as much energy and protein as the average adult, before they can digest the bulkier foods. They must also, therefore, depend on milk to a great extent.

In a weight-reducing diet, the problem is to restrict Calories without reducing the intake of essential protein, vitamins and minerals. A successful reducing diet must meet the basic needs of the body and satisfy the appetite; if not it will become dangerous or will soon be given up. Milk is the ideal basis for a healthy diet.

The value of milk for children has already been emphasised, but it is of equal importance to the elderly. Old people often neglect the preparation of adequate meals because of the trouble entailed and/or lack of means. Many suffer from protein and calcium deficiency as a result. Milk is the cheapest and most digestible source of their needs. In addition to a daily pint, they should add cheese or yogurt to one meal — as well as at least one egg.

The ease with which the nutrients of milk can be digested makes it the primary food recommended by doctors in cases of sickness, diseases of children or convalescence from the more serious illnesses or operations of adults. Milk builds up the reserves and aids healing and restoration of energy.

Milk has been established as the basis of diets for digestive upsets, particularly in peptic ulcer where it has the additional advantage of affording a protective film for the stomach against excess acid. This action may also be of value in health, as a glass of milk before a party will protect the empty stomach.

In certain circumstances, the doctor may need to restrict the amount or type of fat that is eaten. This advice may be given in certain types of heart and liver disease, or because the patient is overweight. The advice of the doctor on this particular point should always be obtained.

Appetisers

Appetisers are usually served before meals or at parties. All those in this section will serve between 4 and 10 people.

1 HOT CHEESE PATTIES

1 recipe Rich Short Crust Pastry (No. 89)
3 oz. cream cheese
1 oz. finely-chopped lean ham
1 oz. stuffed olives
1 level teaspoon finely-grated onion
½ level teaspoon made mustard
1 level dessertspoon fresh white
   breadcrumbs
Salt and pepper to taste
Beaten egg for brushing

1. Roll out Pastry fairly thinly. **2.** Cut into 28 2-in. squares. **3.** Mix cheese with ham, olives, onion, mustard and breadcrumbs. Season to taste with salt and pepper. **4.** Put equal amounts of cheese mixture (about 1 teaspoon) on to 14 squares. Moisten edges of Pastry with water. **5.** Cover with remaining squares. **6.** Press edges well together to seal. 'Ridge' with fork. **7.** Transfer to buttered baking tray and brush with beaten egg. **8.** Decorate tops of Patties with small leaves rolled and cut from trimmings. Brush leaves with more egg. **9.** Bake just above centre of hot oven (425°F. or Gas No. 7) for 15 minutes (or until golden brown). **10.** Serve hot.

2 CREAM CHEESE STICKS

1 recipe Cream Cheese Pastry (No. 101)
Beaten egg for brushing
Celery salt

1. Roll out Pastry fairly thinly. **2.** Cut into fingers and transfer to buttered baking trays. **3.** Brush with egg and sprinkle lightly with celery salt. **4.** Bake towards top of hot oven (450°F. or Gas No. 8) for 10 to 12 minutes (or until puffy and golden). **5.** Serve hot.

3 STUFFED CUCUMBERS

1 large cucumber, unpeeled
12 heaped teaspoons cream cheese
1 level tablespoon finely-chopped chives
GARNISH
12 peeled prawns

1. Cut cucumber into 12 1 to 1½-in. lengths. **2.** Scoop out some of the seedy centres, leaving fairly shallow cavities. **3.** Fill with cream cheese. Sprinkle with chives. Garnish each with a prawn. **4.** Chill lightly before serving.

Stuffed Cucumbers (No. 3)

11

4 HOT SAUSAGE CRISPS

½ lb. skinless pork sausages
1 large egg
1 dessertspoon milk
1½ oz. toasted breadcrumbs
2 level teaspoons dry mustard
½ level teaspoon salt
Deep fat or oil for frying

1. Cut each sausage into 4 pieces. **2.** Beat egg and milk well together. Combine breadcrumbs with mustard and salt. **3.** Coat pieces of sausage with egg and milk. Toss in breadcrumb mixture. **4.** Fry in hot fat or oil until crisp and golden. **5.** Remove from pan, drain on soft kitchen paper. Serve hot.

5 BUTTERED SAVOURY ALMONDS

½ lb. blanched almonds
2 oz. English or Welsh butter
2 teaspoons olive or corn oil
½ level teaspoon salt
1 level teaspoon paprika

1. Fry almonds gently in butter and oil for 3 to 4 minutes (or until pale gold), turning often. **2.** Remove from pan. Drain on soft kitchen paper. Sprinkle with salt mixed with paprika. **3.** Serve hot or cold.

6 AUSTRIAN CHEESE SAVOURIES

3 oz. cream cheese
2 oz. English or Welsh butter, softened
½ level teaspoon paprika
¼ level teaspoon caraway seeds
1 level teaspoon finely-chopped capers
½ level teaspoon anchovy essence
½ level teaspoon French mustard
1 level dessertspoon finely-chopped chives
 or green part of leek
Savoury biscuits

GARNISH
Extra capers

1. Beat cream cheese and butter together until smooth and creamy. **2.** Stir in paprika, caraway seeds, capers, anchovy essence, mustard and chives or leek. **3.** Mix well then pile on to biscuits. **4.** Garnish each with a whole caper.

CURRIED WALNUTS 7

½ lb. shelled walnut halves
2 oz. English or Welsh butter
2 teaspoons olive or corn oil
½ level teasooon salt
3 level teaspoons curry powder

1. Fry walnut halves in butter and oil for 2 to 3 minutes, turning often. **2.** Remove from pan. Drain on soft kitchen paper. Sprinkle with salt mixed with curry powder. **3.** Serve hot or cold.

DEVILLED BRAZILS 8

½ lb. shelled Brazil nuts
2 oz. English or Welsh butter
2 teaspoons olive or corn oil
1 level teaspoon each, dry mustard and
 paprika
1 level teaspoon each, celery and onion
 salt
Shake of both Cayenne pepper and garlic
 salt

1. Slice Brazils fairly thickly. Fry gently in butter and oil for 3 to 4 minutes (or until pale gold), turning often. **2.** Remove from pan. Drain on soft kitchen paper. Sprinkle with mustard mixed with paprika, celery and onion salts, Cayenne pepper and garlic salt. **3.** Serve hot or cold.

HOT CHICKEN & MUSHROOM PUFFS 9

Double recipe Choux Pastry (No.102)
¼ pint Mushroom Sauce (No.113)
1 tablespoon fresh double cream
¼ lb. cooked chicken, chopped
Seasoning to taste

1. Using a teaspoon, place 40 equal amounts of Pastry on buttered and lightly-floured baking trays. **2.** Bake just above centre of fairly hot oven (400°F. or Gas No. 6) for 20 minutes. **3.** Reduce temperature to moderate (325°F. or Gas No. 3). Bake further 20 minutes. **4.** Cool on wire rack. **5.** Combine Sauce with double cream and chicken. Season and heat through gently. **6.** Make slit in each Puff. Fill with chicken mixture. **7.** Transfer to baking trays. Heat through in moderate oven for 5 to 7 minutes. Serve straight away.

10 HOT CHEESE & HAM PUFFS

1. Follow recipe and method for Hot Chicken and Mushroom Puffs (No. 9). **2.** Use Cheese Sauce (No. 116) instead of Mushroom and chopped ham instead of chicken.

11 HOT MUSTARD & BACON PUFFS

1. Follow recipe and method for Hot Chicken and Mushroom Puffs (No. 9). **2.** Use Mustard Sauce (No. 118) instead of the Mushroom and chopped fried bacon instead of chicken.

12 HOT PARSLEY & HADDOCK PUFFS

1. Follow recipe and method for Hot Chicken and Mushroom Puffs (No. 9). **2.** Use Parsley Sauce (No. 107) instead of Mushroom and cooked finely-mashed smoked haddock instead of chicken.

13 CHEESE-STUFFED CELERY

¼ lb. finely-grated English Cheddar cheese
  (stale for preference)
2 oz. English or Welsh butter, softened
½ level teaspoon dry mustard
1 tablespoon fresh double cream or
  soured cream
Well-washed celery stalks

GARNISH
Paprika

1. Beat cheese, butter and mustard well together. Gradually beat in cream. **2.** Fill celery stalks with cheese mixture. Cut into 2-in. lengths. **3.** Chill and before serving dust lightly with paprika.

4 PRAWN-STUFFED CELERY

1. Follow recipe and method for Cheese-Stuffed Celery (No. 13). **2.** Fill celery stalks with Prawn Butter (No. 201) instead of the cheese mixture. **3.** Before serving sprinkle with finely-chopped parsley.

CHEESE & WALNUT PUFFS 15

1 recipe Choux Pastry (No. 102)
3 oz. cream cheese
2 oz. Blue Stilton cheese
1 tablespoon milk
1 oz. finely-chopped shelled walnut halves

1. Using a teaspoon, place 20 equal amounts of Pastry on to buttered and lightly-floured baking tray. **2.** Bake just above centre of fairly hot oven (400°F. or Gas No. 6) for 20 minutes. **3.** Reduce temperature to moderate (325°F. or Gas No. 3). Bake further 20 minutes. **4.** Cool on wire rack. **5.** Just before serving, beat cream cheese, Stilton and milk well together. Stir in nuts. **6.** Cut puffs in half. Fill bottom halves with cheese mixture. Replace tops. **7.** Serve straight away. (If left to stand too long, the Pastry softens slightly.)

CHEESE & PRAWN PUFFS 16

1. Follow recipe and method for Cheese and Walnut Puffs (No. 15). **2.** Use 3 oz. finely-chopped peeled prawns instead of Stilton. **3.** Stir in ½ level teaspoon lemon peel instead of walnuts.

CHEESE AIGRETTES 17

2 oz. finely-grated English Cheddar cheese
  (stale for preference)
1 recipe Choux Pastry (No. 102)
Deep fat or oil for frying

1. Beat 1 oz. cheese into Choux Pastry. **2.** Drop about 20 equal amounts, from a teaspoon, into hot fat or oil. **3.** Fry about 5 minutes (or until Aigrettes are golden and well puffed). **4.** Remove from pan and drain on soft kitchen paper. **5.** Transfer to serving dish. Sprinkle with rest of cheese. **6.** Serve hot.

HAM & ASPARAGUS ROLLS 18

4 slices lean ham (about ¼ lb.)
3 to 4 oz. cream cheese
12 asparagus tips

1. Cut each slice of ham into 3 strips. **2.** Spread with cream cheese. **3.** Roll strips round asparagus tips. Skewer with cocktail sticks. **4.** Chill lightly before serving.

DIPS & DUNKS

The Dips for which recipes are given on these two pages are ideal for 'help-yourself' parties and for serving with drinks before a meal. Spoon the prepared Dips into bowls and stand on large platters or small trays. Surround with potato crisps, small savoury biscuits, thin slices of carrot. 1-in. lengths of celery and slices of peeled cucumber. Guests help themselves by dunking the crisps, biscuits or vegetables into the Dips. For more formal occasions, the Dips can be piled on to small biscuits and garnished to taste with sliced olives and gherkins, red or green peppers, paprika, curry powder, small pieces of tomato and thin slices of cucumber.

19 MUSHROOM & HAM DIP

¼ pint fresh double cream
1 carton (5 oz.) natural yogurt
½ packet mushroom soup
2 oz. very finely-chopped or minced lean ham
GARNISH
Cayenne pepper

1. Lightly whip cream. 2. Stir in yogurt and soup. 3. Chill for 2 or 3 hours. 4. Before serving, stir in ham and transfer to bowl. 5. Dust lightly with Cayenne pepper.

20 COTTAGE CHEESE, BACON & ONION DIP

¼ lb. back bacon
¼ lb. cottage cheese
1 to 2 level teaspoons finely-grated onion
GARNISH
Paprika

1. Chop bacon into small pieces. Fry in own fat until crisp. 2. Drain on soft kitchen paper. Leave until cold. 3. Combine with cottage cheese and onion. Transfer to bowl. 4. Sprinkle with paprika.

21 CREAMED YOGURT DIP

1 carton (5 oz.) natural yogurt
¼ lb. cream cheese
2 level tablespoons finely-chopped peeled cucumber
1 level teaspoon paprika
½ to 1 level teaspoon salt
Good shake of pepper

1. Beat yogurt into cheese. Stir in cucumber and paprika. 2. Season to taste with salt and pepper. Chill. 3. Transfer to bowl before serving.

ASPARAGUS & PRAWN DIP 22

4 tablespoons canned chopped asparagus
2 to 3 oz. peeled prawns, very finely chopped
2 cartons (10 oz.) natural yogurt
Seasoning to taste
GARNISH
Slices of stuffed olives

1. Stir asparagus and prawns into yogurt. 2. Season to taste and chill. 3. Before serving, transfer to bowl. Garnish with olives.

CURRIED CREAM CHEESE DIP 23

½ lb. cream cheese
4 tablespoons Mayonnaise
1 carton (5 oz.) natural yogurt
3 to 4 level teaspoons curry powder
2 level teaspoons finely-grated onion
Salt to taste
GARNISH
About 1 tablespoon sultanas

1. Beat cheese until smooth with Mayonnaise and natural yogurt. 2. Stir in curry powder and onion. Season to taste with salt. 3. Spoon into serving bowl. Sprinkle sultanas over the top.

ONION DIP 24

¼ pint fresh double cream
1 carton (5 oz.) natural yogurt
½ packet onion soup
GARNISH
1 level tablespoon finely-chopped parsley

1. Lightly whip cream. 2. Stir in yogurt and soup. 3. Chill for 2 or 3 hours. 4. Transfer to bowl before serving. Sprinkle with parsley.

A selection of Appetisers: Mushroom & Ham Dip (No. 19), Cheese & Olive Balls (No. 37), Toasted Lancashire Rolls (No. 35) and Buttered Savoury Almonds (No. 5)

25 LEEK DIP

¼ pint fresh double cream
1 carton (5 oz.) natural yogurt
½ packet leek soup
2 oz. Caerphilly cheese, grated

GARNISH
Paprika

1. Lightly whip cream. **2.** Stir in yogurt, soup and cheese. **3.** Chill for 2 or 3 hours. **4.** Transfer to bowl before serving. Sprinkle with paprika.

26 COTTAGE CHEESE & PINEAPPLE DIP

½ lb. cottage cheese
4 tablespoons soured cream
4 heaped tablespoons finely-chopped canned pineapple
Seasoning to taste

GARNISH
Chopped red and/or green peppers

1. Combine cottage cheese with soured cream and pineapple. **2.** Season to taste with salt and a little Cayenne pepper. **3.** Transfer to bowl. Garnish with red or green peppers, or mixture of both.

27 CHEDDAR CHEESE & CELERY DIP

2 oz. English or Welsh butter, softened
½ lb. very finely grated English Cheddar cheese
2 level teaspoons made mustard
¼ lb. very finely-chopped celery
¼ pint fresh single cream
Seasoning to taste

GARNISH
About 1 oz. chopped salted peanuts

1. Beat butter until creamy. Stir in cheese, mustard and celery. **2.** Very gradually beat in cream. Season to taste with salt and pepper. **3.** Before serving, transfer to bowl. Sprinkle top lightly with chopped nuts.

28 HOT CHEESE FLUFFS

12 cream crackers
English or Welsh butter
2 oz. finely-grated English Cheddar cheese
  (stale for preference)
4 tablespoons fresh double cream
$\frac{1}{2}$ level teaspoon made mustard
$\frac{1}{4}$ level teaspoon salt
White of 1 standard egg

1. Spread biscuits with butter. 2. Combine grated cheese and double cream. Add mustard and salt. 3. Beat egg white until stiff. Gently fold into cheese mixture. 4. Pile over biscuits. Grill until golden. 5. Serve straight away.

29 CHEESE & POPPY SEED FLAKES

1 recipe Flaky Pastry (No. 99)
Beaten egg
3 oz. crumbled Lancashire cheese
About 4 level teaspoons poppy seeds

1. Roll out Pastry into 18-in. × 6-in. rectangle. Cut in half lengthwise. (There should be 2 pieces, each measuring 18 in. × 3 in.) 2. Brush one half with egg and sprinkle with cheese. 3. Cover with second half of Pastry and press down well. 4. Cut into 18 strips, each about 1 in. wide × 3 in. long. 5. Transfer to baking tray. Brush with egg. Sprinkle with poppy seeds. 6. Leave in cool 20 to 30 minutes. Bake towards top of hot oven (450°F. or Gas No. 8) for 8 to 10 minutes (or until well puffed and golden). Serve hot.

30 CHEESE & CARAWAY SEED FLAKES

1. Follow recipe and method for Cheese and Poppy Seed Flakes (No. 29). 2. Use caraway seeds instead of poppy seeds.

31 MUSHROOM BUTTONS

16 very fresh button mushrooms
2 oz. cream cheese
2 tablespoons fresh double cream
1 dessertspoon very finely-chopped chives
Salt and pepper to taste

HOT MUSHROOM TARTLETS 32

1 recipe Cheese Pastry (No. 93)
$\frac{1}{4}$ pint Mushroom Sauce (No.113)
GARNISH
10 to 12 lightly-grilled button mushrooms

1. Roll out Pastry thinly. Cut into 10 to 12 rounds with biscuit cutter. 2. Arrange neatly in bun tins. 3. Prick well all over. Line each with aluminium foil (to prevent Pastry rising as it cooks) and bake just above centre of hot oven (425°F. or Gas No. 7) for 5 minutes. 4. Remove foil and return tartlet cases to oven. Bake further 5 to 7 minutes (or until golden). 5. Fill with equal amounts of hot Mushroom Sauce. Garnish each with grilled mushroom. 6. Serve straight away.

COLD CUCUMBER TARTLETS 33

1. Follow recipe and method for Hot Mushroom Tartlets (No. 32). 2. After baking, leave tartlet cases until completely cold. 3. Fill with 1 carton (5 oz.) soured cream mixed with 2 to 3 tablespoons finely-grated cucumber. 4. Season to taste with freshly-milled pepper and salt.

PRUNE & BACON SAVOURIES 34

1 dozen large prunes
2 to 3 oz. cream cheese
12 rashers streaky bacon

1. Soak prunes in hot water for 3 to 4 hours (or until plump and soft). 2. Drain, pat dry and remove stones. 3. Fill cavities with cream cheese. 4. Wrap rasher of bacon round each stuffed prune. Skewer with cocktail sticks. 5. Cook under hot grill until bacon is crisp and golden. 6. Serve straight away.

1. Remove stalks from mushrooms. 2. Gently wipe caps with clean damp cloth. 3. Combine cheese with double cream and chives. Season to taste with salt and pepper. 4. Fill caps with equal amounts of cream cheese mixture then spear cocktail sticks into each.

5 TOASTED LANCASHIRE ROLLS

8 rashers streaky bacon
16 × ½-in. cubes of Lancashire cheese

1. Cut bacon rashers in half. Wrap round cubes of cheese. **2.** Secure with cocktail sticks. **3.** Cook under hot grill until bacon is crisp and golden. **4.** Serve straight away.

6 CHEESE & PINEAPPLE PORCUPINE

1 large grapefruit
6 oz. Leicester cheese
6 oz. Derby cheese
1 medium-sized can pineapple cubes,
  well-drained

1. Stand grapefruit on serving dish. (If necessary, cut small slice off base so it stands without toppling.) **2.** Cut both cheeses into ½-in. cubes. **3.** Put on to cocktail sticks alternately with pineapple, then spear into grapefruit.

37 CHEESE & OLIVE BALLS

¼ lb. cream cheese
1 tablespoon fresh double cream
1 level tablespoon finely-chopped stuffed
  olives
¼ level teaspoon paprika
Seasoning to taste
About 1 oz. finely-chopped shelled
  walnut halves

1. Beat cheese and cream together until smooth. Stir in olives and paprika. **2.** Season to taste with salt and pepper. **3.** Divide into 12 to 14 equal-sized pieces. Shape into balls. **4.** Roll in chopped walnuts and chill. **5.** Spear on to cocktail sticks just before serving.

38 CHEESE & GHERKIN BALLS

1. Follow recipe and method for Cheese and Olive Balls (No. 37). **2.** Use 1 level tablespoon finely-chopped gherkins instead of the olives. **3.** Roll in 1 oz. salted and chopped peanuts instead of the walnuts.

CHEESE & HAM BALLS 39

1. Follow recipe and method for Cheese and Olive Balls (No. 37). **2.** Use 1 oz. finely-chopped ham instead of the olives.

CHEESE & CELERY BALLS 40

1. Follow recipe and method for Cheese and Olive Balls (No. 37). **2.** Use 1 level tablespoon finely-chopped celery instead of the olives. **3.** Roll in 1 oz. blanched, toasted and chopped almonds instead of the walnuts.

CHEESE & TOMATO FLAKES 41

1 recipe Flaky Pastry (No. 99)
2 level tablespoons tomato purée
3 oz. crumbled Lancashire cheese
Beaten egg for brushing

1. Roll out Pastry into 18-in. × 6-in. rectangle. Cut in half lengthwise. (There should be 2 pieces, each measuring 18 in. × 3 in.) **2.** Brush one half with tomato purée. Sprinkle with cheese. **3.** Cover with second half of Pastry and press down well. **4.** Cut into 18 strips, each about 1-in. in width and 3 in. long. **5.** Transfer to baking tray. Brush with egg. Leave in the cool for 20 to 30 minutes. **6.** Bake towards top of hot oven (450°F. or Gas No. 8) 8 to 10 minutes (or until well puffed and golden). Serve hot.

BABY BURGERS 42

1 lb. lean minced beef
4 level tablespoons fresh white
  breadcrumbs
4 tablespoons fresh single cream
2 teaspoons Worcester sauce
½ to 1 level teaspoon salt
1 level teaspoon mixed herbs

1. Combine beef with breadcrumbs, cream, Worcester sauce, salt and herbs. Shape into 2 dozen tiny cakes. **2.** Stand below hot grill and cook 4 to 5 minutes per side. **3.** Spear on to cocktail sticks. Serve hot.

Soups & Soup Garnishes

43 MINESTRONE SOUP

1 medium-sized leek
1 large onion
1 medium-sized carrot
2 large celery stalks
6 oz. white or green cabbage
1 small packet frozen green beans
1 can (14 oz.) tomatoes
2 oz. haricot beans, soaked overnight
2 level tablespoons finely-chopped parsley
1 level teaspoon basil
1 to 2 level teaspoons salt
1 level teaspoon granulated sugar
1½ pints water
2 oz. broken macaroni
2 to 3 oz. finely-grated English Cheddar
  cheese

1. Trim leek and cut in half lengthwise. Wash thoroughly under cold running water. Shred finely. **2.** Thinly slice onion, carrot and celery. **3.** Cut cabbage into thin strips. **4.** Put prepared vegetables in large pan. Add green beans, tomatoes, drained haricot beans, parsley, basil, salt, sugar and water. **5.** Bring to boil. Lower heat and cover pan. **6.** Simmer 1 hour. Add macaroni and simmer further 30 minutes (or until macaroni is plump and tender). **7.** Ladle into 4 warm soup bowls. Sprinkle each thickly with cheese. **Serves 4.**

44 LIVER & BACON SOUP

1 medium-sized onion
¼ lb. lean bacon
1 oz. English or Welsh butter
½ lb. ox or pigs' liver
1 oz. flour
1½ pints water
½ level teaspoon salt
1 dessertspoon lemon juice
½ teaspoon Worcester sauce

GARNISH
1 level tablespoon finely-chopped parsley

1. Finely chop onion and bacon. Fry gently in butter (in saucepan) for 5 to 7 minutes. **2.** Wash liver well and wipe dry. Cut into ½-in. cubes. **3.** Toss in flour until each piece is well coated. Add to pan and fry with onion and bacon further 5 minutes, stirring. **4.** Gradually blend in water. Add salt, lemon juice and Worcester sauce. **5.** Bring slowly to boil, stirring. Lower heat and cover pan. **6.** Simmer gently 1½ hours. Ladle into 4 warm soup bowls. Sprinkle each with parsley. **Serves 4.**

FISH SOUP 45

1 medium-sized celery stalk
1 small lettuce
2 medium-sized tomatoes
1 shallot or small onion
1 garlic clove (optional)
1 pint boiling water
1 pint milk
1 blade mace
1 bay leaf
1 lb. fish trimmings (bones, heads, etc.)
½ oz. English or Welsh butter
½ oz. flour
Seasoning to taste
Yolk of 1 standard egg
2 tablespoons fresh single cream

GARNISH
2 medium-sized tomatoes, skinned and
  chopped
Snipped chives

1. Chop celery, lettuce, tomatoes, shallot or onion and garlic if used. **2.** Put into saucepan with water, milk, mace and bay leaf. **3.** Bring to boil. Remove scum. **4.** Lower heat. Cover pan. **5.** Simmer for 15 minutes. **6.** Add well-washed fish trimmings. **7.** Bring to boil again. **8.** Lower heat. Simmer slowly for further 20 minutes. **9.** Strain fish liquor and reserve (discarding vegetables, etc.) **10.** Melt butter in clean saucepan. Stir in flour. Cook for 2 minutes without browning. **11.** Gradually blend in fish liquor. **12.** Cook, stirring, until soup comes to boil and thickens. **13.** Season to taste. Simmer for 2 minutes. **14.** Remove from heat. **15.** Mix egg yolk and cream well together. **16.** Gradually beat into soup. **17.** Ladle into 4 or 5 warm soup bowls. **18.** Garnish each with chopped tomatoes and chives. **Serves 4 to 5.**

FRENCH ONION SOUP 4

¾ lb. onions
1½ oz. English or Welsh butter
1½ pints beef stock
Salt and freshly-milled black pepper to
  taste
1 or 2 teaspoons dry sherry (optional)
4 slices French bread, each 1 in. thick
2 oz. finely-grated English Cheddar cheese

1. Slice onions thinly. Fry gently in butter (in saucepan) until warm gold. **2.** Pour in stock. Season to taste with salt and pepper. Bring to boil. **3.** Lower heat. Cover pan and simmer 45 minutes. Add sherry if used. **4.** Pour into heatproof dish. Add bread (which will float on top) and sprinkle with cheese. **5.** Brown under hot grill and serve straight away. **Serves 4.**

47 CABBAGE SOUP

1 small head cabbage (about ½ lb.)
1 medium-sized onion
1 oz. English or Welsh butter
1 pint beef stock
Salt and pepper to taste
4 tablespoons soured cream
GARNISH
1 tablespoon very finely-chopped parsley

1. Shred cabbage finely, wash well and drain.
2. Coarsely grate onion. Fry gently in butter (in saucepan) until soft and pale gold. **3.** Add cabbage and stock. Bring to boil. **4.** Season to taste with salt and pepper. Reduce heat and cover pan. **5.** Simmer gently for 15 minutes. **6.** Ladle into 4 warm soup bowls. Pour tablespoon of soured cream on to each. **7.** Sprinkle with parsley and serve very hot. **Serves 4.**

48 CREAM OF POTATO SOUP

1 lb. potatoes
1 large onion
2 medium-sized celery stalks
1½ oz. English or Welsh butter
¾ pint water
1 level teaspoon salt
Shake of pepper
1 oz. cornflour
½ pint milk
2 level tablespoons finely-chopped parsley

1. Cut potatoes into dice. **2.** Thinly slice onion and celery. **3.** Fry vegetables very gently in butter (in saucepan) for 10 minutes. Do not allow to brown. **4.** Add water and salt and pepper. **5.** Bring to boil. Cover pan and simmer very gently for 45 minutes. **6.** Rub through sieve (or liquidise) and return to pan. **7.** Mix cornflour to smooth paste with a little of the cold milk. Stir in remainder. **8.** Add to Soup and bring to boil, stirring. **9.** Simmer 5 minutes. Ladle into 4 warm soup bowls. **10.** Sprinkle each with parsley. **Serves 4.**

49 CREAM OF ARTICHOKE SOUP

1. Follow recipe and method for Cream of Potato Soup (No. 48). **2.** Use 1 lb. Jerusalem artichokes instead of potatoes. **3.** Stir in 2 to 3 tablespoons fresh double cream just before serving. **Serves 4.**

Ingredients for Minestrone Soup
(No. 43)

50 CREAM OF CAULIFLOWER SOUP

1. Follow recipe and method for Cream of Potato Soup (No. 48). **2.** Use 1 lb. cauliflower (divided into small florets) instead of potatoes. **3.** Add large pinch nutmeg with salt and pepper.

51 CHEESE & ONION SOUP

1 large onion
1 oz. English or Welsh butter
1 oz. flour
1 level teaspoon dry mustard
1 pint milk
¼ pint chicken stock or water
Seasoning to taste
¼ lb. Lancashire cheese, finely crumbled
GARNISH
Paprika

1. Chop onion finely. Fry gently in butter (in saucepan) until soft but not brown. **2.** Add flour and mustard. Cook slowly for 2 minutes. Gradually blend in milk and stock or water. **3.** Cook, stirring, until Soup comes to boil and thickens slightly. **4.** Season to taste with salt and pepper. Lower heat and cover pan. **5.** Simmer very gently for 15 minutes. **6.** Remove from heat. Add cheese and stir until melted. **7.** Ladle into 4 warm soup bowls. Dust tops of each lightly with paprika. **Serves 4.**

52 CHEESE & TOMATO SOUP

1 small onion
1 oz. English or Welsh butter
1 oz. flour
¼ pint chicken stock or water
1 pint milk
¼ lb. skinned chopped tomatoes
Seasoning to taste
6 oz. finely-grated English Cheddar cheese

1. Chop onion finely. Fry gently in butter (in saucepan) until soft, not brown. **2.** Add flour and cook slowly for 2 minutes. **3.** Gradually blend in stock or water and milk. Cook, stirring, until Soup comes to boil and thickens slightly. **4.** Add tomatoes and season to taste. **5.** Lower heat and cover pan. **6.** Simmer for 10 minutes. Remove from heat and add 5 oz. cheese. **7.** Stir until cheese melts. Ladle into 4 warm soup bowls. **8.** Sprinkle rest of cheese on top of each. **Serves 4.**

PAPRIKA BEEF SOUP 53

1 medium-sized onion
1 small red or green pepper
1 oz. English or Welsh butter
¾ lb. shin of beef
1 level tablespoon paprika
1 level tablespoon tomato purée
½ level teaspoon granulated sugar
1 level teaspoon salt
½ level teaspoon caraway seeds
2 pints cold water
1 large potato
1 carton (5 oz.) natural yogurt

1. Finely chop onion and pepper. Fry gently in butter (in saucepan) for 5 minutes. **2.** Cut beef into small pieces and add to saucepan. Fry further 5 minutes, turning all the time. **3.** Stir in paprika, purée, sugar, salt, caraway seeds and water. **4.** Coarsely grate potato and add. **5.** Bring Soup to boil. Lower heat and cover. **6.** Simmer gently for 2 hours (or until beef is tender). **7.** Remove from heat. Stir in yogurt. Ladle into 4 or 6 warm soup bowls. **Serves 4 to 6.**

CREAM OF MARROW SOUP 54

1 lb. marrow
1 medium-sized onion
1 oz. English or Welsh butter
Handful of parsley
¾ pint water
Large pinch of grated nutmeg
1 level teaspoon salt
Shake of pepper
1 oz. cornflour
¼ pint milk
4 tablespoons fresh double cream

GARNISH
Paprika

1. Cut marrow into 1-in. cubes. Chop onion finely. **2.** Fry both very gently in butter (in saucepan) for 10 minutes. Do not allow to brown. **3.** Add parsley, water, nutmeg and salt and pepper. Bring to boil. **4.** Lower heat, cover pan and simmer gently 1 hour. **5.** Rub through sieve (or liquidise) and return to pan. **6.** Mix cornflour to smooth paste with cold milk. **7.** Add to soup and bring to boil, stirring. **8.** Simmer for 5 minutes. Ladle into 4 warm soup bowls. **9.** Pour tablespoon of fresh double cream on to each. Sprinkle lightly with paprika. **Serves 4.**

55 CREAM OF LENTIL SOUP

$\frac{1}{4}$ lb. lentils
1 large carrot
1 large onion
1 celery stalk
$\frac{1}{2}$ small turnip
1 medium-sized potato
1$\frac{1}{2}$ oz. English or Welsh butter
Handful of parsley
1 pint milk
$\frac{1}{2}$ pint chicken stock or water
Pinch of grated nutmeg
Seasoning to taste
$\frac{1}{4}$ pint fresh single cream

GARNISH
1 tablespoon finely-chopped parsley

1. Wash lentils and drain. **2.** Thinly slice carrot, onion and celery. Cut turnip and potato into small dice. **3.** Fry very gently in butter (in saucepan) for 7 to 10 minutes. **4.** Add lentils and parsley. Pour in milk and stock or water. **5.** Bring to boil, lower heat and cover pan. **6.** Simmer very gently for 1 hour. **7.** Rub through sieve and return to pan. Add nutmeg and seasoning to taste. **8.** Re-heat gently. Stir in cream just before serving. **9.** Ladle into 4 warm soup bowls. Sprinkle each with parsley. **Serves 4.**

CHICKEN SOUP 57

1 chicken carcass
1 medium-sized onion
1 bay leaf
1 clove
1 pint milk
1 chicken stock cube
4 tablespoons boiling water
1 level tablespoon cornflour
4 tablespoons cold water
$\frac{1}{4}$ level teaspoon nutmeg
$\frac{1}{4}$ lb. cooked chopped chicken
Seasoning to taste

GARNISH
1 oz. blanched, toasted and chopped almonds

1. Break up carcass and put into saucepan. **2.** Chop onion and add with bay leaf and clove. **3.** Pour in milk and stock cube dissolved in boiling water. **4.** Simmer slowly 20 minutes. Strain and return to pan. **5.** Add cornflour mixed to smooth paste with cold water. Cook, stirring, until Soup comes to boil and thickens slightly. **6.** Add nutmeg and chicken. Season to taste. Simmer, covered, for 15 minutes. **7.** Ladle into 4 warm soup bowls. Sprinkle each with almonds. **Serves 4.**

56 CHEESE & VEGETABLE SOUP

4 medium-sized carrots
2 medium-sized onions
2 celery stalks
$\frac{3}{4}$ pint water
1 level teaspoon salt
1 oz. plain flour
$\frac{1}{2}$ pint milk
$\frac{1}{4}$ lb. finely-grated English Cheddar cheese
1 oz. English or Welsh butter
Seasoning to taste

1. Cut carrots into tiny dice. Chop onions and celery finely. **2.** Put vegetables into saucepan. Add $\frac{1}{2}$ pint water and salt. **3.** Cook 20 to 30 minutes (or until tender). Pour in rest of water. **4.** Mix flour to smooth paste with milk and add to saucepan. **5.** Cook, stirring, until Soup comes to boil. Simmer 5 minutes. **6.** Remove from heat. Add 3 oz. cheese and butter. Stir until both have melted. **7.** Season to taste with salt and pepper and ladle into 4 warm soup bowls. Sprinkle with rest of cheese. **Serves 4.**

COCK-A-LEEKIE SOUP 58

3 medium-sized leeks
1 medium-sized joint roasting chicken
1 pint water
1 clove ⎱ tied
1 blade mace ⎰ together
Sprig of parsley ⎱ in muslin
3 peppercorns ⎰ bag
1 level teaspoon salt
2 oz. rice
$\frac{1}{4}$ pint fresh single cream

1. Cut off all but 2 in. of green leaves from leeks. **2.** Cut leeks in half lengthwise. Wash well under cold running water then cut into fine shreds. **3.** Put into saucepan with chicken and water. **4.** Add bag of clove, mace, parsley and peppercorns. Add salt. **5.** Bring to boil and remove scum. **6.** Lower heat, cover pan and simmer gently $\frac{3}{4}$ to 1 hour (or until chicken is tender). **7.** Remove chicken and cut flesh into small pieces. **8.** Add to Soup with rice. **9.** Simmer further 20 to 30 minutes (or until rice is tender). Remove from heat and stir in cream. **10.** Ladle into 4 soup bowls. Serve straight away. **Serves 4.**

21

59 MULLIGATAWNY SOUP

1 large onion
1 small carrot
1 large celery stalk
2 oz. English or Welsh butter
1 oz. flour
1 level dessertspoon curry powder
1½ pints water
1 large cooking apple
2 teaspoons lemon juice
1 oz. boiled rice (about ½ oz. uncooked)
1 oz. finely-chopped cooked chicken (optional)
1 level teaspoon salt
Good shake pepper
4 tablespoons fresh single cream

1. Slice onion thinly. Cut carrot into tiny dice. Chop celery finely. **2.** Fry vegetables gently in butter (in saucepan) for 7 minutes. Do not allow to brown. **3.** Stir in flour and curry powder. Cook 2 minutes then blend in water. **4.** Cook, stirring, until Soup comes to boil and thickens slightly. Lower heat and cover pan. **5.** Simmer very slowly 30 minutes, stirring at least twice. **6.** Peel, core and dice apple. Add to Soup with lemon juice, rice, chicken if used, and salt and pepper. **7.** Simmer further 15 minutes. **8.** Remove from heat. Stir in cream and ladle into 4 warm soup bowls. **Serves 4.**

60 CREAMED SCOTCH BROTH

1 lb. scrag end neck of lamb
2 pints cold water
1 large onion
2 medium-sized celery stalks
1 medium-sized carrot
½ small turnip
1½ to 2 level teaspoons salt
1 oz. well-washed barley
4 tablespoons fresh single cream
GARNISH
2 level tablespoons finely-chopped parsley

1. Cut lamb into small neat sections. Remove as much fat as possible. **2.** Put into large saucepan with water. **3.** Bring to boil and remove scum. **4.** Cover and simmer gently while preparing vegetables. **5.** Chop onion and celery. Cut carrot and turnip into small dice. **6.** Add to saucepan with salt and barley. **7.** Bring to boil again. Lower heat and cover pan. **8.** Simmer very gently for 2 hours. Leave until completely cold. **9.** Remove fat and discard. **10.** Bring Soup just up to boil. Stir in cream. Ladle into 4 warm soup bowls. Sprinkle each with parsley. **Serves 4.**

CREAMY CARROT SOUP 61

1 lb. carrots
1 large potato
1 medium-sized onion
1 oz. English or Welsh butter
¾ pint water
¼ pint milk
1 oz. well-washed rice
Large pinch of grated nutmeg
½ to 1 level teaspoon salt
1 dessertspoon lemon juice
2 to 3 tablespoons fresh single cream

1. Coarsely grate carrots, potato and onion. **2.** Fry gently in butter (in saucepan) for 5 minutes. Do not allow to brown. **3.** Add water, milk, rice, nutmeg and salt. **4.** Bring to boil, lower heat and cover pan. **5.** Simmer very gently for ¾ to 1 hour. **6.** Stir in lemon juice and cream. Re-heat without boiling. Ladle into 4 warm soup bowls. **Serves 4.**

VEGETABLE BROTH 62

1 medium-sized carrot
1 small parsnip
½ small turnip
1 medium-sized onion
2 large celery stalks
1 large leek
1 oz. English or Welsh butter
1½ pints water
1 level tablespoon well-washed barley
1 to 1½ level teaspoons salt
GARNISH
1 level tablespoon finely-chopped parsley

1. Cut carrot, parsnip and turnip into dice. Chop onion and celery. Cut leek into fine shreds. **2.** Melt butter in a saucepan. Add vegetables and cover pan. **3.** Fry very gently, without browning, 7 minutes, shaking pan frequently. **4.** Pour in water. Add barley and salt and bring to boil. **5.** Lower heat. Cover pan and simmer very gently for 1½ hours (or until barley is soft). **6.** Ladle into 4 warm soup bowls. Sprinkle each with parsley. **Serves 4.**

BEEF BROTH 63

1. Follow recipe and method for Vegetable Broth (No. 62). **2.** Fry ¼ lb. lean stewing steak — cut into thin strips — with vegetables. **3.** Use beef stock instead of water. **Serves 4.**

Creamy Carrot Soup (No. 61)

4 ONION VELOUTÉ SOUP

2 large onions
1½ oz. English or Welsh butter
1 level dessertspoon flour
¼ pint water
½ pint milk
½ level teaspoon salt
Yolks of 2 standard eggs
2 tablespoons fresh double cream
Pinch of grated nutmeg
¼ level teaspoon paprika
GARNISH
1 level tablespoon finely-chopped parsley

1. Chop onions fairly finely. Fry very gently in butter (in saucepan) for 10 minutes. Do not allow to brown. **2.** Stir in flour. Cook further minute, then blend in water and milk. Add salt. **3.** Very slowly bring to boil, stirring, then lower heat. **4.** Cover pan. Simmer gently for ¾ to 1 hour (or until onions are tender). **5.** Beat egg yolks with cream, nutmeg and paprika. Stir into Soup. **6.** Heat gently, without boiling, for 1 or 2 minutes. Ladle into 4 warm soup bowls. **7.** Sprinkle parsley over each. **Serves 4.**

CLEAR TOMATO SOUP 66

1 small onion
2 medium-sized celery stalks and leaves
1 oz. English or Welsh butter
1 pint tomato juice
1 small bay leaf
2 cloves
¼ level teaspoon basil
1 level tablespoon coarsely-chopped parsley
2 level teaspoons granulated sugar
1 dessertspoon lemon juice
Salt and pepper to taste
4 tablespoons fresh single cream

1. Chop onion and celery finely. Fry very gently in butter (in saucepan) for 7 minutes. Do not allow to brown. **2.** Pour in tomato juice. **3.** Add bay leaf, cloves, basil, parsley and sugar. Bring to boil and lower heat. **4.** Cover pan. Simmer Soup gently 15 minutes. Strain. **5.** Return to clean pan. Add lemon juice and season to taste with salt and pepper. **6.** Re-heat 1 or 2 minutes. Ladle into 4 warm soup bowls. **7.** Pour 1 tablespoon cream over each. **Serves 4.**

5 JELLIED TOMATO CONSOMMÉ

3 level teaspoons gelatine
5 tablespoons boiling water
1 pint tomato juice
1 level teaspoon finely-grated onion
1 strip lemon peel
2 tablespoons lemon juice or dry sherry
1 or 2 teaspoons Worcester sauce
GARNISH
2 level tablespoons finely-chopped parsley

1. Shower gelatine into boiling water. Stir until dissolved. **2.** Pour tomato juice into saucepan. Add onion and lemon peel. Bring just up to boil. **3.** Strain. Add dissolved gelatine, lemon juice or sherry and Worcester sauce. **4.** Leave until cold. Chill until softly set. **5.** Break up lightly with fork. Spoon into 4 or 6 soup bowls. **6.** Sprinkle each with parsley. **Serves 4 to 6.**

67 ICED CUCUMBER & YOGURT SOUP

1 large unpeeled cucumber
2 cartons (10 oz.) natural yogurt
½ small green pepper
1 garlic clove (optional)
2 tablespoons wine vinegar
1 level tablespoon snipped chives
Seasoning to taste
½ pint chilled milk

GARNISH
2 level tablespoons finely-chopped parsley

1. Grate cucumber on medium grater. Transfer to bowl. Stir in yogurt. **2.** Finely chop green pepper (discarding pips) and garlic if used. **3.** Add to cucumber mixture with vinegar and chives. **4.** Season to taste with salt and pepper. Chill very thoroughly. **5.** Just before serving stir in milk. **6.** Ladle into 4 or 6 soup bowls. Sprinkle each with chopped parsley. **Serves 4 to 6.**

68 HOT BORTSCH (RUSSIAN BEET SOUP)

1 large carrot
2 medium-sized onions
4 medium-sized cooked beetroots
¼ pint water
1 pint beef stock
¼ lb. white cabbage
1 tablespoon lemon juice
Seasoning to taste
4 tablespoons soured cream

1. Finely grate carrot, onions and beetroots. **2.** Put into saucepan. Add water and bring to boil. **3.** Lower heat. Cover pan and simmer very slowly for 30 minutes. **4.** Add stock, cabbage and lemon juice. Season to taste and simmer further 20 minutes. **5.** Ladle into 4 warm soup bowls. Pour 1 tablespoon soured cream over each. **Serves 4.**

69 COLD BORTSCH

1. Follow recipe and method for Hot Bortsch (No. 68). **2.** Leave Soup in saucepan until completely cold. **3.** Strain, ladle into 4 soup bowls and chill. **4.** Just before serving pour tablespoon of soured cream over each. **Serves 4.**

SPLIT PEA & HAM SOUP 70

¼ lb. split peas
1 celery stalk
1 medium-sized onion
2 oz. lean ham
1½ oz. English or Welsh butter
1 medium-sized potato
1½ pints water
1 level teaspoon salt
Good shake pepper
4 tablespoons natural yogurt

1. Cover split peas with cold water. Leave to soak 2 to 3 hours. Drain. **2.** Finely chop celery, onion and ham. Fry gently in butter (in saucepan) for 5 minutes. **3.** Peel and grate potato. Add to saucepan with split peas, water and salt. **4.** Bring to boil. Season to taste with pepper. **5.** Lower heat, cover pan and simmer for 2 hours, stirring frequently. **6.** Ladle into 4 warm soup bowls. Pour tablespoon of natural yogurt on to each. **Serves 4.**

CURRIED CHICKEN SOUP 71

1 oz. English or Welsh butter
2 level teaspoons curry powder
1 level tablespoon cornflour
¾ pint chicken stock or water
½ level teaspoon paprika
2 level tablespoons chutney
2 oz. cooked chopped chicken
Yolk of 1 standard egg
4 tablespoons fresh single cream
Seasoning to taste

GARNISH
1 level tablespoon finely-chopped chives

1. Melt butter in saucepan. Stir in curry powder and cornflour. **2.** Cook gently for 2 minutes. **3.** Very gradually blend in stock and water. Add paprika. **4.** Cook, stirring, until Soup comes to boil and thickens slightly. **5.** Add chutney and chicken. Cover pan and simmer 7 minutes. **6.** Remove from heat and stir in egg yolk beaten with cream. **7.** Season to taste with salt and pepper. Ladle into 4 warm soup bowls. Sprinkle each with chives. **Serves 4.**

24

Stuffings

72   VICHYSSOISE SOUP

2 medium-sized leeks
1 small onion
1 oz. English or Welsh butter
¾ lb. potatoes
1 pint chicken stock
1 level teaspoon salt
Light shake of pepper
1 blade mace
½ pint fresh double cream

GARNISH
2 level tablespoons snipped chives or
finely-chopped watercress

1. Finely chop white part of leeks and onion.
2. Fry gently in butter (in saucepan) for 7 to 10
minutes. Do not allow to brown. **3.** Thinly slice
potatoes and add to saucepan with stock, salt,
pepper and mace. **4.** Bring to boil, lower heat and
cover pan. **5.** Simmer very gently 20 to 30
minutes (or until vegetables are tender). **6.** Rub
Soup through fine sieve (or liquidise). Chill
thoroughly. **7.** Just before serving stir in cream.
Transfer to 4 or 6 soup bowls. **8.** Sprinkle each
with chives or watercress. **Serves 4 to 6.**

73   OYSTER SOUP

1 oz. English or Welsh butter
1 oz. flour
1 pint fish stock
1 dozen oysters
1 blade mace
1 strip lemon peel
½ level teaspoon salt
Light shake of Cayenne pepper
1 teaspoon lemon juice
4 tablespoons fresh single cream

GARNISH
1 level teaspoon finely-grated lemon peel
1 level dessertspoon finely-chopped
parsley

1. Melt butter in saucepan. Add flour and cook
over low heat, stirring, for 2 minutes. Gradually
blend in stock and liquor from oysters. **2.** Add
mace, lemon peel, salt and Cayenne pepper.
3. Cook, stirring, until Soup comes to boil and
thickens slightly. **4.** Simmer for 5 minutes.
Remove mace and strip of lemon peel. Stir in
lemon juice and cream. **5.** Re-heat, without
boiling, for 1 minute. **6.** Place shelled oysters in
4 warm soup bowls. **7.** Pour Soup into each.
Sprinkle tops with lemon peel and parsley.
Serves 4.

*Stuffings should not be made over-wet by the
addition of too much milk, egg, water or stock,
etc. For best results, the stuffing should be fairly
loose and crumbly but at the same time be firm
enough to hold its shape when gathered
together either with fork, spoon or fingertips.*

LEMON, PARSLEY &   74
THYME STUFFING

For veal, poultry and fish.

¼ lb. fresh white breadcrumbs
1 level tablespoon finely-chopped parsley
½ level teaspoon finely-grated lemon peel
½ level teaspoon thyme
½ level teaspoon salt
Shake of white pepper
1 oz. English or Welsh butter, melted
Milk

1. Combine breadcrumbs with parsley, lemon
peel, thyme and salt and pepper. **2.** Bind loosely
with melted butter and milk.

CELERY & TOMATO   75
STUFFING

For lamb, veal, poultry, turkey and whole fish.

¼ lb. fresh white breadcrumbs
2 level tablespoons finely-chopped celery
2 skinned and finely-chopped tomatoes
½ level teaspoon salt
1 oz. English or Welsh butter, melted
Milk

1. Combine breadcrumbs and celery. Stir in
tomatoes and salt. **2.** Bind loosely with butter
and milk.

BACON STUFFING   76

For chicken, turkey and veal.

¼ lb. lean bacon
¼ lb. fresh white breadcrumbs
½ level teaspoon dry mustard
¼ level teaspoon salt
½ level teaspoon mixed herbs
1 oz. English or Welsh butter, melted
Milk

1. Chop bacon fairly finely. Combine with
breadcrumbs, mustard, salt and herbs. **2.** Bind
loosely with butter and milk.

STUFFINGS

77 LIVER & ONION STUFFING

For chicken and turkey.

¼ lb. chicken or calves' liver
1 small onion
1½ oz. English or Welsh butter
¼ lb. fresh white breadcrumbs
½ level teaspoon finely-grated lemon peel
1 teaspoon lemon juice
1 level dessertspoon finely-chopped parsley
½ level teaspoon paprika
½ level teaspoon salt
Milk

1. Cut liver into small dice. Chop onion finely.
2. Fry both gently in butter 5 minutes. 3. Remove from heat. Stir in breadcrumbs, lemon peel and juice, parsley, paprika and salt. 4. Bind loosely with milk.

78 MUSHROOM & LEMON STUFFING

For poultry, whole fish, tomatoes and marrow.

1 small onion
¼ lb. washed mushrooms and stalks
1 oz. English or Welsh butter
¼ lb. fresh white breadcrumbs
½ level teaspoon finely-grated lemon peel
1 teaspoon lemon juice
¼ to ½ level teaspoon salt
Shake of white pepper
1 tablespoon milk

1. Finely chop onion and mushrooms and stalks. Fry very gently in butter 5 minutes. 2. Remove from heat and stir in crumbs, lemon peel and juice and salt and pepper. 3. If necessary, bind loosely with milk.

79 SAGE & ONION STUFFING

For pork, duck and goose.

½ lb. onions
¼ lb. fresh white breadcrumbs
½ level teaspoon sage
½ level teaspoon salt
Shake of white pepper
1 oz. English or Welsh butter, melted
Milk

80 APPLE & WALNUT STUFFING

For pork, lamb, duck, goose, bacon joints and rabbit.

1 lb. cooking apples
1 level tablespoon granulated sugar
¼ lb. fresh white breadcrumbs
1 oz. finely-chopped shelled walnut halves
1 level dessertspoon finely-grated onion (optional)
1 level teaspoon salt
Freshly-milled pepper
2 oz. English or Welsh butter, melted
Beaten egg

1. Peel, core and coarsely chop apples. 2. Combine with sugar, breadcrumbs, walnuts and onion, if used. 3. Season with salt and pepper. Combine loosely with butter (and beaten egg if necessary).

81 ORANGE & PARSLEY STUFFING

For lamb, mutton, duck and whole fish.

1 small onion
1 oz. English or Welsh butter
¼ lb. fresh white breadcrumbs
Finely-grated peel and juice of 1 medium-sized orange
3 level dessertspoons finely-chopped parsley
½ level teaspoon salt
Milk

1. Chop onion finely. Fry in butter very gently until pale gold. 2. Remove from heat. Stir in breadcrumbs, orange peel and juice, parsley and salt. 3. If necessary, bind loosely with milk.

1. Quarter onions. Cook in boiling, salted water until tender. 2. Drain and chop finely. 3. Combine with breadcrumbs. Add sage and salt and pepper. 4. Bind loosely with melted butter and milk.

26

32 CHESTNUT CREAM STUFFING

For chicken and turkey.

¼ lb. dried chestnuts, soaked overnight
¼ lb. fresh white breadcrumbs
2 level teaspoons very finely-grated onion
½ level teaspoon salt
¼ level teaspoon grated nutmeg
Good shake white pepper
2 oz. English or Welsh butter, melted
Fresh single cream

1. Drain chestnuts. Cook in boiling, salted water until tender, 20 to 30 minutes. **2.** Mince finely. Combine with breadcrumbs, onion, salt, nutmeg and pepper. **3.** Bind with melted butter and fresh single cream.

● *If preferred, use ½ lb. fresh chestnuts instead of dried.*

33 SWEETCORN & ONION STUFFING

For lamb, veal, poultry and whole fish.

¼ lb. fresh white breadcrumbs
1 can (¾ lb.) sweetcorn kernels, drained
1 level teaspoon finely-grated onion
½ level teaspoon salt
Shake of pepper
1 oz. English or Welsh butter, melted
Milk

1. Combine breadcrumbs with corn and onion. **2.** Season with salt and pepper. Bind loosely with butter and milk.

34 PORK SAUSAGE STUFFING

For chicken, turkey, veal and beef.

½ lb. pork sausage meat
¼ lb. fresh white breadcrumbs
½ level teaspoon thyme
¼ level teaspoon nutmeg
1 level dessertspoon finely-chopped parsley
½ level teaspoon salt
3 tablespoons milk

1. Put all ingredients into bowl. **2.** Knead well together.

PRAWN STUFFING 85

For fish and tomatoes.

¼ lb. fresh white breadcrumbs
1 level dessertspoon finely-chopped parsley
½ level teaspoon finely-grated lemon peel
2 oz. peeled prawns, coarsely chopped
½ level teaspoon salt
1 oz. English or Welsh butter, melted
Milk

1. Combine breadcrumbs with parsley, lemon peel, prawns and salt. **2.** Bind loosely with butter and milk.

HAM & PINEAPPLE STUFFING 86

For pork, lamb, chicken and duck.

¼ lb. fresh white breadcrumbs
2 oz. finely-chopped lean ham
2 level tablespoons finely-chopped canned pineapple
2 level teaspoons finely-grated onion
¼ level teaspoon salt
1 oz. English or Welsh butter, melted
Milk

1. Combine breadcrumbs with ham, pineapple, onion and salt. **2.** Bind loosely with butter and milk.

SAVOURY RICE STUFFING 87

For chicken and turkey.

1 medium-sized onion
1 oz. English or Welsh butter
¼ lb. long grain rice
½ pint water
½ level teaspoon salt
1 level teaspoon crushed rosemary

1. Chop onion finely. Fry very gently in butter until pale gold. **2.** Add rice. Cook further minute. **3.** Pour in water and add salt and rosemary. Bring to boil, stirring. **4.** Lower heat and cover pan. Simmer 20 minutes (or until rice grains have absorbed all the liquid and are dry and separate). **5.** Leave until cold before using.

● *If preferred, ½ level teaspoon mixed herbs can be used instead of rosemary.*

Pastry

HOME-MADE PASTRY

When a recipe calls for a certain weight of pastry, the weight refers to the amount of flour used and not to the total amount of pastry. For example, if a recipe says you need $\frac{1}{4}$ lb. Short Crust Pastry, it means you start off with $\frac{1}{4}$ lb. flour and then add all the other ingredients.

BOUGHT PASTRY

When a recipe calls for a certain weight of bought pastry, this DOES refer to total weight. Thus if a recipe says you need $\frac{1}{2}$ lb. Puff Pastry, you should buy $\frac{1}{2}$ lb. Puff Pastry.

88   SHORT CRUST PASTRY

For sweet and savoury flans, pies, tarts and tartlets, pasties, patties, turnovers etc.

$\frac{1}{2}$ **lb. plain flour**
$\frac{1}{4}$ **level teaspoon salt**
$\frac{1}{4}$ **lb. English or Welsh butter**
Cold water to mix; allow between 1 to 1$\frac{1}{2}$
  teaspoon per oz. of flour

1. Sift flour and salt into bowl. **2.** Add butter. Cut into flour with a knife then rub in with fingertips. When rubbed in sufficiently, the mixture should look like fine breadcrumbs. **3.** Sprinkle the water over the crumbs. Mix to stiff crumbly-looking paste with round-ended knife. **4.** Draw together with fingertips, turn out on to lightly-floured board. Knead quickly until smooth and crack-free. **5.** Roll out and use as required. **6.** If not to be used straight away, transfer to polythene bag or wrap in aluminium foil and leave in refrigerator or cold larder.

89   RICH SHORT CRUST PASTRY

For same dishes as Short Crust Pastry.

1. Follow recipe and method for Short Crust Pastry (No. 88) but use 5 oz. of butter instead of 4 and mix with 4 to 5 teaspoons cold water. **2.** Transfer to polythene bag or wrap in aluminium foil and chill at least $\frac{1}{2}$ hour before rolling out and using.

NUT PASTRY   90

For savoury flans, pies, pasties, patties and turnovers etc.; especially those filled with chicken, veal, eggs or white fish.

1. Follow recipe and method for Short Crust Pastry (No. 88) but stir in 1 to 1$\frac{1}{2}$ oz. very finely-chopped shelled walnut halves, salted peanuts or salted cashew nuts before adding water. **2.** If using salted nuts, reduce quantity of salt by half.

POPPY SEED PASTRY   9

For same dishes as Nut Pastry (No. 90)

Follow recipe and method for Short Crust Pastry (No. 88) but stir in 1 level tablespoon poppy seeds before adding water.

LEMON PASTRY   9:

For same dishes as Nut Pastry (No. 90)

Follow recipe and method for Short Crust Pastry (No. 88) but stir in 1 level teaspoon very finely-grated lemon peel before adding water.

CHEESE PASTRY   93

For savoury biscuits and straws; savoury tarts, pies, flans, patties and turnovers.

$\frac{1}{4}$ **lb. plain flour**
$\frac{1}{4}$ **level teaspoon dry mustard**
$\frac{1}{4}$ **level teaspoon salt**
Light shake of Cayenne pepper
2$\frac{1}{2}$ oz. English or Welsh butter
2 oz. very finely-grated English Cheddar
  cheese (stale for preference)
Yolk of 1 standard egg
2 to 3 teaspoons cold water

1. Sift flour, mustard, salt and Cayenne pepper into bowl. **2.** Add butter, cut into flour with knife, then rub in with fingertips. **3.** Add cheese and toss ingredients lightly together. Mix to very stiff paste with egg yolk and water. **4.** Turn out on to lightly-floured board. Knead quickly until smooth and crack-free. **5.** Transfer to polythene bag or wrap in aluminium foil. **6.** Chill at least $\frac{1}{2}$ hour before rolling out and using.

94 ROUGH PUFF PASTRY

For sweet and savoury pies, patties, turnovers and sausage rolls.

½ lb. plain flour
¼ level teaspoon salt
6 oz. English or Welsh butter
¼ pint chilled water
1 teaspoon lemon juice

1. Sift flour and salt into bowl. **2.** Cut butter into tiny dice. **3.** Mix together water and lemon juice. **4.** Add butter to flour. Using knife, mix to fairly soft crumbly paste with water and lemon juice, taking care not to cut or break down butter any further. **5.** Draw together with fingertips. Turn out on to floured board and shape into block. **6.** Roll into ¼-in. thick rectangle, measuring about 18 in. × 6 in. Fold in three, envelope style, by bringing bottom third over middle third and folding top third over. **7.** Seal open edges by pressing firmly together with rolling pin. Give pastry a quarter turn so that folded edges are to right and left. **8.** Roll out. Fold and turn three more times. **9.** If possible, put folded pastry into polythene bag (or wrap in aluminium foil) and chill about 15 minutes between rollings.

95 HOT WATER CRUST PASTRY

For raised pies such as pork, veal, veal and ham and game.

¾ lb. plain flour
½ level teaspoon salt
Yolk of 1 standard egg
4 tablespoons milk
4 tablespoons water
1 oz. English or Welsh butter
3 oz. lard

1. Sift flour and salt into bowl and warm slightly. Make a well in centre. **2.** Beat yolk with 1 tablespoon milk and pour into well. **3.** Pour rest of milk and water into saucepan. Add butter and lard. Heat slowly until butter and lard melt. Bring to a brisk boil. **4.** Pour into well. Mix with wooden spoon until ingredients are well blended. **5.** Turn out on to floured board. Knead quickly until smooth. **6.** Put into bowl or basin standing over pan of hot water. Cover with clean tea-towel and leave to rest ½ an hour. **7.** Roll out warm pastry to ¼ in. in thickness and use as required. **8.** When making pies, cut off piece for lid first. Leave it (covered with towel), in bowl over hot water.

PUFF PASTRY 96

For vol-au-vents; pastries such as cream horns, Mille Feuilles.

½ lb. English or Welsh butter
½ lb. plain flour
¼ level teaspoon salt
1 teaspoon lemon juice
Chilled water to mix

1. Put butter into clean cloth. Squeeze well to remove surplus moisture and to make it soft and pliable. Shape into ¾-in. brick. **2.** Sift flour and salt into bowl. Mix to soft paste (about same consistency as butter) with lemon juice and water. **3.** Turn out on to floured board and knead well. Roll into rectangle measuring 12 in. × 6 in. **4.** Stand butter on lower half of rectangle. Bring top half over so that butter is completely enclosed. **5.** Press open edges firmly together with rolling pin. Put into polythene bag or wrap in aluminium foil. Chill 15 minutes. **6.** Remove from bag. With fold on right, roll into 18-in. × 6-in. rectangle. **7.** Fold in three as for Flaky Pastry (No. 99). Seal edges, wrap and chill. **8.** Repeat, until pastry has been rolled, folded and chilled 7 times. **9.** Return to polythene bag or wrap in aluminium foil. Chill at least 30 minutes before rolling out (to ¼ in. in thickness) and using. **10.** After shaping, let dishes etc. rest 30 minutes in cool before baking.

SUET CRUST PASTRY 97

For sweet and savoury roly-polys and boiled and steamed puddings.

½ lb. self-raising flour
½ level teaspoon salt
1 level teaspoon baking powder
¼ lb. finely-grated or shredded beef suet
About ¼ pint cold water to mix

1. Sift flour, salt and baking powder into bowl. **2.** Add suet and toss ingredients lightly together. **3.** Mix to soft paste with water. **4.** Turn out on to floured board. Knead until smooth and roll out to about ⅛ in. in thickness. **5.** Use as required: preferably straight away.

98 SWEET FLAN PASTRY

For sweet flans, tarts, tartlets and small and large pies.

Yolk of 1 standard egg
1 level dessertspoon sifted icing sugar
¼ lb. plain flour
Pinch of salt
2½ oz. English or Welsh butter
1 to 2 teaspoons cold water

1. Mix egg yolk and sugar well together. **2.** Sift flour and salt into bowl. **3.** Add butter, cut into flour with knife, then rub in with fingertips. **4.** Mix to very stiff paste with yolk, sugar and water. **5.** Turn out on to lightly-floured board. Knead quickly until smooth. **6.** Transfer to polythene bag or wrap in aluminium foil. **7.** Chill at least ½ hour before rolling out and using.

99 FLAKY PASTRY

For same dishes as Rough Puff Pastry (No. 94)

6 oz. English or Welsh butter
½ lb. plain flour
¼ level teaspoon salt
¼ pint chilled water
1 teaspoon lemon juice

1. Divide butter into 4 equal portions. Chill 3 portions. **2.** Sift flour and salt into bowl. Rub in unchilled portion of butter. **3.** Mix to soft paste with water and lemon juice. Turn out on to floured board. Knead thoroughly until smooth. **4.** Put into polythene bag or wrap in aluminium foil. Chill ½ an hour. **5.** Roll out into ¼-in. thick rectangle, measuring about 18 in. × 6 in. **6.** Using tip of knife, spread second portion of butter (in small flakes) over top and middle third of rectangle to within 1 in. of edges. Dust lightly with flour. **7.** Fold in three, envelope style, by bringing bottom third over middle third and folding top third over. **8.** Seal open edges by pressing firmly together with rolling pin. Put into polythene bag or wrap in aluminium foil and chill 15 minutes. **9.** Remove from bag or unwrap. With folded edges to left and right, roll out again into 18-in. × 6-in. rectangle. **10.** Cover with third portion of butter as before. Fold, seal and chill. **11.** Repeat again, adding last portion of butter, and chill. **12.** Roll out again. Fold and seal, return to polythene bag or wrap in aluminium foil. Chill at least 30 minutes before rolling out (to ¼ in. in thickness) and using. **13.** After shaping, let dishes etc. rest 30 minutes in cool before baking.

MILK 'PUFF' PASTRY 100

For same dishes as Rough Puff Pastry (No. 94)

½ lb. self-raising flour
¼ level teaspoon salt
6 oz. English or Welsh butter
4 to 5 tablespoons cold milk

1. Sift flour and salt into bowl. **2.** Add butter and cut into flour until pieces are no larger than peas. **3.** Mix to stiff paste with milk. Draw together with fingertips. **4.** Quickly shape into ball and transfer to polythene bag or wrap in aluminium foil. **5.** Chill 1 hour before rolling out and using.

CREAM CHEESE PASTRY 10

This is a light, slightly puffy pastry, particularly good for sausage rolls, little savoury patties and jam turnovers.

¼ lb. plain flour
¼ lb. English or Welsh butter
¼ lb. cream cheese

1. Sift flour into bowl. **2.** Add butter and cheese. Cut both into flour with 2 knives held in same hand until mixture looks like coarse breadcrumbs. **3.** Draw together with fingertips and shape lightly into a ball. **4.** Transfer to polythene bag or wrap in aluminium foil and chill overnight. **5.** Roll out to about ⅛ in. in thickness. Use as soon as it is rolled.

CHOUX PASTRY 10

For sweet and savoury buns and éclairs etc.

2½ oz. plain flour
Pinch of salt
¼ pint water
2 oz. English or Welsh butter
2 standard eggs, well beaten

1. Sift flour and salt twice. **2.** Put water and butter into saucepan. Heat slowly until butter melts, then bring to brisk boil. **3.** Lower heat and tip in all the flour. **4.** Stir briskly until mixture forms soft ball and leaves sides of pan clean. **5.** Remove from heat and cool slightly. Add eggs very gradually, beating hard until mixture is smooth, shiny and firm enough to stand in soft peaks when lifted with spoon. **6.** Use immediately. Otherwise leave in saucepan and cover with lid to prevent pastry drying out.

Sauces

SAVOURY SAUCES

SIMPLE WHITE POURING SAUCE 103

½ oz. cornflour
½ pint milk
Small knob of English or Welsh butter
¼ to ½ level teaspoon salt
Shake of pepper

1. Mix cornflour to smooth paste with a little cold milk. 2. Warm remainder of milk. Pour on to paste and mix well. 3. Return to pan. 4. Cook, stirring, until Sauce comes to boil and thickens. 5. Simmer for 2 minutes. 6. Remove from heat and stir in butter. 7. Season to taste with salt and pepper. **Serves 6.**

SIMPLE WHITE COATING SAUCE 104

1. Follow recipe and method for Simple White Pouring Sauce (No.103). 2. Increase cornflour to ¾ oz. **Serves 4.**

BASIC WHITE POURING SAUCE 105

½ oz. English or Welsh butter
½ oz. flour
½ pint milk
¼ to ½ level teaspoon salt
Shake of pepper

1. Melt butter in pan. Add flour and cook over low heat, stirring, for 2 minutes. Do not allow mixture (roux) to brown. 2. Gradually blend in milk. 3. Cook, stirring, until Sauce comes to boil and thickens. 4. Simmer very gently for 3 minutes. 5. Season to taste with salt and pepper. **Serves 6.**

BASIC WHITE COATING SAUCE 106

1. Follow recipe and method for Basic White Pouring Sauce (No.105). 2. Increase butter and flour to 1 oz. each. **Serves 4.**

Cheese Coating Sauce (No. 116)

107 PARSLEY SAUCE

For bacon, ham and fish dishes; also boiled mutton.

1. Follow recipe and method for either Basic White Pouring Sauce (No.105) or Basic White Coating Sauce (No.106). **2.** After seasoning with salt and pepper stir in 1 or 2 level tablespoons finely-chopped parsley. **Serves 4 to 6.**

108 ONION SAUCE

For tripe, lamb grills and roasts and boiled mutton.

1. Follow recipe and method for either Basic White Pouring Sauce (No.105) or Basic White Coating Sauce (No.106). **2.** Before seasoning with salt and pepper stir in 1 large onion, boiled and finely chopped. **3.** Re-heat gently before using. **Serves 4 to 6.**

109 PRAWN OR SHRIMP SAUCE

For fish dishes.

1. Follow recipe and method for either Basic White Pouring Sauce (No.105) or Basic White Coating Sauce (No.106). **2.** Before seasoning with salt and pepper, stir in 2 oz. finely-chopped peeled prawns or 2 oz. peeled whole shrimps, $\frac{1}{2}$ level teaspoon dried mustard mixed with 2 teaspoons lemon juice and $\frac{1}{2}$ level teaspoon anchovy essence. **3.** Re-heat gently before using. **Serves 4 to 6.**

LEMON SAUCE 11

For fish, poultry, egg and veal dishes.

1. Follow recipe and method for either Basic White Pouring Sauce (No.105) or Basic White Coating Sauce (No.106). **2.** Before seasoning with salt and pepper stir in finely-grated peel of 1 small lemon and 1 tablespoon lemon juice. **3.** Re-heat gently before using. **Serves 4 to 6.**

MAÎTRE D'HÔTEL SAUCE 11

For baked, grilled, poached or steamed fish.

1. Follow recipe and method for either Basic White Pouring Sauce (No. 105) or Basic White Coating Sauce (No. 106). **2.** Use $\frac{1}{4}$ pint milk and $\frac{1}{4}$ pint fish stock instead of all milk. **3.** Before seasoning with salt and pepper stir in juice of $\frac{1}{2}$ medium-sized lemon, 3 level dessertspoons finely-chopped parsley and 2 tablespoons fresh double cream. **4.** Re-heat gently (without boiling) before using. **Serves 4 to 6.**

MUSHROOM SAUCE 11

For fish, poultry, veal, egg and cheese dishes.

1. Follow recipe and method for either Basic White Pouring Sauce (No.105) or Basic White Coating Sauce (No.106). **2.** Before seasoning with salt and pepper stir in 2 to 3 oz. mushrooms – finely chopped and lightly fried in butter. **3.** Re-heat gently before using. **Serves 4 to 6.**

110 RICH WHITE SAUCE (OR BÉCHAMEL)

For fish, poultry, egg and vegetable dishes.

$\frac{1}{2}$ **pint milk**
1 small peeled onion
1 small peeled carrot
$\frac{1}{2}$ **small celery stalk**
2 cloves
6 white peppercorns
1 blade mace
1 sprig parsley
1 oz. English or Welsh butter
1 oz. flour
Seasoning to taste
2 tablespoons fresh double cream

1. Put milk into saucepan. Add quartered onion, thickly-sliced carrot, sliced celery, cloves, peppercorns, mace and parsley. **2.** Slowly bring just up to boil. **3.** Remove from heat and cover. **4.** Leave $\frac{1}{2}$ an hour. Strain, reserving milk liquor. **5.** Melt butter in pan. Add flour and cook over low heat, stirring, for 2 minutes. Do not allow mixture (or roux) to brown. **6.** Gradually blend in flavoured milk. **7.** Cook, stirring, until Sauce comes to boil and thickens. Simmer very gently for 3 minutes. **8.** Remove from heat and season to taste with salt and pepper. Stir in cream. **Serves 4.**

4 ANCHOVY SAUCE

For grilled, baked, steamed, poached and fried fish dishes, and fried veal dishes.

1. Follow recipe and method for either Basic White Pouring Sauce (No.105) or Basic White Coating Sauce (No.106). **2.** Before seasoning with salt and pepper, stir in 2 level teaspoons anchovy essence and 1 teaspoon lemon juice. **Serves 4 to 6.**

5 CAPER SAUCE

For boiled mutton, fried or grilled mackerel and herrings.

1. Follow recipe and method for either Basic White Pouring Sauce (No. 105) or Basic White Coating Sauce (No.106). **2.** Stir in 2 tablespoons chopped capers and 2 teaspoons caper vinegar. **3.** Re-heat gently before using. **Serves 4 to 6.**

6 CHEESE SAUCE

For fish, poultry, ham, bacon, egg and vegetable dishes.

1. Follow recipe and method for either Basic White Pouring Sauce (No.105) or Basic White Coating Sauce (No.106). **2.** Before seasoning with salt and pepper, stir in 2 oz. finely-grated English **Cheddar** or 2 oz. crumbled Lancashire cheese, $\frac{1}{2}$ to 1 level teaspoon made mustard and pinch of Cayenne pepper. **Serves 4 to 6.**

7 EGG SAUCE

For fish, poultry and veal dishes.

1. Follow recipe and method for either Basic White Pouring Sauce (No. 105) or Basic White Coating Sauce (No.106). **2.** Before seasoning with salt and pepper, stir in 1 large, finely-chopped hard-boiled egg. **3.** Re-heat gently before using. **Serves 4 to 6.**

MUSTARD SAUCE 118

For herring, mackerel, cheese, ham and bacon dishes.

1. Follow recipe and method for either Basic White Pouring Sauce (No. 105) or Basic White Coating Sauce (No. 106). **2.** Before seasoning with salt and pepper stir in 2 level teaspoons dry mustard mixed with 2 teaspoons vinegar. **3.** Re-heat gently before using. **Serves 4 to 6.**

AURORE SAUCE 119

For fish and egg dishes.

1. Follow recipe and method for Béchamel Sauce (No. 110). **2.** Before seasoning with salt and pepper, stir in 3 level dessertspoons tomato purée and $\frac{1}{2}$ level teaspoon caster sugar. **3.** Re-heat gently before using. Do not allow to boil. **Serves 4.**

CHAUD-FROID SAUCE 120

For coating portions of cold chicken and whole skinned fish, or cutlets of fish such as salmon and salmon trout.

1. Follow recipe and method for Béchamel Sauce (No. 110). **2.** Before seasoning with salt and pepper stir in 3 level teaspoons gelatine dissolved in $\frac{1}{4}$ pint boiling water. **3.** Use when cold and just on setting point. **Serves 4.**

CUCUMBER SAUCE 121

For all fish dishes.

1. Follow recipe and method for Béchamel Sauce (No. 110). **2.** Before seasoning with salt and pepper stir in 4 level tablespoons finely-grated peeled cucumber and large pinch of nutmeg. **3.** Re-heat gently before using. Do not allow to boil. **Serves 4.**

122 HOT HORSERADISH SAUCE

For beef roasts and grills; grilled, fried trout, mackerel and herrings.

1. Follow recipe and method for Béchamel Sauce (No. 110). **2.** Before seasoning with salt and pepper, stir in 3 level dessertspoons grated horseradish, $\frac{1}{2}$ level teaspoon sugar and 1 teaspoon vinegar. **3.** Re-heat gently before using. Do not allow to boil. **Serves 4.**

123 MORNAY SAUCE

For poultry, fish, shellfish and egg dishes.

1. Follow recipe and method for Béchamel Sauce (No. 110). **2.** Before seasoning with salt and pepper, stir in yolk of standard egg mixed with 2 extra tablespoons fresh double cream and 2 oz. very finely-grated English Cheddar cheese. **3.** Stand over low heat. Whisk until Sauce is smooth. Do not allow to boil. **Serves 4.**

124 MOCK HOLLANDAISE SAUCE

For poultry and steamed, poached or grilled fish dishes.

1. Follow recipe and method for Béchamel Sauce (No. 110). **2.** Before seasoning with salt and pepper, stir in yolk of standard egg mixed with 2 extra tablespoons fresh double cream and 1 dessertspoon lemon·juice. **3.** Re-heat gently before using. Do not allow to boil. **Serves 4.**

125 HOT TARTARE SAUCE

For all hot fish dishes.

1. Follow recipe and method for Béchamel Sauce (No. 110). **2.** Before seasoning with salt and pepper, stir in yolk of standard egg mixed with 2 extra tablespoons fresh double cream, 1 tablespoon very finely-chopped parsley, 1 dessertspoon finely-chopped gherkins and 1 dessertspoon finely-chopped capers. **3.** Re-heat gently before using. Do not allow to boil. **Serves 4.**

BÉARNAISE SAUCE 12

For meat grills and roasts, grilled fish.

2 tablespoons tarragon vinegar
3 tablespoons wine vinegar
1 level tablespoon finely-chopped onion
Yolks of 2 standard eggs
1 dessertspoon cold water
$\frac{1}{4}$ lb. English or Welsh butter, softened
Seasoning to taste

1. Put both vinegars and onion into saucepan. Boil gently until liquid is reduced by about one third. **2.** Leave until cold and strain. **3.** Put egg yolks, reduced vinegar liquor and water into double saucepan (or basin standing over pan of simmering water). Whisk until thick and fluffy. **4.** Gradually add butter, a tiny piece at a time. Continue whisking until each piece has been absorbed by the Sauce and Sauce itself has thickened. **5.** Season to taste with salt and pepper. **Serves 4.**

VELOUTÉ SAUCE 1:

For poultry, veal, and poached, grilled and steamed fish dishes.

1 oz. English or Welsh butter
1 oz. finely-chopped mushrooms
2 or 3 parsley sprigs
1 oz. flour
$\frac{1}{2}$ pint poultry, veal or fish stock (depending on dish)
2 peppercorns
1 dessertspoon lemon juice
4 tablespoons fresh double cream or soured cream
Seasoning to taste

1. Melt butter in saucepan. Add mushrooms and parsley and fry very gently for 5 minutes. **2.** Stir in flour. Gradually blend in stock. Add peppercorns. **3.** Cook, stirring, until Sauce comes to boil and thickens. **4.** Reduce heat, cover pan. Simmer very gently for 30 minutes. **5.** Strain, stir in lemon juice and cream. Season to taste with salt and pepper. **6.** Re-heat gently before using. Do not allow to boil. **Serves 4 to 6.**

28 SUPREME SAUCE

For same dishes as Velouté Sauce.

1. Follow recipe and method for Velouté Sauce (No. 127). **2.** After straining, stir in lemon juice, followed by the cream, mixed with yolk of standard egg. **3.** Season to taste with salt and pepper. **4.** Re-heat gently before using. Do not allow to boil. **Serves 4 to 6.**

29 ALLEMANDE SAUCE

For poached chicken and vegetable dishes.

1½ oz. English or Welsh butter
1 oz. flour
½ pint chicken stock
2 teaspoons lemon juice
Yolks of 2 standard eggs
2 tablespoons fresh single cream
Seasoning to taste

1. Melt 1 oz. butter in pan. Add flour and cook over low heat, stirring, for 2 minutes. Do not allow mixture (roux) to brown. **2.** Gradually blend in stock. **3.** Cook, stirring, until Sauce comes to boil and thickens. **4.** Lower heat. Cover pan and simmer *very gently* for 10 minutes. **5.** Remove from heat. Whisk in remaining butter, followed by lemon juice and egg yolks mixed with cream. **6.** Season to taste with salt and pepper. **7.** Re-heat gently before using. Do not allow to boil. **Serves 4 to 6.**

HOLLANDAISE SAUCE 131

For asparagus and broccoli, poached fish, egg and chicken dishes.

1 teaspoon lemon juice
1 teaspoon wine vinegar
1 tablespoon cold water
3 white peppercorns
½ small bay leaf
Yolks of 4 standard eggs
½ lb. English or Welsh butter, softened
Seasoning to taste

1. Put lemon juice, vinegar, water, peppercorns and bay leaf into saucepan. Boil gently until liquor is reduced by half. **2.** Leave until cold and strain. **3.** Put egg yolks and reduced vinegar liquor into double saucepan (or basin standing over pan of gently simmering water). **4.** Whisk until thick and foamy. **5.** Gradually add butter, a tiny piece at a time. Continue whisking until each piece has been absorbed by the Sauce and Sauce itself is consistency of Mayonnaise. **6.** Season to taste with salt and pepper. Serve straight away. **Serves 6.**

MOUSSELINE SAUCE 132

For same dishes as Hollandaise Sauce.

1. Follow recipe and method for Hollandaise Sauce (No. 131). **2.** Stir in 3 tablespoons lightly-whipped fresh double cream just before serving. **Serves 6.**

30 BROWN (OR ESPAGNOLE) SAUCE

1 oz. English or Welsh butter
1 teaspoon olive or corn oil
1 oz. chopped lean ham or bacon
½ small peeled onion
½ small celery stalk
1 oz. mushrooms and stalks
½ small peeled carrot
1 oz. flour
½ pint beef stock
1 level dessertspoon tomato purée (or
  1 small chopped tomato)
1 small bay leaf
2 sprigs parsley
Seasoning to taste

1. Put butter and oil into pan. Heat until both are sizzling. **2.** Add ham or bacon, chopped onion, celery, mushrooms with stalks and sliced carrot. **3.** Fry gently 7 to 10 minutes (or until golden). **4.** Add flour and cook, stirring, until it turns light brown. **5.** Gradually blend in stock. Cook, stirring, until Sauce comes to boil and thickens. **6.** Add purée or chopped tomato, bay leaf and parsley. Cover pan. **7.** Simmer gently for 30 minutes. **8.** Strain, season to taste with salt and pepper. **9.** Re-heat before using. **Serves 4.**

133 BIGARRADE SAUCE

For duck, goose and game dishes.

1. Follow recipe and method for Brown Sauce (No. 130). **2.** After straining, stir in juice of 1 small lemon and orange and 2 tablespoons dry red wine. **3.** Season to taste with salt and pepper. **4.** Re-heat before serving. **Serves 4.**

134 BROWN ONION SAUCE

For offal and beef dishes.

1. Follow recipe and method for Brown Sauce (No. 130). **2.** After straining add 1 large onion, finely chopped and lightly fried in butter. **3.** Season to taste with salt and pepper. **4.** Re-heat before serving. **Serves 4.**

135 MADEIRA SAUCE

For tongue, game and beef roasts and grills.

1. Follow recipe and method for Brown Sauce (No.130). **2.** After straining, stir in 3 tablespoons Madeira wine. **3.** Season to taste with salt and pepper. **4.** Re-heat before serving. **Serves 4.**

136 PEPPER SAUCE

For beef grills and roast, game.

1. Follow recipe and method for Brown Sauce (No.130). **2.** Before straining, add 4 tablespoons vinegar and about 10 crushed white peppercorns. **3.** Simmer with lid off pan for 15 minutes. **4.** Strain and season to taste with salt. **5.** Re-heat before using. **Serves 4.**

137 RÉFORME SAUCE

For lamb grills, mutton cutlets and beef fillets.

1. Follow recipe and method for Pepper Sauce (No. 136). **2.** Before straining, add 5 dessert-spoons dry red wine and 1 dessertspoon redcurrant jelly. **3.** Simmer with lid off pan for 15 minutes. **4.** Strain and season to taste with salt. **5.** Re-heat before using. **Serves 4.**

PIQUANT SAUCE 138

For pork grills and roasts, ham and bacon dishes and meat rissoles.

1. Follow recipe and method for Brown Sauce (No. 130). **2.** Before straining, add 1 level dessertspoon *each,* finely-chopped gherkins and capers, 1½ teaspoons Worcester sauce and 3 dessertspoons vinegar. **3.** Simmer with lid off pan for 10 minutes. **4.** Strain and season to taste with salt and pepper. **5.** Re-heat before using. **Serves 4.**

BREAD SAUCE 139

For poultry.

4 cloves
1 small peeled onion
6 white peppercorns
1 blade mace or large pinch nutmeg
½ small bay leaf
¼ pint milk
2 oz. fresh white breadcrumbs
1 oz. English or Welsh butter
2 tablespoons fresh single cream
Seasoning to taste

1. Press cloves into onion and put into saucepan. **2.** Add peppercorns, mace or nutmeg, bay leaf and milk. **3.** Slowly bring to boil. Reduce heat, cover pan and simmer 15 minutes. **4.** Strain. Combine hot milk with breadcrumbs, butter and cream. **5.** Season to taste with salt and pepper. **6.** Re-heat gently. **Serves 4 to 6.**

CUMBERLAND SAUCE 140

For ham and game dishes.

¼ pint red wine or port
4 tablespoons redcurrant jelly
Finely-grated peel and juice of 1 medium-
**   sized lemon and orange**
1 level dessertspoon finely-grated onion
1 level teaspoon made mustard
¼ level teaspoon ground ginger
¼ level teaspoon salt
Shake of pepper

1. Put all ingredients into pan. Slowly bring *just* up to boil, stirring occasionally. **2.** Remove from heat. Cover and leave 10 minutes. **3.** Leave unstrained and serve hot or strain and serve cold. **Serves 4.**

41 CURRY SAUCE

For pouring over hard-boiled eggs or combining with pieces of cooked fish, chicken, meat or vegetables.

2 oz. English or Welsh butter
2 teaspoons olive or corn oil
2 large finely-chopped onions
1 finely-chopped garlic clove (optional)
2 level tablespoons curry powder
1 level tablespoon flour
2 cloves
1 level tablespoon tomato purée
$\frac{1}{4}$ level teaspoon *each*, ground ginger and cinnamon
2 level tablespoons sweet pickle or chutney
1 tablespoon lemon juice
3 level teaspoons granulated sugar
$\frac{1}{2}$ pint stock or water
$\frac{1}{2}$ to 1 level teaspoon salt

1. Put butter and oil into pan. Heat until both are sizzling. 2. Add onions and garlic (if used). Fry gently until pale gold. 3. Stir in curry powder and flour. Add cloves, purée, ginger and cinnamon, sweet pickle or chutney, lemon juice and sugar. 4. Gradually blend in stock or water. Slowly bring to the boil, stirring. 5. Lower heat. Season with salt and cover pan. 6. Simmer slowly $\frac{3}{4}$ to 1 hour. 7. Sauce may be strained and re-heated before using. **Serves 4.**

42 QUICK CREAM SAUCE

For veal, poultry, fish, egg and cheese dishes.

1 can condensed cream soup (flavour to taste)
4 tablespoons milk

1. Put soup and milk into saucepan. 2. Heat through gently, stirring. **Serves 4 to 6.**

43 MINT SAUCE

For lamb and mutton roasts

4 level tablespoons finely-chopped mint
3 tablespoons boiling water
3 level teaspoons caster sugar
$\frac{1}{4}$ level teaspoon salt
3 tablespoons vinegar

1. Stir mint into boiling water. Add sugar and salt. 2. Leave until cold. 3. Add vinegar and mix well. **Serves 4 to 6.**

TOMATO SAUCE 144

For meat, fried and baked fish, egg, cheese, spaghetti and macaroni dishes.

2 oz. English or Welsh butter
2 teaspoons olive or corn oil
1 medium-sized sliced onion
1 clove finely-chopped garlic (optional)
2 oz. chopped lean bacon or ham
1 oz. flour
$\frac{1}{2}$ lb. chopped tomatoes
1 level tablespoon tomato purée
$\frac{1}{2}$ pint stock or water
1 bay leaf
1 blade of mace
6 white peppercorns
$\frac{1}{4}$ level teaspoon basil or mixed herbs
1 level teaspoon brown sugar
1 dessertspoon lemon juice
Seasoning to taste

1. Put butter and oil into pan and heat until both are sizzling. 2. Add onion, garlic if used, and bacon or ham. Fry gently until pale gold. 3. Stir in flour, tomatoes, purée, stock or water, bay leaf, mace, peppercorns, basil or mixed herbs and sugar. 4. Bring to the boil, stirring. Reduce heat and cover pan. 5. Simmer gently for 45 minutes. 6. Strain. Add lemon juice. Season to taste with salt and pepper. 7. Re-heat before using. **Serves 4 to 6.**

CRANBERRY SAUCE 145

For poultry, duck, goose, game, turkey, lamb and mutton dishes.

$\frac{1}{2}$ pint water
6 oz. granulated sugar
$\frac{1}{2}$ lb. cranberries

1. Put water and sugar into saucepan. Heat slowly until sugar dissolves. 2. Add cranberries. Cook fairly quickly for 2 to 3 minutes (or until skins pop open). 3. Reduce heat. Simmer very gently for 10 minutes. 4. Serve hot or cold. **Serves 6.**

146 APPLE SAUCE

For pork roasts and grills, duck and goose dishes.

1 lb. cooking apples
3 tablespoons water
Large pinch of salt
2 level teaspoons caster sugar
½ oz. English or Welsh butter

1. Peel, core and slice apples. Put into pan with water. **2.** Cook gently until soft and pulpy. Either beat to a purée or rub through sieve or liquidise. **3.** Return to pan, add salt, sugar and butter. **4.** Re-heat gently. **5.** Serve hot or cold. **Serves 6.**

MEAT OR POULTRY GRAVY 14

Meat or poultry dripping
3 level dessertspoons cornflour
½ pint stock or water
Seasoning to taste

1. Pour off all but 1 tablespoon dripping from roasting tin. **2.** Add cornflour and combine. **3.** Stand tin over very low heat. Gradually blend in stock or water. **4.** Cook, stirring, until gravy comes to boil and thickens. **5.** Lower heat. Simmer for 3 minutes. **6.** Season to taste with salt and pepper. **Serves 4 to 6.**

SAVOURY BUTTER SAUCES

These consist of melted butter with one or two simple additions. To keep the butter a good colour and prevent dark speckles and bitterness, the butter should be clarified first. The method for doing this is as follows:

Put required amount of English or Welsh butter into pan and melt over very low heat. Leave to stand a few minutes then strain through fine muslin into clean basin. Butter will now be clear and free of milky solids.

148 BROWN BUTTER SAUCE

For hot asparagus and broccoli.

3 oz. clarified English or Welsh butter

1. Put butter into saucepan. Cook very slowly until it turns light brown. **2.** Serve straight away. **Serves 4.**

BLACK BUTTER SAUCE WITH CAPERS 15

For poached or steamed fish and brain dishes.

3 oz. clarified English or Welsh butter
1 teaspoon vinegar
1 level tablespoon chopped capers

1. Put butter into saucepan. Cook very slowly until it turns dark brown. **2.** At once stir in vinegar and capers. Serve straight away. **Serves 4.**

149 BLACK BUTTER SAUCE

For poached and steamed fish, egg and vegetable dishes.

3 oz. clarified English or Welsh butter
1 teaspoon vinegar

1. Put butter into saucepan. Cook very slowly until it turns dark brown. **2.** Stir in vinegar at once. Serve straight away. **Serves 4.**

LEMON BUTTER SAUCE 1

For poached and steamed fish dishes.

3 oz. clarified English or Welsh butter
1 level tablespoon finely-chopped parsley
1 teaspoon lemon juice
Shake of pepper

1. Put butter into saucepan. Cook very slowly until it turns light brown. **2.** Stir in remaining ingredients. Serve straight away. **Serves 4.**

BARBECUE SAUCES

These are brushed on to foods during cooking. Use them on meat or fish and vegetables on skewers (Kebabs), chops, steaks and portions of poultry in a rotisserie, under the grill or over a barbecue pit. They should be brushed on to the foods during the latter part of cooking: prolonged heating would make the spices bitter.

152 MEAT BARBECUE SAUCE

For all types of meat.

1 oz. English or Welsh butter
1 teaspoon olive or corn oil
1 medium-sized onion, finely chopped
3 tablespoons water
2 tablespoons vinegar
1 tablespoon Worcester sauce
2 tablespoons lemon juice
1 level dessertspoon soft brown sugar
2 level teaspoons made mustard
½ level teaspoon salt
½ level teaspoon paprika
¼ level teaspoon chilli powder

1. Put butter and oil into saucepan. Heat until both are sizzling. **2.** Add onion. Fry gently until pale gold. **3.** Add all remaining ingredients. Bring slowly to boil, stirring. **4.** Reduce heat. Cover pan and simmer gently 30 minutes.

MILD BARBECUE SAUCE 153

For meat, poultry or fish.

½ pint tomato ketchup
1 oz. English or Welsh butter
3 tablespoons vinegar
¼ level teaspoon chilli powder
1 level teaspoon brown sugar
½ level teaspoon celery salt
½ level teaspoon mixed herbs

1. Put all ingredients into pan. **2.** Bring slowly to the boil, stirring. **3.** Cover pan and simmer gently for 15 minutes.

POULTRY BARBECUE SAUCE 154

For poultry and duck.

½ pint dry cider, apple juice or white wine
1 level teaspoon crushed rosemary
1 finely-chopped garlic clove (optional)
1 small onion, finely grated
2 teaspoons Worcester sauce
3 oz. English or Welsh butter
2 level teaspoons paprika
½ level teaspoon salt

1. Put all ingredients into pan. **2.** Bring slowly to the boil, stirring. **3.** Cover pan. Simmer gently for 15 minutes.

SWEET SAUCES

155 FUDGE SAUCE

For ice cream, steamed and baked puddings.

1 oz. plain chocolate
½ oz. English or Welsh butter
2 tablespoons warm milk
¼ lb. soft brown sugar
3 level teaspoons golden syrup
½ teaspoon vanilla essence

1. Break up chocolate. Put into basin standing over saucepan of hot water. Add butter. **2.** Leave until chocolate and butter have melted, stirring once or twice. **3.** Blend in milk. Transfer to saucepan. Add sugar and golden syrup.

4. Stand over low heat. Stir until sugar has dissolved. **5.** Bring to the boil. Boil steadily without stirring for 5 minutes. **6.** Remove from heat. Add vanilla and mix well. Serve hot. **Serves 4.**

● *For a Sauce that hardens quickly over ice cream, boil an extra 2 to 3 minutes. If there is any Sauce left over, it can be re-heated in double saucepan (or in basin standing over saucepan of simmering water).*

156 RUM OR BRANDY FUDGE SAUCE

For same dishes as Fudge Sauce.

1. Follow recipe and method for Fudge Sauce (No. 155). **2.** Add 2 teaspoons rum or brandy instead of vanilla essence. **Serves 4.**

157 COFFEE FUDGE SAUCE

For same dishes as Fudge Sauce.

1. Follow recipe and method for Fudge Sauce (No. 155). **2.** Add 1 level teaspoon instant coffee powder with the butter. **Serves 4.**

158 RED JAM SAUCE

For steamed and baked puddings.

2 level teaspoons arrowroot or cornflour
¼ pint cold water
4 level tablespoons raspberry, strawberry, plum or blackcurrant jam
1 dessertspoon lemon juice
1 level tablespoon caster sugar

1. Mix arrowroot or cornflour to smooth paste with a little of the cold water. **2.** Put rest of water into pan. Add jam, lemon juice and sugar. **3.** Heat gently, stirring, until sugar is dissolved. Combine with arrowroot or cornflour paste. **4.** Return to pan. Cook, stirring, until Sauce comes to boil and both thickens and clears. **5.** Simmer for 2 minutes. **Serves 4 to 6.**

159 APRICOT JAM SAUCE

For steamed and baked puddings.

1. Follow recipe and method for Red Jam Sauce (No. 158). **2.** Use apricot jam instead of red jam. **Serves 4 to 6.**

160 MARMALADE SAUCE

For steamed and baked puddings.

1. Follow recipe and method for Red Jam Sauce (No. 158). **2.** Use orange marmalade instead of the red jam. **Serves 4 to 6.**

SWEET WHITE SAUCE 161

For steamed and baked puddings.

½ oz. cornflour
½ pint milk
¼ oz. English or Welsh butter
1 level tablespoon caster sugar

1. Mix cornflour to smooth paste with a little of the cold milk. **2.** Warm remainder. Pour on to paste and mix well. **3.** Return to pan. **4.** Cook, stirring, until Sauce comes to boil and thickens. **5.** Simmer for 2 minutes. **6.** Remove from heat. Stir in butter and sugar. **Serves 4 to 6.**

VANILLA SAUCE 162

For steamed and baked puddings.

1. Follow recipe and method for Sweet White Sauce (No. 161). **2.** Add ½ to 1 teaspoon vanilla essence with butter and sugar. **Serves 4 to 6.**

BRANDY SAUCE 163

For Christmas Puddings, baked and steamed fruit puddings.

1. Follow recipe and method for Sweet White Sauce (No. 161). **2.** Add 1 or 2 tablespoons brandy with the butter and sugar. **Serves 4 to 6.**

GOLDEN SYRUP SAUCE 164

For steamed and baked puddings.

2 level teaspoons arrowroot or cornflour
4 tablespoons cold water
4 level tablespoons golden syrup
Finely-grated peel and juice of 1 small lemon

1. Mix arrowroot or cornflour to smooth paste with cold water. **2.** Put into saucepan with syrup and grated peel and juice. **3.** Heat gently, stirring, until Sauce comes to boil and both thickens and clears. **4.** Simmer for 2 minutes. **Serves 4 to 6.**

65 BUTTERSCOTCH SAUCE

For steamed and baked puddings, for serving over sliced bananas, for ice cream.

1 level tablespoon cornflour
$\frac{1}{4}$ pint milk
1 oz. English or Welsh butter
$\frac{1}{4}$ lb. soft brown sugar
$\frac{1}{2}$ to 1 teaspoon vanilla essence

1. Mix cornflour to smooth paste with a little of the cold milk. **2.** Pour rest of milk into saucepan. Add butter and sugar. **3.** Stand over low heat. Stir until sugar dissolves. **4.** Pour on to cornflour paste and return to pan. **5.** Cook, stirring, until Sauce comes to boil and thickens. Add vanilla. **6.** Simmer 3 minutes. **Serves 4 to 6.**

66 ORANGE OR LEMON BUTTERSCOTCH SAUCE

For steamed and baked puddings, for serving over sliced bananas, for ice cream.

1. Follow recipe and method for Butterscoth Sauce (No. 165). **2.** Add $\frac{1}{2}$ level teaspoon finely-grated orange or lemon peel to cornflour paste. **3.** Omit vanilla. **Serves 4 to 6.**

67 BRANDY HARD SAUCE

For Christmas Puddings, baked and steamed fruit puddings.

$\frac{1}{4}$ lb. English or Welsh butter, softened
$\frac{1}{4}$ lb. sifted icing sugar
$\frac{1}{4}$ lb. caster sugar
1 tablespoon milk
1 tablespoon brandy
2 oz. ground almonds
Cinnamon

1. Beat butter until creamy. **2.** Gradually beat in icing and caster sugars alternately with milk and brandy. Cream until light and fluffy. **3.** Add almonds and mix well. **4.** Pile into small dish. Sprinkle lightly with cinnamon. **Serves 6 to 8.**

RUM HARD SAUCE 168

For same dishes as Brandy Hard Sauce.

1. Follow recipe and method for Brandy Hard Sauce (No. 167). **2.** Use rum instead of brandy. **3.** Sprinkle Sauce lightly with mixed spice instead of cinnamon. **Serves 6 to 8.**

COFFEE CREAM SAUCE 169

For ice cream, hot gingerbread, Christmas Pudding, mince pies.

2 standard eggs
6 tablespoons hot strong coffee
2 oz. caster sugar
Pinch of salt
$\frac{1}{4}$ pint fresh double cream

1. Beat eggs well. Gradually beat in coffee. **2.** Put into double saucepan (or basin standing over pan of simmering water). **3.** Add sugar and salt. Cook, without boiling, until Sauce is thick enough to coat back of spoon. Stir frequently. **4.** Remove from heat and chill. **5.** Just before serving, whip cream until thick. Gently stir in Coffee Sauce. **Serves 4 to 6.**

WHIPPED SHERRY SAUCE 170

For steamed and baked puddings, ice cream, stewed fruit and fruit pies.

Yolks of 2 standard eggs
2 level tablespoons sifted icing sugar
4 tablespoons sweet sherry

1. Put all ingredients into basin standing over pan of simmering water. **2.** Whisk until thick, light and foamy. **3.** Serve at once. **Serves 4.**

171 CUSTARD SAUCE

For steamed and baked puddings, fruit and mince pies, stewed fruit.

2 standard eggs
1 level dessertspoon caster sugar
$\frac{1}{2}$ pint milk
$\frac{1}{4}$ teaspoon vanilla essence (optional)

1. Beat eggs with sugar and 3 tablespoons milk. **2.** Heat rest of milk to lukewarm. **3.** Beat into eggs. Pour into double saucepan (or basin standing over pan of simmering water). **4.** Cook, without boiling, until custard thickens enough to coat back of spoon thinly. Stir frequently. **5.** Pour into cold jug and stir in vanilla. **6.** Serve hot or cold. **Serves 4 to 6.**

172 COFFEE CUSTARD SAUCE

For steamed and baked puddings.

1. Follow recipe and method for Custard Sauce (No. 171). **2.** Add 1 or 2 level teaspoons instant coffee powder to the milk while it is warming. **3.** Omit vanilla. **Serves 4 to 6.**

173 CHOCOLATE CUSTARD SAUCE

For steamed and baked puddings.

1. Follow recipe and method for Custard Sauce (No. 171). **2.** Melt 1 oz. grated plain chocolate in the milk while it is warming. **Serves 4 to 6.**

174 LEMON CUSTARD SAUCE

For steamed and baked puddings, fruit pies and stewed fruit.

1. Follow recipe and method for Custard Sauce (No. 171). **2.** Add $\frac{1}{2}$ level teaspoon finely-grated lemon peel to the milk while it is warming. Omit vanilla. **Serves 4 to 6.**

ORANGE CUSTARD SAUCE 175

For same dishes as Lemon Custard Sauce.

1. Follow recipe and method for Custard Sauce (No. 171). **2.** Add $\frac{1}{2}$ level teaspoon finely-grated orange peel to the milk while it is warming. **3.** Omit vanilla. **Serves 4 to 6.**

QUICK CHOCOLATE SAUCE 176

For ice cream, steamed and baked puddings, Profiteroles.

3 oz. caster sugar
3 oz. soft brown sugar
3 oz. cocoa powder
$\frac{1}{2}$ pint milk
1 teaspoon vanilla essence
1 oz. English or Welsh butter

1. Put all ingredients into saucepan. Stand over low heat. **2.** Stir until sugar has dissolved. Slowly bring to boil. **3.** Boil briskly, without stirring, for 2 minutes (or until Sauce coats back of spoon). **Serves 4 to 6.**

● *If a more fudge-like Sauce is preferred, boil an extra 2 to 3 minutes.*

CHOCOLATE SAUCE 177

For steamed and baked puddings.

1 level tablespoon cornflour
$\frac{1}{2}$ pint milk
2 oz. grated plain chocolate
$\frac{1}{2}$ teaspoon vanilla essence
$\frac{1}{2}$ oz. English or Welsh butter
1 to 1$\frac{1}{2}$ level tablespoons caster sugar

1. Mix cornflour to smooth paste with a little of the cold milk. **2.** Put remainder of milk into saucepan and add chocolate. Heat very slowly until chocolate melts. **3.** Pour on to cornflour paste and mix well. Return to pan. **4.** Cook, stirring, until Sauce comes to boil and thickens. **5.** Add vanilla, butter and sugar. Simmer 3 minutes. **Serves 4 to 6.**

Marinades & Savoury Butters

MARINADES

Marinades are used to tenderise uncooked foods and to improve their flavour and preserve their colour. Once raw foods have been coated with the chosen Marinade they should be covered, put into a cold larder or refrigerator and left for the required amount of time. As a general rule, cubed meat and fish should be marinated from 1 to 3 hours; large joints of meat and whole fish, overnight. As most Marinades contain an acid they, together with the food to be marinated, should be put into a glass, stainless steel or enamel dish or tray. Any turning or stirring should be done with a wooden spoon.

178 YOGURT MARINADE

For cubes of lamb.

1 carton (5 oz.) natural yogurt
1 tablespoon lemon juice
1 level tablespoon finely-grated onion
½ level teaspoon salt

1. Combine ingredients well together. 2. Add cubes of lamb. Toss until well coated. 3. Cover and chill at least 3 hours, turning frequently.

179 LEMON MARINADE

For cubes or small fillets of fish; cubes or cutlets of lamb.

2 tablespoons lemon juice
3 tablespoons olive or corn oil
½ to 1 level teaspoon salt
Freshly-milled pepper

1. Combine ingredients well together. 2. Add fish or meat. Coat all over with Marinade mixture. 3. Cover and chill at least 3 hours, turning frequently.

180 SPICE MARINADE

For cubes or small fillets of fish; cubes or cutlets of lamb.

½ level teaspoon finely-grated lemon peel
½ level teaspoon turmeric
¼ level teaspoon ginger
1 small garlic clove, very finely chopped
1 tablespoon lemon juice
½ level teaspoon salt

1. Combine ingredients well together. 2. Add fish or meat. Coat all over with Marinade mixture. 3. Cover and chill 5 hours, turning frequently.

SWEET-SOUR MARINADE 181

For cubes of pork and pork fillet; cubes or cutlets of lamb.

4 tablespoons pineapple juice
1 dessertspoon soy sauce
1 dessertspoon lemon juice
1 small garlic clove, very finely chopped
¼ level teaspoon salt

1. Combine ingredients well together. 2. Add meat. Coat all over with Marinade mixture. 3. Cover and chill 2 hours, turning frequently.

BEER MARINADE 182

For joints of beef and thick steaks.

6 tablespoons olive or corn oil
½ pint beer
1 garlic clove, finely chopped
2 tablespoons lemon juice
1 level tablespoon caster sugar
½ to 1 level teaspoon salt

1. Gradually beat oil into beer then stir in remaining ingredients. 2. Pour over meat. 3. Cover and refrigerate 4 to 5 hours, turning at least twice.

FIERY MARINADE 183

For pork fillet and chops.

1 level teaspoon Cayenne pepper
3 dessertspoons lemon juice
1 small onion, finely grated
¼ level teaspoon dried mustard
1 dessertspoon Worcester sauce
½ level teaspoon salt

1. Combine ingredients well together. 2. Add meat. Coat all over with Marinade mixture. 3. Cover and chill 2 to 3 hours, turning frequently.

184 WINE MARINADE

For large legs and shoulders of lamb and mutton; game.

6 tablespoons dry red wine
3 tablespoons wine vinegar
3 tablespoons olive or corn oil
1 sprig *each* parsley and thyme
2 small bay leaves, crumbled
1 garlic clove, finely chopped
1 small onion, sliced
¼ level teaspoon nutmeg
1 level tablespoon caster sugar
Shake of Cayenne pepper

1. Combine ingredients well together. **2.** Pour over meat. **3.** Cover and refrigerate 8 to 12 hours, turning at least twice.

CHICKEN MARINADE 185

For portions of roasting chicken.

3 tablespoons olive or corn oil
6 tablespoons dry white wine or cider
1 garlic clove, very finely chopped
  (optional)
1 small onion, very finely chopped
½ level teaspoon celery salt
Good shake pepper
½ level teaspoon thyme or crushed
  rosemary

1. Gradually beat oil into wine or cider. Stir in rest of ingredients. **2.** Add chicken portions. Coat all over with Marinade mixture. **3.** Cover and chill 2 to 3 hours, turning at least twice.

SAVOURY BUTTERS

These are highly-seasoned butters which add piquancy and flavour to grilled or fried meat and fish. After making, they should be well chilled, cut into penny-sized pats of ¼ inch in thickness, and put on to the hot food immediately before serving. **All quantities are for 4.**

186 DEVILLED BUTTER

For shellfish, ham, bacon and pork.

2 oz. English or Welsh butter
½ level teaspoon dry mustard
1 teaspoon Worcester sauce
1 teaspoon lemon juice
Pinch Cayenne pepper

1. Cream butter until soft. **2.** Beat in remaining ingredients. **3.** Chill.

187 GARLIC BUTTER

For steaks.

2 garlic cloves
2 oz. English or Welsh butter

1. Peel garlic cloves and boil in a little water for about 5 minutes. **2.** Drain and chop very finely. **3.** Cream butter until soft. **4.** Gradually beat in garlic. **5.** Chill.

GREEN BUTTER 188

For fish.

1 level teaspoon fresh tarragon
1 level teaspoon fresh chervil
1 level teaspoon fresh parsley
2 small spinach leaves
2 oz. English or Welsh butter
1 level teaspoon finely-grated onion

1. Put tarragon, chervil, parsley and spinach into bowl. **2.** Cover with boiling water and leave 5 minutes. **3.** Drain. **4.** Cover with cold water, drain and dry in tea-towel. **5.** Chop finely. **6.** Cream butter until soft. **7.** Gradually beat in chopped herbs and onion. **8.** Chill.

SMOKED COD'S 189
ROE BUTTER

For fish.

2 oz. English or Welsh butter
1 oz. smoked cod's roe
1 teaspoon lemon juice
Freshly-milled black pepper to taste

1. Cream butter until soft. **2.** Gradually beat in cod's roe and lemon juice. **3.** Season well with pepper. **4.** Chill.

90 MAÎTRE D'HÔTEL BUTTER

For fish and meat

2 oz. English or Welsh butter
1 level teaspoon very finely-chopped
parsley
2 teaspoons lemon juice
Shake of pepper

1. Cream butter until soft. **2.** Gradually beat in remaining ingredients. **3.** Chill.

91 HAM BUTTER

For veal and chicken.

2 oz. English or Welsh butter
2 oz. very finely-minced ham
¼ level teaspoon made mustard
2 teaspoons lemon juice

1. Cream butter until soft. **2.** Gradually beat in remaining ingredients. **3.** Chill.

92 HERRING ROE BUTTER

For fish.

2 oz. English or Welsh butter
2 oz. canned herring roes (soft)
¼ level teaspoon made mustard
1 teaspoon lemon juice

1. Cream butter until soft. **2.** Gradually beat in small pieces of roe. Continue beating until smooth. **3.** Work in mustard and lemon juice. **4.** Chill.

93 TUNA BUTTER

For veal and fish.

2 oz. English or Welsh butter
2 oz. canned, drained tuna, very finely
mashed
1 level teaspoon very finely-chopped
parsley
1 teaspoon lemon juice
Freshly-milled black pepper to taste

1. Cream butter until soft. **2.** Gradually beat in tuna, parsley and lemon juice. **3.** Season with pepper. **4.** Chill.

ANCHOVY BUTTER 194

For fish or steak.

2 oz. English or Welsh butter
1 teaspoon anchovy essence
½ teaspoon lemon juice

1. Cream butter until soft. **2.** Beat in essence and lemon juice. **3.** Chill.

CURRY BUTTER 195

For shellfish and lamb.

2 oz. English or Welsh butter
1 level teaspoon curry powder
¼ level teaspoon turmeric
1 teaspoon lemon juice

1. Cream butter until soft. **2.** Beat in remaining ingredients. **3.** Chill.

CHIVE BUTTER 196

For steaks and chicken.

2 oz. English or Welsh butter
2 teaspoons very finely-chopped chives
1 teaspoon lemon juice

1. Cream butter until soft. **2.** Gradually beat in chives and lemon juice. **3.** Chill.

LEMON BUTTER 197

For fish, veal and chicken.

2 oz. English or Welsh butter
1 level teaspoon finely-grated lemon peel
1 teaspoon lemon juice

1. Cream butter until soft. **2.** Gradually beat in lemon peel and juice. **3.** Chill.

HORSERADISH BUTTER 198

For beef, herrings and mackerel.

2 oz. English or Welsh butter
2 level teaspoons grated horseradish

1. Cream butter until soft. **2.** Gradually beat in horseradish. **3.** Chill.

Hors-d'Œuvres

199 MUSTARD BUTTER

For beef, lamb, bacon, ham, shellfish, herrings and mackerel.

2 oz. English or Welsh butter
1 level teaspoon made mustard (or 2 level teaspoons French mustard)

1. Cream butter until soft. **2.** Gradually beat in mustard. **3.** Chill.

200 PAPRIKA BUTTER

For veal, bacon, ham and shellfish.

2 oz. English or Welsh butter
1 level teaspoon paprika
¼ level teaspoon onion salt
Good shake pepper

1. Cream butter until soft. **2.** Gradually beat in remaining ingredients. **3.** Chill.

201 PRAWN BUTTER

For fish.

2 oz. English or Welsh butter
2 oz. shelled prawns, very finely chopped
1 teaspoon lemon juice
¼ level teaspoon made mustard

1. Cream butter until soft. **2.** Gradually beat in remaining ingredients. **3.** Chill.

202 TOMATO BUTTER

For veal, lamb, bacon, ham and shellfish.

2 oz. English or Welsh butter
2 level teaspoons tomato purée
¼ level teaspoon caster sugar
¼ teaspoon Worcester sauce

1. Cream butter until soft. **2.** Gradually beat in remaining ingredients. **3.** Chill.

LIVER SAUSAGE PÂTÉ 20

¾ lb. soft liver sausage
2 oz. English or Welsh butter, softened
1 level tablespoon very finely-chopped parsley
1 dessertspoon brandy or dry sherry
¼ level teaspoon thyme
Freshly-milled black pepper and salt to taste

1. Beat sausage with butter until smooth and creamy. **2.** Blend in parsley, brandy or sherry and thyme. **3.** Season to taste with pepper and salt. **4.** Turn into small serving bowl. Chill 2 to 3 hours. **5.** Serve by spooning portions on to plates and accompanying with crisp toast. **Serves 4.**

BUTTERED BUCKLING 20

1 large buckling
¼ lb. English or Welsh butter, softened
1 level tablespoon finely-chopped parsley
1 dessertspoon bottled horseradish sauce
1 tablespoon lemon juice
Freshly-milled black pepper

1. Cover buckling with boiling water, leave 1 minute and drain. **2.** Remove skin and bones and flake up flesh very finely. **3.** Beat to smooth cream with softened butter. Stir in parsley, horseradish sauce and lemon juice. **4.** Season to taste with pepper. Arrange equal amounts on 4 serving plates. **5.** Shape into neat mounds with fork. Accompany with hot toast. **Serves 4.**

HOT CHEESE CUPS 20

2 standard eggs
¼ pint fresh double cream
1 level teaspoon made mustard
Large pinch Cayenne pepper
¼ level teaspoon salt
¼ lb. crumbled Lancashire cheese

1. Beat eggs, cream and mustard together. **2.** Season with Cayenne pepper and salt. Stir in 3 oz. cheese. **3.** Pour into 4 individual buttered heatproof dishes, and sprinkle with rest of cheese. Bake in centre of fairly hot oven (400°F. or Gas No. 6) for 20 to 25 minutes (or until top is pale gold). **4.** Serve straight away with crisp toast. **Serves 4.**

06 STILTON-FILLED EGGS

4 large hard-boiled eggs
2 oz. Blue Stilton cheese
1 level teaspoon paprika
2 tablespoons fresh single cream
Salt and pepper to taste
4 level tablespoons mustard and cress
GARNISH
8 small slices of tomato

1. Halve eggs lengthwise and carefully remove yolks. **2.** Transfer to basin and mash finely with Stilton cheese. **3.** Stir in paprika and cream then season to taste with salt and pepper. **4.** Pile back into egg white halves. **5.** Cover 4 serving plates with mustard and cress and place 2 egg halves on each. Garnish each with slice of tomato. **6.** Chill lightly before serving. **7.** Accompany with brown bread and butter. **Serves 4.**

CURRIED EGG & SHRIMP COCKTAIL 208

½ round lettuce, washed and dried
3 tablespoons Mayonnaise (No. 577)
4 tablespoons natural yogurt
2 level teaspoons curry powder
4 level tablespoons chutney
2 tablespoons lemon juice
1 level dessertspoon sultanas
¼ lb. peeled shrimps
2 standard eggs, hard boiled and
   coarsely chopped

1. Shred lettuce and use to half-fill 4 large wine glasses. Leave on one side. **2.** Combine Mayonnaise with yogurt, curry powder, chutney and lemon juice. Stir in sultanas, shrimps and eggs. **3.** Mix well and chill lightly. **4.** Spoon equal amounts into glasses and accompany with brown bread and butter. **Serves 4.**

07 INDIVIDUAL KIPPER CREAMS

½ lb. kipper fillets
1 dessertspoon finely-chopped onion
3 oz. English or Welsh butter, softened
¼ pint cold Béchamel Sauce (No. 110)
1 dessertspoon lemon juice
1 dessertspoon dry white wine
Seasoning to taste
¼ pint fresh double cream
GARNISH
¼ pint cold aspic jelly
4 cucumber slices

1. Skin kipper fillets. Fry gently with onion in 1 oz. butter for 5 to 7 minutes. **2.** Remove from pan and mince finely. **3.** Put into bowl and add pan juices. Gradually beat in rest of butter, cold sauce, lemon juice and wine. Season to taste with salt and pepper. **4.** Whip cream fairly stiffly. Gently fold into kipper mixture. **5.** Transfer equal amounts to 4 individual dishes. Smooth tops with a knife. **6.** Spoon aspic jelly over each and chill. **7.** Just before serving, garnish with cucumber. **Serves 4.**

Individual Kipper Creams (No. 207)

209 CREAM CHEESE-FILLED EGGS

4 large hard-boiled eggs
2 oz. cream cheese
1 level tablespoon finely-chopped celery
1 tablespoon milk
Salt and pepper to taste
4 heaped tablespoons shredded lettuce
GARNISH
8 thin strips canned pimento

1. Halve eggs lengthwise and carefully remove yolks. **2.** Transfer to basin and mash finely. **3.** Mix well with cream cheese, celery and milk then season to taste with salt and pepper. **4.** Pile back into egg white halves. **5.** Cover 4 serving plates with shredded lettuce and place 2 egg halves on each. Garnish with pimento. **6.** Chill lightly before serving. **Serves 4.**

210 HOT SOLE FRITTERS

1 lb. sole fillets
Salt and pepper
1 recipe Savoury Fritter Batter (No. 665)
Deep fat or oil for frying
2 oz. very finely-grated English Cheddar
    cheese
4 lemon wedges

1. Using sharp knife or kitchen scissors, cut sole into strips measuring about 2 in. × ½ in. **2.** Sprinkle lightly with salt and pepper. Coat with Fritter Batter. **3.** Fry in hot fat or oil (about a quarter at a time) for 2 to 3 minutes (or until crisp and golden). **4.** Remove from pan and drain on soft kitchen paper. Transfer to serving dish lined with paper napkin. **5.** Sprinkle with cheese. Serve straight away. **6.** Hand lemon separately. **Serves 4.**

211 POTTED TONGUE

½ lb. tongue
3 oz. English or Welsh butter, softened
¼ level teaspoon made mustard
Seasoning to taste
1 extra oz. English or Welsh butter, melted

1. Mince tongue finely. **2.** Gradually beat in 3 oz. butter and mustard. **3.** Season to taste with salt and pepper then press equal amounts into 4 small jars or pots. **4.** Cover tops completely with remaining butter. Leave in cool until butter is set. **5.** Serve with crisp toast. **Serves 4.**

POTTED HAM   21

1. Follow recipe and method for Potted Tongue (No. 211).**2.** Use ½ lb. ham instead of tongue. **Serves 4.**

POTTED BEEF   21

1. Follow recipe and method for Potted Tongue (No. 211). **2.** Use ½ lb. cooked beef instead of tongue and 1 teaspoon bottled horseradish sauce instead of mustard. **Serves 4.**

EGG MAYONNAISE   21

½ box mustard and cress
4 large hard-boiled eggs, halved
8 tablespoons Chantilly Mayonnaise
    (No. 581)
Paprika
GARNISH
4 anchovy fillets, each halved lengthwise

1. Line 4 serving plates with mustard and cress. **2.** Arrange 2 hard-boiled egg halves on each, cut sides down. **3.** Spoon Mayonnaise over eggs. Sprinkle lightly with paprika. **4.** Garnish each serving with 2 strips of anchovy. **Serves 4.**

EGG & SMOKED   21
SALMON MAYONNAISE

1. Follow recipe and method for Egg Mayonnaise (No. 214). **2.** Garnish each serving with small strips of smoked salmon. **Serves 4.**

CREAM-FILLED AVOCADOS   21

2 medium-sized ripe Avocados
Lemon juice
1 recipe Cream Cheese and Celery
    Dressing (No. 563)

1. Cut Avocados in half about 5 minutes before serving. **2.** Remove stones. Brush Avocado flesh with lemon juice to prevent browning. **3.** Fill cavities with Dressing. **4.** Pass rest of Dressing separately. **Serves 4.**

17 AVOCADOS WITH YOGURT

1. Follow recipe and method for Cream-filled Avocados (No. 216). **2.** Fill cavities with Basic Yogurt Dressing (No. 566). **3.** Pass rest of Dressing separately. **Serves 4.**

18 AVOCADOS WITH SHELLFISH

1. Follow recipe and method for Cream-filled Avocados (No. 216). **2.** Fill cavities with 4 level dessertspoons peeled prawns or crabmeat mixed with 4 dessertspoons Thousand Island Mayonnaise (No. 586). **Serves 4.**

19 CHICKEN & MUSHROOM VOL-AU-VENTS

½ recipe Puff Pastry (No. 96) or ½ lb. bought Puff Pastry
Beaten egg for brushing
FILLING
¼ lb. cooked chicken
2 oz. chopped mushrooms
½ oz. English or Welsh butter
¼ pint freshly-made Béchamel Sauce (No. 110)
1 dessertspoon lemon juice
Seasoning to taste

1. Roll home-made Pastry out to ¼-in thickness and bought Pastry as directed on packet. **2.** Cut into 4 rounds with 3½-in. fluted biscuit cutter dipped in hot water. **3.** Stand upside down on damp baking tray. Cut circle in centre of each round by pressing a quarter of the way through Pastry with 1½-in. cutter. **4.** Brush with beaten egg and leave for 30 minutes. **5.** Bake just above centre of hot oven (450°F. or Gas No. 8) for 10 to 15 minutes (or until well risen and crisp). **6.** Lift off centre pieces from baked Pastry cases and reserve for lids. Scoop out remaining soft centres underneath and discard. **7.** Return cases to oven (with heat switched off and door left open). Leave 5 to 10 minutes. **8.** Cut chicken into bite-sized pieces. Lightly fry mushrooms in butter. **9.** Add chicken and mushrooms to Sauce with lemon juice. Heat through gently, then adjust seasoning to taste. **10.** Spoon equal amounts of filling into hot Pastry cases. Top with lids and serve straight away. **Serves 4.**

PRAWN VOL-AU-VENTS 220

1. Follow recipe and method for Chicken and Mushroom Vol-au-Vents (No. 219). **2.** Instead of chicken and fried mushrooms, use ¼ lb. peeled prawns and 2 oz. cooked and flaked white fish. **Serves 4.**

HAM & MUSHROOM VOL-AU-VENTS 221

1. Follow recipe and method for Chicken and Mushroom Vol-au-Vents (No. 219). **2.** Instead of chicken, use ¼ lb. coarsely-chopped ham. **Serves 4.**

LARGE VOL-AU-VENT 222

1 recipe Puff Pastry (No. 96)
Beaten egg for brushing
Fillings (double quantity) as for small Vol-au-Vents (Nos. 219-221)

1. Roll out Pastry to ½ to ¾-in. thickness. **2.** Cut into 7-in. round (with knife dipped in hot water), using 7-in. cake tin as guide. **3.** Stand upside down on damp baking tray. Cut circle in centre by pressing half-way through Pastry with 4-in. round biscuit cutter. **4.** Brush with egg. Leave for ½ an hour then bake just above centre of hot oven (450°F. or Gas No. 8) for 15 minutes. **5.** Reduce temperature to fairly hot (375°F. or Gas No. 5). Bake further 15 to 20 minutes. **6.** Remove lid from baked Pastry case and reserve. Scoop out remaining soft centre and discard. **7.** Return case to oven (with heat switched off and door left open) for 5 to 10 minutes. **8.** Fill as for small Vol-au-Vents. **Serves 4 to 6.**

GRILLED GRAPEFRUITS 223

2 grapefruits
4 teaspoons sweet sherry
8 level teaspoons caster sugar
4 teaspoons melted English or Welsh butter

1. Halve grapefruits and loosen flesh. Sprinkle with sherry. **2.** Cover with equal amounts of caster sugar. Spoon butter over each. **3.** Stand under hot grill. Leave until sugar just starts turning brown. **Serves 4.**

224 PRAWN COCKTAIL

½ round lettuce, washed and dried
2 tablespoons Mayonnaise (No. 577)
4 tablespoons natural yogurt
3 tablespoons tomato ketchup
2 teaspoons Worcester sauce
2 level teaspoons bottled horseradish
  sauce
2 tablespoons lemon juice
½ lb. peeled prawns

1. Shred lettuce and use to half-fill 4 large wine glasses. Leave on one side. **2.** Combine Mayonnaise with natural yogurt, ketchup, Worcester and horseradish sauces and lemon juice. **3.** Add prawns and mix well. Chill lightly. **4.** Spoon equal amounts into glasses. Accompany with brown bread and butter. **Serves 4.**

225 ONION-STUFFED TOMATOES

4 large tomatoes
3 level tablespoons fresh white
  breadcrumbs
1 small onion, finely grated
1 level tablespoon very finely-chopped
  parsley
1½ oz. English or Welsh butter, melted
Salt and pepper to taste
GARNISH
Parsley

1. Cut tops off tomatoes and keep on one side for lids. **2.** Scoop tomato centres into basin and discard any hard pieces. **3.** Add breadcrumbs, onion, parsley and melted butter to tomato pulp. Mix well together. **4.** Season to taste with salt and pepper. Leave to stand 10 minutes. **5.** Pile back into tomato cases and put lid on to each. **6.** Transfer to lightly-buttered heatproof dish and heat through towards top of fairly hot oven (400°F. or Gas No. 6) 15 minutes. **7.** Transfer to 4 warm serving plates and garnish with parsley. Serve hot. **Serves 4.**

226 HAM-STUFFED TOMATOES

1. Follow recipe and method for Onion-stuffed Tomatoes (No. 225). **2.** Use 2 oz. very finely-chopped ham instead of onion. **3.** Add ½ level teaspoon made mustard with finely-chopped parsley. **Serves 4.**

PRAWN-STUFFED TOMATOES 22⁷

1. Follow recipe and method for Onion-stuffed Tomatoes (No. 225). **2.** Use 2 oz. peeled and chopped prawns instead of onion. **Serves 4.**

LAMB-STUFFED TOMATOES 228

1. Follow recipe and method for Onion-stuffed Tomatoes (No. 225). **2.** Use 2 oz. very finely-chopped cooked lamb instead of onion. **3.** Add ½ level teaspoon mixed herbs with finely-chopped parsley. **Serves 4.**

CHEESE-STUFFED TOMATOES 22

1. Follow recipe and method for Onion-stuffed Tomatoes (No. 225). **2.** Use 2 oz. finely-crumbled Lancashire cheese instead of onion. **Serves 4.**

CREAMED PICKLED MUSHROOMS 23

½ lb. button mushrooms
1 tablespoon lemon juice
½ level teaspoon salt
4 tablespoons wine vinegar
1 bay leaf
2 cloves
1 small sliced onion
¼ pint fresh double cream
Freshly-milled pepper and salt
GARNISH
Paprika

1. Wash mushrooms, put into pan and cover with water. **2.** Add lemon juice and salt. Bring to boil and drain. **3.** Slice thinly. Transfer to bowl. **4.** Pour vinegar into pan. Add bay leaf, cloves and onion and bring slowly to boil. Boil 5 minutes, then strain over mushrooms. **5.** Leave mushrooms to cool in liquor. Chill 2 to 3 hours. **6.** Before serving, lift mushrooms out of bowl with draining spoon. Transfer equal amounts to 4 serving plates. **7.** Combine fresh double cream with 3 tablespoons vinegar liquor. Season to taste with pepper and salt. **8.** Spoon over mushrooms. Dust each lightly with paprika. **Serves 4.**

1 CHICKEN & BACON PÂTÉ

1 oz. English or Welsh butter
¼ lb. pigs' liver, sliced
¼ lb. gammon, coarsely chopped
¼ lb. cold cooked chicken
1 garlic clove
1 dessertspoon brandy or dry sherry
3 dessertspoons fresh double cream
Freshly-milled pepper and salt to taste
1 extra oz. English or Welsh butter, melted

1. Melt butter in pan. Add liver slices and gammon. Fry gently 7 to 10 minutes. **2.** Remove from heat. Mince finely with chicken and garlic. **3.** Stir in brandy or sherry and cream. Season to taste with pepper and salt. **4.** Transfer to small earthenware dish and smooth top with knife. **5.** Pour melted butter over top. Chill before serving. **Serves 4.**

2 ASPARAGUS MOUSSE

3 level teaspoons gelatine
¼ pint boiling water
¼ pint fresh single cream
Yolks and whites of 2 standard eggs
1 level teaspoon paprika
½ level teaspoon salt
1 tablespoon lemon juice
6 oz. canned asparagus tips, very finely
  chopped
GARNISH
8 extra asparagus tips

1. Shower gelatine into boiling water and stir briskly until dissolved. Leave until lukewarm. **2.** Warm cream then beat into egg yolks. **3.** Combine with dissolved gelatine and stir in paprika, salt and lemon juice. **4.** When cold and just beginning to thicken, stir in chopped asparagus. **5.** Beat egg whites to stiff snow and gently fold into asparagus mixture. **6.** Spoon into 4 large wine glasses and chill until firm. **7.** Just before serving decorate each with 2 asparagus tips. **Serves 4.**

3 SALMON MOUSSE

1. Follow recipe and method for Asparagus Mousse (No. 232). **2.** Use 1 medium-sized can red salmon (about ½ lb.), well drained and finely mashed, instead of asparagus. **3.** Garnish with lemon slices and parsley. **Serves 4.**

CRAB COCKTAIL 234

½ round lettuce, washed and dried
¼ pint Mayonnaise (No. 577)
3 tablespoons tomato ketchup
½ teaspoon Tabasco sauce
1 tablespoon lemon juice
2 tablespoons fresh double cream
½ lb. flaked crab meat

1. Shred lettuce and use to half-fill 4 large wine glasses. Leave on one side. **2.** Combine Mayonnaise with ketchup, Tabasco sauce, lemon juice and cream. **3.** Stir in crab meat, mix well and chill lightly. **4.** Spoon equal amounts into glasses. Accompany with brown bread and butter. **Serves 4.**

MUSHROOM COCKTAIL 235

½ round lettuce, washed and dried
½ lb. button mushrooms
¼ pint fresh double cream
2 tablespoons bottled salad cream
2 tablespoons tomato ketchup
1 tablespoon lemon juice

1. Shred lettuce and use to half-fill 4 large wine glasses. **2.** Wash mushrooms and stalks, cover with boiling water and leave 2 minutes. **3.** Drain and slice. **4.** Combine fresh double cream with salad cream, ketchup and lemon juice. **5.** Add sliced mushrooms. Mix well and chill lightly. **6.** Spoon equal amounts into glasses. Accompany with brown bread and butter. **Serves 4.**

TUNA COCKTAIL 236

½ round lettuce, washed and dried
1 carton (5 oz.) natural yogurt
2 tablespoons tomato ketchup
2 tablespoons lemon juice
2 teaspoons Worcester sauce
4 level tablespoons grated cucumber
1 × 7 oz. can middle-cut tuna

1. Shred lettuce and use to half-fill 4 large wine glasses. Leave on one side. **2.** Combine natural yogurt with ketchup, lemon juice, Worcester sauce and cucumber. **3.** Drain tuna, divide into small chunks and add to soured cream mixture. **4.** Mix well and chill lightly. **5.** Spoon equal amounts into glasses. Accompany with brown bread and butter. **Serves 4.**

237 STEAK TARTARE

1 lb. rump, sirloin or fillet steak, very
  finely minced
1 tablespoon finely-chopped capers
1 teaspoon Worcester sauce
½ to 1 level teaspoon salt
Freshly-milled black pepper
1 small onion, peeled and coarsely grated
Yolks of 4 standard eggs

1. Combine meat with capers, Worcester sauce
and salt. Season to taste with pepper. **2.** Put
equal amounts on to 4 plates. Shape into neat
mounds, then make hole in centre of each.
3. Sprinkle with onion. Fill with egg yolks.
Serves 4.

238 COLD SPAGHETTI CREAMS

6 oz. spaghetti
1 recipe Mixed Cheese Dressing (No.576)
1 level teaspoon paprika

GARNISH
4 tomato slices and watercress

1. Break spaghetti into 1-in. lengths and cook in
boiling salted water until tender. **2.** Drain and
leave until cold. **3.** Turn into large bowl, add
Dressing and toss lightly together. **4.** Transfer to
4 individual plates. Sprinkle with paprika and
garnish each with slice of tomato and watercress.
Serves 4.

239 AVOCADO CREAMS

¼ pint fresh double cream
1 tablespoon wine vinegar
4 finely-chopped anchovy fillets
1 level teaspoon very finely-chopped onion
2 level teaspoons caster sugar
2 medium-sized ripe avocados
Salt and Cayenne pepper
1 level teaspoon paprika

GARNISH
4 lemon slices

1. Whip cream until thick. **2.** Combine vinegar
with anchovies, onion and sugar. **3.** Halve
avocados, remove flesh and mash finely. **4.**
Combine with cream and vinegar mixture.
Season to taste with salt and Cayenne pepper.
5. Pile back into avocado shells and sprinkle
lightly with paprika. **6.** Garnish each with slice
of lemon. **Serves 4.**

FRENCH COUNTRY-STYLE PÂTÉ 24

6 oz. pigs' liver, sliced
¼ lb. lean bacon
¼ lb. stewing veal
1 small peeled onion
2 oz. fresh white breadcrumbs
1 level tablespoon finely-chopped parsley
2 standard eggs, beaten
¼ pint milk
½ to 1 level teaspoon salt
Freshly-milled pepper
3 bay leaves

1. Cover liver with boiling water and leave 5
minutes. Drain. **2.** Mince with bacon, veal and
onion. **3.** Stir in breadcrumbs and parsley.
Combine with beaten eggs and milk. **4.** Season
to taste with salt and pepper. Pack mixture into
well-buttered 1-lb. loaf tin. **5.** Put bay leaves on
top and cover with aluminium foil. Bake in
centre of moderate oven (325°F. or Gas No. 3)
for 1 hour. **6.** Leave in tin 5 minutes. Remove bay
leaves then turn out. **7.** Serve cold, cut in slices,
and accompany with crisp toast. **Serves 4 to 5.**

STUFFED MUSHROOMS 24

8 large mushrooms
1 oz. English or Welsh butter
1 level tablespoon finely-grated onion
1 oz. lean bacon, finely chopped
3 level dessertspoons fresh white
  breadcrumbs
1 level dessertspoon finely-chopped
  parsley
¼ to ½ level teaspoon salt
Freshly-milled pepper

1. Wash and peel mushrooms. **2.** Chop stalks
finely. Retain caps. **3.** Melt butter in pan. Add
mushroom stalks, onion and bacon. Fry very
gently, without browning, for 5 minutes. **4.** Stir in
breadcrumbs and parsley. Season to taste with
salt and pepper. **5.** Pile equal amounts on to
mushroom caps. Transfer to buttered heatproof
dish. **6.** Bake towards top of fairly hot oven
(375°F. or Gas No. 5) for 10 to 12 minutes.
7. Serve straight away. Accompany with crisp
toast and butter. **Serves 4.**

Fish

Where whole fish are used, and where the method does not specify, heads can be removed or retained according to personal preferences.

242 SOUSED HERRINGS

4 large herrings
1 large onion
1 level tablespoon mixed pickling spice
2 small bay leaves, halved
5 tablespoons water
$\frac{1}{4}$ pint malt vinegar
1 level teaspoon granulated sugar
$\frac{1}{2}$ level teaspoon salt

1. Scale, bone and wash herrings. **2.** Roll up from head end to tail (with skin outside). Arrange in 1 to $1\frac{1}{2}$-pint heatproof dish. **3.** Slice onion thinly and arrange over herrings. **4.** Sprinkle with pickling spice and halved bay leaves. **5.** Combine water with vinegar, sugar and salt. **6.** Pour over fish. **7.** Cover with lid or aluminium foil. **8.** Bake in centre of cool oven (300°F. or Gas No. 2) for $1\frac{1}{2}$ hours. **9.** Leave herrings to cool in dish. **10.** Chill thoroughly before serving. **Serves 4.**

243 SOUSED HERRINGS WITH CIDER

1. Follow recipe and method for Soused Herrings (No. 242). **2.** Use dry cider instead of vinegar. **Serves 4.**

244 FOIL-WRAPPED BAKED HERRINGS OR MACKEREL

4 herrings or mackerel
Salt and pepper
1 oz. English or Welsh butter, melted
GARNISH
Lemon wedges and parsley

1. Scale and wash herrings or mackerel. Wipe dry. **2.** Sprinkle with salt and pepper. **3.** Stand each fish on piece of foil. Brush with melted butter. **4.** Seal foil loosely round each and stand on baking tray. **5.** Bake just above centre of fairly hot oven (375°F. or Gas No. 5) for 20 minutes. **6.** Unwrap and serve each garnished with lemon and parsley. **Serves 4.**

FRIED HERRINGS   245

4 large herrings
About 4 level tablespoons flour
Good shake of pepper
$\frac{1}{2}$ level teaspoon salt
2 oz. English or Welsh butter
2 teaspoons olive or corn oil

GARNISH
4 lemon wedges

1. Scale and wash herrings. Wipe dry. **2.** Coat with flour mixed with pepper and salt. **3.** Fry in hot butter and oil, allowing 4 to 5 minutes per side. **4.** Drain on soft kitchen paper. **5.** Transfer to serving dish and garnish with lemon. **Serves 4.**

FRIED MACKEREL   246

1. Follow recipe and method for Fried Herrings (No. 245). **2.** Use mackerel instead of herrings. **Serves 4.**

FRIED HERRINGS —   247
SCOTS-STYLE

1. Follow recipe and method for Fried Herrings (No. 245). **2.** Instead of flour, coat with 3 level tablespoons oatmeal or 4 level tablespoons porridge oats mixed with pepper and $\frac{1}{2}$ level teaspoon salt. **Serves 4.**

KEDGEREE   248

6 oz. cooked smoked haddock
6 oz. cooked fresh haddock
3 oz. English or Welsh butter
$\frac{3}{4}$ lb. cooked long grain rice (about 6 oz. raw)
2 chopped large hard-boiled eggs
About 4 tablespoons fresh single cream
Salt and freshly-milled pepper to taste
GARNISH
2 level tablespoons finely-chopped parsley

1. Flake fish with 2 forks. **2.** Melt butter in large saucepan. **3.** Add fish, rice, eggs and cream. **4.** Mix well. Add a little extra cream if mixture seems on dry side. **5.** Season well to taste with salt and pepper. **6.** Transfer to $1\frac{1}{2}$ to 2-pint buttered heatproof dish. **7.** Cover with lid or aluminium foil. **8.** Re-heat just above centre of moderate oven (325°F. or Gas No. 3) for 30 minutes. **9.** Uncover and sprinkle with parsley. **10.** Serve straight away. **Serves 4.**

FISH

249 JUGGED KIPPERS

4 medium-sized kippers
1 to 1½ oz. English or Welsh butter

1. Put kippers into tall jug and cover completely with boiling water. **2.** Leave for 5 minutes and drain. **3.** Serve straight away and top each with piece of butter. **Serves 4.**

250 SMOKED HADDOCK FLORENTINE

1 large packet frozen spinach
¾ lb. cooked and flaked smoked haddock
1 recipe Cheese Coating Sauce (No. 116)
1 extra oz. finely-grated Cheddar cheese
GARNISH
Parsley

1. Cook spinach as directed on packet. **2.** Meanwhile, add fish to Sauce and heat through gently. **3.** Drain spinach well. Use to cover base of 1½-pint buttered heatproof dish. **4.** Cover with fish and Sauce. **5.** Sprinkle top with cheese. **6.** Brown under hot grill. **7.** Garnish with parsley. **Serves 4.**

251 SAVOURY HADDOCK CASSEROLE

1½ lb. fillet of fresh haddock
About 2 level tablespoons flour
½ level teaspoon salt
2 oz. English or Welsh butter
Juice of 1 small lemon
Freshly-milled pepper
¼ lb. mushrooms and stalks
1 medium-sized onion
½ lb. skinned tomatoes
1 small green pepper (optional)
3 level teaspoons soft brown sugar
GARNISH
Parsley

1. Skin fish and cut flesh into 4 portions. **2.** Coat with flour mixed with salt. **3.** Fry quickly in 1 oz. butter until golden on both sides. **4.** Transfer to 1½-pint buttered heatproof dish. Sprinkle with lemon juice and pepper. **5.** Finely chop mushrooms, onion, tomatoes and green pepper if used. **6.** Mix well together and spread over fish. **7.** Scatter brown sugar over vegetables. Dot with remaining butter. **8.** Cover dish with lid or aluminium foil. Bake in centre of fairly hot oven (375°F. or Gas No. 5) for 30 to 40 minutes. **9.** Uncover and garnish with parsley. **Serves 4.**

CHEESE-BAKED HADDOCK 252

1½ lb. fillet of fresh haddock
Salt and pepper
1 medium-sized onion
1 garlic clove (optional)
1 medium-sized can (about 15 oz.) tomatoes
1 oz. English or Welsh butter
¼ level teaspoon thyme
2 level tablespoons finely-chopped parsley
1 oz. fresh white breadcrumbs
2 oz. crumbled Lancashire cheese

1. Skin fish and cut flesh into 4 portions. **2.** Arrange in shallow heatproof dish. Sprinkle with salt and pepper. **3.** Finely chop onion and garlic if used. **4.** Put into saucepan with tomatoes, butter, thyme and parsley. **5.** Simmer slowly for 10 minutes. **6.** Cover fish with tomato mixture. **7.** Sprinkle with breadcrumbs mixed with cheese. **8.** Bake just above centre of moderate oven (350°F. or Gas No. 4) for 30 minutes. **Serves 4.**

TROUT WITH ALMONDS 253

4 medium-sized trout
4 level tablespoons flour
½ level teaspoon salt
Shake of Cayenne pepper
¼ lb. English or Welsh butter
2 teaspoons olive or corn oil
3 oz. blanched and halved almonds
GARNISH
Lemon wedges
Parsley

1. Wash trout. Wipe dry with soft kitchen paper. **2.** Coat well with flour mixed with salt and pepper. **3.** Fry in the oil and 3 oz. butter until cooked through and golden (about 4 to 5 minutes per side). **4.** Remove to serving dish and keep warm. **5.** Add remaining butter to pan and stand over low heat until melted. **6.** Add almonds and fry gently until golden. **7.** Pour hot butter and almonds over fish. **8.** Garnish with lemon and parsley. **9.** Serve straight away. **Serves 4.**

Baked Stuffed Haddock Fillet (No. 255)

1 whole fresh haddock (about 2 lb.)
Salt and pepper
1 oz. English or Welsh butter, softened
2 tablespoons lemon juice
1 level teaspoon made mustard
1 small grated onion
1 teaspoon Worcester sauce
¼ pint fresh double cream

GARNISH
1 level tablespoon finely-chopped parsley
Paprika

1. Scale and wash haddock. Wipe dry with soft kitchen paper. 2. Sprinkle inside with salt and pepper then spread with butter. 3. Stand fish in buttered shallow heatproof dish. 4. Combine lemon juice with mustard, onion and Worcester sauce. Pour over fish. 5. Coat with cream. Bake, uncovered, in centre of fairly hot oven (375°F. or Gas No. 5) for 35 to 40 minutes (or until fish is tender). 6. Sprinkle with parsley and paprika. **Serves 4 to 5.**

● *If preferred, a 1½ to 2-lb. portion of cod may be used instead of haddock.*

2 fillets of fresh haddock, each about ¾ lb.
1 recipe either Celery and Tomato Stuffing (No. 75) or Lemon, Parsley and Thyme Stuffing (No. 74)
2 large sliced tomatoes
2 level tablespoons chopped parsley
2 oz. English or Welsh butter, melted

1. Place 1 fillet of fish flesh side uppermost in buttered shallow heatproof dish. 2. Cover with Stuffing. 3. Put second fillet of fish, skin side uppermost, on top. 4. Stand a line of tomato slices along centre. Sprinkle with parsley. 5. Coat with melted butter. 6. Bake, uncovered, in centre of moderate oven (350°F. or Gas No. 4) for 40 minutes. **Serves 4.**

256 FISH QUENELLES

½ lb. haddock, hake or whiting fillet
(weighed after boning and skinning)
1 recipe freshly-made Choux Pastry
(No. 102)
¼ level teaspoon nutmeg
½ level teaspoon salt
3 dessertspoons fresh double cream

1. Mince raw fish finely. **2.** Beat into Choux Pastry with nutmeg and salt. **3.** Chill for at least 2 hours. Beat in cream. **4.** Half-fill large, fairly shallow pan with water and bring slowly to boil. **5.** Reduce heat. Gently lower dessertspoons of fish mixture into pan, allowing room between each for swelling. **6.** Poach very gently for 15 to 20 minutes. **7.** Lift out of water and drain. **8.** Serve hot with suitable savoury sauce (see Sauce Section). **Serves 4.**

257 DANISH-STYLE COD

¼ lb. streaky bacon
¼ lb. button mushrooms
¼ lb. cooked peas
4 cod cutlets (each about 4 to 6 oz.)
Salt and pepper
1 oz. English or Welsh butter

1. Chop bacon and arrange, with whole mushrooms and peas, over base of well-buttered shallow heatproof dish. **2.** Sprinkle cod with salt and pepper. Place on top of bacon and vegetables. **3.** Put a piece of butter on each cutlet. **4.** Cover dish with lid or aluminium foil. **5.** Bake just above centre of moderate oven (350°F. or Gas No. 4) for 20 minutes. **6.** Remove lid or foil. Continue to bake for further 20 minutes. **Serves 4.**

BAKED STUFFED COD CUTLETS   25

4 cod cutlets (each about 4 to 6 oz.)
Salt and pepper
1 small onion
½ oz. English or Welsh butter
1 oz. fresh white breadcrumbs
1 level teaspoon finely-chopped parsley
2 teaspoons lemon juice
½ pint Cheese Coating Sauce (No. 116)

1. Sprinkle fish with salt and pepper. Stand each on large square of aluminium foil. **2.** Chop onion finely. Fry gently in butter until pale gold. **3.** Stir in breadcrumbs, parsley and lemon juice. Season if necessary with salt and pepper. **4.** Divide into 4 equal portions and use to fill fish cavities. **5.** Seal foil loosely round each cutlet. Transfer to baking tray. **6.** Bake just above centre of moderate oven (350°F. or Gas No. 4) for 30 minutes. **7.** Unwrap and accompany with Cheese Sauce. **Serves 4.**

FISH FRITTERS   26

1 recipe Savoury Fritter Batter (No. 665)
½ lb. cooked and finely-flaked fish
2 level tablespoons finely-chopped drained
capers
Deep fat or oil for frying
1 oz. finely-grated English Cheddar cheese

1. Make up Batter as directed but, before folding in beaten egg white, stir in flaked fish and capers. **2.** Drop dessertspoon mixture into hot fat or oil. **3.** Fry until well puffed and golden (2 to 3 minutes). **4.** Drain on soft kitchen paper. **5.** Transfer to serving plate and sprinkle with cheese. **6.** Accompany with suitable savoury sauce (see Sauce Section). **Serves 4.**

258 COD WITH ORANGE & WALNUTS

2 oz. English or Welsh butter
3 oz. fresh brown breadcrumbs
1 finely-chopped garlic clove (optional)
1 oz. very finely-chopped shelled walnut
halves
Finely-grated peel and juice of 1 medium
orange
4 cod cutlets (each about 4 to 6 oz.)
Salt and pepper
GARNISH
Watercress

1. Melt butter in pan. Stir in breadcrumbs, garlic if used, walnuts and orange peel. **2.** Leave over low heat, stirring frequently, until butter has been absorbed by crumbs. **3.** Sprinkle fish with salt and pepper. Stand in buttered shallow heatproof dish. **4.** Moisten with orange juice. Cover with breadcrumb mixture. **5.** Bake, uncovered, just above centre of moderate oven (350°F. or Gas No. 4) for 20 to 30 minutes (or until fish is tender). **6.** Garnish with watercress. **Serves 4.**

261 LEMON BUTTERED SKATE

1 small sliced onion
1 small bay leaf
1 parsley sprig
1 tablespoon vinegar
$\frac{1}{2}$ level teaspoon salt
2 lb. skate
1 recipe Lemon Butter Sauce (No. 151)

GARNISH
4 lemon wedges
Parsley

1. Pour about 3 in. water into large, fairly shallow, saucepan. **2.** Add onion, bay leaf, parsley sprig, vinegar and salt. **3.** Bring to boil. Carefully put in fish (cut into 4 portions). **4.** Lower heat, cover pan and simmer gently for 25 minutes. **5.** Drain skate. If preferred, remove bones. **6.** Transfer to serving dish. Coat with Lemon Butter Sauce. **7.** Garnish with lemon and parsley. **8.** Serve straight away. **Serves 4.**

262 SKATE WITH CIDER SAUCE

$\frac{1}{2}$ pint dry cider
1 small sliced onion
1 small bay leaf
1 parsley sprig
1 tablespoon vinegar
$\frac{1}{2}$ level teaspoon salt
2 lb. skate
1 oz. English or Welsh butter
1 oz. flour
2 tablespoons fresh double cream

GARNISH
4 slices unpeeled orange
Watercress

1. Put cider into large, fairly shallow, pan. **2.** Add onion, bay leaf, parsley, vinegar and salt. **3.** Bring to boil. Carefully put in fish (cut into 4 portions). **4.** Lower heat. Cover pan and simmer very gently for 25 minutes. **5.** Drain and reserve $\frac{1}{2}$ pint liquor. If preferred, take bones out of skate. Transfer fish to heatproof dish. Keep warm. **6.** Melt butter in pan. Stir in flour. Cook gently, without browning, 1 minute. **7.** Gradually blend in cider liquor. **8.** Cook, stirring, until sauce comes to boil and thickens. **9.** Simmer for 3 minutes. Stir in cream. **10.** Pour over skate. **11.** Garnish with orange slices and watercress. **Serves 4.**

SALMON FISH CAKES 263

1 lb. potatoes (after peeling)
3 oz. English or Welsh butter
1 medium-sized can (about $\frac{1}{2}$ lb.) red salmon
1 level tablespoon finely-chopped parsley
1 level teaspoon finely-grated lemon peel
Onion salt to taste
Pepper
1 tablespoon olive or corn oil

GARNISH
Parsley
Lemon slices

1. Cook potatoes in boiling salted water until tender. **2.** Mash finely with 1 oz. butter, drained salmon, parsley and lemon peel. **3.** Season to taste with onion salt and pepper. Leave mixture to cool. **4.** Turn out on to floured board. Divide into 8 equal-sized pieces. **5.** Shape into cakes. Fry in remaining butter and oil until crisp and golden, allowing about 3 to 4 minutes per side. **6.** Drain on soft kitchen paper. **7.** Garnish with parsley and lemon. **Serves 4.**

HALIBUT AU GRATIN 264

1 small onion
$\frac{1}{4}$ lb. mushrooms and stalks
2 level tablespoons finely-chopped parsley
4 halibut steaks (each about 6 oz.)
Salt and pepper
1 teaspoon lemon juice
4 tablespoons fresh single cream
3 level tablespoons toasted breadcrumbs
2 oz. English or Welsh butter

GARNISH
4 lemon wedges
Watercress

1. Finely chop onion and mushrooms with stalks. **2.** Arrange, with parsley, over base of buttered shallow heatproof dish. **3.** Stand fish on top. Sprinkle with salt, pepper and lemon juice. **4.** Pour cream into dish. Coat fish with breadcrumbs. **5.** Dot with small pieces of butter. **6.** Bake in centre of fairly hot oven (375°F. or Gas No. 5) for 30 to 35 minutes. **7.** Garnish with lemon and watercress. **Serves 4.**

TURBOT AU GRATIN 265

1. Follow recipe and method for Halibut au Gratin (No. 264). **2.** Use turbot steaks instead of halibut. **Serves 4.**

FISH

266 CREAMED HALIBUT

1½ lb. boned halibut
Salt and pepper
Juice of ½ medium-sized lemon
¼ pint fresh double cream
5 level tablespoons grated English Cheddar
 cheese
1½ oz. English or Welsh butter
GARNISH
1 level tablespoon finely-chopped parsley

1. Skin fish. Cut flesh into 4 serving portions.
2. Arrange in buttered shallow heatproof dish.
3. Sprinkle with salt, pepper and lemon juice.
4. Coat fish with cream. Sprinkle with grated
cheese. 5. Cover top with flakes of butter. Bake
uncovered, in centre of moderate oven (350°F.
or Gas No. 4) for 25 to 30 minutes. 6. Scatter
parsley over top. 7. Serve straight away.
Serves 4.

267 SCALLOPED HAKE

1 lb. hake
1 recipe Cheese Pouring Sauce (No.116)
¼ lb. fresh white breadcrumbs
1 level teaspoon celery salt
2 oz. crumbled Lancashire cheese
GARNISH
Parsley

1. Poach hake gently in boiling salted water for
8 to 10 minutes. 2. Lift out of pan. Remove skin
and bones. Flake up flesh with forks. 3. Fill
1½-pint buttered heatproof dish with alternate
layers fish, Sauce and breadcrumbs mixed with
celery salt. 4. Finish with layer of breadcrumbs.
Sprinkle cheese over top. 5. Re-heat just above
centre of fairly hot oven (375°F. or Gas No. 5)
20 to 30 minutes or until top is golden. 6. Garnish
with parsley. Serves 4.

268 FRIED FISH

4 cutlets of fish or 8 medium-sized fillets
 (about 1½ lb.)
Deep fat or oil for frying
Coating Batter (No.659)
GARNISH
Lemon wedges

GRECIAN SOLE 269

½ lb. freshly-boiled rice (about ¼ lb. raw)
8 sole fillets (each about 3 oz.)
2 level tablespoons flour
½ level teaspoon salt
2 oz. English or Welsh butter
1 dessertspoon olive or corn oil
1 recipe Tomato Sauce (No.144)
GARNISH
1 canned red pepper

1. Arrange rice on serving platter. Keep warm
and dry in very cool oven. 2. Coat sole fillets with
flour mixed with salt. 3. Fry until crisp and golden
in butter and oil, allowing 3 to 4 minutes per side.
4. Place on top of rice. 5. Coat with hot Tomato
Sauce. 6. Garnish with red pepper, cut into strips.
Serves 4.

SOLE WITH CUCUMBER SAUCE 270

4 large sole fillets (each about 6 oz.)
2 tablespoons dry white wine
1 small sliced onion
½ small bay leaf
½ level teaspoon salt
1 recipe freshly-made Cucumber Sauce
 (No.121)
GARNISH
Paprika

1. With skin outside, roll up sole fillets. Secure
with wooden sticks. 2. Stand in shallow pan.
Cover with water. 3. Add wine, onion, bay leaf
and salt. Slowly bring to boil. 4. Reduce heat.
Cover pan. Simmer fish for 6 to 7 minutes.
5. Transfer to warm serving dish. Remove sticks.
6. Coat with hot Cucumber Sauce. 7. Sprinkle
lightly with paprika. Serves 4.

1. Wash fish well. Wipe dry with soft kitchen
paper. 2. Half-fill deep frying pan with melted fat
or oil. 3. Heat until faint haze rises from it (or
until bread cube sinks to bottom of pan, rises to
top immediately and turns golden in 50 seconds).
4. Coat fish with Batter. Lift into pan with fork or
kitchen tongs. 5. Fry until crisp and golden,
allowing about 6 to 8 minutes for cutlets and
4 to 5 minutes for fillets. 6. Remove from pan.
7. Drain on soft kitchen paper. 8. Garnish with
lemon. Serves 4.

Portugese Plaice (No. 271)

271 PORTUGUESE PLAICE

8 sardines (canned)
8 level tablespoons fresh white
 breadcrumbs
2 level tablespoons finely-chopped parsley
Finely-grated peel and juice of 1 medium-
 sized lemon
1 level teaspoon finely-grated onion
¼ level teaspoon salt
Beaten egg to bind
8 small plaice fillets (each about 3 oz.)
1 oz. English or Welsh butter, melted

1. Mash sardines finely. Combine with crumbs, parsley, lemon peel, onion and salt. **2.** Bind loosely with egg. **3.** Spread sardine mixture over plaice fillets. Roll up. **4.** Arrange in buttered shallow heatproof dish. Coat with lemon juice combined with melted butter. **5.** Cover dish with lid or aluminium foil. **6.** Bake just above centre of moderate oven (350°F. or Gas No. 4) for 30 minutes. **Serves 4.**

BUTTERED PLAICE WITH BANANAS 272

4 large plaice fillets (each about 6 oz.)
Salt and pepper
3 oz. English or Welsh butter
1 oz. salted cashew nuts
2 medium-sized bananas
Juice of 1 lemon

1. Arrange plaice fillets in buttered shallow heatproof dish. Season with salt and pepper. **2.** Melt 1 oz. butter. Pour over fish. **3.** Cover dish with lid or aluminium foil. Bake in centre of moderate oven (350°F. or Gas No. 4) for 20 minutes. **4.** After 15 minutes, melt remaining butter in pan. Add nuts and slice in bananas. **5.** Fry very gently for 3 minutes. **6.** Remove dish from oven and uncover. Arrange nuts and banana slices on top of fish. **7.** Sprinkle with lemon juice. Serve straight away. **Serves 4.**

273 GRILLED WHOLE PLAICE

4 whole plaice (each about 6 oz.)
2 oz. English or Welsh butter, melted
Salt and pepper
GARNISH
4 lemon wedges
Parsley

1. Line grill pan or grill rack with aluminium foil. **2.** Arrange 2 plaice on top. **3.** Brush with melted butter. Sprinkle with salt and pepper. **4.** Grill for 5 to 6 minutes. **5.** Turn over. Brush with more butter. Sprinkle with salt and pepper. **6.** Grill for further 5 to 6 minutes. Transfer to warm platter and keep hot. **7.** Cook remaining 2 plaice and transfer to platter. **8.** Garnish with lemon and parsley. **Serves 4.**

274 PLAICE WITH STILTON SAUCE

4 large plaice fillets (each about 6 oz.)
2 level tablespoons flour
½ level teaspoon salt
1½ oz. English or Welsh butter
2 teaspoons olive or corn oil
¼ pint freshly-made Basic White Coating Sauce (No.106)
3 oz. Blue Stilton cheese, finely chopped
2 level tablespoons toasted breadcrumbs
GARNISH
Watercress

1. Cut each fillet into 4 pieces. Coat with flour mixed with salt. **2.** Fry fairly briskly in butter and oil, allowing 3 minutes per side. **3.** Transfer to 1½-pint buttered heatproof dish. **4.** Stand Sauce over low heat. Add cheese. **5.** Whisk gently until smooth. Pour over fish. **6.** Sprinkle breadcrumbs over top. **7.** Re-heat in centre of fairly hot oven (375°F. or Gas No. 5) for 20 minutes. **8.** Garnish with watercress. **Serves 4.**

275 GRILLED SOLE

1. Follow recipe and method for Grilled Plaice (No. 273). **2.** Use 4 medium-sized soles, skinned on both sides, instead of plaice. **3.** Whether the heads are left on is a matter of personal choice. **Serves 4.**

CRUMBED WHITING MEUNIÈRE 27

4 medium-sized boned whiting
2 level tablespoons flour
½ level teaspoon salt
Shake of pepper
1 small egg, beaten
8 level tablespoons fresh white breadcrumbs
¼ lb. English or Welsh butter
2 teaspoons olive or corn oil
Juice of ½ medium-sized lemon
GARNISH
Parsley

1. Cut head and tail off each fish. **2.** Wash fish well. Pat dry with soft kitchen paper. **3.** Toss in flour mixed with salt and pepper. **4.** Coat with beaten egg and crumbs. **5.** Fry in the oil and 3 oz. butter until crisp and golden, allowing 3 to 4 minutes per side. **6.** Remove from pan. Transfer to warm serving dish. **7.** Add rest of butter to pan. Heat gently until it just begins to turn brown. **8.** Add lemon juice and pour over whiting. **9.** Garnish with parsley. **Serves 4.**

NORMANDY WHITING 27

4 medium-sized boned whiting
Salt and pepper
1 small onion
1 level tablespoon French mustard
4 tablespoons dry white wine or cider
Juice of ½ medium-sized lemon
1½ oz. butter
1 level tablespoon finely-chopped parsley
GARNISH
Parsley

1. Wash whiting. Arrange in buttered shallow heatproof dish. Season with salt and pepper. **2.** Chop onion very finely. Sprinkle over fish. **3.** Put mustard, wine or cider, lemon juice, butter and parsley into small saucepan. **4.** Leave over low heat until butter has melted. **5.** Pour over fish. **6.** Cover dish with lid or aluminium foil. **7.** Bake in centre of moderate oven (350°F. or Gas No. 4) for 15 minutes. **8.** Uncover and continue to bake for further 10 minutes. **9.** Garnish with parsley. **Serves 4.**

Shellfish

CRABS

Fresh crabs are at their best between May and September. They should have rough shells and large claws and feel heavy for their size. When buying a cooked crab from the fishmonger make sure that it has been freshly boiled.

78 DEVILLED CRAB

1 small onion or 2 shallots
2 oz. English or Welsh butter
$\frac{1}{4}$ pint freshly-made Béchamel Sauce
  (No. 110)
1 tablespoon brandy, dry sherry or lemon
  juice
1 teaspoon Worcester sauce
1 level teaspoon Dijon mustard
1 level tablespoon finely-chopped parsley
$\frac{3}{4}$ to 1 lb. cooked crabmeat
Salt to taste
1 oz. finely-grated English Cheddar cheese
1 level tablespoon fresh white
  breadcrumbs

1. Chop onion or shallots finely. Fry very gently in butter until soft. **2.** Stir in Sauce, brandy, sherry or lemon juice, Worcester sauce, mustard, parsley and crabmeat. **3.** Mix well and season. Transfer to buttered shallow heatproof dish. **4.** Sprinkle with cheese mixed with crumbs. **5.** Bake towards top of hot oven (425°F. or Gas No. 7) for 10 to 15 minutes. **Serves 4.**

79 CRAB TARTARE

$\frac{3}{4}$ to 1 lb. cooked crabmeat
1 recipe freshly-made Hot Tartare Sauce
  (No. 125)
1 tablespoon toasted breadcrumbs
1 oz. English or Welsh butter, melted
GARNISH
Parsley

1. Combine crabmeat with Sauce. Heat through gently without boiling. **2.** Transfer to shallow heatproof dish. **3.** Sprinkle with crumbs and melted butter. **4.** Brown under hot grill. **5.** Garnish with parsley. **Serves 4.**

80 CRAB NEWBURG

1. Follow recipe and method for Lobster Newburg (No. 281). **2.** Use $\frac{3}{4}$ to 1 lb. crabmeat instead of lobster. **Serves 4.**

LOBSTERS

These are in season from March to October. Cooked lobsters should be bright red, feel heavy for their size and have their tails curled tightly under their bodies. Although the female or hen lobster is held in greater esteem than the male, the flesh of the male lobster is firmer in texture and therefore more suitable for cooked lobster dishes. A 1 to 1$\frac{1}{2}$-lb. lobster serves 2.

LOBSTER NEWBURG 281

2 cooked lobsters (each about 1 lb.)
Salt and freshly-milled pepper to taste
3 oz. English or Welsh butter
5 tablespoons dry sherry
$\frac{1}{4}$ pint fresh double cream
Yolks of 3 standard eggs
$\frac{1}{2}$ lb. freshly-boiled rice (about $\frac{1}{4}$ lb. raw)
GARNISH
Paprika

1. Cut lobsters in half and discard stomachs. **2.** Remove meat from shells. Cut into neat cubes. **3.** Season with salt and pepper. Fry gently in butter for about 4 to 5 minutes. **4.** Pour in sherry. Simmer slowly until liquid is reduced by about half. **5.** Put cream and egg yolks (broken) into double saucepan (or into basin standing over saucepan of gently-simmering water). **6.** Cook, stirring, until sufficiently thick to coat back of a wooden spoon. Do not allow to boil. Adjust seasoning to taste. **7.** Arrange hot rice on 4 warm serving plates. Place equal amounts of lobster meat and liquor from pan on to centre of each. **8.** Pour cream and egg yolk sauce over each. **9.** Sprinkle lightly with paprika. **Serves 4.**

LOBSTER THERMIDOR 282

2 cooked lobsters (each about 1 lb.)
$\frac{1}{2}$ pint freshly-made Béchamel Sauce
  (No. 110)
3 tablespoons fresh double cream
1 level teaspoon dry mustard
Salt and pepper to taste
6 level tablespoons finely-grated English
  Cheddar cheese

1. Halve lobsters lengthwise. Discard stomachs. **2.** Remove meat and cut into neat cubes. **3.** Combine Sauce with cream and mustard. Heat through gently without boiling. Season to taste. **4.** Cover base of lobster shells with a little sauce. Arrange lobster meat on top. **5.** Coat with remaining Sauce. **6.** Sprinkle with cheese. **7.** Brown under hot grill. **Serves 4.**

SCALLOPS

These are in season during the winter months, from about November to March. If they have not already been opened and cleaned by the fishmonger, put them into a hot oven and leave for a few minutes until the shells open. Remove dark frill (beard) which is round the scallop, then carefully wash the white portion and bright orange roe.

283 CREAMED SCALLOPS

8 scallops
½ level teaspoon salt
¼ pint fresh double cream
Yolk of 1 standard egg
1 level tablespoon finely-chopped parsley
Seasoning to taste
1 level tablespoon toasted breadcrumbs
1 oz. English or Welsh butter

1. Put washed scallops into pan. Cover with cold water. Add salt. **2.** Slowly bring to boil. Cover pan and lower heat. **3.** Poach for 5 minutes in water that is barely simmering. **4.** Lift out and drain on soft kitchen paper. **5.** Cut each scallop, depending on size, into 4 or 6 pieces. Transfer to buttered heatproof dish. **6.** Combine cream with egg yolk, parsley and seasoning to taste. Heat through gently without boiling. **7.** Pour over scallops. **8.** Sprinkle with breadcrumbs. Add flakes of butter and brown under hot grill. **Serves 4.**

284 CRUMBED & FRIED SCALLOPS

8 scallops
Salt and pepper
1 tablespoon lemon juice
3 level tablespoons flour
2 standard eggs, beaten
Fresh white breadcrumbs
3 oz. English or Welsh butter
1 dessertspoon olive or corn oil
GARNISH
Lemon wedges

1. Cut washed scallops in half. Pat dry with soft kitchen paper. **2.** Season well with salt and pepper. Sprinkle with lemon juice. **3.** Toss in flour. Coat twice with egg and breadcrumbs. **4.** Leave 15 minutes in the cool. **5.** Fry in hot butter and oil until golden, allowing about 4 minutes per side. **6.** Drain on soft kitchen paper and transfer to warm serving dish. **7.** Garnish with lemon wedges. **Serves 4.**

FRIED SCALLOPS 285

8 scallops
Salt and pepper
1 tablespoon lemon juice
3 level tablespoons flour
2 oz. English or Welsh butter
1 dessertspoon olive or corn oil
GARNISH
4 lemon wedges

1. Cut washed scallops in half. Pat dry with soft kitchen paper. **2.** Season well with salt and pepper. Sprinkle with lemon juice. **3.** Toss in flour. **4.** Fry in hot butter and oil until golden, allowing about 4 minutes per side. **5.** Transfer to warm dish. **6.** Garnish with lemon. **Serves 4.**

MUSSELS

These are in season from about October to March. The shells of fresh mussels must be tightly closed and intact. Any that are cracked, or remain open after tapping with a knife, should be thrown away: this indicates that the mussels inside are dead. Mussels have beards. These may be left on or cut away with scissors. To clean mussels, put into colander and wash under cold running water. Shake the colander all the time to prevent mussel shells from opening. Scrub with a stiff brush and wash again.

MOULES MARINIÈRE 286

2 oz. English or Welsh butter
6 chopped shallots or chopped small onions
1 garlic clove
¼ pint dry white wine
1 small bay leaf
2½ to 3 quarts washed and bearded mussels
3 level tablespoons fresh white breadcrumbs
3 level tablespoons finely-chopped parsley

1. Melt butter in large saucepan. **2.** Add shallots or onions and garlic. Fry gently until pale gold. **3.** Pour in wine. Add bay leaf. Simmer gently for 7 minutes. **4.** Add mussels. Cook over brisk heat, shaking pan all the time, until shells open (about 6 to 8 minutes). **5.** Stir in breadcrumbs. Pour into 4 warm serving dishes. **6.** Sprinkle with parsley. Serve straight away. **Serves 4.**

Moules Marinière (No. 286)

OYSTERS

Oysters are in season from September to April. Like mussels, their shells should be tightl, closed and intact.

2 dozen oysters
1 oz. English or Welsh butter
1 oz. flour
$\frac{1}{4}$ pint milk
1 tablespoon dry sherry
2 tablespoons fresh double cream
$\frac{1}{2}$ level teaspoon salt
Pinch of Cayenne pepper
4 slices hot buttered toast

GARNISH
Paprika

1. Open oysters and reserve liquor. 2. Melt butter in pan. Add flour. Cook gently, without browning, for 1 minute. 3. Gradually blend in oyster liquor and milk. 4. Cook, stirring, until sauce comes to boil and thickens. 5. Add oysters, sherry and cream. Season to taste with salt and Cayenne pepper. 6. Simmer for 4 minutes. Spoon on to hot toast. 7. Sprinkle with paprika. 8, Serve straight away. **Serves 4.**

2 dozen oysters
1 large egg
2 tablespoons fresh single cream
$\frac{1}{4}$ level teaspoon salt
Freshly-milled black pepper
Fresh white breadcrumbs
$\frac{1}{4}$ lb. English or Welsh butter
2 tablespoons olive or corn oil

GARNISH
Lemon wedges

1. Shell oysters. Dry well with soft kitchen paper. 2. Beat egg with cream and salt. Season to taste with pepper. 3. Coat oysters with egg mixture. Toss in crumbs. Repeat coating and tossing once more. 4. Leave oysters for $\frac{1}{2}$ hour in the cool. 5. Fry in hot butter and oil until crisp and golden (about 4 to 5 minutes). 6. Serve straight away and garnish with lemon. **Serves 4.**

289 ANGELS ON HORSEBACK

8 rashers streaky bacon
16 shelled oysters
4 slices hot buttered toast

1. Cut each bacon rasher in half. **2.** Wrap round oysters. Secure with cocktail sticks. **3.** Grill until bacon is crisp, turning once. **4.** Stand 4 on each slice of toast. **5.** Remove sticks. **6.** Serve straight away. **Serves 4.**

SCAMPI & PRAWNS

290 FRIED SCAMPI

2 dozen large frozen or fresh scampi
1 recipe Savoury Fritter Batter (No. 665)
Deep fat or oil for frying

GARNISH
Lemon wedges

ACCOMPANIMENT
Tartare Mayonnaise (No. 589)

1. Defrost scampi if frozen. Dry well with kitchen paper. **2.** Coat with Batter. **3.** Fry in hot fat or oil until pale gold (about 3 to 4 minutes). **4.** Drain thoroughly. Transfer to warm serving dish. **5.** Garnish with lemon wedges. **6.** Hand Tartare Mayonnaise separately. **Serves 4.**

291 CREAMED SCAMPI WITH WINE

2 dozen large frozen or fresh scampi
3 level tablespoons flour
½ level teaspoon salt
Freshly-milled pepper
2 oz. English or Welsh butter
2 tablespoons dry white wine
¼ pint fresh single cream
2 level tablespoons finely-chopped parsley
½ lb. freshly-boiled rice (about ¼ lb. raw)

1. Defrost scampi if frozen. Dry well with kitchen paper. **2.** Coat thickly with flour mixed with salt and pepper. **3.** Melt butter in shallow frying pan. **4.** Add scampi. Fry gently for 7 minutes, turning at least twice. **5.** Pour in wine and cream. Add parsley. **6.** Cook, stirring, until liquor thickens. Adjust seasoning to taste. **7.** Cover 4 warm serving plates with rice. **8.** Put equal amounts of scampi and sauce on to centres of each. **9.** Serve straight away. **Serves 4.**

CREAMED SCAMPI WITH LEMON 292

1. Follow recipe and method for Creamed Scampi with Wine (No. 291). **2.** Use 1 tablespoon lemon juice instead of wine. **Serves 4.**

CURRIED PRAWNS 293

¾ to 1 lb. peeled prawns
1 recipe Curry Sauce (No. 141)
¾ lb. freshly-boiled rice (about 6 oz. raw)

ACCOMPANIMENTS
1 large banana
1 tablespoon lemon juice
2 tomatoes
1 small onion
2 tablespoons desiccated coconut
Chutney

1. Add prawns to Curry Sauce. Heat through gently. **2.** Cover base of large serving platter with rice. Top with prawns and Curry Sauce. **3.** Accompany with separate dishes of sliced banana sprinkled with lemon juice, sliced tomatoes covered with onion rings, coconut and chutney. **Serves 4.**

PRAWNS IN SOURED CREAM SAUCE 29

½ lb. peeled prawns
2 oz. English or Welsh butter
2 teaspoons lemon juice
4 tablespoons soured cream
Yolks of 2 standard eggs
Seasoning to taste
4 slices hot dry toast

GARNISH
Paprika

1. Put prawns and butter into frying pan. Warm through gently for 5 minutes. **2.** Stir in lemon juice, soured cream and egg yolks. **3.** Cook over very low heat, stirring, until sauce thickens. Do not allow to boil. **4.** Season to taste with salt and pepper. **5.** Spoon equal amounts on to hot toast. **6.** Sprinkle lightly with paprika. **Serves 4.**

Lamb & Mutton

95 ROAST LAMB

Choose leg, shoulder, loin, best end neck or stuffed boned breast.

1 oz. English or Welsh butter, melted

QUANTITY
Allow approximately ¾ lb. of any cut per person

ACCOMPANIMENTS
Gravy (No.147)
Mint Sauce (No. 143) or Onion Sauce (No. 108)
Roast and/or Boiled Potatoes
Green vegetables to taste

1. Tie or skewer joint into neat shape. **2.** Stand in roasting tin. **3.** Brush with butter. **4.** Put into centre of hot oven (450°F. or Gas No. 8). **5.** Immediately reduce temperature to moderate (350°F. or Gas No. 4). **6.** Continue roasting for required amount of time, allowing 25 minutes per lb. and 25 minutes over. **7.** Do not baste. **8.** Transfer joint to carving board or dish. Remove string or skewers. **9.** Serve with accompaniments.

96 ROAST MUTTON

1. Follow recipe and method for Roast Lamb (No. 295). **2.** Allow 30 minutes per lb. roasting time and 30 minutes over.

97 LANCASHIRE HOT POT

1½ lb. best end neck of lamb
2 lambs' kidneys
1 lb. potatoes
½ lb. onions
Salt and pepper
¼ pint stock or water
1 oz. English or Welsh butter, melted

1. Cut lamb into cutlets. Remove surplus fat. **2.** Peel and core kidneys. Cut into slices. **3.** Thinly slice potatoes and onions. **4.** Cover base of 2 to 3-pint casserole dish with some of potato slices. **5.** Stand lamb on top. **6.** Cover with kidneys and onions. **7.** Sprinkle with salt and pepper. **8.** Arrange overlapping rings, of rest of potatoes attractively on top. Pour in stock or water. **9.** Brush heavily with butter. **10.** Cover dish with lid or aluminium foil. **11.** Cook in centre of moderate oven (350°F. or Gas No. 4) for 1¼ hours. **12.** Uncover. Continue to cook for further 30 minutes (or until potatoes are golden brown). **Serves 4.**

● *8 shelled oysters may be added if desired.*

LAMB & MUSHROOM HOT POT 298

1. Follow recipe and method for Lancashire Hot Pot (No. 297). **2.** Add 3 to 4 oz. sliced mushrooms and stalks with kidneys and onions. **Serves 4.**

CROWN ROAST OF LAMB 299

1 crown of lamb
Suitable Stuffing (see Stuffings Section)
1 oz. English or Welsh butter, melted
6 or 7 glacé cherries
6 or 7 cutlet frills

GARNISH
Parsley sprigs

ACCOMPANIMENTS
Same as Roast Lamb (No. 295)

1. Ask butcher (in advance if possible) to prepare crown from 2 best end necks of lamb, each with 6 or 7 cutlets. **2.** Alternatively, to make crown yourself, buy 2 best end necks, already chined. **3.** Cut half way down between each bone to separate cutlets. **4.** Scrape fat from upper parts of bones, leaving 2 to 3 in. bare. **5.** With skin side inside, curve both necks round to form crown. **6.** Hold together by stitching ends with fine string or thick thread. **7.** Transfer to roasting tin. Pack Stuffing into centre of crown. **8.** Cover tops of bones with squares of fat, or pieces of aluminium foil, to prevent over-browning. **9.** Brush joints with butter. Roast exactly as for Roast Lamb (No. 295). **10.** Remove from oven. Transfer to carving board or plate. **11.** Take fat or foil off bones. **12.** Put glacé cherries on to alternate bones and cutlet frills on to remainder. **13.** Serve with accompaniments. **Serves 6.**

IRISH STEW 300

2 lb. potatoes
½ lb. onions
2½ lb. middle neck of lamb
¾ pint stock or water
1 level teaspoon salt
Pepper
3 level tablespoons finely-chopped parsley

1. Thinly slice potatoes and onions. **2.** Divide lamb into neat pieces. Cut away surplus fat. **3.** Put vegetables and lamb into saucepan. **4.** Pour in stock. Season with salt and pepper. **5.** Bring to boil and lower heat. **6.** Cover pan. Simmer gently for 1½ hours (or until meat is tender). **7.** Transfer to warm dish and sprinkle thickly with parsley. **Serves 4.**

301 SHEPHERD'S (OR COTTAGE) PIE

¾ lb. cold cooked lamb (or other cold
  minced meat)
1 recipe Brown Sauce (No. 130)
Creamed Potatoes (No. 440)
2 oz. crumbled Lancashire cheese

1. Finely mince meat. Combine with Sauce.
2. Turn into 1½-pint pie dish. 3. Cover with
Creamed Potatoes. 4. Sprinkle with cheese.
5. Re-heat and brown towards top of hot oven
(425°F. or Gas No. 7) for 15 to 20 minutes.
Serves 4.

302 GRILLED LAMB CUTLETS

8 best end neck cutlets
1 oz. English or Welsh butter
GARNISH
Curry, Maître d'Hôtel, Mustard or Tomato
  Butter (see Savoury Butters Section)
4 grilled mushrooms and/or tomato halves
Watercress

1. Trim away surplus fat from cutlets. 2. Stand in
grill pan. Brush with melted butter. 3. Cook under
pre-heated hot grill for 1 minute. 4. Turn over.
Brush with more butter. 5. Grill for further
minute. 6. Continue to grill for total of 7 to
9 minutes. turning cutlets frequently. 7. Transfer
to 4 individual plates or warm serving dish.
8. Top each with piece of savoury butter.
Garnish with mushrooms and/or tomatoes and
watercress. Serves 4.

GRILLED LAMB CHOPS 30

1. Follow recipe and method for Grilled Lamb
Cutlets (No. 302). 2. Use 4 loin chops instead of
cutlets. 3. Grill for total of 10 to 18 minutes,
depending on thickness. Serves 4.

BRAISED SHOULDER OF 30 MUTTON OR LAMB

2 oz. English or Welsh butter
½ lb. chopped onions
1 chopped garlic clove
¼ lb. chopped lean bacon
½ lb. sliced carrots
¼ lb. diced turnip
2 large chopped celery stalks
¼ pint red wine
¼ pint water
1 level teaspoon crushed rosemary
1 level teaspoon salt
3 lb. shoulder of mutton or lamb, boned
  and rolled
ACCOMPANIMENTS
Boiled potatoes
Green vegetables

1. Heat butter in large saucepan. 2. Add onions,
garlic, bacon, carrots, turnip and celery. 3. Cover
pan. Fry gently for 10 minutes, shaking pan
frequently. 4. Pour in wine and water. Add
rosemary and salt. 5. Bring to boil. Stand lamb
on top. 6. Cover saucepan. 7. Simmer very gently
for 2 to 2½ hours (or until meat is tender).
8. Transfer lamb to warm serving dish and
surround with vegetables from saucepan.
9. Strain liquor and pour into clean saucepan.
10. Boil briskly until reduced by half. 11. Pour
over meat. 12. Serve with accompaniments.
Serves 4 to 5.

Braised Shoulder of Lamb (No. 304)

05

MIXED GRILL

4 best end neck cutlets
4 lambs' kidneys, peeled and cored
1½ oz. English or Welsh butter, melted
4 small pork or beef sausages
8 mushrooms
4 medium-sized halved tomatoes
4 rashers back bacon
Maître d'Hôtel Butter (No. 190)
GARNISH
Watercress
Potato crisps

1. Trim away surplus fat from cutlets. **2.** Stand in grill pan with kidneys. **3.** Brush with some of butter. **4.** Cook under pre-heated hot grill for 3 minutes. Turn. **5.** Add sausages and mushrooms. **6.** Brush all ingredients with butter. Grill for 4 minutes. **7.** Turn and add tomatoes and bacon. **8.** Brush all ingredients with remaining butter. Grill for further 4 minutes. **9.** Transfer to warm serving dish. **10.** Top cutlets and kidneys with small pieces of Maître d'Hôtel Butter. **11.** Garnish with watercress and crisps. **Serves 4.**

06

GOLDEN CREAMED LAMB

½ lb. cold cooked lamb
¾ pint Basic White Coating Sauce (No. 106)
½ lb. cooked diced carrots and peas
2 oz. crumbled Lancashire cheese

1. Chop lamb. Add to Sauce with carrots and peas. **2.** Turn into 1½-pint buttered heatproof dish. **3.** Sprinkle cheese over top. **4.** Brown towards top of fairly hot oven (400°F. or Gas No. 6) for 15 to 20 minutes. **Serves 4.**

Lamb Kebabs (No. 307)

7

LAMB KEBABS

1 lb. fillet of lamb (cut from leg)
Yogurt Marinade (No. 178)
4 shallots or small onions
8 rashers long back bacon
8 small skinned tomatoes
8 button mushrooms
1½ oz. English or Welsh butter
¾ lb. freshly-boiled rice (about 6 oz. raw)

1. Cut lamb into 1-in. cubes. **2.** Soak in Yogurt Marinade for 3 hours. **3.** Cook shallots or onions in boiling salted water for 10 minutes. Drain and halve. **4.** Cut bacon rashers in half. Roll up each one like a Swiss roll. **5.** Put lamb on to 4 skewers alternately with halved onions, bacon rolls, whole tomatoes and mushrooms. **6.** Stand in grill pan. Brush well with melted butter. **7.** Cook under pre-heated hot grill for 8 minutes. **8.** Turn and brush with more butter. **9.** Grill for further 8 minutes. **10.** Serve on bed of rice. **Serves 4.**

LAMB & MUTTON

308 BLANQUETTE OF LAMB

1¼ lb. fillet of lamb (cut from leg)
1 large sliced carrot
2 medium-sized sliced onions
1 bay leaf
1 level teaspoon salt
1½ oz. English or Welsh butter
1½ oz. flour
Yolk of 1 standard egg
¼ pint fresh single cream
1 dessertspoon lemon juice
Seasoning to taste

GARNISH
Parsley
Lemon wedges

1. Cut lamb into neat cubes. 2. Put into saucepan. Cover with water. 3. Bring to boil. Remove scum. 4. Add vegetables, bay leaf and salt. 5. Cover pan. Simmer gently for 1½ hours (or until meat is tender). 6. Strain lamb liquor and reserve ¾ pint. 7. Transfer lamb and vegetables to warm dish and keep hot. 8. Melt butter in clean saucepan. 9. Stir in flour and cook gently for 2 minutes. 10. Gradually blend in lamb liquor. 11. Cook, stirring, until sauce comes to boil and thickens. Simmer for 2 minutes. 12. Beat yolk, cream and lemon juice well together. 13. Stir into sauce. Heat through very gently without boiling. 14. Adjust seasoning to taste. Pour over meat. 15. Garnish with parsley and lemon. Serves 4.

309 BOILED MUTTON WITH CAPER SAUCE

3 lb. piece of mutton, cut from leg
1 level teaspoon salt
2 medium-sized sliced onions
2 large sliced carrots
¼ lb. diced swede
¼ lb. diced turnip

ACCOMPANIMENTS
Caper Sauce (No. 115)
Boiled potatoes

1. Put mutton into large saucepan. 2. Cover with cold water. 3. Bring slowly to boil. Remove scum. 4. Add salt and vegetables. 5. Lower heat and cover pan. 6. Simmer for required amount of time, allowing 25 minutes per lb. and 25 minutes over. 7. Transfer mutton to warm dish. 8. Surround with vegetables. 9. Serve with accompaniments. Serves 4.

LAMB CURRY 31

2 lb. middle neck of lamb
2 medium-sized onions
1 garlic clove (optional)
1 oz. English or Welsh butter
1 level tablespoon curry powder
1 level tablespoon flour
2 large tomatoes, skinned and chopped
1 bay leaf
4 cloves
1 level teaspoon cinnamon
1 oz. sultanas or seedless raisins
1 large cooking apple, peeled and grated
1 level tablespoon sweet pickle
1 level teaspoon salt
½ pint stock or water

ACCOMPANIMENTS
¾ lb. freshly-boiled rice (about 6 oz. raw)
1 carton (5 oz.) natural yogurt
Chopped salted peanuts
Thinly-sliced cucumber
Chutney

1. Cut lamb into neat pieces. Remove as much surplus fat as possible. 2. Thinly slice onions and garlic if used. 3. Fry gently in hot butter (in saucepan) until pale gold. 4. Stir in curry powder, flour, tomatoes, bay leaf, cloves, cinnamon, sultanas or raisins, apple, sweet pickle and salt. 5. Gradually blend in stock or water. 6. Add lamb and bring slowly to boil. 7. Lower heat. Cover pan. 8. Simmer gently for 1¼ to 1¾ hours (or until meat is tender). 9. Serve with accompaniments. Serves 4.

LAMB STEW 31

2½ lb. scrag neck of lamb
2 level tablespoons flour
Salt and pepper
1 oz. English or Welsh butter
1 large chopped onion
2 level tablespoons pearl barley
¾ pint stock or water
Seasoning to taste

1. Divide lamb into neat pieces. Cut away surplus fat. 2. Toss in flour seasoned with salt and pepper. 3. Fry briskly (in saucepan) in hot butter until crisp and brown, turning all the time. 4. Transfer to plate. 5. Add onion to remaining butter in pan. Fry slowly until pale gold. 6. Replace lamb. Add barley, stock or water and salt and pepper to taste. 7. Bring slowly to boil. Lower heat. 8. Cover pan. Simmer gently for 1½ to 2 hours (or until meat is tender). Serves 4.

Beef

312 ROAST BEEF

Choose sirloin, all the rib cuts, topside, rump or fillet in one piece

2 oz. English or Welsh butter, melted

QUANTITIES
Allow ½ to ¾ lb. per person for beef with bone
Allow 4 to 6 oz. per person for beef without bone.

ACCOMPANIMENTS
Gravy (No. 147)
Yorkshire Pudding (No. 641)
Whipped Cream Horseradish Dressing (No. 597)
Roast and/or boiled potatoes
Green vegetables to taste

1. Tie or skewer joint into neat shape. **2.** Stand in roasting tin. **3.** Brush with butter. **4.** Pour remaining butter into tin. **5.** Put into centre of hot oven (450°F. or Gas No. 8). **6.** Immediately reduce heat to moderate (350°F. or Gas No. 4). **7.** Continue roasting for required amount of time, allowing 20 minutes per lb. and 20 minutes over. **8.** Baste frequently. **9.** Stand joint on carving board. **10.** Remove string or skewers. **11.** Serve with accompaniments.

313 POT ROASTED BEEF

2 lb. topside or thick flank of beef
2 oz. English or Welsh butter
1 dessertspoon olive or corn oil
1 medium-sized chopped onion
2 large sliced carrots
2 large chopped celery stalks
1 large skinned and chopped tomato
½ pint stock or water
1 wine glass red wine (optional)
1 level teaspoon salt
Shake of pepper
12 small peeled onions or shallots

1. Brown joint briskly in hot butter and oil (in large saucepan or flameproof casserole). **2.** Transfer to plate. **3.** Add onion, carrots and celery to remaining butter in pan. Fry gently until golden. **4.** Replace beef. Add tomatoes, stock or water, wine if used, and salt and pepper. **5.** Bring to boil. Lower heat. **6.** Cover pan tightly. **7.** Simmer very gently for 1 hour, turning at least twice. **8.** Add whole onions. Continue to simmer further for 45 minutes to 1 hour (or until meat is tender). **9.** Serve with vegetables from pan. **Serves 4.**

STEWED BEEF 314

1½ lb. stewing beef (shin, flank, skirt or chuck)
2 level tablespoons flour
Salt and pepper
1½ oz. English or Welsh butter
2 medium-sized chopped onions
3 medium-sized sliced carrots
½ small diced turnip (optional)
¾ pint water

1. Cut beef into 1-in. cubes. **2.** Toss in flour seasoned with salt and pepper. **3.** Fry briskly in hot butter until well browned, turning all the time. **4.** Remove to plate. **5.** Add onions, carrots and turnip (if used) to remaining butter in pan. Fry for 7 minutes (or until pale gold). **6.** Replace meat. Pour in water. **7.** Bring slowly to boil. **8.** Lower heat. Cover pan. **9.** Simmer very gently for 1¾ to 2¼ hours (or until meat is tender). **10.** Stir occasionally. **Serves 4.**

BEEF CASSEROLE 315

1. Follow recipe and method for Stewed Beef (No. 314). **2.** After frying meat and vegetables, transfer to heatproof casserole dish. **3.** Pour in water and cover dish. **4.** Cook in centre of moderate oven (325°F. or Gas No. 3) for 3 to 3½ hours (or until meat is tender). **Serves 4.**

SEA PIE 316

1. Follow recipe and method for Stewed Beef (No. 314), Stewed Beef with Beer (No. 318) or Stewed Beef with Tomato (No. 319). **2.** Half an hour before serving, remove lid of saucepan. **3.** Cover top of meat with ½ recipe Suet Crust Pastry (No. 97), rolled into a round a little smaller than top of saucepan. **4.** Cover with lid. **5.** Continue to simmer for further ½ hour. **6.** Cut pastry into 4 portions before serving. **Serves 4.**

STEWED BEEF WITH DUMPLINGS 317

1. Follow recipe and method for Stewed Beef (No. 314). **2.** 20 minutes before serving, add 8 small dumplings, made from ½ recipe Suet Crust Pastry (No. 97). **3.** Simmer with meat. **Serves 4.**

Boiled Silverside & Carrots (No. 321)

STEWED BEEF WITH BEER 318

1. Follow recipe and method for Stewed Beef (No. 314). **2.** Use ½ beer and ½ water instead of all water. **3.** If liked, a small chopped garlic clove may also be added. **Serves 4.**

STEWED BEEF WITH TOMATO 319

1. Follow recipe and method for Stewed Beef (No. 314). **2.** Use ½ pint tomato juice instead of water, or ½ lb. skinned and chopped tomatoes and ¼ pint water. **3.** Add also 1 level teaspoon sugar. **Serves 4.**

BEEF CRUMBLE 320

1. Follow recipe and method for Stewed Beef (No. 314), Stewed Beef with Beer (No. 318) or Stewed Beef with Tomato (No. 319). **2.** Transfer cooked meat to 2-pint pie dish. **3.** Cover with crumble made by rubbing 3 oz. English or Welsh butter into 6 oz. plain flour. **4.** Add 3 oz. crumbled Lancashire cheese. **5.** Put into centre of fairly hot oven (375°F. or Gas No. 5). Bake for 30 to 35 minutes (or until top is pale gold). **Serves 4.**

BOILED SILVERSIDE & CARROTS 321

2 lb. salted silverside
3 cloves
1 large onion
1 large chopped celery stalk
Sprig of parsley
½ lb. sliced carrots
½ recipe Suet Crust Pastry (No. 97)
ACCOMPANIMENT
1 recipe Parsley Coating Sauce (No. 107)

1. Cover beef with cold water. Soak for 8 to 12 hours, changing water as often as possible (to remove excess salt). **2.** Drain. Put into saucepan. **3.** Cover with fresh water. Slowly bring to boil. **4.** Remove scum. **5.** Press cloves into onion. Add to pan with celery and parsley. **6.** Lower heat. Cover pan. **7.** Simmer gently for 1½ hours. Add carrots. Continue to simmer for further 1 to 1½ hours (or until meat is tender). **8.** 20 minutes before serving shape pastry into 8 small dumplings. Lower into pan. **9.** Simmer with meat. **10.** Transfer beef to warm platter. **11.** Surround with carrot slices and dumplings. **12.** Serve Parsley Coating Sauce separately. **Serves 4.**

22 STEAK & KIDNEY PUDDING

1 recipe Suet Crust Pastry (No. 97)
1 lb. stewing steak (flank, shin or chuck)
6 oz. ox kidney
1 level tablespoon flour
Salt and pepper
1 large chopped onion
3 tablespoons cold water

1. Roll out two-thirds pastry. **2.** Use to line well-buttered 1½-pint pudding basin. **3.** Cut steak and kidney into cubes. **4.** Toss in flour seasoned with salt and pepper. **5.** Put into pastry-lined basin alternately with layers of onion. **6.** Pour in water. **7.** Moisten edges of lining pastry with water. **8.** Cover with lid, rolled from rest of pastry. **9.** Press pastry edges well together to seal. **10.** Cover with double thickness of buttered greaseproof paper or single thickness of buttered aluminium foil. **11.** Steam steadily for 3½ hours. Replenish boiling water if necessary. **12.** Serve from the basin with clean table napkin folded round it. **Serves 4.**

23 STEAK, KIDNEY & OYSTER PUDDING

1. Follow recipe and method for Steak and Kidney Pudding (No. **322**). **2.** Reduce kidneys to ¼ lb. **3.** Include 12 shelled oysters with meat filling. **Serves 4.**

STEAK & KIDNEY PLATE PIE   324

1 lb. stewing beef (shin, flank, skirt or chuck)
6 oz. ox kidney
2 level tablespoons flour
Salt and pepper
1½ oz. English or Welsh butter
1 large chopped onion
½ pint stock or water
1 recipe Milk 'Puff' Pastry (No. 100)
Milk for brushing

1. Cut stewing steak and kidney into small cubes. **2.** Toss in flour seasoned with salt and pepper. **3.** Fry briskly in hot butter until well browned, turning all the time. **4.** Remove to plate. **5.** Add onion to remaining butter in pan. Fry gently until pale gold. **6.** Replace meat. Pour in stock or water. **7.** Bring to boil. Lower heat. **8.** Cover pan. Simmer gently for 1¾ to 2 hours (or until meat is tender) stirring occasionally. **9.** Leave until completely cold. **10.** Roll out half the pastry. Use to cover lightly-buttered 8 to 9-in. heatproof plate. **11.** Pile cold meat filling in centre. **12.** Moisten edges of pastry with water. **13.** Cover with lid, rolled from rest of pastry. **14.** Press edges well together to seal. Flake by cutting with back of knife. **15.** Press into flutes. **16.** Stand pie on baking tray. **17.** Brush with milk. **18.** Bake just above centre of hot oven (425°F. or Gas No. 7) for 25 to 30 minutes (or until golden brown). **Serves 4.**

Steak & Kidney Pudding (No. 322)

BEEF

325 QUICK-BAKING STEAK & KIDNEY PIE

1. Prepare meat and kidney filling as in recipe for Steak and Kidney Plate Pie (No. 324). **2.** Transfer to 1-pint pie dish. **3.** Cover with Milk 'Puff' Pastry (No. 100), Rough Puff Pastry (No. 94) or Flaky Pastry (No. 99). **4.** Bake towards top of hot oven (450°F. or Gas No. 8) for 15 to 20 minutes (or until pastry is well puffed and golden). **Serves 4.**

326 DEEP DISH STEAK PIE

1½ lb. stewing beef (shin, flank, skirt or chuck)
2 level tablespoons plain flour
Salt and pepper
1 large sliced onion
¼ pint stock or water
¼ level teaspoon salt
1 recipe Milk 'Puff' Pastry (No. 100), Rough Puff Pastry (No. 94) or Flaky Pastry (No. 99)
Milk for brushing

1. Cut meat into small cubes. **2.** Toss in flour seasoned with salt and pepper. **3.** Put into 1-pint lipped pie dish with sliced onion. Dome meat in centre of dish. **4.** Combine stock or water with salt. Pour into dish over meat. **5.** Roll out pastry to just under ½-in. thickness. **6.** From it cut lid, 1½ in. larger all the way round than top of dish. **7.** Moisten edge of dish with water. Line with strip of pastry. **8.** Moisten strip with water. Cover with lid. **9.** Press edges well together to seal. Flake by cutting with back of knife. **10.** Press into flutes. **11.** Stand pie on baking tray. **12.** Brush with milk. Decorate with pastry leaves, rolled and cut from trimmings. **13.** Brush leaves with more milk. **14.** Make small hole in centre to allow steam to escape. **15.** Bake just above centre of hot oven (450°F. or Gas No. 8) for 15 minutes. **16.** Reduce temperature to moderate (350°F. or Gas No. 4). Continue to cook for further 2 hours. **17.** Cover pastry with piece of greaseproof paper during the latter part of cooking if it seems to be browning too much. **Serves 4.**

327 DEEP DISH STEAK & MUSHROOM PIE

1. Follow recipe and method for Deep Dish Steak Pie (No. 326). **2.** Use small onion instead of large. **3.** Include 2 to 3 oz. mushrooms and stalks. **Serves 4.**

MEAT & VEGETABLE PASTIES 328

6 oz. rump steak
¼ lb. ox liver or kidney
1 medium-sized chopped onion
1 large diced potato
1 tablespoon water
½ level teaspoon salt
Shake of pepper
1 recipe Short Crust Pastry (No. 88)
Milk for brushing

1. Cut steak and liver or kidney into very small pieces. **2.** Combine with onion, potato dice, water, salt and pepper. **3.** Divide pastry into 4 equal-sized pieces. **4.** Roll each out into 6 or 7-in. round. **5.** Moisten edges with water. **6.** Put equal amounts of filling into centres of each. **7.** Fold rounds in half over filling to form semi-circles. **8.** Press edges well together to seal. Ridge with fork. **9.** Transfer to lightly-buttered baking tray. **10.** Brush with milk. **11.** Bake just above centre of hot oven (425°F. or Gas No. 7) for 20 minutes. **12.** Reduce heat to moderate (325°F. or Gas No. 3). Bake for further 45 minutes. Serve hot or cold. **Serves 4.**

HAMBURGERS 329

1 lb. raw lean minced beef
2 oz. fresh white breadcrumbs
4 tablespoons milk
1 small finely-grated onion
½ level teaspoon made mustard
1 teaspoon Worcester sauce
Seasoning to taste
1½ oz. English or Welsh butter

1. Combine all ingredients (except butter) well together. **2.** Divide into 8 equal-sized pieces. Shape each into ½-in. thick cake. **3.** Heat butter in frying pan. **4.** Add Hamburgers, 3 or 4 at a time. **5.** Fry briskly for 1 minute each side. **6.** Reduce heat. Cook more slowly for further 6 to 8 minutes, turning twice. **Serves 4.**

MEAT BALLS IN TOMATO SAUCE 330

1. Follow recipe and method for Hamburgers (No. 329). **2.** Shape mixture into 16 small balls. **3.** Drop into saucepan containing freshly-made Tomato Sauce (No. 144). **4.** Cover and simmer for 30 minutes. **5.** Serve with freshly-boiled rice, noodles or potatoes. **Serves 4.**

BEEF

331 BEEF CURRY

¾ lb. cold cooked beef (such as remains of joint)
1 recipe Curry Sauce (No. 141)
ACCOMPANIMENTS
¾ lb. freshly-boiled rice (about 6 oz. raw)
1 oz. desiccated coconut
Chutney
4 skinned and sliced tomatoes
1 carton (5 oz.) natural yogurt

1. Chop beef coarsely. **2.** Add to Sauce. Heat through gently. **3.** Arrange border of rice on warm serving dish. **4.** Fill centre with Hot Beef Curry. **5.** Serve with accompaniments. **Serves 4.**

332 BEEF STROGANOFF

1¼ to 1½ lb. rump or fillet steak
1 small grated onion
3 oz. English or Welsh butter
¾ lb. sliced button mushrooms
Salt and pepper
3 tablespoons white wine
¼ pint fresh double cream
ACCOMPANIMENT
Freshly-boiled rice or noodles

1. Cut steak into ½-in. thick slices. **2.** Beat until very thin with rolling pin. **3.** Cut into ½-in. wide strips. **4.** Fry onion gently in 1½ oz. butter for 5 minutes. **5.** Add steak strips. Fry for further 5 minutes, turning all the time. **6.** Remove steak to plate. **7.** Add rest of butter to pan and heat. **8.** Add mushrooms. Fry for 3 minutes, turning. **9.** Replace steak. Sprinkle with salt and pepper. **10.** Gently stir in wine and cream. **11.** Re-heat gently without boiling. **12.** Serve with rice or noodles. **Serves 4.**

333 GRILLED STEAK

4 pieces of either fillet, rump or sirloin steak, each at least 1-in. thick and weighing between 4 and 6 oz.
1 oz. English or Welsh butter, melted
GARNISH
Anchovy, Chive, Garlic, Horseradish or Mustard Butter (see Savoury Butters Section)
4 whole grilled tomatoes
Watercress
Potato crisps

334 GRILLED TOURNEDO STEAK

1. Follow recipe and method for Grilled Steak (No. 333). **2.** Allow 2 steaks per person, each about 2 in. thick and approximately 3 oz. in weight. **3.** Allow approximately 1 to 3 extra minutes grilling time each side. **Serves 4.**

335 GRILLED STEAK AU POIVRE

1. Follow recipe and method for Grilled Steak (No. 333). **2.** An hour before grilling, press 2 tablespoons crushed black peppercorns (use rolling pin for crushing) well into steaks with palm of hand. **3.** Leave in a cool place until ready to cook. **Serves 4.**

336 FRIED STEAK & ONIONS

¾ lb. onions
2 oz. English or Welsh butter
4 pieces rump steak, each about 6 oz.

1. Slice onions thinly. Fry gently in butter until golden, turning frequently. **2.** Transfer to warm plate and keep hot. **3.** Add steak to pan. Fry briskly for 1 minute each side. **4.** Lower heat. Continue to fry further for 3 to 4 minutes for underdone steak; 4 to 5 minutes for medium-cooked steak; about 7 to 8 minutes for well-done steak. **5.** Turn steaks about every minute to ensure even cooking. **6.** Transfer to 4 individual warm plates. **7.** Top with fried onions. **Serves 4.**

1. Stand steak on grill rack. **2.** Brush with butter. **3.** Stand under pre-heated hot grill. **4.** Grill for 1 minute. **5.** Turn over. Brush with more butter. **6.** Grill for 1 minute. **7.** Turn over. Continue to grill for further 2 to 3 minutes each side for rare or underdone steak; 4 to 5 minutes each side for medium-cooked steak; up to 6 or 7 minutes each side for well-done steak. **8.** Transfer to 4 individual plates. **9.** Top each with piece of savoury butter. **10.** Garnish with tomatoes, watercress and crisps. **Serves 4.**

Roast Pork (No. 337)

Pork

Choose hand and spring, blade, loin, leg or spare rib.

1 oz. English or Welsh butter, melted
Salt

QUANTITIES
Allow $\frac{1}{2}$ to $\frac{3}{4}$ lb. per person for pork with bone
Allow 4 to 6 oz. per person for pork without bone

ACCOMPANIMENTS
Gravy (No. 147)
Apple Sauce (No. 146) or Cranberry Sauce (No. 145)
Sage and Onion Stuffing (No. 79)
Creamed or roast potatoes
Green vegetables to taste

1. Tie or skewer joint into neat shape. **2.** For crisp crackling, score skin at $\frac{1}{4}$-in. intervals (or ask butcher to do this for you). **3.** Brush with butter. Sprinkle thickly with salt. **4.** Stand joint on rack in roasting tin (this helps to keep crackling dry and crisp). **5.** Put into centre of hot oven (450°F. or Gas No. 8). **6.** Immediately reduce temperature to moderate (350°F. or Gas No. 4). **7.** Continue roasting for required amount of time, allowing total of 30 minutes per lb. and 30 minutes over. **8.** Stand roast on carving board and remove string or skewers. **9.** Serve with accompaniments.

2 large chopped onions
1 chopped garlic clove
$1\frac{1}{2}$ oz. English or Welsh butter
$1\frac{1}{4}$ lb. lean diced pork (weighed without bone)
1 level tablespoon flour
1 to 2 level tablespoons curry powder (depending on strength preferred)
4 canned pineapple rings, drained and chopped
1 level tablespoon tomato purée
2 oz. seedless raisins or sultanas
1 tablespoon lemon juice
1 bay leaf
1 level teaspoon ground ginger
1 level teaspoon salt
$\frac{1}{2}$ pint water
$\frac{1}{4}$ pint milk

ACCOMPANIMENTS
$\frac{3}{4}$ lb. freshly-boiled rice (6 oz. raw)
Chutney
Wedges of lemon

1. Fry onion and garlic gently in butter until pale gold. **2.** Add pork. Fry briskly for 5 minutes, turning all the time. **3.** Stir in flour and curry powder. **4.** Add remaining ingredients and bring to boil, stirring. **5.** Lower heat. Cover pan. **6.** Simmer slowly for 2 to $2\frac{1}{4}$ hours (or until pork is cooked through and tender). **7.** Stir frequently. **8.** Serve with accompaniments. **Serves 4.**

339 PORK WITH FRIED PEACHES

4 loin of pork chops, each about 6 oz.
2 oz. English or Welsh butter, melted
4 canned peach halves, well drained
4 canned or glacé cherries

GARNISH
Watercress

1. Stand chops in grill pan. Brush with melted butter. **2.** Grill for 7 to 10 minutes, depending on thickness. **3.** Turn over. Brush with more butter. **4.** Grill for further 7 to 10 minutes. **5.** Meanwhile, pour rest of butter into frying pan. **6.** Add peach halves. Fry gently until golden on both sides. **7.** Arrange chops on warm serving dish. **8.** Top each with peach half, cut side up. **9.** Fill centres of peaches with cherries. **10.** Garnish with watercress. **Serves 4.**

340 PORK WITH FRIED PINEAPPLE

1. Follow recipe and method for Pork with Fried Peaches (No. 339). **2.** Use 4 fried pineapple rings instead of peaches. **3.** Fill centres of rings with 4 grilled button mushrooms instead of cherries. **4.** Garnish with grilled or fried tomatoes. **Serves 4.**

CHINESE-STYLE FRIED PORK 341

1 lb. pork fillet
1 tablespoon soy sauce
1 level teaspoon salt
1 level teaspoon brown sugar
1 tablespoon dry white wine
1 level tablespoon flour
3 oz. English or Welsh butter
1 medium-sized chopped onion
¼ lb. sliced mushrooms and stalks
2 large tomatoes, skinned and chopped
4 tablespoons cooked peas

ACCOMPANIMENTS
Freshly-boiled cabbage
¾ lb. freshly-boiled flat noodles

1. Cut pork into wafer-thin slices. **2.** Cut slices into 1-in. squares. **3.** Combine soy sauce, salt, sugar, wine and flour. **4.** Add pork squares. Toss well in soy sauce mixture. **5.** Melt 2 oz. butter in frying pan. **6.** Add onion. Fry gently until soft (but not brown). **7.** Transfer to plate. **8.** Melt rest of butter in pan. **9.** Add pork. Fry fairly briskly for 5 minutes, turning all the time. **10.** Add fried onion, mushrooms and stalks, tomatoes and peas. Cook gently for further 10 minutes, stirring and turning frequently. **11.** Serve with accompaniments. **Serves 4.**

Pork With Fried Peaches (No. 339)

342 GRILLED GAMMON WITH TOMATO BUTTER

4 gammon rashers, each 4 to 6 oz.
1 oz. English or Welsh butter, melted
1 recipe Tomato Butter (No. 202)

1. Remove rinds from gammon. **2.** Snip fat with scissors at 1-in. intervals to prevent gammon from curling as it cooks. **3.** Stand in grill pan. Brush with melted butter. **4.** Grill for 5 to 7 minutes (or until fat becomes transparent). **5.** Turn over. Brush with more melted butter. **6.** Grill for further 5 to 7 minutes. **7.** Transfer to warm dish. **8.** Top each with pat of Tomato Butter. **Serves 4.**

343 GRILLED GAMMON WITH MUSTARD OR DEVILLED BUTTER

1. Follow recipe and method for Grilled Gammon with Tomato Butter (No. 342). **2.** Use Mustard Butter (No. 199) or Devilled Butter (No. 186) instead of Tomato Butter. **Serves 4.**

344 GRILLED GAMMON MARYLAND

1. Grill gammon as in recipe for Grilled Gammon with Tomato Butter (No. 342). **2.** Transfer to warm platter and surround with hot Corn Fritters (No. 465) and halved bananas fried in English or Welsh butter. **Serves 4.**

345 PORK WITH CHEESE & BEER

4 loin of pork chops, each about 6 oz.
1 oz. English or Welsh butter, melted
6 oz. crumbled Lancashire cheese
1 level dessertspoon made mustard
4 tablespoons brown ale

GARNISH
4 grilled tomato halves

1. Stand chops in grill pan. Brush with melted butter. **2.** Grill for 7 to 10 minutes, depending on thickness. **3.** Turn over. Brush with more butter. **4.** Grill for further 7 to 10 minutes. **5.** Combine cheese with mustard and beer. **6.** Spread equal amounts over chops. **7.** Grill until brown. **8.** Transfer to warm serving dish. **9.** Garnish each with ½ grilled tomato. **Serves 4.**

346 BAKED GAMMON STEAK WITH APPLES

2 level tablespoons soft brown sugar
1 level teaspoon dry mustard
Pepper
1½-in. thick gammon steak (about 1¼ lb.)
12 very small onions or shallots
¼ pint apple juice or cider
2 medium-sized cooking apples
3 cloves
1 oz. English or Welsh butter

1. Combine 1 tablespoon brown sugar with mustard and shake of pepper. **2.** Rub on to both sides of gammon steak. **3.** Transfer to buttered heatproof dish. Surround with whole onions or shallots. **4.** Pour in apple juice. **5.** Cover tightly with lid or aluminium foil. **6.** Bake in centre of hot oven (425°F. or Gas No. 7) for 30 minutes. **7.** Turn gammon steak over. **8.** Cover with peeled, cored and sliced apples, rest of sugar and 3 cloves. **9.** Dot with butter and re-cover. **10.** Continue to cook in moderate oven (350°F. or Gas No. 4) for further hour. Uncover during the last 15 minutes. **Serves 4.**

347 PARTY GAMMON

1 piece corner or middle cut of gammon, 3½ to 4 lb. after boning
Cloves

GLAZE
3 oz. soft brown sugar
2 level teaspoons dry mustard
2 oz. English or Welsh butter, melted
2 tablespoons cider or apple juice
1 teaspoon Worcester sauce

1. Put gammon into large pan. Cover with cold water. **2.** Soak for 8 to 10 hours, changing water at least 3 times to get rid of excess salt. **3.** Drain. Cover with fresh cold water. **4.** Bring slowly to boil. Remove scum. **5.** Lower heat. Cover pan. **6.** Simmer very slowly, allowing 30 minutes per lb. **7.** Drain and cool slightly. **8.** Strip off skin. Score fat into diamond pattern with sharp knife. **9.** Press a clove into each alternate diamond. **10.** Put joint into roasting tin. **11.** Combine sugar with mustard, melted butter, cider or apple juice and Worcester sauce. **12.** Coat fat with mixture. **13.** Cook in centre of fairly hot oven (375°F. or Gas No. 5) for 30 minutes (or until fat is golden brown). Baste 3 or 4 times. **14.** Serve hot or cold. **Serves 12 to 14.**

348 STEAMED BACON PUDDING

1 lb. streaky bacon
¾ lb. self-raising flour
Good shake of pepper
¼ lb. English or Welsh butter
¼ lb. grated onions
½ level teaspoon mixed herbs
1 level tablespoon finely-chopped parsley
2 large eggs, beaten
5 tablespoons cold milk

ACCOMPANIMENTS
Gravy (No. 147)
Grilled tomato halves
Apple Sauce (No. 146)

1. Line 2-pint lightly-buttered pudding basin with 8 to 10 bacon rashers. Chop rest of bacon finely. **2.** Sift flour and pepper into bowl. **3.** Rub in butter finely. **4.** Add chopped bacon, onions, herbs and parsley. **5.** Mix to soft batter with eggs and milk, stirring briskly without beating. **6.** Transfer to prepared basin. **7.** Cover securely with buttered greaseproof paper or aluminium foil. **8.** Steam steadily for 2 hours. **9.** Turn out on to warm dish. **10.** Serve with accompaniments. **Serves 4.**

PORK PIE 350

1 recipe Hot Water Crust Pastry (No. 95)
1 lb. lean diced pork (weighed without bone)
1 small grated onion
1 level teaspoon sage
Large pinch of nutmeg
Good shake of pepper
¼ pint water
Beaten egg for brushing
1½ level teaspoons gelatine

1. Roll out two-thirds pastry. **2.** Mould over outside of well-floured 6-in. round cake tin, covering base and sides completely. **3.** Turn over on to buttered baking tray. Carefully remove cake tin. **4.** Combine diced pork with onion, sage, nutmeg, pepper and 4 tablespoons water. **5.** Pack into pastry case. Moisten edges of pastry with water. **6.** Roll out rest of pastry into lid. Cover pie, pressing pastry edges well together to seal. **7.** Tie strip of double-thickness aluminium foil round outside of pie to keep it in shape. **8.** Make hole in the top to allow steam to escape. **9.** Brush with beaten egg. **10.** Decorate with pastry leaves, cut from trimmings. Brush with more egg. **11.** Bake pie in centre of fairly hot oven (400°F. or Gas No. 6) for 15 minutes. **12.** Reduce temperature to moderate (350°F. or Gas No. 4) and bake for further 1¾ hours. **13.** Remove from oven. **14.** Bring rest of water to boil. Add gelatine. Stir briskly until dissolved. **15.** Pour into hot pie through hole in top, using small plastic or paper funnel. **16.** Leave until completely cold before cutting. **Serves 4 to 6.**

349 DEVILLED PORK SAUSAGES

1 lb. skinless pork sausages
1 oz. English or Welsh butter
1 medium-sized chopped onion
2 level tablespoons flour
¼ pint water
2 level tablespoons sweet pickle
1 dessertspoon Worcester sauce
2 tablespoons tomato ketchup
1 level teaspoon made mustard
1 tablespoon vinegar
½ level teaspoon salt

1. Fry sausages briskly in butter until golden. **2.** Remove to plate. **3.** Add onion to remaining butter in pan. Fry gently until pale gold. **4.** Stir in flour. Cook for 1 minute. **5.** Gradually blend in water. **6.** Add all remaining ingredients. **7.** Slowly bring to boil, stirring. **8.** Replace sausages. Lower heat. Cover pan. **9.** Simmer gently for 30 minutes. **Serves 4.**

PORK PATTIES 351

½ lb. cooked minced pork
¼ lb. finely-chopped or minced lean bacon
¼ lb. fresh white breadcrumbs
½ level teaspoon sage or mixed herbs
1 standard egg
¼ pint milk
Seasoning to taste
½ pint Mustard Coating Sauce (No. 118)

1. Combine pork with bacon, breadcrumbs and sage or mixed herbs. **2.** Beat egg and milk well together. **3.** Add to breadcrumb mixture. Mix well. **4.** Season to taste with salt and pepper. **5.** Turn mixture out on to lightly-floured board. **6.** Divide into 8 equal-sized pieces. Shape each into a 1-in. thick cake. **7.** Transfer to heatproof dish. **8.** Coat with Mustard Sauce. **9.** Bake, uncovered, in centre of fairly hot oven (375°F. or Gas No. 5) for 20 minutes. **Serves 4.**

PORK

4 loin of pork chops, each about 6 oz.
2 level tablespoons flour
1 level teaspoon salt
Shake of pepper
1½ oz. English or Welsh butter
1 large chopped onion
4 medium-sized potatoes, sliced
2 large chopped celery stalks
½ lb. skinned and chopped tomatoes
2 level teaspoons granulated sugar
1 teaspoon Worcester sauce

1. Toss chops in flour seasoned with salt and pepper. 2. Fry briskly in butter until crisp and golden on both sides. Transfer to plate. 3. Add onion to remaining butter in pan. Fry gently until golden. 4. Cover base of fairly shallow heatproof dish with potatoes. 5. Add celery, tomatoes, sugar and Worcester sauce to onion in pan. 6. Mix well. Pour over potatoes. 7. Arrange chops on top. 8. Cover with lid or aluminium foil. 9. Bake in centre of moderate oven (350°F. or Gas No. 4) for 1 to 1¼ hours. **Serves 4.**

1 lb. fillet of pork
4 level tablespoons flour
Salt and pepper
1½ oz. English or Welsh butter
1 large chopped onion
½ lb. skinned tomatoes
1 large chopped celery stalk
1 small chopped green pepper
¼ level teaspoon salt
4 tablespoons tomato juice

1. Cut pork into thin slices. 2. Toss in flour seasoned with salt and pepper. 3. Fry briskly in butter until golden. Transfer to plate. 4. Add onion to remaining butter in pan. Fry gently until pale gold. 5. Arrange pork in casserole dish. 6. Cover with fried onion, tomatoes, celery and green pepper. 7. Sprinkle with salt. 8. Pour tomato juice into dish. Cover with lid or aluminium foil. 9. Bake in centre of moderate oven (350°F. or Gas No. 4) for 1 hour. 10. Uncover. Continue to cook for further 15 minutes. **Serves 4.**

2 lb. spare ribs of pork
1 large onion
1 large carrot
2 celery stalks
1 bay leaf
6 peppercorns
1 level teaspoon salt
ACCOMPANIMENTS
Sweet Sour White Cabbage (No. 470)
Pease Pudding (No. 460)
Creamed potatoes (No. 440)

1. Divide spare ribs into cutlets. 2. Put into large saucepan. Cover with boiling water. 3. Add whole onion, carrot, halved celery stalks, bay leaf, peppercorns and salt. 4. Bring to boil and remove scum. 5. Lower heat. Cover pan. 6. Simmer gently for 1½ to 2 hours (or until tender). 7. Drain. 8. Arrange cabbage on warm plate. 9. Place spare ribs on top. 10. Serve with accompaniments. **Serves 4.**

¼ pint milk
1 teaspoon Worcester sauce
2 standard eggs
¼ lb. fresh white breadcrumbs
1 medium-sized chopped onion
1 finely-chopped garlic clove (optional)
1 oz. English or Welsh butter
¾ lb. cold cooked pork, finely minced
½ level teaspoon mixed herbs
Seasoning to taste
ACCOMPANIMENT
Mushroom Sauce (No. 113) or Onion Sauce (No. 108)

1. Beat milk with Worcester sauce and eggs. 2. Combine with breadcrumbs. 3. Fry onion and garlic (if used) gently in butter until pale gold. 4. Add to breadcrumb mixture with minced pork and herbs. 5. Season to taste. Mix well. 6. Transfer to 2-lb. buttered loaf tin. 7. Bake in centre of moderate oven (350°F. or Gas No. 4) for ¾ to 1 hour (or until firm). 8. Serve hot with Sauce. **Serves 4.**

Swiss Veal (No. 359)

Veal

WIENER SCHNITZEL

4 pieces of veal fillet, each 4 to 6 oz.
4 level tablespoons flour
½ level teaspoon salt
1 large egg, beaten
8 slightly rounded tablespoons fine white
  breadcrumbs
3 oz. English or Welsh butter
1 tablespoon olive or corn oil

GARNISH
4 slices lemon
2 teaspoons capers

1. Beat each piece of veal until very very thin.
2. Nick edges with scissors to prevent meat from
curling up as it cooks. **3.** Toss in flour seasoned
with salt. **4.** Dip in beaten egg and coat with
crumbs. **5.** Shake off surplus crumbs. **6.** Heat
butter and oil in frying pan. **7.** Add no more than
1 or 2 pieces of veal at a time so that there is
sufficient room for them to float about. **8.** Fry
gently for 8 to 10 minutes, turning once.
9. Drain on soft kitchen paper. **10.** Transfer to
warm dish. **11.** Garnish centres of each with
slices of lemon topped with capers. **Serves 4.**

WIENER SCHNITZEL HOLSTEIN 357

1. Follow recipe and method for Wiener
Schnitzel (No. 356) but omit garnish. **2.** Top
each Schnitzel with fried egg and accompany
with lemon wedges. **Serves 4.**

ITALIAN VEAL 358

1. Follow recipe and method for Wiener
Schnitzel (No. 356). **2.** After dipping veal in egg,
coat with 5 level tablespoons breadcrumbs mixed
with 4 level tablespoons finely-grated English
Cheddar cheese. **3.** Omit capers. Garnish each
with lemon slices and 2 black or stuffed olives.
Accompany with Tomato Sauce (No. 144).
Serves 4.

SWISS VEAL 359

1. Follow recipe and method for Wiener
Schnitzel (No. 356) but omit garnish. **2.** Coat
Schnitzel with sauce made by heating gently
1 carton (5 oz.) soured cream with yolks of
2 standard eggs. **3.** Dust lightly with chopped
parsley. **Serves 4.**

VEAL

360 ROAST VEAL

Choose loin, leg, boned shoulder, stuffed breast

2 oz. English or Welsh butter

QUANTITIES
Allow ½ to ¾ lb. per person for veal with bone
Allow 4 to 6 oz. per person for veal without bone

ACCOMPANIMENTS
Gravy (No. 147)
Grilled bacon rolls
Lemon wedges
Roast or boiled potatoes
Peas, beans, cauliflower, carrots or mixture of vegetables to taste

1. Skewer or tie joint into neat shape. **2.** Stand in roasting tin. **3.** Brush with butter. **4.** Pour remaining butter into tin. **5.** Put into centre of hot oven (450°F. or Gas No. 8). **6.** Immediately reduce to moderate (350°F. or Gas No. 4). **7.** Continue roasting for required amount of time, allowing 30 minutes per lb. and 30 minutes over. Baste frequently. **8.** Stand joint on carving board. **9.** Remove string or skewers. **10.** Serve with accompaniments.

361 VEAL MARENGO

1½ lb. boned breast or knuckle of veal
3 level tablespoons flour
1 level teaspoon salt
2 oz. English or Welsh butter
1 tablespoon olive or corn oil
1 large chopped onion
1 chopped garlic clove
¼ pint water
1 wine glass dry white wine
¾ lb. skinned and chopped tomatoes
½ lb. sliced mushrooms and stalks
1 level teaspoon granulated sugar
2 level tablespoons finely-chopped parsley
¾ lb. freshly-boiled rice (about 6 oz. raw)

1. Cut veal into 1-in. cubes. **2.** Toss in flour seasoned with salt. **3.** Fry in hot butter and oil until crisp and golden, turning all the time. **4.** Remove to plate. **5.** Add onion and garlic to remaining butter in pan. Fry gently until pale gold. **6.** Return veal to pan. **7.** Pour in water and wine. **8.** Add tomatoes, mushrooms and sugar. **9.** Bring slowly to boil. Lower heat. Cover pan. **10.** Simmer gently for 1 to 1¼ hours (or until veal is tender). **11.** Transfer to a warm dish. Sprinkle with parsley. **12.** Serve rice separately. **Serves 4.**

POT-ROASTED VEAL BREAST 36

2½ lb. boned veal breast
1 recipe Celery and Tomato Stuffing (No. 75)
3 oz. English or Welsh butter
1 tablespoon olive or corn oil

ACCOMPANIMENT
Gravy (No. 147)

1. Spread veal with Stuffing. **2.** Roll up. Tie at 1½-in. intervals with fine string or thick thread. **3.** Heat butter and oil in flameproof casserole or heavy saucepan. **4.** Add joint. Brown well all over. **5.** Cover pan tightly. Cook over very low heat, allowing 45 minutes per lb. **6.** Turn occasionally. **7.** Transfer to carving board. **8.** Remove string or thread. **9.** Accompany with gravy. **Serves 4 to 6.**

FRICASSÉE OF VEAL 36

1½ lb. boned breast or knuckle of veal
½ pint stock or water
½ pint milk
3 cloves
1 large onion
½ small bay leaf
1 blade mace
1 sprig parsley
1 level teaspoon salt
1 oz. English or Welsh butter
1 oz. flour
¼ lb. button mushrooms
Seasoning to taste

GARNISH
8 grilled bacon rolls
4 lemon wedges
Parsley sprigs

1. Cut veal into 2-in. cubes. Put into saucepan. **2.** Pour in stock or water and milk. **3.** Press cloves into onion. Add to saucepan with bay leaf, mace, parsley and salt. **4.** Bring to boil. Remove scum. **5.** Lower heat. Cover pan. **6.** Simmer gently for 1 to 1¼ hours (or until veal is tender). **7.** Strain liquor and reserve. **8.** Transfer veal to warm platter. Keep hot. **9.** Melt butter in clean saucepan. **10.** Stir in flour. Cook for 2 minutes without browning. **11.** Gradually blend in veal liquor. **12.** Cook, stirring, until sauce comes to boil and thickens. **13.** Add mushrooms. Simmer for 5 minutes. Season to taste. **14.** Pour over veal. **15.** Garnish with bacon, lemon and parsley. **Serves 4.**

64 BLANQUETTE OF VEAL

1. Follow recipe and method for Fricassée of Veal (No. 363). **2.** After sauce has simmered for 5 minutes, remove from heat and cool slightly. **3.** Stir in yolks of 2 standard eggs and 1 dessertspoon lemon juice. **4.** Pour over veal. **Serves 4.**

65 VEAL CASSEROLE WITH CREAM

1½ lb. boned breast or knuckle of veal
2 oz. English or Welsh butter
1 medium-sized chopped onion
1 large chopped celery stalk
¼ lb. sliced mushrooms and stalks
1 level teaspoon paprika
½ level teaspoon mixed herbs
2 tablespoons lemon juice or dry sherry
½ to 1 level teaspoon salt
Shake of pepper
¼ pint fresh double cream

1. Cut veal into 1-in. cubes. **2.** Fry gently in butter with onion, celery and mushrooms until pale gold. **3.** Transfer to casserole dish. **4.** Stir in paprika, herbs, lemon juice or sherry and salt and pepper. **5.** Cover dish with lid or aluminium foil. **6.** Cook in centre of moderate oven (350°F. or Gas No. 4) for 1 to 1¼ hours (or until veal is tender). **7.** Stir in cream. **8.** Serve straight away. **Serves 4.**

66 VEAL & EGG PIE

Double recipe Cheese Pastry (No. 93)
½ pint cold Basic White Coating Sauce (No. 106)
½ lb. cooked chopped veal
2 large chopped hard-boiled eggs
2 tablespoons cooked peas
Seasoning to taste
Milk for brushing

1. Divide pastry into 2 equal portions. **2.** Roll out 1 portion. Use to line lightly-buttered 8-in. heatproof plate. **3.** Combine Sauce with veal, eggs and peas. **4.** Season to taste with salt and pepper. **5.** Spread over pastry to within 1 in. of edges. **6.** Moisten edges with water. **7.** Cover with lid, rolled from rest of pastry. **8.** Press edges well together to seal. Ridge with fork. **9.** Brush with milk. Stand Pie on baking tray. **10.** Bake just above centre of hot oven (425°F. or Gas No. 7) for 25 to 30 minutes (or until golden). Serve hot or cold. **Serves 4 to 6.**

VEAL GOULASH 367

½ lb. chopped onions
1 chopped garlic clove
2 oz. lean chopped bacon
3 oz. English or Welsh butter
1½ lb. boned breast or knuckle of veal
1 level tablespoon paprika
1 large chopped green pepper
6 oz. skinned tomatoes, chopped
½ level teaspoon caraway seeds
1 level teaspoon salt
1 carton (5 oz.) natural yogurt

ACCOMPANIMENT
Boiled potatoes or noodles

1. Gently fry onion, garlic and bacon in butter (in saucepan) until pale gold. **2.** Cut veal into 2-in. cubes and add. **3.** Fry fairly briskly for 5 minutes, turning all the time. **4.** Stir in paprika. **5.** Add all remaining ingredients except yogurt. **6.** Very slowly bring to boil. **7.** Lower heat. Cover pan. **8.** Simmer gently for 1 to 1¼ hours (or until veal is tender). **9.** Remove from heat. Stir in yogurt. **10.** Serve with potatoes or noodles. **Serves 4.**

● *An authentic Goulash has no liquid added to it; the meat and vegetables provide their own.*

ESCALOPES WITH YOGURT SAUCE 368

4 pieces of veal fillet, each 4 to 6 oz.
2 oz. English or Welsh butter
1 dessertspoon olive or corn oil
1 carton (5 oz.) natural yogurt
1 level teaspoon paprika

1. Beat each piece of veal until very thin. **2.** Nick edges with scissors to prevent meat from curling up as it cooks. **3.** Fry gently in hot butter and oil, allowing about 5 minutes per side. **4.** Transfer to warm plate. Keep warm. **5.** Add yogurt and paprika to remaining butter in pan. Heat through gently. **6.** Pour over veal. **7.** Serve straight away. **Serves 4.**

ESCALOPES IN LEMON SAUCE 369

1. Follow recipe and method for Escalopes with Yogurt Sauce (No. 368). **2.** Coat fried veal with ½ pint Lemon Coating Sauce (No. 111) instead of yogurt sauce. **3.** Garnish by sprinkling with finely-chopped parsley. **Serves 4.**

Offal

2 lb. dressed tripe
½ lb. onions
¾ pint milk
1 level teaspoon salt
1 level tablespoon corn flour
3 extra tablespoons cold milk
½ oz. English or Welsh butter
Pepper to taste

ACCOMPANIMENT
Creamed Potatoes (No. 440)

1. Wash tripe well. Cut into 2-in. squares. **2.** Slice onions thinly. **3.** Put both into saucepan. **4.** Add milk and salt. **5.** Bring to boil. Lower heat. **6.** Cover pan. Simmer very gently for 35 to 45 minutes (or until tripe is tender). **7.** Mix cornflour to smooth paste with extra cold milk. **8.** Add to tripe and onions in saucepan. Cook, stirring, until mixture comes to boil and thickens. **9.** Add butter. Season to taste with pepper. **10.** Serve with Creamed Potatoes. **Serves 4.**

2 lb. dressed tripe
1 pint water (or 1 pint milk if preferred)
1 level teaspoon salt
1 large onion
1 garlic clove
2 oz. English or Welsh butter
1 level tablespoon finely-chopped parsley
1 dessertspoon malt vinegar

ACCOMPANIMENTS
4 slices hot fried bread

1. Wash tripe well. Cut into 1-in. squares. **2.** Put into saucepan. Add water and salt. **3.** Bring to boil. Lower heat. **4.** Cover pan. Simmer very gently for 35 to 45 minutes (or until tripe is tender). Drain. **5.** Chop onion and garlic. Fry gently in butter until pale gold. **6.** Add tripe, parsley and vinegar. Heat briskly for 2 to 3 minutes, shaking pan frequently. **7.** Pile equal amounts on to fried bread. **8.** Serve straight away. **Serves 4.**

2 lb. dressed tripe
1 pint water (or 1 pint milk, if preferred)
1 level teaspoon salt
2 oz. English or Welsh butter
1 garlic clove
½ lb. crumbled Lancashire cheese
¼ pint extra milk (unless tripe is cooked in milk)

ACCOMPANIMENT
Salad to taste (see Salad Section)

1. Wash tripe well. Cut into strips. **2.** Put into saucepan with water or milk and salt. **3.** Bring to boil. Lower heat. **4.** Cover pan. Simmer very gently for 35 to 45 minutes (or until tripe is tender). Drain. (If milk used in cooking, reserve ¼ pint tripe liquor). **5.** Put butter and halved garlic clove into saucepan. **6.** Melt over low heat. Remove garlic. **7.** Add tripe. Cook briskly in butter for 1 minute, shaking pan frequently. **8.** Arrange layers of tripe and crumbled cheese in heatproof dish, beginning with tripe and ending with cheese. **9.** Pour in tripe liquor (or extra milk). **10.** Re-heat towards top of fairly hot oven (375°F. or Gas No. 5) for 20 to 25 minutes. **11.** Serve hot and accompany with salad. **Serves 4.**

4 pigs' kidneys
2 level tablespoons flour
Salt and pepper
2 oz. English or Welsh butter
1 medium-sized chopped onion
½ pint water
2 teaspoons Worcester sauce
2 level teaspoons made mustard
1 dessertspoon tomato purée
1 level tablespoon finely-chopped parsley
4 slices hot buttered toast

1. Skin and core kidneys. **2.** Cut into ¼-in. thick slices. **3.** Toss in flour seasoned with salt and pepper. **4.** Melt butter in saucepan. **5.** Add onion. Fry until pale gold. **6.** Add kidney and any remaining flour. Cook slowly for further 5 minutes, turning frequently. **7.** Combine water with Worcester sauce, mustard, purée and parsley. **8.** Pour into pan. **9.** Cook slowly, stirring, until mixture comes to boil and thickens. **10.** Lower heat. Cover pan. **11.** Simmer for 15 minutes. **12.** Serve on toast. **Serves 4.**

Tongue With Mustard Sauce (No. 376)

74 KIDNEYS ESPAGNOLE

4 calves' kidneys
2 oz. English or Welsh butter
1 recipe Espagnole Sauce (No. 130)
¾ lb. freshly-boiled rice (about 6 oz. raw)
1 level tablespoon finely-chopped parsley

1. Skin and core kidneys. **2.** Cut into slices. Fry in hot butter for 5 minutes, turning frequently. **3.** Remove from pan. Add to Espagnole Sauce. **4.** Heat through gently. **5.** Arrange border of rice on warm serving dish. **6.** Fill centre with kidney mixture. **7.** Sprinkle with chopped parsley. **Serves 4.**

75 KIDNEYS EN BROCHETTE

8 lambs' kidneys
Cold milk
8 rashers streaky bacon
½ lb. freshly-boiled rice (about ¼ lb. raw)

1. Skin and core kidneys. **2.** Cut each in half. **3.** Put into saucepan. Cover with milk. Bring slowly to boil. **4.** Reduce heat. Simmer for 3 minutes. **5.** Lift out of pan. Drain on soft kitchen paper. **6.** Cut bacon rashers in half. Wrap round pieces of kidney. **7.** Thread on to 4 skewers. **8.** Brown under hot grill for 2 to 3 minutes. **9.** Turn over and grill for further 2 to 3 minutes. **10.** Serve with rice. **Serves 4.**

TONGUE WITH MUSTARD SAUCE 376

1 fresh ox tongue (2½ to 3 lb.)
½ lb. onions
2 medium-sized carrots
3 celery stalks
Handful of parsley
1 bay leaf
8 peppercorns
1 level teaspoon salt
Double recipe Mustard Coating Sauce
 (No. 118)

1. Remove excess fat from root end of tongue. **2.** Put tongue into large bowl. Cover with cold water. **3.** Soak for 2 hours. Drain. **4.** Transfer to large saucepan. Cover with cold water. **5.** Bring slowly to boil. Drain. **6.** Cover with fresh water. Add whole onions, thickly-sliced carrots, halved celery stalks, parsley, bay leaf, peppercorns and salt. **7.** Bring slowly to boil. Lower heat. **8.** Cover pan. Simmer for 3 to 3½ hours (or until tongue is tender). **9.** Drain. Leave until cool enough to handle. **10.** Remove wind and food pipe, small bones and gristle at root end. **11.** Strip off skin. **12.** Carve hot tongue into thin slices. **13.** Serve with Mustard Sauce. **Serves 6 to 8.**

TONGUE WITH MADEIRA SAUCE 377

1. Follow recipe and method for Tongue with Mustard Sauce (No. 376). **2.** Serve tongue with Madeira Sauce (No. 135) instead of Mustard Sauce. **Serves 6 to 8.**

OFFAL

378 BAKED STUFFED HEARTS

4 calves' hearts
½ recipe Pork Sausage Stuffing (No. 84)
2 oz. English or Welsh butter
3 tablespoons stock or water

ACCOMPANIMENTS
Creamed Potatoes (No. 440)
Brown Sauce (No. 130)
Redcurrant jelly

1. Wash hearts well. **2.** Remove veins and fat. Dry thoroughly. **3.** Cut through centre divisions to make 1 cavity in each heart. **4.** Fill loosely with equal amounts of Stuffing. **5.** Transfer to casserole dish. **6.** Dot with butter. Pour in stock or water. **7.** Cook, tightly covered, in centre of moderate oven (325°F. or Gas No. 3) for 1½ hours. **8.** Baste well. **9.** Continue to cook, uncovered, for further 30 minutes (or until tender). **10.** Serve with accompaniments. **Serves 4.**

379 POACHED SWEETBREADS IN CREAM SAUCE

1 lb. calves' sweetbreads
1 dessertspoon lemon juice
½ pint milk
1 small chopped onion
2 peppercorns
1 small celery stalk
1 oz. English or Welsh butter
1 oz. flour
¼ level teaspoon finely-grated lemon peel
Salt and pepper to taste
4 slices hot buttered toast

1. Soak sweetbreads in lukewarm salted water for 1 hour. Drain. **2.** Put into saucepan. Cover with cold water. **3.** Add lemon juice. Bring slowly to boil. **4.** Boil for 5 minutes. Drain. **5.** Plunge at once into cold water. **6.** When sweetbreads are cool enough to handle, lift out of water. Cut away gristle and tissues. **7.** Bring milk to boil. **8.** Lower heat. Add sweetbreads, onion, peppercorns and halved celery stalk. **9.** Simmer gently for 15 to 20 minutes. **10.** Strain sweetbread liquor. Make up to ½ pint with extra cold milk if necessary. **11.** Melt butter in clean saucepan and stir in flour. **12.** Cook slowly for 2 minutes, without browning. **13.** Gradually blend in sweetbread liquor. Add lemon peel. **14.** Cook, stirring, until sauce comes to boil and thickens. **15.** Add sweetbreads. Season to taste. **16.** Heat through gently for 5 minutes. **17.** Arrange on buttered toast and serve straight away. **Serves 4.**

CRUMBED & FRIED SWEETBREADS 38

1. Prepare sweetbreads as in recipe for Poached Sweetbreads in Cream Sauce (No. 379). **2.** After simmering sweetbreads in milk for 15 to 20 minutes, remove from saucepan and drain. **3.** Toss in 4 to 5 level teaspoons flour seasoned with salt and pepper. **4.** Coat twice in 1 large beaten egg and 5 to 6 level tablespoons toasted breadcrumbs. **5.** Fry until crisp and golden in 2 oz. English or Welsh butter. Drain on soft kitchen paper. **6.** Serve with Mock Hollandaise Sauce (No. 124). **Serves 4.**

BRAIN SAUTÉ 3

2 calves' brains
2 tablespoons lemon juice
Salt and pepper
2 level tablespoons flour
2 oz. English or Welsh butter
1 recipe Black Butter Sauce with Capers (No. 150)

1. Put brains into bowl. **2.** Cover with cold water and 1 dessertspoon lemon juice. Soak for 3 hours. Drain. **3.** Soak briefly in lukewarm water to remove all traces of blood. **4.** Drain. Put into saucepan. **5.** Cover with cold water and rest of lemon juice. **6.** Bring slowly to boil. **7.** Lower heat at once. Simmer very gently for 20 minutes. Drain. **8.** Cut each brain in half lengthwise. Wipe dry with soft kitchen paper. **9.** Sprinkle lightly with salt and pepper. **10.** Toss in flour. **11.** Heat butter in frying pan. Add brains. Cook for 2 to 3 minutes each side. **12.** Transfer to warm platter. **13.** Coat with Black Butter Sauce with Capers. **Serves 4.**

CREAMED LIVER 38

½ lb. calves' or lambs' liver
2 level tablespoons flour
Salt and pepper
1 oz. English or Welsh butter
½ pint milk

1. Cut liver into small pieces. **2.** Roll in flour seasoned with salt and pepper. **3.** Fry gently in hot butter until cooked through and golden brown. **4.** Stir in remaining flour. **5.** Gradually blend in milk. **6.** Cook slowly, stirring, until mixture comes to boil and thickens. **7.** Simmer gently for 5 minutes. **Serves 4.**

383 GRILLED LIVER

1 lb. calves' liver
Cold milk
1 oz. English or Welsh butter, melted

1. Slice liver thinly. **2.** Put into soup plate or shallow dish. Cover with milk. **3.** Soak for 30 minutes. **4.** Drain. Pat dry with soft kitchen paper. **5.** Stand on grill rack. Brush with melted butter. **6.** Cook under hot grill for $1\frac{1}{2}$ minutes. **7.** Turn over. Brush with more butter. **8.** Grill for further $1\frac{1}{2}$ minutes. **9.** Serve straight away. **Serves 4.**

384 CREAMED FRIED LIVER

1 lb. lambs' or pigs' liver
Cold milk
4 level tablespoons flour
Salt and pepper
1 large egg, beaten
6 to 8 level tablespoons toasted
  breadcrumbs
3 oz. English or Welsh butter

GARNISH
Lemon slices
Watercress

1. Cut liver into thin slices. **2.** Put into soup plate or shallow dish. Cover with milk. **3.** Soak for 30 minutes. **4.** Drain. Pat dry with soft kitchen paper. **5.** Toss in flour seasoned with salt and pepper. **6.** Coat twice in egg and breadcrumbs. Leave for 15 minutes. **7.** Heat butter in frying pan. **8.** Add liver, 1 or 2 pieces at a time. **9.** Fry until crisp and golden, allowing 2 to 3 minutes per side. **10.** Drain on soft kitchen paper. **11.** Transfer to warm platter. **12.** Garnish with lemon and parsley. **Serves 4.**

385 BRAISED LIVER

1 lb. ox liver
4 level tablespoons flour
Salt and pepper
2 oz. English or Welsh butter
1 medium-sized chopped onion
2 medium-sized grated carrots
1 large grated potato
2 chopped celery stalks
2 level tablespoons chopped parsley
$\frac{1}{2}$ level teaspoon salt
$\frac{1}{2}$ pint water
1 medium-sized sliced lemon

1. Cut liver into 1-in. cubes. **2.** Toss in flour seasoned with salt and pepper. **3.** Fry briskly (in saucepan) in hot butter until crisp and well sealed, turning all the time. **4.** Remove to plate. **5.** Add onion to remaining butter. Fry slowly until pale gold. **6.** Stir in any left-over flour, together with carrots, potato, celery, parsley, salt and water. **7.** Mix well. Bring slowly to boil. **8.** Replace liver. Top with lemon slices. **9.** Lower heat. Cover pan. **10.** Simmer for 30 to 40 minutes (or until liver is tender). **Serves 4.**

STEWED OXTAIL 386

1 medium-sized oxtail (2 to $2\frac{1}{2}$ lb.)
1 oz. English or Welsh butter
1 large sliced onion
1 medium-sized sliced carrot
$\frac{1}{2}$ small turnip, diced
1 bay leaf
6 peppercorns } tied together in
3 cloves   } muslin bag
3 parsley sprigs
$\frac{3}{4}$ pint boiling water
1 level teaspoon salt
2 level tablespoons flour
3 tablespoons cold water
1 dessertspoon vinegar
Seasoning to taste

GARNISH
2 level tablespoons finely-chopped parsley

1. Wash and dry oxtail. **2.** Cut into neat joints. Remove excess fat. **3.** Heat butter in large saucepan. **4.** Add onion. Fry gently until pale gold. **5.** Add oxtail and rest of vegetables. **6.** Fry briskly for 5 minutes, turning all the time. **7.** Add bag of herbs, boiling water and salt. **8.** Bring to boil. Lower heat. **9.** Cover pan. Simmer for 3 hours (or until oxtail is tender). **10.** Remove bag of herbs. **11.** Leave overnight in cold place. **12.** Before serving, remove hard layer of fat from surface and discard. **13.** Bring oxtail up to the boil. **14.** Pour in flour mixed to smooth paste with cold water and vinegar. **15.** Cook, stirring until liquor comes to boil and thickens. **16.** Simmer for 5 minutes. Season. **17.** Transfer to warm dish. **18.** Sprinkle with parsley. **Serves 4.**

Chicken

4 lb. roasting chicken
3 oz. English or Welsh butter
Salt and pepper
ACCOMPANIMENTS
Gravy (No. 147)
Bread Sauce (No. 139)
Small cooked sausages
Grilled bacon rolls
Roast and boiled potatoes
Assorted vegetables to taste

1. If chicken is frozen, thaw completely and remove giblet pack. **2.** Wash fresh or thawed bird well. Dry thoroughly with soft kitchen paper or clean cloth. **3.** Stand in roasting tin. **4.** Put 1½ oz. butter into body cavity. **5.** Melt rest of butter. Pour over chicken. **6.** Cover bird loosely with aluminium foil. **7.** Put into centre of hot oven (450°F. or Gas No. 8). **8.** Immediately reduce heat to moderate (350°F. or Gas No. 4). **9.** Continue to roast, allowing 25 minutes per lb. **10.** Uncover half way through cooking time and baste well. **11.** Sprinkle with salt and pepper and replace foil. **12.** Uncover for last 30 minutes to brown bird. **13.** Transfer to board or carving dish. Leave for 5 minutes before carving. **14.** Serve with accompaniments. **Serves 4 to 6.**

1. Follow recipe and method for Buttered Roast Chicken (No. 387). **2.** Instead of butter, fill body cavity with suitable stuffing (see Stuffings Section). **3.** Allow extra 5 minutes per lb. roasting time. **Serves 4 to 6.**

1. Follow recipe and method for Buttered Roast Chicken (No. 387). **2.** Fill body cavity with 1½ oz. English or Welsh butter creamed with 1 level teaspoon finely-crushed rosemary and ¼ to 1 level teaspoon French mustard. **Serves 4 to 6.**

4 medium-sized joints roasting chicken, washed and dried
4 level tablespoons flour
1 level teaspoon salt
2 oz. English or Welsh butter
1 tablespoon olive or corn oil
1 large chopped onion
1 chopped garlic clove
¼ lb. chopped lean bacon
8 small onions or 10 shallots
2 level tablespoons finely-chopped parsley
1 small bay leaf
½ pint dry red wine
4 tablespoons water
¼ lb. sliced mushrooms and stalks

1. Toss chicken joints in flour seasoned with salt. **2.** Heat butter and oil in large saucepan. **3.** Add chicken. Fry until crisp and golden on both sides. **4.** Remove to plate. **5.** Add chopped onion, garlic and bacon to remaining butter and oil in pan. **6.** Fry gently until pale gold. **7.** Replace chicken. **8.** Add small onions or shallots, parsley, bay leaf, wine and water. **9.** Bring to boil and lower heat. **10.** Cover pan. Simmer for 1 hour. **11.** Add mushrooms and simmer for further 15 minutes. **Serves 4.**

1 oz. blanched and toasted almonds
1 small chopped onion
2 oz. sliced mushroom and stalks
1 oz. English or Welsh butter
1 level dessertspoon cornflour
¼ pint milk
¾ lb. cooked chicken
¼ level teaspoon ground ginger
¼ level teaspoon grated nutmeg
1 carton (5 oz.) natural yogurt
Yolks of 2 standard eggs
Salt and pepper
1 oz. blanched and toasted almonds

1. Cut almonds into strips. **2.** Fry onion and mushrooms in butter (in saucepan) until pale gold. **3.** Add cornflour. Cook for 1 minute. **4.** Gradually blend in milk. **5.** Cook, stirring, until sauce comes to boil. **6.** Add chicken (cut into bite-size pieces), ginger and grated nutmeg. Heat through gently for 5 to 7 minutes. **7.** Beat yogurt and egg yolks well together. **8.** Add to chicken mixture. Cook very slowly, without boiling, until thickened. **9.** Season to taste and pour into warm serving dish. **10.** Scatter almonds over the top. **Serves 4.**

4 medium-sized joints roasting chicken,
  washed and dried
Milk
4 to 5 level tablespoons flour
Salt and pepper
6 level tablespoons toasted breadcrumbs
3 oz. English or Welsh butter
1 tablespoon olive or corn oil
GARNISH
Watercress

ACCOMPANIMENTS
Gravy (No. 147)
Corn Fritters (No. 465)
Halved bananas fried in English or Welsh
  butter

1. Dip chicken joints in milk. **2.** Toss in flour
seasoned with salt and pepper. Leave to dry for
30 minutes. **3.** Dip in milk again. Coat with
breadcrumbs. **4.** Shake surplus crumbs from
each chicken portion. **5.** Put butter and oil into
roasting tin. Heat for 10 minutes just above
centre of fairly hot oven (375°F. or Gas No. 5).
6. Add chicken and baste with hot butter and oil.
7. Return to oven. Cook, uncovered, for 30
minutes (or until chicken is tender). **8.** Drain
well on soft kitchen paper. **9.** Garnish with
watercress. **10.** Serve with accompaniments.
Serves 4.

4 medium-sized joints roasting chicken,
  washed and dried
Milk
2 level tablespoons flour
Salt and pepper
3 oz. English or Welsh butter
1 tablespoon olive or corn oil
1 tablespoon lemon juice
1 level tablespoon finely-chopped parsley

1. Dip chicken joints in milk. **2.** Coat with flour
seasoned with salt and pepper. **3.** Heat butter and
oil in large frying pan. **4.** Add chicken joints, skin
side up. **5.** Fry until golden. **6.** Turn over and
cover pan. **7.** Continue to fry gently until tender
(20 to 30 minutes). Turn joints at least twice.
8. Transfer to warm serving dish. Keep hot.
9. Add lemon juice and parsley to remaining
butter and oil in pan. Heat through quickly.
Pour over chicken. **Serves 4.**

Chicken Maryland (No. 392)

CHICKEN

394 CHICKEN & PARSLEY CASSEROLE

4 medium-sized joints roasting chicken, washed and dried
3 oz. English or Welsh butter
¼ lb. streaky bacon
2 large onions
2 oz. flour
1 pint milk
1 bay leaf
1 level teaspoon mixed herbs
1 chicken stock cube
Seasoning to taste
¼ lb. sliced mushrooms and stalks

GARNISH
2 level tablespoons finely-chopped parsley

1. Fry chicken joints in 2 oz. butter until golden on both sides. **2.** Transfer to large casserole. **3.** Chop bacon and onions. Add to butter in pan. Fry gently until pale gold. **4.** Sprinkle over chicken. **5.** Melt remaining oz. of butter in frying pan. Stir in flour. **6.** Cook, without browning, for 2 minutes. **7.** Gradually blend in milk. **8.** Add bay leaf, herbs and crumbled stock cube. **9.** Cook, stirring, until sauce comes to boil and thickens. Season to taste. **10.** Pour over chicken. Cover casserole with lid or aluminium foil. **11.** Cook in centre of moderate oven (325°F. or Gas No. 3) for 1 hour. **12.** Add mushrooms and stalks. Cook, covered, for further 30 minutes. **13.** Sprinkle with chopped parsley. **Serves 4.**

395 GRILLED CHICKEN

4 medium-sized joints roasting chicken, washed and dried
2 oz. English or Welsh butter, melted
1 tablespoon lemon juice
¼ level teaspoon paprika
¼ level teaspoon mixed herbs (optional)
Shake of pepper

GARNISH
Watercress

1. Brush chicken joints with some of the melted butter. **2.** Stand in grill pan, skin side down. **3.** Stand below pre-heated hot grill. **4.** Grill for about 30 minutes, turning frequently and brushing with rest of butter mixed with lemon juice, paprika, herbs and pepper. **5.** Transfer to warm serving dish. **6.** Garnish with watercress. **Serves 4.**

DEVILLED CHICKEN 396

1. Follow recipe and method for Grilled Chicken (No. 395). **2.** Mix melted butter with ½ level teaspoon dry mustard, 2 teaspoons Worcester sauce, 1 level teaspoon paprika and large pinch Cayenne pepper. **Serves 4.**

FRICASSÉE OF CHICKEN 397

1 roasting chicken (about 3 to 4 lb.)
½ pint stock or water
½ pint milk
¼ lb. streaky bacon, chopped
4 cloves
1 large onion
¼ level teaspoon grated nutmeg
2 oz. mushrooms and stalks
¼ level teaspoon mixed herbs
½ level teaspoon salt
1 oz. English or Welsh butter
1 oz. flour

GARNISH
4 rashers streaky bacon, halved, rolled and grilled
4 lemon wedges
1 level tablespoon finely-chopped parsley

1. Cut chicken into 8 joints. **2.** Put into saucepan with stock or water and milk. **3.** Add chopped bacon. **4.** Press cloves into onion. Add to pan with grated nutmeg, mushrooms and stalks, herbs and salt. **5.** Bring to boil. Remove scum. **6.** Lower heat. Cover pan. Simmer gently for 1¼ to 1¾ hours (or until chicken is tender). **7.** Strain liquor and reserve. Transfer chicken to warm plate and keep hot. **8.** Melt butter in clean saucepan. Add flour. Cook for 2 minutes without browning. **9.** Gradually blend in chicken liquor. **10.** Cook, stirring, until sauce comes to boil and thickens. **11.** Simmer for 2 minutes. Pour over chicken. **12.** Garnish with bacon rolls, lemon and parsley. **Serves 4.**

BLANQUETTE OF CHICKEN 398

1. Follow recipe and method for Fricassée of Chicken (No. 397). **2.** After sauce has cooked for 2 minutes remove from heat and cool slightly. **3.** Stir in yolks of 2 standard eggs and 1 dessertspoon lemon juice. **4.** Pour over chicken. **Serves 4.**

88

399 CHICKEN PIE

4 joints boiling fowl (about 3 lb.)
2 medium-sized carrots
2 medium-sized onions
2 medium-sized celery stalks
2 pints water
2 level teaspoons salt
1½ oz. English or Welsh butter
1½ oz. plain flour
½ pint milk
4 tablespoons fresh double cream
Seasoning to taste
1 recipe Milk 'Puff' Pastry (No. 100)
Beaten egg for brushing

1. Put chicken joints into saucepan. **2.** Add whole carrots, onions and celery broken into small lengths. **3.** Pour in water and salt. **4.** Bring to boil. Remove scum. **5.** Lower heat. Cover pan. Simmer for 2¼ to 2¾ hours (or until chicken is tender). If preferred, pressure-cook for 30 minutes at 15 lb. pressure. **6.** Lift chicken out of saucepan. Discard skin and bones. Cut chicken meat into bite-size pieces. **7.** Strain chicken liquor and reserve ¼ pint (if liked, retain vegetables for soup). **8.** Melt butter in clean saucepan. Add flour. Cook for 2 minutes without browning. **9.** Gradually blend in chicken stock and milk. **10.** Cook, stirring, until sauce comes to boil and thickens. **11.** Remove from heat. Stir in chicken and cream. **12.** Adjust seasoning to taste. Transfer to 1½-pint pie dish. **13.** Roll out Pastry to ¼-in. thickness. From it, cut lid about 1½ in. wider, all the way round, than top of dish. **14.** Moisten edge of dish with water. Line with strip of Pastry. **15.** Moisten strip. Cover with lid. **16.** Press edges well together to seal. **17.** Flake by cutting lightly with back of knife. **18.** Flute edges or ridge with fork. **19.** Brush with beaten egg. **20.** Stand Pie on baking tray. **21.** Bake just above centre of hot oven (425°F. or Gas No. 7) for 25 to 30 minutes (or until golden). **Serves 4 to 6.**

400 CHICKEN CACCIATORE

4 medium-sized joints roasting chicken, washed and dried
4 level tablespoons flour
1 level teaspoon salt
2 oz. English or Welsh butter
1 tablespoon olive or corn oil
1 large chopped onion
1 chopped garlic clove
1 lb. skinned and chopped tomatoes
1 level teaspoon sugar
¼ pint chicken stock
¼ lb. sliced mushrooms and stalks

CURRY OF CHICKEN 401

4 medium-sized joints roasting chicken, washed and dried
4 level tablespoons flour
1 level teaspoon salt
1½ oz. English or Welsh butter
1 tablespoon olive or corn oil
2 large chopped onions
1 large peeled and chopped cooking apple
1 chopped garlic clove (optional)
½ level teaspoon salt
1 level tablespoon curry powder
½ level teaspoon ground ginger
½ level teaspoon cinnamon
1 level tablespoon chutney
¼ pint milk
¼ pint water
1 carton (5 oz.) natural yogurt

ACCOMPANIMENTS
¾ lb. freshly-boiled rice (about 6 oz. raw)
2 large sliced tomatoes
2 oz. chopped salted peanuts
Chutney

1. Toss chicken joints in flour seasoned with salt. **2.** Heat butter and oil in large saucepan. **3.** Add chicken. Fry until crisp and golden on both sides. **4.** Remove to plate. **5.** Add onions, apples and garlic (if used) to remaining butter and oil in pan. **6.** Fry gently until pale gold. **7.** Stir in salt, curry powder, ginger, cinnamon, chutney, milk and water. **8.** Bring to boil. Replace chicken. **9.** Cover pan. **10.** Simmer slowly for 45 minutes to 1 hour (or until chicken is tender). **11.** Stir in yogurt. Heat through for further 5 minutes. **12.** Serve straight away with accompaniments. **Serves 4.**

1. Toss chicken in flour seasoned with salt. **2.** Heat butter and oil in large pan. **3.** Add chicken. Fry until crisp and golden on both sides. **4.** Remove to plate. **5.** Fry onion and garlic in remaining butter and oil in pan until pale gold. **6.** Add tomatoes, sugar and stock. **7.** Replace chicken. **8.** Slowly bring to boil. Cover pan. **9.** Lower heat. Simmer for 45 minutes. **10.** Add mushrooms. Continue to simmer for further 15 to 25 minutes (or until chicken is tender). **11.** Serve with noodles, macaroni or spaghetti. **Serves 4.**

Duckling & Goose

ROASTING TIME

Allow 25 minutes per lb.

QUANTITY

Allow 1 to 1¼ lb. raw weight per person.

402 ROAST DUCKLING OR GOOSE

1 duckling or goose
Stuffing (see Stuffings Section)
Salt

ACCOMPANIMENTS
Gravy (No. 147)
Apple Sauce (No. 146)
Roast and/or boiled potatoes
Cooked green peas

1. Wash duckling or goose inside and out under cold running water. **2.** Dry with cloth or soft kitchen paper. **3.** Fill with stuffing through vent end (or leave unstuffed if preferred). **4.** Stand in roasting tin. **5.** Prick skin all over with fork. Sprinkle well with salt. **6.** Stand bird (on grid) in roasting tin. **7.** Put into centre of moderate oven (350°F. or Gas No. 4). Roast for required amount of time. Do not baste or cover. **8.** Transfer to board or carving dish and carve. **9.** Serve with accompaniments.

403 DUCKLING OR GOOSE BIGARRADE

1. Follow recipe and method for Roast Duckling or Goose (No. 402). **2.** After carving meat transfer to warm platter. **3.** Coat with hot Bigarrade Sauce (No. 133). **4.** Garnish edge of dish with Duchesse Potatoes (No. 442).

404 DUCKLING OR GOOSE WITH APPLES & PRUNES

1. Follow recipe and method for Roast Duckling or Goose (No. 402). **2.** Before roasting, stuff bird with 1 or 2 lb. peeled, cored and thickly-sliced cooking apples and 8 to 12 soaked, stoned and halved prunes. **3.** Accompany with Cranberry Sauce (No. 145) or pickled red cabbage instead of Apple Sauce.

DUCKLING WITH ORANGE SAUCE 405

1 duckling (4 to 5 lb.)
1 level tablespoon flour
Coarsely-grated peel and juice of 2
  medium-sized oranges
2 tablespoons dry red wine
2 level tablespoons redcurrant jelly
½ wine glass dry sherry
Seasoning to taste

GARNISH
2 thinly-sliced peeled oranges
Watercress

1. Roast duckling for required amount of time (see Roast Duckling or Goose, Recipe (No. 402)). **2.** Transfer to warm platter and keep hot. **3.** Pour off all but 1 tablespoon fat from roasting tin. **4.** Stand tin over medium heat. **5.** Stir in flour. **6.** Cook for 2 minutes without browning. **7.** Add orange peel, juice, wine, jelly and sherry. **8.** Cook gently, stirring, until jelly dissolves and sauce comes to boil and thickens. Season to taste. **9.** Simmer for 2 minutes. Pour over duck. **10.** Garnish with border of orange slices. Stand watercress at either end of dish. **Serves 4.**

DUCKLING WITH PINEAPPLE & CHERRIES 406

1 duckling (4 to 5 lb.)
1 level tablespoon flour
4 canned pineapple rings, chopped
¼ pint pineapple syrup (taken from can)
1 wine glass dry white wine
Seasoning to taste

GARNISH
2 halved pineapple rings
Canned red cherries

1. Roast duckling for required amount of time (see Roast Duckling or Goose, Recipe (No. 402)). **2.** Transfer to warm platter and keep hot. **3.** Pour off all but 1 tablespoon fat from roasting tin. **4.** Stand tin over medium heat and stir in flour. **5.** Cook for 2 minutes without browning. **6.** Add chopped pineapple, pineapple syrup and wine. **7.** Cook gently, stirring, until sauce comes to boil and thickens. **8.** Simmer for 2 minutes. Season to taste. **9.** Pour over duckling. **10.** Garnish dish with pineapple and small mounds of cherries. **Serves 4.**

Right: Duckling With Orange Sauce (No. 405)

407 DUCKLING & APPLE CASSEROLE

1 × 4 lb. duckling or 4 duckling portions
1 medium-sized onion
½ lb. cooking apples
1 oz. English or Welsh butter
1 level tablespoon flour
½ pint apple juice
2 level tablespoons raisins
¼ level teaspoon sage
Salt and pepper to taste

GARNISH
2 level tablespoons chopped parsley

1. Cut whole duckling into 4 joints. **2.** Wash and dry joints (or portions if used). **3.** Cut away excess fat from either. Stand duckling in casserole dish. **4.** Chop onion and peeled and cored apples. **5.** Fry gently in butter until pale gold and soft. **6.** Stir in flour. Cook for 2 minutes. **7.** Gradually blend in apple juice. **8.** Cook, stirring, until sauce comes to boil and thickens. **9.** Add raisins and sage. **10.** Season to taste with salt and pepper. **11.** Pour into dish over duckling. **12.** Cover casserole with lid or aluminium foil. **13.** Cook in centre of moderate oven (350°F. or Gas No. 4) until duckling is tender (about 1½ to 2 hours). **14.** Uncover. Sprinkle with parsley. **Serves 4.**

408 DUCKLING & CELERY CASSEROLE

1 × 4 lb. duckling or 4 duckling portions
1 medium-sized onion
3 rashers lean bacon
1 oz. English or Welsh butter
1 level tablespoon flour
½ pint water
Salt and pepper
¼ level teaspoon mixed herbs
1 small head celery

1. Cut whole duckling into 4 joints. **2.** Wash and dry joints (or portions if used). **3.** Cut away excess fat from either. Stand duckling in large casserole dish. **4.** Chop onion and bacon. Fry gently in butter until pale gold. **5.** Stir in flour and cook for 2 minutes. **6.** Gradually blend in water. **7.** Cook, stirring, until sauce comes to boil and thickens. **8.** Season to taste with salt and pepper. **9.** Add herbs. Pour sauce over duckling. **10.** Cut celery into 1-in. lengths and add to casserole. **11.** Cover with lid or aluminium foil. **12.** Cook in centre of moderate oven (350°F. or Gas No. 4) until duckling is tender (about 1½ to 2 hours). **Serves 4.**

DUCKLING PROVENÇALE-STYLE 4

1 × 4 lb. duckling or 4 duckling portions
4 level tablespoons flour
2 oz. English or Welsh butter
½ lb. onions
2 small garlic cloves
1 medium-sized green pepper
2 oz. stuffed olives
1 level tablespoon tomato purée
1 level dessertspoon caster sugar
¾ pint water
1 medium-sized lemon
½ level teaspoon salt

ACCOMPANIMENTS
Boiled rice or potatoes
Salad to taste (see Salad Section)

1. Cut whole duckling into 4 joints. **2.** Wash and dry joints (or portions if used). **3.** Coat thickly with flour. **4.** Fry briskly in butter until crisp and golden. Remove to plate. **5.** Chop onions, garlic and green pepper. **6.** Add to butter in pan. Fry gently until soft and golden. **7.** Slice olives thinly. Add with purée and sugar. **8.** Blend in water. Bring to boil. **9.** Replace duckling. **10.** Slice lemon thinly. Add to saucepan with salt. **11.** Cover. Simmer very slowly for 1½ to 1¾ hours (or until duckling is tender). **12.** Serve with accompaniments. **Serves 4.**

DUCK & HAM LOAF 41

6 oz. cooked minced duck meat
6 oz. lean minced ham
¼ lb. fresh white breadcrumbs
½ level teaspoon finely-grated orange peel
1 small minced onion
3 oz. finely-chopped mushrooms and stalks
½ level teaspoon sage
2 level tablespoons finely-chopped parsley
2 large beaten eggs
¼ pint milk
Seasoning to taste

1. Combine duck, ham, breadcrumbs, orange peel, onion, mushrooms and stalks, sage and parsley. **2.** Add beaten eggs and milk. **3.** Season to taste with salt and pepper. Mix well. **4.** Transfer to well-buttered 2-lb. loaf tin. **5.** Smooth top with knife. **6.** Bake in centre of moderate oven (350°F. or Gas No. 4) for 1 hour (or until firm). **7.** Leave in tin for 5 minutes. **8.** Turn out on to serving dish. **9.** Serve hot or cold. **Serves 4 to 6.**

Turkey

ROASTING TIMES

For small turkeys weighing between 6 to 12 lb. allow 25 minutes per lb.
For medium-sized turkeys weighing between 12 to 16 lb. allow 20 minutes per lb.
For large turkeys weighing between 16 and 25 lb. allow 15 to 18 minutes per lb.

QUANTITIES

Allow $\frac{3}{4}$ lb. raw weight per person for small and medium-sized turkeys. Allow $\frac{1}{2}$ lb. raw weight per person for turkeys weighing 16 lb. and over.

11 ROAST TURKEY

1 turkey
Stuffings to taste (see Stuffings Section)
2 to 4 oz. melted English or Welsh butter, depending on size of bird
Salt and pepper

ACCOMPANIMENTS
Same as for Roast Chicken (No. 387) but include Cranberry Sauce (No. 145)

1. If turkey is frozen, thaw completely and remove giblet pack. **2.** Wash fresh or thawed bird well. Dry thoroughly with soft kitchen paper. **3.** Fill crop and body cavity with 2 different stuffings. **4.** Stand bird in roasting tin. Brush heavily with melted butter. Pour remaining butter into tin. **5.** Cover bird loosely with aluminium foil. Put into centre of hot oven (450°F. or Gas No. 8). **6.** Immediately reduce temperature to moderate (325°F. or Gas No. 3). Continue to roast for required length of time. **7.** Uncover half way through cooking time and baste well. **8.** Sprinkle with salt and pepper. Replace foil. Return to oven to continue roasting. **9.** Remove foil for last 30 minutes (45 minutes if turkey is medium sized or large) to brown bird. **10.** Leave 5 minutes before carving (meat will be less crumbly and easier to slice). **11.** Serve with accompaniments.

1 large chopped onion
1 small chopped green pepper
1½ oz. English or Welsh butter
1 dessertspoon olive or corn oil
1 level tablespoon flour
1½ level tablespoons paprika
1 level tablespoon tomato purée
1 level teaspoon caster sugar
½ pint stock or water
½ level teaspoon salt
¼ level teaspoon caraway seeds (optional)
¾ lb. cooked turkey
1 carton (5 oz.) natural yogurt

ACCOMPANIMENTS
Freshly-boiled potatoes or rice

1. Fry onion and pepper in hot butter and oil until pale gold and soft. **2.** Remove from heat. **3.** Stir in flour, paprika, purée and sugar. **4.** Gradually blend in stock or water, salt and caraway seeds. **5.** Cook, stirring, until sauce comes to boil and thickens. **6.** Cover. Simmer gently for 15 minutes. **7.** Cut turkey into bite-size pieces. Add to pan with yogurt. **8.** Heat through for further 5 minutes without boiling. **9.** Accompany with potatoes or rice. **Serves 4.**

1 recipe Savoury Fritter Batter (No. 665)
½ lb. cooked minced turkey
1 level teaspoon finely-grated lemon peel
1 level teaspoon curry powder
Deep fat or oil for frying
2 oz. grated Wensleydale cheese

1. Make Fritter Batter as directed but stir in turkey, lemon peel and curry powder before folding in egg whites. **2.** Drop dessertspoonsful of mixture into hot fat or oil. **3.** Fry until well puffed and golden. **4.** Remove from pan and drain on soft kitchen paper. **5.** Transfer to paper-lined serving dish and sprinkle with cheese. **6.** Serve hot. **Serves 4.**

½ lb. cold cooked turkey, cut into bite-size pieces
1 recipe Mushroom Coating Sauce (No. 113)
4 slices hot buttered toast
GARNISH
Watercress

1. Add turkey to Sauce. Heat through gently. **2.** Stand toast on 4 serving plates. **3.** Top with equal amounts of turkey mixture. **4.** Garnish with watercress. **5.** Serve straight away. **Serves 4.**

415 TURKEY & WALNUT FRITTERS

1. Follow recipe and method for Turkey Fritters (No. 414). **2.** Include 1 oz. very finely-chopped shelled walnut halves. **3.** Sprinkle with 2 oz. grated Leicester cheese instead of Wensleydale. **Serves 4.**

416 TURKEY FLAN

Nut Pastry made with ¼ lb. flour (No. 90)
1 recipe Mixed Cheese Dressing (No 576)
6 oz. cooked chopped turkey

GARNISH
1 large sliced tomato
8 black or green olives

1. Roll out Pastry. Use to line 6-in. flan ring resting on lightly-buttered baking tray. **2.** Prick well all over with fork. **3.** Line with aluminium foil to prevent pastry rising as it cooks. **4.** Bake towards top of hot oven (425°F. or Gas No. 7) for 15 minutes. **5.** Remove foil. Continue to bake for further 7 to 10 minutes (or until pastry is pale gold). **6.** Remove from oven. Lift off flan ring. Cool pastry case on wire rack. **7.** Combine Dressing with turkey. **8.** Spoon into cold pastry case. **9.** Garnish centre with slices of tomato and olives. **Serves 4 to 5.**

417 CHEESE & TURKEY FLAN

1 recipe Cheese Pastry (No. 93)
½ recipe Chantilly Mayonnaise (No. 581)
6 oz. cooked chopped turkey
1 level tablespoon finely-chopped
  watercress

GARNISH
4 level tablespoons finely-grated carrot
Watercress

1. Roll out Pastry. Use to line 6-in. flan ring resting on lightly-buttered baking tray. **2.** Prick well all over. **3.** Line with aluminium foil to prevent Pastry from rising as it cooks. **4.** Bake towards top of hot oven (425°F. or Gas No. 7) for 15 minutes. **5.** Remove foil. Continue to bake for further 7 to 10 minutes (or until Pastry is pale gold). **6.** Remove from oven. Lift off flan ring. Cool pastry case on wire rack. **7.** Combine Mayonnaise with turkey and chopped watercress. **8.** Spoon into cold pastry case. **9.** Garnish edges with small mounds of grated carrot. Arrange watercress in centre. **Serves 4 to 5.**

TURKEY À LA KING 418

1 medium-sized chopped green pepper
2 oz. English or Welsh butter
1 dessertspoon olive or corn oil
¼ lb. sliced mushrooms and stalks
1 oz. flour
¼ pint turkey stock or water
¼ pint milk
¾ lb. cooked turkey, cut into bite-size pieces
¼ pint fresh single cream
Yolks of 2 standard eggs
1 tablespoon dry sherry or lemon juice
Seasoning to taste

1. Fry green pepper gently in butter and oil for 5 minutes. **2.** Add mushrooms and stalks. Fry gently with pepper for further 5 minutes. **3.** Remove from pan and transfer to plate. **4.** Stir flour into remaining butter and oil in pan. Cook for 2 minutes without browning. **5.** Gradually blend in stock or water and milk. **6.** Cook, stirring, until sauce comes to boil and thickens. **7.** Lower heat. Add green pepper, mushrooms and turkey. **8.** Cover pan. Heat through gently for 10 minutes. **9.** Beat cream with egg yolks and sherry or lemon juice. **10.** Add to turkey mixture. **11.** Cook for further 2 to 3 minutes without boiling. **12.** Season to taste with salt and pepper. **Serves 4.**

TURKEY PILAF 419

1 large chopped onion
2 oz. English or Welsh butter
1 dessertspoon olive or corn oil
½ lb. long-grain rice
1 pint water
1 level teaspoon salt
½ lb. cooked turkey, cut into bite-size
  pieces
2 oz. seedless raisins
½ level teaspoon finely-grated orange peel
¼ lb. skinned and chopped tomatoes
1 oz. blanched, toasted and chopped
  almonds
1 level tablespoon finely-chopped parsley

1. Fry onion in hot butter and oil until pale gold. **2.** Add rice. Fry further minute, turning all the time. **3.** Pour in water and salt. Bring to boil. **4.** Cover pan. Lower heat. Simmer for 15 minutes. **5.** Add all remaining ingredients. **6.** Continue simmering for further 7 to 10 minutes (or until rice grains have absorbed all the liquid). **7.** Serve straight away. **Serves 4.**

Roast Turkey (No. 411)

¾ lb. cooked minced turkey
¼ lb. fresh white breadcrumbs
½ level teaspoon dry mustard
1 small minced onion
3 oz. finely-chopped mushrooms and stalks
½ level teaspoon celery salt
1 level teaspoon finely-grated lemon peel
2 level tablespoons chopped parsley
2 large eggs, beaten
¼ pint milk
1 teaspoon Worcester sauce
Seasoning to taste

1. Combine turkey, breadcrumbs, mustard, onion, mushrooms and stalks, celery salt, lemon peel and parsley. **2.** Stir in beaten eggs, milk and Worcester sauce. **3.** Season to taste with salt and pepper. **4.** Transfer to well-buttered 2-lb. loaf tin. **5.** Smooth top with knife. **6.** Bake in centre of moderate oven (350°F. or Gas No. 4) for 1 hour (or until firm). **7.** Leave in tin for 5 minutes. **8.** Turn out on to serving dish. **9.** Serve hot or cold. **Serves 4 to 6.**

1. Follow recipe and method for Turkey Loaf (No. 420). **2.** Add 1½ oz. blanched, toasted and finely-chopped almonds with parsley. **Serves 4 to 6.**

½ lb. cold cooked turkey, cut into bite-size
 pieces
1 recipe Lemon Coating Sauce (No. 111)
4 slices hot buttered toast

GARNISH
4 button mushrooms, grilled or fried

1. Add turkey to Sauce. Warm through gently. **2.** Stand toast on 4 individual plates. **3.** Top with equal amounts of turkey mixture. **4.** Garnish each with a mushroom. **5.** Serve straight away. **Serves 4.**

¼ lb. cold cooked turkey, cut into bite-size
 pieces
¼ lb. boiled bacon, chopped
1 recipe Mustard Coating Sauce (No. 118)
4 slices hot buttered toast

GARNISH
4 grilled tomato slices

1. Add turkey and bacon to Sauce. Heat through gently. **2.** Stand toast on 4 serving plates. **3.** Top with equal amounts of turkey mixture. **4.** Garnish each with slices of tomato. **5.** Serve straight away. **Serves 4.**

Game

1 recipe Hot Water Crust Pastry (No. 95)
½ lb. pork sausage meat
1 lb. raw game (pheasant, partridge,
  pigeon or mixture)
¾ lb. rump steak
¼ lb. lean bacon
2 pickled walnuts
1 small peeled onion
½ level teaspoon mixed herbs
½ pint stock
Beaten egg for brushing
2 level teaspoons gelatine

1. Roll out two-thirds of Pastry. Use to line raised pie mould or 7-in. loose-bottomed cake tin. **2.** Cover base neatly with sausage meat. **3.** Cut game into neat pieces. Discard bones, skin and gristle. **4.** Cut steak into dice. Chop bacon and pickled walnuts. Grate onion. **5.** Put game, steak, bacon, walnuts and onion into bowl. **6.** Add herbs and mix well. **7.** Put into pie mould or cake tin. Pour in ¼ pint stock. **8.** Roll out remaining Pastry into lid. Moisten edges with water and cover pie. **9.** Press edges of lining Pastry and lid well together to seal. Trim away any surplus. **10.** Brush top with egg. **11.** Decorate with pastry leaves (cut from trimmings). Brush with more egg. **12.** Make hole in top to allow steam to escape. Stand on baking tray. **13.** Transfer to centre of fairly hot oven (400°F. or Gas No. 6). Bake for 30 minutes. **14.** Reduce temperature to moderate (350°F. or Gas No. 4). Bake further 1¾ to 2 hours. Cover top with greaseproof paper during last ½ hour to prevent the pastry from browning too much. **15.** Remove pie from oven. **16.** Bring remaining stock to boil. Shower in gelatine and stir until dissolved. **17.** Pour into pie through hole in top. **18.** Leave Pie in cool for 12 hours. Remove cake tin or mould just before serving. **Serves 6 to 8.**

Broadly speaking, game is in season during the autumn and winter months. There is no close season for rabbit, hare or pigeon, but the sale of hare is prohibited between March and July. Neither hare nor rabbit should be eaten when in kindle.

Game is generally hung to improve the flavour and make the flesh more tender. Whether or not to hang game at all is very much a matter of personal taste; there are no hard-and-fast rules.

Hanging time is affected by the weather and length of time the game has been dead. It is always wise to ask the advice of the poulterer or butcher when the game is bought.

*The following table is a guide to the seasons and **approximate** hanging times—*

GAME	SEASON	HANGING TIME
PARTRIDGE	Sep. 1 – Feb. 1	Up to 7 or 8 days
PHEASANT	Oct. 1 – Feb. 1	Up to 7 or 8 days
GROUSE	Aug. 12 – Dec. 10	4 – 5 days
PIGEON	No Close Season	2 – 3 days
WOODCOCK	Oct. 1 – Jan. 31	4 – 5 days
SNIPE	Aug. 12 – Jan. 31	5 – 8 days
HARE	No Close Season, but sale prohibited between March and July	7 – 8 days
RABBIT	No Close Season	4 – 5 days

WATER GAME	SEASON	HANGING TIME
MALLARD TEAL WIDGEON	Sep. 1 – Feb. 20 (but inland season ends Jan. 21)	2 – 3 days

2 young wild ducks
2 oz. English or Welsh butter, melted
Pepper and salt
Maître d'Hôtel Butter (No. 190)

GARNISH
Watercress

1. Halve ducks. **2.** Stand in grill pan, skin sides down. **3.** Brush thickly with some of the butter. **4.** Sprinkle with salt and pepper. **5.** Grill for 5 minutes. Turn over. **6.** Brush with more butter. **7.** Sprinkle with salt and pepper. **8.** Grill for total of 20 to 25 minutes, turning frequently and brushing with rest of melted butter. **9.** Transfer to a warm platter. **10.** Top each portion with piece of Maître d'Hôtel Butter. **11.** Garnish with watercress. **Serves 4.**

426 PIGEONS IN CREAM SAUCE

4 pigeons, plucked and drawn
Salt and pepper to taste
¼ lb. English or Welsh butter
¼ pint fresh double cream
1 tablespoon redcurrant jelly

GARNISH & ACCOMPANIMENT
Watercress
Boiled potatoes

1. Wipe insides of pigeons with clean damp cloth. Sprinkle outside with salt and pepper. **2.** Melt butter in large flameproof casserole. **3.** Add pigeons and fry gently until brown, turning frequently. **4.** Cover with lid and leave over very low heat 45 minutes, turning birds once or twice. **5.** Transfer pigeons to warm serving dish and keep hot. **6.** Add cream and redcurrant jelly to remaining butter in casserole and heat through gently, without boiling, until jelly has melted. **7.** Season to taste and pour over the pigeons. **8.** Garnish with watercress and serve with potatoes. **Serves at least 4.**

427 ROAST PIGEONS

4 pigeons, plucked and drawn
Salt and pepper
¼ lb. English or Welsh butter
4 slices white bread
Extra English or Welsh butter

GARNISH & ACCOMPANIMENTS
Watercress
Brown Sauce (No. 130)
Very thin chips
Green Salad (see Salad Section)

1. Wipe insides of pigeons with clean damp cloth. Sprinkle outsides with salt and pepper. **2.** Place ½-oz. piece of butter inside each bird. Melt remaining butter. **3.** Stand birds in roasting tin and cover each with melted butter. **4.** Bake just above centre of fairly hot oven (400°F. or Gas No. 6) for 20 to 30 minutes, basting frequently with butter. **5.** About 5 minutes before pigeons are ready, fry bread in butter until crisp on both sides. **6.** Drain on soft kitchen paper. Transfer to warm serving plate. **7.** Serve Roast Pigeons on each slice. Garnish with watercress. **8.** Accompany with Brown Sauce, chips and green salad. **Serves at least 4.**

STEWED PIGEONS 428

4 pigeons, plucked and drawn
2 oz. English or Welsh butter
2 teaspoons olive or corn oil
½ pint Brown Sauce (No. 130)
1 glass red wine
4 slices white bread
Extra English or Welsh butter

ACCOMPANIMENTS
Cooked peas
Cooked carrots
Boiled potatoes

1. Cut pigeons in half. **2.** Fry gently in butter and oil until golden brown. **3.** Add Brown Sauce and wine to pan. **4.** Very slowly bring to boil. Cover pan and lower heat. **5.** Simmer pigeons gently for 35 to 45 minutes (or until tender). **6.** About 5 minutes before pigeons are ready, fry bread in butter until crisp on both sides. **7.** Drain on soft kitchen paper. Transfer to large warm serving platter. **8.** Stand 2 pigeon halves on each slice. Coat with sauce from pan. **9.** Place mounds of peas, carrots and potatoes round edge of dish. **Serves at least 4.**

MILKY RABBIT CASSEROLE 429

4 rabbit joints
1 medium-sized onion
1 rasher lean bacon
2 medium-sized carrots
1 pint milk
½ teaspoon salt
Shake of pepper
¼ level teaspoon nutmeg
½ oz. cornflour
2 extra tablespoons cold milk
½ oz. English or Welsh butter

GARNISH
1 level tablespoon chopped parsley

1. Wash rabbit well. Wipe dry and arrange in 2-pint heatproof dish. **2.** Chop onion and bacon. Slice carrot. Add to dish. **3.** Pour milk over rabbit. Sprinkle with salt, pepper and nutmeg. **4.** Cover with lid or aluminium foil. Cook in centre of moderate oven (350°F. or Gas No. 4) for 1¾ to 2 hours (or until rabbit is tender). **5.** Transfer to warm serving dish and keep hot. **6.** Mix cornflour to smooth paste with 2 tablespoons cold milk. Combine with rabbit liquor left in dish. **7.** Pour into clean saucepan. Cook, stirring, until sauce comes to boil and thickens. **8.** Add butter and simmer 3 minutes. **9.** Pour over rabbit and sprinkle with parsley. **Serves 4.**

430 ROAST RABBIT

1 whole rabbit (young for preference),
  skinned and cleaned
4 rashers streaky bacon
3 oz. English or Welsh butter, melted
ACCOMPANIMENTS
Gravy (No. 147)
Cranberry Sauce (No. 145)
Vegetables to taste

1. Weigh rabbit and allow 15 minutes per lb.
roasting time and 15 minutes over. **2.** Stand in
roasting tin. Top with bacon and coat with melted
butter. **3.** Put into centre of hot oven (425°F. or
Gas No. 7) and roast for 15 minutes. **4.** Reduce
temperature to moderate (350°F. or Gas No. 4).
Continue to roast for required amount of time,
basting frequently with butter. **5.** Accompany
with Gravy, Cranberry Sauce and vegetables.
Serves 4.

431 FRICASSÉE OF RABBIT

1 rabbit (young for preference), jointed
½ pint stock or water
½ pint milk
¼ lb. streaky bacon, chopped
4 cloves
1 large onion
1 blade mace
¼ level teaspoon mixed herbs
2 oz. chopped mushrooms
½ level teaspoon salt
1 oz. English or Welsh butter
1 oz. flour
GARNISH
2 slices toast
1 level tablespoon chopped parsley
2 lemon wedges

1. Put rabbit joints into saucepan. **2.** Pour in
stock (or water) and milk. **3.** Add bacon. **4.** Press
cloves into onion. Add to saucepan with mace,
herbs, mushrooms and salt. **5.** Bring to boil and
remove scum. **6.** Lower heat and cover pan.
Simmer very gently for 1½ to 1¾ hours (or until
rabbit is tender). **7.** Strain liquor and reserve.
Transfer rabbit to warm platter and keep hot.
8. Melt butter in clean saucepan. Add flour and
cook 2 minutes without browning. **9.** Gradually
blend in rabbit liquor. **10.** Cook, stirring until
sauce comes to boil and thickens. **11.** Simmer
2 minutes and pour over rabbit. **12.** Cut toast
into 8 triangles and arrange round edge of dish.
13. Sprinkle centre with parsley. Garnish with
lemon. **Serves 4.**

JUGGED HARE 43

1 hare
2 oz. English or Welsh butter
2 medium-sized onions
2 medium-sized carrots
1 medium-sized celery stalk
1½ pints water
1 level teaspoon salt
1 bay leaf
1 blade mace ⎫ bouquet garni
6 peppercorns ⎬ tied in muslin bag
2 cloves ⎭
1 oz. flour
2 extra tablespoons water
1 wine glass port
1 tablespoon redcurrant jelly
GARNISH
¼ lb. fresh white breadcrumbs
2 oz. finely-shredded suet
1 level teaspoon mixed herbs
½ level teaspoon finely-grated lemon peel
½ level teaspoon salt
Milk to bind
2 oz. English or Welsh butter
ACCOMPANIMENT
Extra redcurrant jelly

1. Joint hare (and reserve blood if liked). **2.** Melt
butter in large flameproof casserole. Add hare
and fry until brown. Remove to plate. **3.** Slice
vegetables. Add to pan and fry gently for 6 to
7 minutes. **4.** Replace hare. **5.** Add water and
salt and bouquet garni. **6.** Cover casserole. Cook
in centre of moderate oven (350°F. or Gas No. 4)
for 2 to 3 hours (or until hare is tender).
7. Transfer joints of hare to warm serving dish
and keep hot. **8.** Strain liquor from casserole.
Pour into clean pan. **9.** Add flour, mixed to
smooth paste with water, port and redcurrant
jelly. **10.** Cook, stirring, until sauce comes to boil
and thickens. Simmer 2 minutes. **11.** Remove
from heat (and stir in reserved blood, if wanted).
12. To make Forcemeat Ball garnish, combine
breadcrumbs with suet, herbs, lemon peel and
salt and bind with milk. **13.** Shape into 12 small
balls. Fry gently in butter until crisp and golden.
14. Pour sauce over hare. Arrange Forcemeat
Balls on top. **15.** Accompany with extra
redcurrant jelly. **Serves 4.**

Right: A mixed bag of game – mallard (duc
and drake), hare, pheasant and pigeon

98

433 ROAST PHEASANT

1 pheasant (young for preference)
plucked, drawn and trussed
2 oz. rump steak
4 rashers streaky bacon
3 oz. English or Welsh butter, melted
Plain flour

GARNISH & ACCOMPANIMENTS
Watercress
2 or 3 tail feathers (optional)
2 oz. fresh breadcrumbs fried in 2 oz.
English or Welsh butter
Bread Sauce (No. 139)
Thin Gravy (No. 147)
Thin chips
Green Salad (see Salad Section)

1. Stand pheasant in roasting tin. Place steak inside bird (this helps to keep it moist during cooking). **2.** Cover pheasant breast with bacon rashers. **3.** Coat with melted butter. **4.** Roast just above centre of fairly hot oven (400°F. or Gas No. 6) for 30 minutes, basting frequently. **5.** Remove from oven, lift off bacon and 'froth' the breast. (To do this, baste breast well with butter, dredge with flour and baste again.) **6.** Return to oven for further 15 to 20 minutes (or until golden brown and frothy). **7.** Transfer to warm serving platter. Remove trussing string. Garnish with watercress in the vent (and the feathers if used). **8.** Accompany with small dish of fried breadcrumbs (for sprinkling over each portion), Bread Sauce, Gravy, chips and Salad. **Serves 4.**

434 ROAST PARTRIDGE

1. Follow recipe and method for Roast Pheasant (No. 433). **2.** Use 2 partridges. **3.** Put 1 oz. English or Welsh butter, instead of steak, inside each bird. **4.** Garnish with watercress but not feathers. The accompaniments remain the same as for Pheasant. **Serves 4.**

435 ROAST GROUSE

1. Follow recipe and method for Roast Pheasant (No. 433). **2.** Use 2 plucked, drawn and trussed grouse instead of pheasant. **3.** Put 1 oz. English or Welsh butter, instead of steak, inside each bird and roast 30 to 35 minutes. **4.** Garnish with watercress but no feathers. The accompaniments remain the same as for Pheasant but Cranberry Sauce (No. 145) should be included also. **Serves 4.**

SALMI OF PHEASANT 43

1 pheasant (young for preference)
plucked, drawn and trussed
¾ pint Brown Sauce (No. 130)
3 to 4 tablespoons port
1 dessertspoon redcurrant jelly
6 oz. button mushrooms
2 slices bread
English or Welsh butter

1. Prepare the pheasant for roasting (see Roast Pheasant, No. 433). **2.** Roast for 20 minutes. **3.** Cut into neat joints and remove skin. **4.** Place in fairly large flameproof casserole. **5.** Add Brown Sauce, port and redcurrant jelly. **6.** Cover and simmer very gently for 30 minutes. **7.** Add mushrooms and continue to simmer for further 10 to 15 minutes (or until pheasant is tender). **8.** Meanwhile, cut each slice of bread into 4 triangles. Fry gently in butter until crisp and golden. **9.** Uncover casserole and stand triangles of fried bread round edge of dish. **Serves 4.**

SALMI OF PARTRIDGE 43

Follow recipe and method for Salmi of Pheasant (No. 436) but use 2 partridges instead. **Serves 4.**

SALMI OF GROUSE 43

1. Follow recipe and method for Salmi of Pheasant (No. 436) but use 2 grouse instead. **2.** Roast birds 15 minutes only. **Serves 4.**

CURRIED GAME 43

¾ lb. cooked game
1 recipe Curry Sauce (No. 141)

ACCOMPANIMENT
¾ lb. freshly-boiled long grain rice
(about 6 oz. raw)

GARNISH
4 lemon wedges

1. Cut game into bite-sized pieces. Add to Curry Sauce. **2.** Heat through gently. **3.** Arrange rice in ring on warm serving dish. Fill centre with hot Curry Sauce and game. **4.** Garnish with lemon. **Serves 4.**

Vegetables

440 CREAMED POTATOES

1½ lb. potatoes, peeled and washed
1½ oz. English or Welsh butter
3 tablespoons milk

GARNISH
About 1 level tablespoon finely-chopped
parsley (optional)

1. Cook potatoes in boiling salted water until tender. Drain. **2.** Mash finely with fork or potato masher (or rub through sieve). **3.** Return to saucepan. **4.** Add butter and milk. **5.** Beat over low heat until light and creamy. **6.** Pile into warm dish. **7.** Sprinkle with parsley if used. **Serves 4.**

441 SNOW (OR MOUSSELINE) POTATOES

1 lb. potatoes, peeled and washed
1 oz. English or Welsh butter
¼ pint hot milk

1. Cook potatoes in boiling salted water until tender. Drain. **2.** Mash very finely with fork or potato masher (or rub through fine sieve). **3.** Return to saucepan. Stand over low heat. **4.** Add butter. **5.** Gradually beat in hot milk. **6.** Continue beating until potatoes are very light (the consistency of softly-whipped cream). **7.** Serve straight away. **Serves 4.**

442 DUCHESSE POTATOES

1 lb. potatoes, peeled and washed
1 oz. English or Welsh butter
Yolks of 2 small eggs
1 dessertspoon hot milk
A little egg white

1. Cook potatoes in boiling salted water until tender. Drain. **2.** Mash with fork. **3.** Rub through fine sieve and return to saucepan. **4.** Stand over low heat. **5.** Add butter, egg yolks and milk. **6.** Beat until smooth. **7.** Transfer to forcing bag fitted with large star-shaped icing pipe. **8.** Pipe fairly small mounds or whirls on to buttered baking tray. **9.** Leave until cold. **10.** Brush with egg white. **11.** Bake just above centre of hot oven (425°F. or Gas No. 7) for 15 minutes (or until golden. **12.** Serve hot. **Serves 4.**

443 SAUTÉ POTATOES

1½ lb. potatoes, peeled and washed
2 oz. English or Welsh butter
2 tablespoons olive or corn oil
Salt and pepper

GARNISH
1 level tablespoon finely-chopped parsley

1. Cook potatoes in boiling salted water for 5 to 7 minutes. **2.** Drain and cool. **3.** Cut into ¼-in. thick slices. **4.** Heat butter and oil in large heavy frying pan. Add potato slices. **5.** Fry until golden-brown on both sides, turning occasionally. **6.** Transfer to warm serving dish. **7.** Sprinkle with salt, pepper and parsley. **Serves 4.**

444 POTATOES LYONNAISE

1. Follow recipe and method for Sauté Potatoes (No. 443). **2.** When Potatoes in pan are golden brown, add ½ lb. sliced onions, fried in 2 oz. butter until golden. Mix well. **3.** Transfer to warm serving dish. **4.** Sprinkle with parsley. **Serves 4.**

445 CASSEROLED POTATOES

1½ lb. potatoes, peeled and washed
Salt and pepper
2 oz. English or Welsh butter
½ pint milk

1. Cut potatoes into thin slices. **2.** Dry well in clean tea towel. **3.** Fill 2-pint buttered pie dish with layers of potato slices, sprinkling salt and pepper between layers. **4.** Melt 1½ oz. butter and combine with milk. **5.** Pour into pie dish. **6.** Cover top with rest of butter, cut into thin flakes. **7.** Put into centre of fairly hot oven (375°F. or Gas No. 5). **8.** Bake, uncovered, for 1 hour (or until potatoes are tender). **Serves 4.**

446 CASSEROLED POTATOES WITH PARSLEY

1. Follow recipe and method for Casseroled Potatoes (No 445). **2.** Sprinkle 2 level tablespoons finely-chopped parsley between layers with salt and pepper. **Serves 4.**

VEGETABLES

447 CASSEROLED POTATOES WITH CHEESE

1. Follow recipe and method for Casseroled Potatoes (No. 445). **2.** Sprinkle 2 to 3 oz. finely-grated English Cheddar cheese or crumbled Lancashire cheese between layers with salt and pepper. **Serves 4.**

448 STEWED POTATOES

1½ lb. potatoes, peeled and washed
½ pint Basic White Pouring Sauce (No. 105)
GARNISH
1 level tablespoon snipped chives or green part of leek, chopped

1. Cut potatoes into ¼-in. thick slices. **2.** Put into saucepan with Sauce. **3.** Cover pan. Simmer gently until potatoes are tender (15 to 25 minutes, depending on type of potato). **4.** Transfer to warm serving dish. **5.** Sprinkle with chives or chopped leek. **Serves 4.**

449 STEWED POTATOES WITH CHEESE

1. Follow recipe and method for Stewed Potatoes (No. 448). **2.** Omit chives or leek. **3.** After turning into warm serving dish, sprinkle top with 2 oz. crumbled Lancashire cheese and brown under hot grill. **Serves 4.**

450 POTATOES ANNA

1½ lb. potatoes, washed and peeled
3 oz. English or Welsh butter, melted
Salt and pepper

1. Slice potatoes very thinly. **2.** Dry well in clean tea towel. **3.** Brush 1½ to 2-pint pie dish with butter. Fill with layers of potato slices arranged in overlapping circles. **4.** Brush each layer thickly with butter. Sprinkle with salt and pepper. **5.** Brush top layer with butter. **6.** Cover dish with buttered aluminium foil. **7.** Bake in centre of fairly hot oven (375°F. or Gas No. 5) for 1¼ hours. **8.** Turn out on to warm heatproof plate (potatoes should stay moulded in pie-dish shape). **9.** Return to oven for further 20 to 30 minutes (or until outside is golden brown). **Serves 4.**

JACKET POTATOES WITH BUTTER 45

4 large potatoes
Salad oil
2 to 3 oz. English or Welsh butter

1. Wash, scrub and dry potatoes. **2.** Prick well all over with fork or make small slits in each with sharp knife (to prevent potatoes from bursting in oven). **3.** Brush with salad oil. Stand on baking tray. **4.** Bake just above centre of fairly hot oven (375°F. or Gas No. 5) for 1½ to 2 hours (or until potatoes feel tender when gently pressed). **5.** Remove from oven. Cut a large cross on top of each. **6.** Holding potato in clean tea towel, squeeze base firmly to enlarge cut. **7.** Put a large piece of butter on to each. **8.** Serve straight away. **Serves 4.**

JACKET POTATOES WITH CREAM & CHIVES 45

1. Follow recipe and method for Jacket Potatoes with Butter (No. 451). **2.** Instead of butter, top each potato with 1 or 2 dessertspoons fresh double cream and sprinkle thickly with snipped chives. **Serves 4.**

STUFFED BAKED POTATOES 45

4 large potatoes
Salad oil
1 oz. English or Welsh butter
4 tablespoons milk
1 level teaspoon made mustard
¼ lb. grated English Cheddar cheese or crumbled Lancashire cheese
Salt and pepper to taste

1. Prepare potatoes and bake exactly as for Jacket Potatoes with Butter (No. 451). **2.** When tender, remove from oven and cut each in half lengthwise. **3.** Spoon insides into bowl. Mash finely with butter, milk and mustard. **4.** Add cheese and mix well. Season to taste with salt and pepper. **5.** Return mixture to potato cases. **6.** Re-heat towards top of hot oven (425°F. or Gas No. 7) for 10 to 15 minutes. **Serves 4.**

STUFFED POTATOES WITH BACON 45

1. Follow recipe and method for Stuffed Baked Potatoes (No. 453). **2.** Use 6 oz. finely-chopped fried bacon instead of cheese. **Serves 4.**

102

Jacket Potatoes With Cream & Chives (No. 452)

455 STUFFED POTATOES WITH HAM & CHEESE

1. Follow recipe and method for Stuffed Baked Potatoes (No. 453). **2.** Use 3 oz. grated Derby cheese instead of English Cheddar cheese or Lancashire cheese. **3.** Add 2 oz. finely-chopped ham to potato mixture. **Serves 4.**

456 STUFFED POTATOES WITH CHEESE & PARSLEY

1. Follow recipe and method for Stuffed Baked Potatoes (No. 453). **2.** Use ¼ lb. grated Double Gloucester cheese instead of English Cheddar cheese or Lancashire cheese. **3.** Add 1 or 2 level tablespoons finely-chopped parsley to potato mixture. **Serves 4.**

457 STUFFED POTATOES WITH SMOKED HADDOCK

1. Follow recipe and method for Stuffed Baked Potatoes (No. 453). **2.** Use ¼ lb. cooked and flaked smoked haddock instead of cheese. **Serves 4.**

BUTTERED ROAST POTATOES 458

1 to 1½ lb. potatoes, peeled and washed
2 oz. English or Welsh butter
1 dessertspoon olive or corn oil

1. Cut potatoes into quarters or leave whole if new. **2.** Cook in boiling salted water for 5 to 7 minutes. Drain. **3.** Heat butter and oil in roasting tin. **4.** Add potatoes and turn in tin until well coated with butter and oil. **5.** Roast towards top of fairly hot oven (400°F. or Gas No. 6) for ¾ hour (or until crisp and golden), basting at least twice. **Serves 4.**

BUTTERED & MINTED NEW POTATOES 459

1½ lb. new potatoes, peeled and washed
1½ oz. English or Welsh butter
3 fresh mint leaves

GARNISH
1 level tablespoon finely-chopped parsley (optional)

1. Cook potatoes in boiling salted water until tender. Drain. **2.** Stand saucepan of potatoes over low heat. **3.** Add butter and mint. **4.** Cover with lid. **5.** Leave over low heat for 2 to 3 minutes, shaking pan frequently. **6.** Remove mint. **7.** Transfer potatoes to warm serving dish. **8.** Sprinkle with parsley if used. **Serves 4.**

460 PEASE PUDDING

1 lb. split peas
$\frac{1}{2}$ level teaspoon salt
$\frac{1}{2}$ oz. English or Welsh butter, melted
Yolk of 1 standard egg
Seasoning to taste

1. Soak peas overnight. Drain. **2.** Put into saucepan. Cover with water. **3.** Add salt and bring slowly to boil. **4.** Reduce heat and cover pan. **5.** Simmer gently for $1\frac{3}{4}$ to 2 hours, stirring occasionally. **6.** Add a little extra boiling water if peas begin to get dry. **7.** Rub through sieve. **8.** Add butter and egg yolk. Mix well. **9.** Season to taste with pepper and salt if needed. **10.** Transfer to 1-pint buttered heatproof dish. **11.** Re-heat in centre of moderate oven (350°F. or Gas No. 4) for 30 minutes. **Serves 4 to 6.**

461 BUTTERED PEAS

$\frac{3}{4}$ to 1 lb. shelled peas (or 1 large packet frozen peas)
$\frac{1}{2}$ level teaspoon salt
2 fresh mint leaves
$\frac{1}{2}$ level teaspoon caster sugar
$\frac{1}{2}$ oz English or Welsh butter

1. Put peas into saucepan. **2.** Cover with boiling water. **3.** Add salt and mint. **4.** Cover pan. Simmer for 10 to 15 minutes (or until tender). **5.** Drain and add sugar and butter. **6.** Cover pan. **7.** Toss peas gently. **8.** Remove mint and serve. **Serves 4.**

462 SWISS PEAS WITH RICE

$\frac{3}{4}$ lb. shelled peas (or 1 large packet frozen peas)
$\frac{1}{2}$ level teaspoon salt
6 oz. cooked rice (about 3 oz. raw)
1 small chopped onion
1 small chopped garlic clove (optional)
2 oz. English or Welsh butter
2 oz. sliced stuffed olives
2 level tablespoons finely-chopped parsley

1. Put peas into saucepan. **2.** Cover with boiling water. **3.** Add salt. **4.** Cover pan and simmer for 10 to 15 minutes (or until peas are tender). **5.** Drain and combine with rice. **6.** Fry onion and garlic, if used, in butter until pale gold. **7.** Add rice, peas, olives and parsley. Mix well. **8.** Heat through, gently, for about 5 to 7 minutes. Stir frequently. **9.** Transfer to warm serving dish. **Serves 4.**

FRENCH-STYLE PEAS 46

$\frac{3}{4}$ to 1 lb. shelled peas (or 1 large packet frozen peas)
6 large lettuce leaves, shredded
2 oz. English or Welsh butter
2 level teaspoons finely-grated onion
$\frac{1}{4}$ level teaspoon salt
$\frac{1}{2}$ level teaspoon caster sugar
5 tablespoons water

1. Put all ingredients into saucepan. **2.** Slowly bring to boil. **3.** Lower heat and cover pan. **4.** Simmer very gently for 15 to 20 minutes (or until peas are tender). **5.** Add a little extra water if peas become dry. **Serves 4.**

BUTTERED CORN 46
ON THE COB

4 corn on the cob
2 to 3 oz. English or Welsh butter
Salt and pepper

1. Remove husks and silk from corn. **2.** Put into large frying pan, half full of gently boiling water. **3.** Boil for 4 to 5 minutes only, turning corn over once if water is insufficiently deep to cover them. **4.** Drain and serve with butter, allowing at least $\frac{1}{2}$ oz. per person. **5.** Pass salt and pepper separately. **Serves 4.**

CORN FRITTERS 46

$\frac{1}{4}$ lb. self-raising flour
Pinch of nutmeg
$\frac{1}{2}$ level teaspoon salt
$\frac{1}{2}$ level teaspoon dry mustard
2 standard eggs, beaten
2 tablespoons milk
$\frac{1}{2}$ lb. cooked sweetcorn, frozen or canned
Deep fat or oil for frying

1. Sift together flour, nutmeg, salt and mustard. **2.** Whisk egg and milk well together. **3.** Gradually beat into dry ingredients. **4.** When smooth and creamy, stir in corn. **5.** Drop about 16 dessertspoons of mixture into hot fat or oil. **6.** Fry for about 5 minutes (or until well puffed and golden). **7.** Drain on soft kitchen paper. **Serves 4.**

466 CORN WITH ALMONDS

2 oz. blanched almonds
3 oz. English or Welsh butter
1 can (¾ lb.) sweetcorn

1. Cut almonds into strips. **2.** Fry slowly in butter until pale gold. **3.** Add drained corn. Heat through gently. **4.** Transfer to warm serving dish. **Serves 4.**

467 POACHED ASPARAGUS

2 dozen asparagus spears
Hollandaise Sauce (No. 131) or Brown Butter Sauce (No. 148)

1. Wash asparagus well and trim. **2.** Put into large fairly shallow saucepan or frying pan. **3.** Half-fill with unsalted water. **4.** Bring slowly to boil. **5.** Lower heat. **6.** Cover pan. Simmer for 12 to 15 minutes (or until tender). **7.** Drain and serve with Sauce. **Serves 4.**

468 CRISP BOILED CABBAGE

1½ to 2 lb. young cabbage
2 oz. English or Welsh butter

1. Wash cabbage and shred finely, discarding hard stalks. **2.** Plunge into 2 or 3 in. of rapidly boiling salted water (in saucepan). **3.** Cover pan and lower heat. **4.** Boil 6 to 8 minutes. **5.** Tip into colander and drain well. **6.** Return to pan and add butter. **7.** Cover. Stand over low heat for further 5 minutes, shaking pan frequently. **8.** Serve straight away. **Serves 4.**

469 SAVOURY CABBAGE

1½ lb. young cabbage
2 oz. English or Welsh butter
1 medium-sized grated onion
2 rashers chopped streaky bacon
Pinch of grated nutmeg

1. Wash cabbage and shred finely, discarding hard stalks. **2.** Heat butter in large saucepan. **3.** Add all remaining ingredients. **4.** Cover pan. **5.** Cook very gently for 20 to 30 minutes (or until cabbage is just tender), shaking pan frequently. **Serves 4.**

SWEET-SOUR WHITE CABBAGE 470

1 head white cabbage (1½ to 2 lb.)
2 oz. English or Welsh butter
2 tablespoons water
2 tablespoons vinegar
Pinch of mixed spice
1 level dessertspoon soft brown sugar
¼ level teaspoon salt

1. Wash cabbage. Shred finely. **2.** Put into saucepan with all remaining ingredients. **3.** Cover. Cook over low heat for 15 to 20 minutes (or until cabbage is just tender but still slightly crisp). **4.** Shake pan frequently while cabbage is cooking. **5.** Uncover and cook fairly briskly until no liquid remains (about 5 minutes). **Serves 4.**

BAKED CABBAGE WITH CREAM 471

1 lb. cabbage
¼ pint fresh single cream
1 level teaspoon caster sugar
½ level teaspoon salt
½ level teaspoon paprika
4 level tablespoons toasted breadcrumbs
3 oz. grated English Cheddar cheese

1. Wash cabbage and shred finely, discarding hard stalks. **2.** Transfer to large buttered heatproof dish. **3.** Cover with cream mixed with sugar, salt and paprika. **4.** Sprinkle breadcrumbs over top. Cover dish. **5.** Bake in centre of moderate oven (325°F. or Gas No. 3) for 45 minutes. **6.** Remove from oven and cover with cheese. **7.** Brown under hot grill. **Serves 4.**

FRIED AUBERGINE 472

1 medium-sized aubergine
Salt
Milk
Flour
¼ lb. English or Welsh butter
1 tablespoon olive or corn oil

1. Cut aubergine into ¼-in. thick slices. **2.** Sprinkle with salt and cover. **3.** Leave ½ an hour. **4.** Drain thoroughly. Wipe each slice dry with kitchen paper. **5.** Dip in milk. Toss in flour. **6.** Fry gently in hot butter and oil until crisp, golden brown and tender (5 to 7 minutes). Drain on soft kitchen paper. **Serves 4.**

473 STUFFED AUBERGINE

1 medium-sized aubergine
1 small onion
2 rashers streaky bacon
½ small green pepper
½ lb. skinned tomatoes
1 oz. English or Welsh butter
2 oz. sliced mushrooms
1½ to 2 oz. fresh white breadcrumbs
Seasoning to taste
3 oz. crumbled Lancashire cheese

1. Halve aubergine lengthwise. **2.** Scoop out pulp, leaving ¼-in. thick shells. **3.** Chop pulp and put into saucepan. **4.** Finely chop onion, bacon, green pepper and tomatoes. **5.** Add to aubergine pulp with butter. **6.** Simmer gently until pulp is tender. **7.** Remove from heat. Stir in mushrooms and sufficient breadcrumbs to thicken the mixture. **8.** Season to taste with salt and pepper. **9.** Pile back into aubergine shells. **10.** Sprinkle with cheese. **11.** Re-heat towards top of fairly hot oven (400°F. or Gas No. 6) for 15 to 20 minutes. **Serves 4.**

474 BAKED BUTTERED CARROTS

1 medium-sized onion
2 oz. English or Welsh butter
1 lb. carrots, coarsely grated
½ level teaspoon salt
5 tablespoons water

1. Chop onion finely. Fry gently in butter until pale gold. **2.** Add grated carrots and salt. Mix well. **3.** Transfer to 1-pint heatproof dish. **4.** Add water. **5.** Cover dish and bake in centre of moderate oven (350°F. or Gas No. 4) for 35 to 45 minutes (or until carrots are tender). **Serves 4.**

475 VICHY CARROTS

1 lb. carrots
2 oz. English or Welsh butter
1 level teaspoon caster sugar
¼ level teaspoon salt
1 teaspoon lemon juice

GARNISH
1 level tablespoon finely-chopped parsley

1. Slice carrots thinly. **2.** Put into saucepan with water to cover, butter, sugar, salt and lemon juice. **3.** Cover. Simmer gently for 15 to 20 minutes (or until tender). **4.** Turn into warm serving dish. **5.** Sprinkle with parsley. **Serves 4.**

CARROTS IN PARSLEY SAUCE 47

1 lb. new carrots
½ pint Parsley Coating Sauce (No. 107)

1. Cook whole carrots in boiling salted water until tender. Drain. **2.** Transfer to warm serving dish. **3.** Coat with hot Sauce. **Serves 4.**

HARICOT BEANS WITH 47 TOMATOES

¾ lb. haricot beans, soaked overnight
1 level teaspoon salt
½ lb. skinned tomatoes
¼ lb. lean bacon
1 medium-sized onion
3 oz. crumbled Lancashire cheese

1. Drain beans. **2.** Transfer to saucepan and cover with water. **3.** Add salt. **4.** Bring slowly to boil. Lower heat and cover pan. **5.** Simmer gently until tender. **6.** Meanwhile chop tomatoes, bacon and onion. Combine with drained cooked beans. **7.** Transfer to 2-pint heatproof dish. **8.** Sprinkle with cheese. **9.** Bake towards top of fairly hot oven (375°F. or Gas No. 5) for 30 minutes. **Serves 4.**

CREAMED GREEN BEANS 47

1 lb. French or runner beans
2 oz. sliced mushrooms and stalks
1 oz. English or Welsh butter
¼ pint fresh double cream

1. Top and tail beans. Remove stringy sides if necessary. **2.** Slice runner beans diagonally into thin strips. **3.** Cook in boiling salted water for 15 to 20 minutes (or until tender). **4.** Meanwhile fry mushrooms in butter and keep warm. **5.** Drain beans in colander. **6.** Return to pan. **7.** Add mushrooms and pan juices with fresh cream. **8.** Mix well. Re-heat gently. **Serves 4.**

CREAMED BROAD BEANS 47

1. Follow recipe and method for Creamed Green Beans (No. 478). **2.** Use 1 lb. shelled broad beans instead of French or runner beans. **3.** If preferred, serve cooked, drained beans with ½ pint Basic White Coating Sauce (No. 106). **Serves 4.**

80 CHINESE-STYLE GREEN BEANS

1 lb. runner beans
4 rashers lean bacon
1 small grated onion
½ chopped garlic clove
1½ oz. English or Welsh butter
2 tablespoons soy sauce

1. Top and tail beans. Remove stringy sides. **2.** Slice beans diagonally into thin strips. **3.** Cook in boiling salted water for 15 to 20 minutes (or until tender). **4.** Meanwhile chop bacon. Fry with onion and garlic in butter until pale gold. **5.** Drain beans and return to pan. **6.** Add bacon, onion and garlic and any remaining butter from pan. **7.** Pour in soy sauce. **8.** Heat through gently, shaking pan frequently. **Serves 4.**

81 ARTICHOKES MORNAY

1 lb. Jerusalem artichokes
½ level teaspoon salt
1 dessertspoon lemon juice
1 recipe Mornay Sauce (No. 123)
2 oz. grated English Cheddar cheese

1. Put peeled artichokes into saucepan. **2.** Cover with cold water. **3.** Add salt and lemon juice. **4.** Bring to boil and lower heat. Cover pan. **5.** Simmer for 20 minutes. Drain. **6.** Transfer to warm serving dish. **7.** Coat with Sauce. **8.** Sprinkle with cheese. **9.** Brown under hot grill. **Serves 4.**

82 RATATOUILLE

1 large onion
1 garlic clove
2 oz. English or Welsh butter
2 tablespoons olive or corn oil
2 medium-sized aubergines
½ lb. courgettes or young marrow
1 medium-sized green pepper
½ lb. skinned tomatoes
½ level teaspoon salt
2 level tablespoons finely-chopped parsley

1. Thinly slice onion. Chop garlic. **2.** Fry both gently in hot butter and oil (in saucepan) for 3 to 4 minutes. **3.** Slice unpeeled aubergines and courgettes or marrow fairly thinly. **4.** Chop de-seeded green pepper and tomatoes. **5.** Add to saucepan with salt and parsley. **6.** Cover pan. Simmer gently for 1 hour. **7.** Serve hot or cold. **Serves 4.**

Ratatouille (No. 482)

107

483 BEETROOTS IN YOGURT

¾ lb. cooked beetroots
6 tablespoons natural yogurt
1 level tablespoon snipped chives
2 level teaspoons finely-grated onion
½ level teaspoon salt

1. Coarsely grate beetroots. **2.** Put into saucepan with remaining ingredients. **3.** Heat through gently. **Serves 4.**

484 CRUMBED BRUSSELS SPROUTS

1 lb. Brussels sprouts
1½ oz. English or Welsh butter
2 level tablespoons breadcrumbs
¼ level teaspoon dry mustard

1. Remove outer leaves from sprouts if necessary. **2.** Make cross-cut in stem end of each. **3.** Soak for 10 minutes in cold salted water. Drain. **4.** Cook in boiling salted water for 10 minutes. **5.** Meanwhile melt butter in saucepan. Add crumbs and mustard. Fry gently until golden. **6.** Drain sprouts and transfer to warm serving dish. **7.** Coat with fried crumbs and any remaining butter from pan. **Serves 4.**

485 BRUSSELS SPROUTS & CHESTNUTS

1. Prepare and boil sprouts as in recipe for Crumbed Brussels Sprouts (No. 484). **2.** Drain and return to pan. Add 6 oz. freshly-cooked and halved chestnuts and 1½ oz. English or Welsh butter. Stand over low heat for 5 to 7 minutes, shaking pan frequently. **Serves 4.**

486 BROCCOLI ALLEMANDE

2 lb. fresh broccoli
½ level teaspoon salt
1 recipe Allemande Sauce (No. 129)

1. Soak broccoli in cold water for 10 minutes. Drain. **2.** Remove large leaves and cut away tough parts of stalks. **3.** Put into saucepan. Add 1 in. boiling water. **4.** Cover pan and simmer steadily for 10 to 12 minutes. **5.** Drain thoroughly and sprinkle with salt. **6.** Transfer to warm dish. **7.** Coat with Sauce. **Serves 4.**

CAULIFLOWER WITH CHEESE SAUCE 487

1 medium-sized cauliflower
½ pint Cheese Coating Sauce (No. 116)
3 oz. crumbled Lancashire or grated English Cheddar cheese

1. Cook cauliflower in boiling salted water until tender (12 to 15 minutes). **2.** Drain and divide into florets. **3.** Transfer to warm serving dish. **4.** Coat with hot Sauce. **5.** Sprinkle with cheese. **6.** Brown under hot grill. **Serves 4.**

CAULIFLOWER SAUTÉ 488

1 medium-sized cauliflower
2 oz. English or Welsh butter
1 level dessertspoon finely-grated onion
GARNISH
¼ level teaspoon paprika

1. Cook cauliflower in boiling salted water until tender (12 to 15 minutes). **2.** Drain and divide into florets. **3.** Melt butter in saucepan. Add onion and fry 2 minutes. **4.** Add cauliflower and fry gently, turning frequently, until golden. **5.** Transfer to warm serving dish. **6.** Sprinkle with paprika. **Serves 4.**

CHICORY AU BEURRE 489

4 heads of chicory
Juice of ½ lemon
1 level teaspoon granulated sugar
1½ oz. English or Welsh butter, melted
GARNISH
1 level tablespoon chopped parsley

1. Cut thin slice off base of each head of chicory. **2.** Wash chicory under cold running water. **3.** Put into saucepan of boiling salted water. Add lemon juice and sugar. **4.** Simmer for 20 minutes. **5.** Drain and arrange in warm serving dish. **6.** Cover with melted butter. **7.** Sprinkle with parsley. **Serves 4.**

CHICORY BÉCHAMEL 490

1. Follow recipe and method for Chicory au Beurre (No. 489). **2.** Coat with ½ pint hot Béchamel Sauce (No. 110) instead of butter. **3.** Garnish with 1 level tablespoon toasted breadcrumbs instead of parsley. **Serves 4.**

491 CHICORY WITH CREAM

1. Follow recipe and method for Chicory au Beurre (No. 489). **2.** Cover with $\frac{1}{4}$ pint fresh single cream, heated through gently, instead of butter. **3.** Garnish with a light dusting of paprika instead of parsley. **Serves 4.**

492 BRAISED CELERY

1 medium-sized head of celery
Juice of 1 medium-sized lemon
$\frac{1}{2}$ level teaspoon salt
5 tablespoons water
2 oz. English or Welsh butter, melted
1 level dessertspoon cornflour
2 tablespoons milk

1. Remove leaves from celery. **2.** Cut sticks into 3 or 4-in. lengths. Wash thoroughly. **3.** Transfer to saucepan. **4.** Sprinkle with lemon juice and salt. **5.** Pour in water and melted butter. **6.** Cover with lid. Simmer gently for 25 minutes (or until tender). **7.** Transfer celery to warm serving dish. Keep hot. **8.** Reduce liquor left in pan, by boiling briskly, to about $\frac{1}{4}$ pint. **9.** Mix cornflour to smooth paste with milk. **10.** Add to celery liquor in pan. **11.** Cook, stirring, until mixture comes to boil and thickens. **12.** Simmer for 1 minute. Pour over celery. **Serves 4.**

493 LEEKS AURORE

4 medium-sized leeks
1 recipe Aurore Sauce (No. 119)

1. Trim leeks. Remove all but 2 or 3 in. of green leaves. **2.** Cut each leek in half lengthwise. Wash very thoroughly under cold running water to remove grit. **3.** Put into saucepan containing 2 in. boiling salted water. **4.** Cover. Simmer for 15 to 20 minutes (or until tender). **5.** Drain. Transfer to serving dish. Coat with hot Sauce. **Serves 4.**

494 LEEKS WITH WHITE OR HOLLANDAISE SAUCE

1. Follow recipe and method for Leeks Aurore (No. 493). **2.** Coat with $\frac{1}{2}$ pint Basic White Coating Sauce (No. 106) or Hollandaise Sauce (No. 131) instead of Aurore Sauce. **Serves 4.**

MUSHROOMS WITH CREAM 495

$\frac{3}{4}$ lb. mushrooms and stalks
2 oz. English or Welsh butter
$\frac{1}{4}$ level teaspoon salt
1 level tablespoon snipped chives
1 level tablespoon finely-chopped parsley
$\frac{1}{4}$ pint fresh double cream

1. Slice mushrooms and stalks. Fry gently in butter for 5 minutes. **2.** Add all remaining ingredients. **3.** Heat through gently, without boiling. **4.** Transfer to warm serving dish. **Serves 4.**

MUSHROOM FRITTERS 496

$\frac{3}{4}$ lb. button mushrooms
$\frac{1}{2}$ recipe Savoury Fritter Batter (No. 665)
Deep fat or oil for frying

GARNISH
1 level tablespoon finely-chopped parsley

1. Trim ends of mushroom stalks. **2.** Wash mushrooms and dry thoroughly. **3.** Coat with Batter. **4.** Fry in deep hot fat or oil until golden. **5.** Drain on soft kitchen paper. **6.** Transfer to warm serving dish. **7.** Sprinkle with parsley. **Serves 4.**

STEWED MUSHROOMS 497

$\frac{1}{2}$ to $\frac{3}{4}$ lb. mushrooms
1 oz. English or Welsh butter
$\frac{1}{4}$ pint milk
$\frac{1}{4}$ level teaspoon salt
3 level teaspoons cornflour
3 teaspoons lemon juice

GARNISH
1 level tablespoon chopped parsley

1. Wash and dry mushrooms and stalks. **2.** Fry gently in butter for 5 minutes. **3.** Pour in milk. Add salt. **4.** Cover pan. Simmer for 10 minutes. **5.** Mix cornflour to smooth paste with lemon juice. **6.** Add to pan. **7.** Cook, stirring, until mixture comes to boil and thickens. **8.** Simmer for 1 minute. **9.** Transfer to warm serving dish. **10.** Sprinkle with parsley. **Serves 4.**

498 FRIED MUSHROOMS

½ to ¾ lb. mushrooms
2 oz. English or Welsh butter

1. Peel and wash mushrooms. Dry thoroughly. **2.** Remove stalks and trim. Cut each in half. **3.** Melt butter in saucepan. **4.** Add mushrooms and stalks. Toss until well coated with butter. **5.** Fry briskly, uncovered, for 5 minutes. Shake pan often. **6.** Serve straight away. **Serves 4.**

499 GRILLED MUSHROOMS

½ to ¾ lb. mushrooms
1½ to 2 oz. English or Welsh butter
Pepper and salt

1. Wipe mushrooms with dry cloth. Remove stalks. **2.** Stand mushrooms, brown sides down, in buttered grill pan. **3.** Grill for 2 to 2½ minutes, depending on size. **4.** Turn over. Put knob of butter on each. **5.** Sprinkle with salt and pepper. **6.** Grill for further 2 to 2½ minutes. **7.** Serve straight away. **Serves 4.**

500 ONIONS IN CHEESE SAUCE

8 small onions
½ pint Cheese Coating Sauce (No. 116)
GARNISH
1 level tablespoon toasted breadcrumbs

1. Peel onions. **2.** Cook in boiling salted water for 25 to 40 minutes (or until tender). **3.** Drain. Transfer to warm serving dish. **4.** Coat with hot Sauce. **5.** Sprinkle with breadcrumbs. **Serves 4.**

501 BUTTERED BOILED ONIONS

1. Follow recipe and method for Onions in Cheese Sauce (No. 500). **2.** Coat with 2 oz. melted English or Welsh butter instead of Cheese Sauce. **3.** Garnish by sprinkling lightly with nutmeg. **Serves 4.**

FRIED ONIONS 50

3 medium-sized onions
2 oz. English or Welsh butter

1. Peel onions and cut into thin slices of even thickness. **2.** Heat butter in frying pan. **3.** Add onion slices and fry until golden brown, stirring frequently to prevent burning. **Serves 4.**

GLAZED & SUGARED ONIONS 50

12 small onions
2 oz. English or Welsh butter
½ level teaspoon salt
1 level tablespoon soft brown sugar

1. Cook onions in boiling salted water for 25 minutes. **2.** Drain and dry. **3.** Melt butter in frying pan. **4.** Add salt and sugar. **5.** Heat for 1 minute. **6.** Add onions. Toss in butter mixture until well coated. **7.** Cook over very low heat 15 minutes or until glazed and golden. **Serves 4.**

BACON-STUFFED ONIONS 50

4 large onions
2 oz. fresh white breadcrumbs
¼ lb. chopped lean bacon
Fresh single cream
Seasoning to taste
1 oz. English or Welsh butter

1. Cook onions in boiling salted water for 30 minutes. Drain and reserve 5 tablespoons onion water. **2.** Cut slice off top of each onion. **3.** Carefully remove centres, leaving ½-in. to ¾-in. thick onion shells. **4.** Chop onion centres finely. Mix with breadcrumbs and bacon. **5.** Bind with cream. Season to taste with salt and pepper. **6.** Return mixture to onion shells. **7.** Stand filled onions in shallow heatproof dish. Pour in onion water. **8.** Top each with knob of butter. **9.** Bake, uncovered, in centre of fairly hot oven (375°F. or Gas No. 5) until tender (about 45 minutes). **10.** Baste at least twice. **Serves 4.**

CHEESE & PARSLEY– STUFFED ONIONS 50

1. Follow recipe and method for Bacon-Stuffed Onions (No. 504). **2.** Use ¼ lb. grated Wensleydale or Derby cheese instead of bacon. **3.** Add 1 level tablespoon finely-chopped parsley. **Serves 4.**

French-Fried Onion Rings (No. 506)

4 medium-sized onions
Cold milk
Self-raising flour seasoned with salt and
  pepper
Deep fat or oil for frying

1. Slice onions thinly. Separate into rings.
2. Dip in milk. **3.** Toss in seasoned flour. **4.** Fry
in hot fat or oil until crisp and golden. **5.** Drain on
soft kitchen paper. **6.** Serve straight away.
Serves 4.

4 medium-sized parsnips
2 oz. English or Welsh butter, melted
½ level teaspoon salt
¼ pint water
GARNISH
1 level tablespoon finely-chopped parsley

1. Halve parsnips. Arrange in heatproof dish.
2. Coat with butter. Sprinkle with salt. **3.** Pour
water into dish. Cover with lid or aluminium
foil. **4.** Bake in centre of fairly hot oven (375°F.
or Gas No. 5) for 45 minutes (or until tender).
5. Uncover. Sprinkle with parsley. **Serves 4.**

4 medium-sized green peppers
1 medium-sized grated onion
1 oz. English or Welsh butter
½ lb. raw minced beef
½ lb. freshly-cooked rice (about ¼ lb. raw)
1 teaspoon Worcester sauce
Salt and pepper to taste
5 tablespoons cold water
1 oz. English or Welsh butter

1. Cut tops off peppers. Remove inside seeds
and fibres. **2.** Put into saucepan. Cover with
boiling salted water. **3.** Simmer for 2 minutes.
4. Carefully lift out of pan. Stand upside down to
drain on soft kitchen paper. **5.** Fry onion gently in
butter until pale gold. **6.** Add beef. Fry for
7 minutes, turning frequently. **7.** Stir in rice and
Worcester sauce. **8.** Season to taste with salt and
pepper. **9.** Stand peppers in shallow heatproof
dish. **10.** Fill with meat and rice mixture. **11.** Pour
water into dish. **12.** Put ¼ oz. butter on top of
each. **13.** Re-heat in centre of moderate oven
(350°F. or Gas No. 4) for 15 minutes. **Serves 4.**

509 STUFFED PEPPERS WITH RICE & CHEESE

4 medium-sized green peppers
$\frac{1}{2}$ lb. freshly-boiled rice (about $\frac{1}{4}$ lb. raw)
$\frac{1}{4}$ lb. crumbled Lancashire or grated English
  Cheddar cheese
$\frac{1}{2}$ level teaspoon made mustard
$\frac{1}{4}$ pint fresh single cream
Salt and pepper to taste
5 tablespoons cold water
1 oz. English or Welsh butter

1. Cut tops off peppers. Remove inside seeds and fibres. **2.** Put into saucepan. Cover with boiling salted water. **3.** Simmer for 2 minutes. **4.** Carefully lift out of pan. Stand upside down to drain on soft kitchen paper. **5.** Combine rice with cheese, mustard and cream. **6.** Season to taste with salt and pepper. **7.** Stand peppers in shallow heatproof dish. **8.** Fill with equal amounts of rice mixture. **9.** Pour water into dish. **10.** Put $\frac{1}{4}$ oz. butter on top of each. **11.** Re-heat in centre of moderate oven (350°F. or Gas No. 4) for 15 minutes. **Serves 4.**

510 CREAMED SWEDES

1 lb. swedes
1 oz. English or Welsh butter
4 tablespoons fresh single cream
Large pinch of nutmeg
Seasoning to taste
GARNISH
1 level tablespoon finely-chopped parsley

1. Dice peeled swedes. Cook, uncovered, in boiling salted water for about 30 minutes (or until tender). **2.** Drain and mash finely. **3.** Stand pan over low heat. Add butter, cream and nutmeg. **4.** Beat until smooth and creamy. **5.** Season to taste. Transfer to warm serving dish. **6.** Sprinkle with parsley. **Serves 4.**

511 CREAMED TURNIPS

1. Follow recipe and method for Creamed Swedes (No. 510). **2.** Use 1 lb. young turnips instead of swedes. **Serves 4.**

MARROW PROVENÇALE 51

1 medium-sized marrow
3 oz. English or Welsh butter
1 medium-sized grated onion
1 small chopped garlic clove (optional)
1 small chopped green pepper
$\frac{1}{2}$ lb. skinned and chopped tomatoes
$\frac{1}{4}$ lb. crumbled Lancashire or grated
  English Cheddar cheese

1. Peel marrow. Cut into 1-in. rings. **2.** Remove seeds from centres. **3.** Cut rings into 1-in. cubes. **4.** Melt butter in large saucepan. Add marrow. Fry for 6 to 7 minutes (or until gold). **5.** Transfer to plate. **6.** Add onion, garlic (if used) and green pepper to remaining butter in pan. Fry gently until pale gold. **7.** Add tomatoes and marrow. Mix well. **8.** Arrange half the mixture in fairly large heatproof dish. **9.** Cover with 2 oz. cheese. **10.** Add rest of marrow mixture. **11.** Sprinkle with remaining cheese. **12.** Bake, uncovered, in centre of fairly hot oven (375°F. or Gas No. 5) for 30 minutes. **Serves 4.**

SPINACH WITH CREAM SAUCE 51

$1\frac{1}{2}$ lb. spinach
1 oz. English or Welsh butter
1 level dessertspoon flour
$\frac{1}{4}$ pint fresh single cream
1 level teaspoon caster sugar
Seasoning to taste

1. Cut away tough stems from spinach. **2.** Wash leaves thoroughly under cold running water to remove grit. **3.** Tear into small pieces. Put into saucepan. **4.** Add 1 in. boiling salted water. **5.** Cover. Cook for 7 to 8 minutes (or until tender). Drain well. **6.** Melt butter in second saucepan. **7.** Stir in flour. Cook for 2 minutes without browning. **8.** Gradually blend in cream. **9.** Cook, stirring, until sauce comes to boil and thickens. **10.** Add sugar and spinach. **11.** Season to taste. **12.** Heat through gently. **Serves 4.**

14 BUTTER-BAKED TOMATOES

4 large tomatoes
1 oz. English or Welsh butter, melted
Salt and pepper

1. Stand tomatoes, stem sides down, in heatproof dish. **2.** Cut a shallow cross on top of each with sharp knife. **3.** Brush with butter. Sprinkle with salt and pepper. **4.** Bake in centre of fairly hot oven (400°F. or Gas No. 6) for 15 minutes. **Serves 4.**

15 STEWED TOMATOES

1 medium-sized grated onion
1 oz. English or Welsh butter
1 lb. skinned tomatoes
$\frac{1}{2}$ level teaspoon salt
2 level teaspoons granulated sugar
2 oz. fresh white breadcrumbs
Pepper to taste

GARNISH
1 level tablespoon finely-chopped parsley
or chives

1. Fry onion gently in butter for 3 minutes (in saucepan). **2.** Cut tomatoes into quarters. Add with salt and sugar. **3.** Cover pan. Simmer gently for 15 minutes, stirring frequently. **4.** Add breadcrumbs. Heat through further minute. **5.** Season to taste with pepper. **6.** Transfer to warm serving dish. **7.** Sprinkle with parsley or chives. **Serves 4.**

6 FRIED TOMATOES WITH CREAM

6 medium-sized tomatoes
Flour seasoned with salt and pepper
1 garlic clove
2 oz. English or Welsh butter
2 teaspoons olive or corn oil
$\frac{1}{4}$ pint fresh single cream
1 level dessertspoon finely-chopped
parsley

1. Cut tomatoes into $\frac{1}{4}$-in. thick slices. **2.** Coat with seasoned flour. **3.** Rub cut clove of garlic round inside of frying pan. **4.** Add butter and oil. Heat. **5.** Add tomato slices. Fry on both sides until crisp and golden. **6.** Drain on soft kitchen paper. Transfer to hot dish. **7.** Stir cream and parsley into reminining butter in frying pan. **8.** Heat through gently. Do not allow to boil. **9.** Pour over tomato slices and serve straight away. **Serves 4.**

COLD GLOBE ARTICHOKES 517

4 medium-sized globe artichokes
1 tablespoon vinegar or lemon juice
French Dressing (No. 598)

1. To clean artichokes, hold by stem end (at base) and plunge heads in and out of a large deep bowl of cold water. **2.** Cut off stems. **3.** Pull away bottom row of leaves from each (these are tough). **4.** With kitchen scissors, trim off tips of remaining leaves. **5.** Stand grill pan rack in large saucepan containing 2-in. boiling water. **6.** Add vinegar or lemon juice. **7.** Place artichokes, upright, on grid. **8.** Bring water to boil. Cover pan. **9.** Lower heat. Cook artichokes gently for 45 minutes to 1 hour. **10.** Drain thoroughly. Chill. **11.** Serve with Dressing. **Serves 4.**

● *To eat artichokes, pull off leaves with fingers one at a time. Dip base of each leaf (the edible part) in Dressing and pass between teeth. Discard rest of leaf. Continue until you come to a pale cone of leaves. Lift these off and discard. Discard also the fuzzy centre underneath. Eat remaining heart with dressing.*

HOT GLOBE ARTICHOKES 518

1. Follow recipe and method for Cold Globe Artichokes (No. 517). **2.** Serve artichokes immediately after draining. **3.** Accompany with either 3 to 4 oz. melted English or Welsh butter or Hollandaise Sauce (No. 131). **Serves 4.**

Salads

SIDE SALADS

1 Webb, Cos or round lettuce
1 clove garlic, peeled (optional)
1 recipe French Dressing (No. 598)

1. Wash lettuce well and shake dry. **2.** Halve clove garlic. Press cut sides against base and sides of salad bowl. **3.** Tear lettuce into bite-size pieces and put into bowl. **4.** Just before serving, pour over dressing. **5.** With wooden spoon and fork, toss lettuce in dressing until every piece is coated. **6.** Serve with meat, poultry, offal, duck, turkey, fish, cheese or egg dishes. **Serves 4.**

● For mixed salad, add torn-up watercress and/or curly endive.
● For summer salad, add slices of cucumber, tomatoes, radishes, strips of red or green pepper and spring onions.

1 lb. tomatoes
1 recipe French Dressing (No. 598)
1 level tablespoon finely-chopped onion
1 heaped tablespoon finely chopped parsley

1. Put tomatoes into bowl. **2.** Cover with boiling water, leave $\frac{1}{2}$ a minute and drain. **3.** Slide off skins and discard. **4.** Return tomatoes to bowl and cover with very cold water. **5.** Leave 5 minutes and drain. **6.** Cut tomatoes into very thin slices. **7.** Arrange in large shallow serving dish. **8.** Pour over dressing and sprinkle with onion and parsley. **9.** Serve chilled with meat, poultry, duck, turkey, fish, shellfish, cheese or egg dishes. **Serves 4.**

1 lb. cold cooked potatoes
1 level teaspoon finely-grated onion, or
  2 spring onions, finely chopped (optional)
$\frac{1}{4}$ pint Mayonnaise (No. 577)
5 tablespoons fresh double cream
GARNISH
Snipped chives or paprika

1. Cut potatoes into small cubes. **2.** Put into a large bowl and mix in grated or chopped onion. **3.** Add Mayonnaise and cream and stir gently with spoon until potato cubes are thickly coated. **4.** Pile into a serving dish and sprinkle with chives or paprika. **5.** Serve with meat, poultry, duck, turkey, fish, cheese or egg dishes. **Serves 4.**

$\frac{1}{2}$ Cos or Webb lettuce
1 small cucumber
1 carton (5 oz.) natural yogurt
2 tablespoons Mayonnaise (No. 577)
1 tablespoon lemon juice
$\frac{1}{4}$ to $\frac{1}{2}$ level teaspoon salt
Freshly-milled pepper

1. Wash lettuce and shake dry. **2.** Tear leaves into bite-size pieces and put into serving dish. **3.** Add cucumber, peeled and cut into tiny dice, and mix well. **4.** Combine yogurt with Mayonnaise and lemon juice. Season to taste with salt and pepper. **5.** Pour over lettuce and cucumber and toss well. **6.** Serve with poultry, turkey, fish, cheese or egg dishes. **Serves 4.**

6 large tomatoes
1 recipe Cream Cheese and Nut Dressing (No. 561)
GARNISH
4 level tablespoons finely-chopped parsley

Left: Cucumber Salad (No. 523)
    with Mayonnaise (No. 577)

1. Put tomatoes into bowl. **2.** Cover with boiling water, leave $\frac{1}{2}$ a minute and drain. **3.** Slide off skins and discard. **4.** Return tomatoes to bowl. Cover with very cold water. **5.** Leave 5 minutes and drain. **6.** Cut into thin slices and use to cover base of serving dish. **7.** Coat with dressing and garnish with rows of parsley. **8.** Serve with meat, offal, poultry, fish, shellfish and egg dishes. **Serves 4.**

524 GREEN BEAN SALAD

1 lb. young green beans
4 tablespoons olive oil
$\frac{1}{4}$ level teaspoon salt
$\frac{1}{4}$ level teaspoon dry mustard
$\frac{1}{4}$ level teaspoon icing sugar
Freshly-milled black pepper
1 clove garlic, very finely chopped
  (optional)
2 tablespoons wine vinegar
2 level tablespoons finely-chopped parsley
2 level tablespoons snipped chives or green
  part of leek
4 tablespoons fresh double cream

1. Trim beans and slice. **2.** Cook in boiling salted water until tender. **3.** Meanwhile, beat olive oil with salt, mustard, sugar, freshly-milled pepper to taste and the garlic. **4.** Gradually beat in vinegar and continue beating until dressing is thick. **5.** Stir in 1 tablespoon each parsley, chives or finely-chopped leek. **6.** Drain beans. While still hot, toss with dressing. **7.** Leave in cool for 2 hours. Just before serving, stir in cream and sprinkle top with rest of parsley and chives. **8.** Serve with meat, poultry, offal, duck, turkey, fish, cheese or egg dishes. **Serves 4.**

525 WINTER COLE SLAW

1 small or $\frac{1}{2}$ medium-sized head of white
  cabbage (about $\frac{1}{2}$ lb.)
2 eating apples
1 level tablespoon finely-grated onion
  (optional)
2 heaped tablespoons finely-chopped
  parsley
2 oz. Leicester cheese, grated
1 carton (5 oz.) soured cream
2 tablespoons milk
1 tablespoon lemon juice
2 teaspoons rose hip syrup
$\frac{1}{2}$ teaspoon Worcester sauce
$\frac{1}{2}$ level teaspoon salt

1. Shred or grate cabbage finely, wash well and drain. **2.** Peel apples and grate coarsely. **3.** Put cabbage and apples into large bowl. **4.** Add onion, parsley and cheese and mix well. **5.** Mix soured cream with milk, lemon juice, rose hip syrup, Worcester sauce and salt. **6.** Pour over cabbage mixture. Toss well with spoon and fork. **7.** Transfer to serving dish. **8.** Serve with meat, poultry, duck, turkey or fried fish dishes. **Serves 4.**

CREAMED CABBAGE & CARAWAY SALAD 5:

1 small or $\frac{1}{2}$ medium-sized head of white
  cabbage (about $\frac{1}{2}$ lb.)
1 level tablespoon finely-grated onion
1 level teaspoon caraway seeds
2 cartons (10 oz.) soured cream
4 tablespoons lemon juice
2 level teaspoons soft brown sugar
Salt and pepper to taste

1. Shred or grate cabbage finely, wash well and drain. **2.** Put into large bowl. Add onion and caraway seeds and mix well. **3.** Combine soured cream with lemon juice, brown sugar and salt and pepper to taste. **4.** Pour over cabbage mixture and toss well. **5.** Transfer to serving dish. **6.** Serve with Frankfurters or cold assorted sausages. **Serves 4.**

CREAMED AVOCADO SALAD SLICES 5:

1 oz. Blue Stilton cheese
$\frac{1}{4}$ lb. cream cheese
2 level tablespoons finely-chopped stuffed
  olives
2 level tablespoons toasted almonds
1 level tablespoon snipped chives
Finely-grated peel and juice of 1 medium-
  sized lemon
1 dessertspoon fresh single cream
$\frac{1}{4}$ level teaspoon salt
1 level teaspoon paprika
Pinch of Cayenne pepper
1 large avocado pear
$\frac{1}{2}$ curly endive

GARNISH
Strips of canned pimento

1. Crumble Stilton and mash finely with cream cheese. Stir in olives, almonds, chives, lemon peel and juice, cream, salt, paprika and pepper. Mix well. **2.** Cut avocado in half, peel and remove stone. **3.** Enlarge cavity in each half by scooping out some of the avocado flesh (which can be mashed and added to cheese mixture). Brush both halves – inside and out – with lemon juice to prevent discolouration. **4.** Pack cheese filling into cavities. Press both halves of avocado together. **5.** Immediately wrap in aluminium foil and chill. **6.** Before serving, wash endive, shake dry and use to cover base of serving platter. **7.** Unwrap avocado, cut into 4 slices and arrange on top of endive. **8.** Garnish each with strips of pimento. **9.** Serve with poultry, turkey, fish or egg dishes. **Serves 4.**

528 APPLE & WALNUT SALAD

½ Cos or small Webb lettuce
6 celery stalks
3 large eating apples
3 oz. shelled walnut halves, coarsely
  chopped
¼ pint Mayonnaise (No. 577)
5 tablespoons fresh double cream or
  soured cream
1 tablespoon vinegar
Juice of 1 medium-sized lemon

1. Wash lettuce leaves and shake dry. 2. Tear into bite-size pieces and use to cover base of serving dish. 3. Cut celery into thin slices and put into bowl. 4. Peel and core 2 apples and cut into thin slices. Add to celery, together with chopped nuts, and mix well. 5. Combine Mayonnaise with cream and vinegar. 6. Pour over apple mixture and toss until ingredients are thickly coated. 7. Arrange over lettuce. 8. Cut third apple, unpeeled, into thin slices. 9. Dip in lemon juice to prevent browning then arrange on top of salad. 10. Serve with meat, poultry, duck, or turkey dishes. Serves 4.

529 STUFFED PEPPER SALAD

2 medium-sized red or green peppers
¼ lb. cream cheese
2 tablespoons fresh double cream
1 level teaspoon finely-grated onion
3 level tablespoons very finely-chopped
  ham or chopped and salted cashew nuts
1 level teaspoon paprika
Seasoning to taste
½ round lettuce
1 large tomato

1. Wash peppers and wipe dry. Cut a slice from the stem end of each. Remove all inside pips. 2. Mix cream cheese with cream, onion, paprika and ham or nuts. Season to taste. 3. Stuff peppers with cheese mixture. Wrap in foil and refrigerate overnight. 4. Before serving, wash lettuce, shake leaves dry and use to cover base of serving dish. 5. Cut each pepper into 6 slices and arrange in a ring on top of lettuce. 6. Fill centre with wedges of tomato. 7. Serve with lamb, poultry, fish, shellfish or egg dishes. Serves 4.

BRUSSELS SPROUTS & CELERY SALAD 530

¾ lb. Brussels sprouts
1 recipe Cream Cheese & Celery Dressing
  (No. 563)

GARNISH
1 finely-grated carrot
8 shelled walnut halves

1. Trim and wash sprouts. Shred with sharp knife. 2. Put into large bowl, add dressing and toss well. 3. Transfer to serving dish. Garnish with mounds of grated carrot and nuts. 4. Serve with meat, offal or egg dishes. Serves 4.

RUSSIAN SALAD 531

1 lettuce heart
½ lb. cooked potatoes
½ lb. cooked carrots
¼ lb. cooked peas
¼ lb. cooked green beans
Mayonnaise (No. 577)

GARNISH
1 large hard-boiled egg
4 gherkins, sliced

1. Wash lettuce and shake leaves dry. 2. Arrange in salad bowl. 3. Cut potatoes and carrots into cubes. 4. Put into large bowl. 5. Add peas and beans and mix well. 6. Combine gently with Mayonnaise, adding enough to coat vegetables fairly thickly. 7. Pile on top of lettuce. Garnish with wedges of hard-boiled egg and slices of gherkin. 8. Serve with meat, poultry, duck, turkey, fish, cheese or egg dishes. Serves 4.

TROPICANA SALAD 532

2 large oranges
4 large tomatoes
2 large bananas
1 carton (5 oz.) soured cream
1 tablespoon lemon juice
1 level teaspoon grated horseradish
¼ level teaspoon salt

1. Peel oranges and remove all traces of pith. Cut into thin slices. Cut each slice into 4 and arrange over base of serving dish. 2. Blanch and skin tomatoes, slice very thinly and place over oranges. 3. Top with sliced bananas. Cover completely with the soured cream mixed with lemon juice, horseradish and salt. 4. Serve with cold poultry, duck or turkey dishes. Serves 4.

533 GREEN PEPPER & ONION SALAD

½ curly endive
2 medium-sized green peppers
2 medium-sized onions
1 recipe Basic Cream Cheese Dressing
(No. 562)
GARNISH
1 large hard-boiled egg
Paprika

1. Wash endive, shake dry and use to cover base of serving dish. 2. Wash green peppers, de-seed and cut into thin strips. 3. Peel and wash onions and slice thinly. 4. Arrange pepper strips and onion slices on top of endive. Spoon over dressing. 5. Garnish with slices of hard-boiled egg and paprika. 6. Serve with veal, lamb, poultry, duck or egg dishes. **Serves 4.**

SYRIAN SALAD 5.

½ Cos or Webb lettuce
¼ lb. *each* cooked green beans, cooked peas
and cooked diced carrot
¼ lb. coarsely-grated cucumber
1 carton (5 oz.) natural yogurt
4 tablespoons fresh single cream
¼ to ½ level teaspoon salt
GARNISH
Chopped fresh mint

1. Wash lettuce and shake leaves dry. 2. Tear into bite-size pieces and use to cover bases of 4 individual plates. 3. Arrange beans, peas, carrot and cucumber in separate piles on top. 4. Spoon over yogurt, well mixed with the cream and salt. 5. Garnish with chopped mint. 6. Serve with meat, offal, poultry, duck or egg dishes. **Serves 4.**

MAIN COURSE SALADS

535 SWEET CORN & CHICKEN SALAD

1 head of chicory
1 can (approximately ¾ lb.) sweet corn
½ lb. cooked chicken
¼ lb. Cheshire cheese
1 recipe Banana Dressing (No. 572)
GARNISH
Canned pimento

1. Separate leaves of chicory, wash well and drain. Arrange on round platter, radiating from the centre. 2. Drain sweet corn. Tip into a bowl. 3. Cut chicken into bite-size pieces. Cut cheese into small cubes. Add to corn and mix well. 4. Pour Dressing over corn mixture and toss. 5. Pile on to centre of dish over chicory leaves. Garnish with trellis of pimento strips. **Serves 4.**

Cheese Platter Salad (No. 536)

Sweet Corn & Chicken Salad (No. 535)

536 CHEESE PLATTER SALAD

½ round lettuce
1 head of chicory
1 dessertspoon lemon juice
½ lb. back bacon
¼ lb. Blue Stilton cheese
2 large cartons (1 lb.) cottage cheese
5 tablespoons fresh single cream
1 heaped tablespoon chopped stuffed
  olives or chopped gherkins

GARNISH
4 unpeeled orange slices

1. Wash lettuce and shake leaves dry. **2.** Tear into bite-size pieces and put into a bowl. **3.** Slice chicory, wash well and drain. Sprinkle with lemon juice to prevent browning, then add to lettuce. Mix well together. **4.** Chop bacon and fry in own fat until crisp. Drain on soft kitchen paper. **5.** Mash Stilton cheese finely then combine with cottage cheese, cream and olives or gherkins. **6.** Put lettuce, chicory and bacon on to 4 individual plates. Top with equal amounts of cheese mixture. **7.** Garnish with orange slices. **Serves 4.**

TONGUE & CUCUMBER SALAD 537

6 large lettuce leaves
6 oz. tongue
6 oz. Caerphilly cheese
½ medium-sized cucumber, peeled
1 carton (5 oz.) natural yogurt
2 tablespoons fresh single cream
1 level tablespoon snipped chives or green
  part of leek
¼ level teaspoon dry mustard
¼ level teaspoon salt
½ level teaspoon icing sugar
1 teaspoon lemon juice

GARNISH
1 large tomato

1. Wash lettuce leaves and shake dry. **2.** Tear into bite-size pieces and use to cover base of serving dish. **3.** Cut tongue into thin strips. Cut cheese and cucumber into small dice. Put into bowl. **4.** Combine yogurt with cream, chives (or finely-chopped leek), mustard, salt, sugar and lemon juice. **5.** Beat well then pour over tongue and cucumber. **6.** Toss thoroughly and arrange mounds over lettuce. **7.** Garnish with sliced tomato. **Serves 4.**

538 COTTAGE CHEESE SUMMER SALAD

1 round lettuce
1 dozen radishes
$\frac{1}{2}$ large cucumber, peeled
1 bunch spring onions
2 cartons (1 lb.) cottage cheese
1 carton (5 oz.) soured cream
1 dessertspoon lemon juice
$\frac{1}{2}$ level teaspoon salt
Good shake of pepper

GARNISH
Paprika

1. Wash lettuce, shake leaves dry then tear into bite-size pieces. **2.** Slice radishes and cucumber thinly. **3.** Peel onions and coarsely chop. **4.** Put vegetables into bowl and mix well together. **5.** Arrange equal amounts on 4 individual plates. Place a mound of cottage cheese in centre of each. **6.** Mix soured cream with lemon juice, salt and pepper and pour over salads. **7.** Sprinkle lightly with paprika. **Serves 4.**

539 HERRING SALAD

$\frac{1}{2}$ Cos lettuce
3 rollmops
1 carton (5 oz.) soured cream
2 tablespoons milk
$\frac{1}{4}$ level teaspoon paprika
$\frac{1}{2}$ level teaspoon finely-grated lemon peel
2 large hard-boiled eggs
1 small pickled cucumber

1. Wash lettuce and shake leaves dry. **2.** Tear into bite-size pieces and use to cover base of serving dish. **3.** Drain rollmops well and cut into wide strips. Put into a bowl and add soured cream, milk, paprika, lemon peel and chopped eggs. **4.** Mix well then pile over lettuce. **5.** Garnish with slices of pickled cucumber. Serve very cold. **Serves 4.**

540 EGG & SARDINE SALAD

1 round lettuce
1 can sardines in pure olive oil
2 large hard-boiled eggs
1 large stalk celery
1 recipe Soured Cream with Chives
Dressing (No. 549)

GARNISH
Paprika
4 lemon wedges

SPINACH & COTTAGE CHEESE SALAD 54

1 lb. fresh spinach
1 Webb or medium-sized Cos lettuce
$\frac{1}{2}$ lb. back bacon
$\frac{1}{4}$ pint olive or corn oil
1 level teaspoon dry mustard
1 level teaspoon salt
2 level teaspoons icing or caster sugar
1 level tablespoon very finely-grated onion
4 tablespoons wine or cider vinegar
1 large carton ($\frac{1}{2}$ lb.) cottage cheese

1. Thoroughly wash and drain spinach. **2.** Repeat with lettuce. **3.** Tear spinach and lettuce leaves into bite-size pieces (discarding stems) and put into large salad bowl. Mix well. **4.** Coarsely chop bacon and fry in own fat until crisp. Drain on soft kitchen paper. Add to greens when cold. **5.** Mix oil with mustard, salt, sugar and onion. Beat in the vinegar. **6.** Pour half over salad greens and bacon and toss well. **7.** Mix cottage cheese with remaining dressing. Add to greens in bowl. **8.** Toss again. **Serves 4.**

TUNA & BACON SALAD 54

$\frac{1}{2}$ lb. back bacon
$\frac{1}{2}$ Cos lettuce
1 level tablespoon finely-chopped onion
1 x 7 oz. can middle-cut tuna
2 large hard-boiled eggs
Double recipe Watercress & Yogurt
Dressing (No. 567)

1. Chop bacon and fry in own fat until crisp. **2.** Drain on soft kitchen paper. **3.** Wash lettuce and shake leaves dry. **4.** Tear into bite-size pieces and put into a large bowl. **5.** Add bacon, onion, drained and flaked tuna, chopped eggs and dressing. **6.** Toss well and transfer to serving dish. **Serves 4.**

1. Wash lettuce and shake leaves dry. **2.** Tear into bite-size pieces and use to cover 4 individual plates. **3.** Skin and bone sardines. Chop eggs finely. **4.** Wash celery and cut into thin slices. **5.** Put sardines into bowl and mash finely with eggs. **6.** Add celery. Blend in Dressing. **7.** Pile equal amounts over lettuce. Sprinkle lightly with paprika and top each with wedge of lemon. **Serves 4.**

543 PRAWN & PINEAPPLE SALAD

1 Webb or Cos lettuce
1 medium-sized can pineapple cubes, well drained
6 oz. fresh or frozen peeled prawns
6 oz. Derby cheese, diced
1 recipe Soured Cream with Stilton Dressing (No. 558)
2 tablespoons fresh single cream

GARNISH
Paprika
Unpeeled cucumber slices

1. Wash lettuce and shake leaves dry. 2. Tear into bite-size pieces and use to cover 4 individual plates. 3. Mix pineapple cubes well together with the prawns and cheese. Pile equal amounts on top of lettuce. 4. Pour over Dressing mixed with the cream. Garnish lightly with paprika and cucumber slices. Serves 4.

544 HAM, CHEESE & CABBAGE TOSS

1 recipe Cream Cheese and Onion Dressing (No. 565)
6 tablespoons Mayonnaise (No. 577)
1 small green pepper
1 small head of white cabbage (about ½ lb.)
3 eating apples
6 oz. lean ham
6 oz. Wensleydale cheese
1 tablespoon lemon juice

1. Combine Dressing with Mayonnaise. 2. Add washed, finely-chopped and de-seeded green pepper. Chill thoroughly. 3. Before serving, shred or grate cabbage finely, wash well and drain. Peel and core 2 apples and cut into dice. Cut ham into shreds and cheese into small cubes. 4. Put cabbage, apples, ham and cheese into large bowl and add dressing. 5. Toss well and transfer to serving dish. 6. Garnish with third apple, unpeeled, cut into slices and dipped in the lemon juice to prevent browning. Serves 4.

545 SWEDISH SAUSAGE SALAD

1 round lettuce
¾ lb. cold, cooked pork sausages
½ lb. cold cooked potatoes
1 recipe Swedish Mayonnaise (No. 588)
GARNISH
Parsley

ENGLISH CHEDDAR CHEESE 546 & APPLE SALAD

½ round lettuce
1 carton (5 oz.) soured cream
3 tablespoons milk
1 teaspoon lemon juice
1 level teaspoon icing or caster sugar
¼ level teaspoon salt
2 eating apples, peeled and cored
½ lb. English Cheddar cheese
2 canned pineapple rings

GARNISH
4 slices unpeeled orange
8 black olives

1. Wash lettuce and shake leaves dry. 2. Tear into bite-size pieces and use to cover base of serving dish. 3. Combine soured cream with milk, lemon juice, sugar and salt. 4. Cut apples and cheese into small dice. Chop pineapple coarsely. 5. Add to soured cream mixture and toss lightly together. 6. Pile over lettuce. 7. Garnish with orange slices and olives. Serves 4.

COTTAGE CHEESE 547 & PEACH SALAD

½ Cos lettuce
½ recipe French Dressing (No. 598)
1½ large cartons (¾ lb.) cottage cheese
5 tablespoons Mayonnaise (No. 577) or soured cream
¼ lb. salted cashew nuts

GARNISH
1 medium can peach slices
4 black olives or grapes

1. Wash lettuce and shake leaves dry. 2. Tear into bite-size pieces and toss with French Dressing. 3. Use to cover base of 4 individual serving plates. 4. Put cottage cheese into bowl. Combine with Mayonnaise or soured cream and the nuts. 5. Pile equal amounts on to plates. Garnish with the peach slices (well drained) and olives or grapes. Serves 4.

1. Wash lettuce, shake leaves dry and use to cover base of a serving dish. 2. Cut sausages into slices. Dice potatoes. 3. Put both into bowl and add Dressing. 4. Toss well together. Arrange over lettuce. 5. Garnish with parsley. Serves 4.

Salad Dressings

All quantities of dressings are sufficient for 4 to 6 servings.

548 BASIC SOURED CREAM DRESSING

For green and mixed salads; potato salads; meat, poultry, fish, cheese and egg salads.

1 carton (5 oz.) soured cream
1 tablespoon milk
1 tablespoon lemon juice or vinegar
½ to 1 level teaspoon icing or caster sugar
¼ level teaspoon salt
Shake of pepper

1. Beat soured cream well together with milk and lemon juice or vinegar. **2.** Stir in sugar. Season to taste with salt and pepper. **3.** If a thinner dressing is preferred, add a little extra milk. **4.** Leave 15 minutes in the cool before using.

549 SOURED CREAM WITH CHIVES DRESSING

For same salads as Basic Soured Cream Dressing.

1. Follow recipe and method for Basic Soured Cream Dressing (No. 548). **2.** Stir in 1 heaped tablespoon snipped chives before seasoning with salt and pepper.

550 SOURED CREAM WITH PARSLEY DRESSING

For same salads as Basic Soured Cream Dressing.

1. Follow recipe and method for Basic Soured Cream Dressing (No. 548). **2.** Stir in 1 heaped tablespoon finely-chopped parsley before seasoning with salt and pepper.

551 SOURED CREAM WITH MUSTARD DRESSING

For beef, ham and tongue salads; salads made with canned fish.

1. Follow recipe and method for Basic Soured Cream Dressing (No. 548). **2.** Add 1 level teaspoon made mustard with lemon juice or vinegar.

552 SOURED CREAM WITH HORSERADISH DRESSING

For cold roast beef and salad.

1. Follow recipe and method for Basic Soured Cream Dressing (No. 548). **2.** Stir in 2 level teaspoons grated horseradish before seasoning with salt and pepper.

553 SOURED CREAM WITH CUCUMBER DRESSING

For all poultry and fish salads.

1. Follow recipe and method for Basic Soured Cream Dressing (No. 548). **2.** Stir in 4 level tablespoons very finely-grated peeled cucumber before seasoning with salt and pepper.

554 SOURED CREAM WITH TOMATO DRESSING

For vegetable, poultry, fish and egg salads

1. Follow recipe and method for Basic Soured Cream Dressing (No. 548). **2.** Stir in 1 dessertspoon tomato purée and 1 finely-chopped, skinned tomato before seasoning with salt and pepper.

555 SOURED CREAM WITH LEMON DRESSING

For poultry, fish and egg salads.

1. Follow recipe and method for Basic Soured Cream Dressing (No. 548). **2.** Stir in 1 level teaspoon finely-grated lemon peel before seasoning with salt and pepper.

556 SOURED CREAM WITH PAPRIKA DRESSING

For veal, poultry and egg salads.

1. Follow recipe and method for Basic Soured Cream Dressing (No. 548). **2.** Stir in 2 level teaspoons paprika before seasoning with salt and pepper.

7 SOURED CREAM WITH NUTS DRESSING

For poultry, fish and egg salads.

1. Follow recipe and method for Basic Soured Cream Dressing (No. 548). **2.** Add 2 oz. finely-chopped walnuts or finely-chopped salted almonds before seasoning with salt and pepper.

SOURED CREAM WITH DATES DRESSING 559

For winter vegetable salads.

¼ **lb. dates (stoned)**
3 tablespoons water
1 carton (5 oz.) soured cream

1. Put dates and water into a pan. Bring slowly to the boil. **2.** Cover pan and simmer gently for 10 minutes. **3.** Cool dates, chop finely and beat into soured cream.

8 SOURED CREAM WITH STILTON DRESSING

For all green and mixed salads.

2 oz. Blue Stilton cheese
1 carton (5 oz.) soured cream
2 tablespoons milk
¼ **level teaspoon salt**
Freshly–milled pepper

1. Put Stilton into a bowl. Mash finely with a fork. **2.** Gradually blend in soured cream and milk. **3.** Season to taste with salt and pepper. **4.** Leave in cool 15 minutes before using. **5.** If thinner dressing is preferred, add a little more milk.

DAIRY SALAD DRESSING 560

For green and mixed salads; salads with white fish, poultry, eggs or cheese.

4 tablespoons *each* **milk, vinegar and salad oil**
½ **level teaspoon icing or caster sugar**
¼ **level teaspoon** *each* **made mustard and salt**
Pepper

1. Beat milk, vinegar and oil together until smooth and well blended. **2.** Beat in sugar, mustard and salt. **3.** Season to taste with pepper.

**Prawn & Pineapple Salad (No. 543) with
Soured Cream With Stilton Dressing (No. 558)**

561 CREAM CHEESE & NUT DRESSING

For green and mixed salads; combination salads of fruit and vegetables.

½ lb. cream cheese
4 tablespoons fresh single cream
1 tablespoon lemon juice
2 tablespoons salted cashew nuts, very
    finely-chopped
2 oz. finely-grated English Cheddar cheese
1 level teaspoon icing or caster sugar
Shake of pepper
¼ to ½ level teaspoon salt

1. Beat cream cheese, cream and lemon juice together until smooth. **2.** Stir in chopped nuts, grated cheese and sugar. **3.** Season to taste with pepper and salt. **4.** If thinner dressing is preferred, add a little more cream.

562 BASIC CREAM CHEESE DRESSING

For green and mixed salads; salads with poultry, fish or eggs.

¼ lb. cream cheese
1 tablespoon fresh single cream
¼ level teaspoon salt
1 level teaspoon icing or caster sugar
3 teaspoons lemon juice or vinegar

1. Put cream cheese into a bowl. Gradually blend in cream. **2.** Stir in remaining ingredients. **3.** Leave in cool 15 minutes before using. **4.** If thinner dressing is preferred, add a little more cream.

563 CREAM CHEESE & CELERY DRESSING

For same dishes as Basic Cream Cheese Dressing.

1. Follow recipe and method for Basic Cream Cheese Dressing (No. 562). **2.** Use ½ level teaspoon celery salt instead of plain salt.

564 CREAM CHEESE & GARLIC DRESSING

For green and tomato salads.

1. Follow recipe and method. for Basic Cream Cheese Dressing (No. 562). **2.** Use ¼ level teaspoon garlic salt instead of the plain salt.

CREAM CHEESE & ONION DRESSING 5●

For beef, tongue and ham salads.

1. Follow recipe and method for Basic Cream Cheese Dressing (No. 562). **2.** Add 1 level teaspoon very finely-grated onion with the lemon juice or vinegar.

BASIC YOGURT DRESSING 5●

For green and mixed salads; potato salads; meat, poultry, fish, cheese and egg salads.

1 carton (5 oz.) natural yogurt
2 tablespoons fresh single cream
3 teaspoons lemon juice
1 level teaspoon icing or caster sugar
¼ level teaspoon salt
Shake of pepper

1. Pour yogurt into a bowl. Beat in cream, lemon juice and sugar. **2.** Season to taste with salt and pepper. **3.** Leave 15 minutes in cool before using.

WATERCRESS & YOGURT DRESSING 5●

For poultry, fish and egg salads.

1. Follow recipe and method for Basic Yogurt Dressing (No. 566). **2.** Stir in 2 or 3 level tablespoons very finely-chopped watercress before seasoning with salt and pepper.

EGG, ANCHOVY & YOGURT DRESSING 5●

For green and fish salads.

1. Follow recipe and method for Basic Yogurt Dressing (No. 566). **2.** Add 2 finely-chopped, large hard-boiled eggs and 1 oz. canned and finely-chopped anchovy fillets before seasoning with salt.

CURRY YOGURT DRESSING 5●

For poultry, fish and egg salads.

1. Follow recipe and method for Basic Yogurt Dressing (No. 566). **2.** Add 2 level teaspoons curry powder and 1 level tablespoon sweet pickle before seasoning with salt and pepper.

70 PIQUANT YOGURT DRESSING

For green and mixed salads; meat, poultry and egg salads.

1. Follow recipe and method for Basic Yogurt Dressing (No. 566). **2.** Stir in 1 teaspoon Worcester Sauce, large pinch of Cayenne pepper, 1 level teaspoon paprika and $\frac{1}{2}$ finely-chopped clove of garlic (optional).

71 FRUITY YOGURT DRESSING

For fresh fruit salads; canned fruits.

1 carton (5 oz.) natural yogurt
3 tablespoons fresh orange juice
1 tablespoon lemon juice
1 tablespoon rose hip syrup

1. Pour yogurt into a bowl. Beat in remaining ingredients. **2.** Chill at least 30 minutes before using.

72 BANANA DRESSING

For winter vegetable salads.

2 medium-sized bananas
3 dessertspoons lemon juice
5 tablespoons Mayonnaise (No.577)
1 carton (5 oz.) natural yogurt
1 level teaspoon bottled horseradish sauce
$\frac{1}{2}$ level teaspoon icing or caster sugar
$\frac{1}{2}$ level teaspoon salt
Pinch of Cayenne pepper

1. Mash bananas finely. **2.** Beat in lemon juice, Mayonnaise, yogurt, horseradish sauce and sugar. **3.** Season to taste with salt and pepper. **4.** Use straight away.

3 CREAM CHEESE & APRICOT DRESSING

For fresh fruit salads; canned fruits

$\frac{1}{4}$ lb. cream cheese
6 level tablespoons apricot purée (made from canned or stewed apricots)
1 tablespoon lemon juice
3 tablespoons Mayonnaise (No.577)
Pinch of salt

1. Put cream cheese into bowl. Mash finely with fork. Beat in apricot purée. **2.** Add lemon juice, Mayonnaise and salt. Beat until smooth.

COTTAGE CHEESE SALAD DRESSING 574

For green and mixed salads; salads with poultry, fish and eggs.

1 carton ($\frac{1}{2}$ lb.) cottage cheese
3 tablespoons French Dressing (No.598)
3 dessertspoons lemon juice
1 level tablespoon finely-grated English Cheddar cheese
Large pinch of garlic salt (optional)
$\frac{1}{4}$ level teaspoon salt
Shake of pepper

1. Put cottage cheese, French Dressing, lemon juice, Cheddar cheese and garlic salt (if used) into bowl. Beat with whisk until smooth. **2.** Season to taste with salt and pepper. **3.** Leave 15 minutes in cool before using. **4.** For an even smoother dressing, sieve cottage cheese first.

COTTAGE CHEESE & MINT DRESSING 575

For canned fruit; fresh fruit salads.

1 small carton ($\frac{1}{4}$ lb.) cottage cheese
2 to 3 level teaspoons mint jelly
Finely-grated peel and juice of 1 medium-sized lemon
3 tablespoons fresh orange juice

1. Rub cottage cheese through a fine sieve. **2.** Put into bowl. Beat in mint jelly, lemon peel and juice and orange juice. **3.** Chill before using.

MIXED CHEESE DRESSING 576

For green and mixed salads.

2 oz. Blue Stilton cheese
$\frac{1}{4}$ lb. cream cheese
4 level tablespoons very finely-grated English Cheddar cheese
$\frac{1}{2}$ garlic clove, finely chopped (optional)
5 tablespoons milk
$\frac{1}{4}$ level teaspoon salt
Good shake of pepper

1. Mash the Stilton and cream cheese together. Add Cheddar cheese and garlic (if used). **2.** Gradually beat in milk. Season to taste with salt and pepper.

125

577 MAYONNAISE

Yolks of 2 standard eggs
$\frac{1}{2}$ level teaspoon *each* dry mustard, salt and caster sugar
$\frac{1}{4}$ teaspoon Worcester sauce (optional)
Shake of pepper
$\frac{1}{2}$ pint salad oil
2 tablespoons vinegar or lemon juice
1 tablespoon boiling water

1. Put yolks, mustard, salt, sugar, Worcester sauce (if used) and pepper into a bowl. Beat until smooth. **2.** Beating more quickly, add $\frac{1}{4}$-pint oil, *a drop at a time,* and continue beating until Mayonnaise is very thick. **3.** Stir in 1 tablespoon vinegar or lemon juice. **4.** Beat in rest of oil gradually, about a dessertspoon at a time. **5.** When all the oil has been added, stir in last tablespoon of vinegar or lemon juice and the boiling water. (The water helps to prevent separation.) **6.** Adjust seasoning to taste. Transfer to covered container. Will keep in cool up to 2 weeks.

578 AIOLI MAYONNAISE

For all vegetable salads; salads with hard-boiled eggs, beef and lamb.

Add 1 very finely-chopped clove of garlic to Mayonnaise (No. 577) after stirring in the boiling water.

579 CAMILLA MAYONNAISE

For cold poultry, fish and egg salads.

Stir 1 carton (5 oz.) Soured Cream into Mayonnaise (No. 577) before stirring in the boiling water.

580 GREEN DRAGON MAYONNAISE

For all cold fish and shellfish dishes.

1. Mince finely 1 garlic clove, 3 anchovy fillets, 2 tablespoons chives and handful of parsley. **2.** Add to the Mayonnaise (No. 577) after stirring in boiling water. Blend in 1 dessertspoon tarragon vinegar and lemon juice and 1 carton (5 oz.) soured cream. **3.** Adjust salt and pepper to taste.

CHANTILLY MAYONNAISE 58

For cold poultry, fish and egg salads.

Stir $\frac{1}{4}$ pint fresh whipped double cream into Mayonnaise (No. 577) before stirring in the boiling water.

CURRY MAYONNAISE 58

For cold poultry and egg salads.

Add to Mayonnaise (No. 577) after stirring in the boiling water: 2 level teaspoons curry powder, 1 level teaspoon finely-grated onion, pinch of Cayenne pepper and 1 level tablespoon sweet pickle.

LOUIS MAYONNAISE 58

For cold shellfish and winter vegetable salads.

Add to Mayonnaise (No. 577) after stirring in boiling water: 3 tablespoons fresh double cream, 2 to 3 tablespoons bottled chilli sauce, 1 teaspoon Worcester sauce, finely-chopped $\frac{1}{2}$ small green pepper, 1 level tablespoon finely-grated onion and 3 dessertspoons lemon juice.

RÉMOULADE MAYONNAISE 58

For cold fish and shellfish dishes; cold meat and poultry dishes.

Add to Mayonnaise (No. 577) after stirring in boiling water: 2 level teaspoons made mustard, 1 level teaspoon finely-chopped parsley, 1 level tablespoon *each* finely-chopped gherkins and capers, 1 level teaspoon *each* fresh chervil and tarragon and 1 level teaspoon anchovy essence.

RUSSIAN MAYONNAISE 58

For green and mixed salads; cold shellfish and egg dishes.

Add to Mayonnaise (No. 577) after stirring in boiling water: 1 carton (5 oz.) soured cream, 1 dessertspoon bottled chilli sauce, 2 level tablespoons finely-chopped canned pimento, 1 teaspoon vinegar, 1 level teaspoon paprika and 1 large chopped hard-boiled egg.

86 THOUSAND ISLAND MAYONNAISE

For all green and egg salads.

Add to Mayonnaise (No. 577) after stirring in boiling water: 4 tablespoons fresh double cream, 1½ tablespoons tomato ketchup, 1½ level tablespoons bottled chilli sauce (or use all ketchup), 2 level tablespoons finely-chopped stuffed olives, 2 level teaspoons finely-grated onion, 1 level tablespoon finely-chopped green pepper, I finely-chopped small hard-boiled egg and 1 heaped tablespoon finely-chopped parsley.

87 SPANISH MAYONNAISE

For green and egg salads.

Add to Mayonnaise (No. 577) after stirring in boiling water: 2 level tablespoons tomato purée and 3 level tablespoons finely-chopped canned pimento.

88 SWEDISH MAYONNAISE

For cold pork, lamb and mutton dishes; cold sausage platters.

Add to Mayonnaise (No. 577) after stirring in boiling water: ¼ pint thick and unsweetened apple purée, 1 or 2 level teaspoons grated horseradish and 5 tablespoons soured cream.

89 TARTARE MAYONNAISE

For fried fish dishes.

Add to Mayonnaise (No. 577) after stirring in boiling water: 1 level tablespoon *each* finely-chopped capers and parsley and 2 tablespoons finely-chopped gherkins.

0 VERTE MAYONNAISE

For cold salmon and salmon trout.

1. Mince very finely a handful of parsley, 2 level tablespoons fresh tarragon and chives, 2 heaped tablespoons torn-up spinach leaves and 2 level tablespoons watercress. **2.** Add to Mayonnaise (No. 577) after stirring in boiling water.

1 TIVOLI MAYONNAISE

For poultry, tongue, ham, fish and egg salads.

Add 1 carton (5 oz.) natural yogurt to Mayonnaise (No. 577) before stirring in boiling water.

TOMATO YOGURT DRESSING 592

For all green and mixed salads.

1. Beat French Dressing (No. 598) into 1 can condensed tomato soup. **2.** Stir in 1 carton (5 oz.) natural yogurt, 1 teaspoon Worcester sauce and 2 level teaspoons finely-grated onion. **3.** Pour into screw-top jar and refrigerate. This dressing keeps up to 2 weeks but should be shaken well before using.

CREAMED ONION DRESSING 593

For all green and mixed salads; salads with poultry and eggs.

1. Gradually beat French Dressing (No. 598) into 3 to 4 oz. cream cheese. **2.** Add 1 level teaspoon finely-grated onion and 1 level tablespoon very finely-chopped parsley.

BUTTER DRESSING 594

For green and mixed salads; salads with poultry, turkey, fish or cheese.

2 oz. English or Welsh butter
2 standard eggs
1 carton (5 oz.) soured cream
3 tablespoons white vinegar
½ level teaspoon salt
Shake of pepper

1. Melt butter. Beat well with eggs and soured cream. **2.** Bring vinegar to boil and gradually beat into egg mixture. **3.** Pour into double saucepan (or basin standing over pan of gently simmering water). **4.** Cook, stirring, until mixture thickens. On no account allow to boil. **5.** Remove from heat. Season and chill before using.

WHIPPED CREAM DRESSING 595

For cold poultry, fish and egg salads.

¼ pint fresh double cream
2 tablespoons milk
3 teaspoons lemon juice or wine vinegar
¼ level teaspoon salt
Shake of Cayenne pepper

1. Beat milk and cream together until thick. **2.** Gradually stir in lemon juice or vinegar. **3.** Season to taste with salt and pepper.

Meringue

596 FLUFFY WHIPPED CREAM DRESSING

For cold poultry, fish and egg salads.

Follow recipe and method for Whipped Cream Dressing (No. 595). **2.** Fold in 1 stiffly-whisked egg white after seasoning with salt and pepper.

597 WHIPPED CREAM HORSERADISH DRESSING

For cold roast beef and salad.

1. Follow recipe and method for Whipped Cream Dressing (No. 595). **2.** Stir in 2 level tablespoons grated horseradish with the lemon juice or vinegar. **2.** Season to taste with salt, pepper and $\frac{1}{2}$ to 1 level teaspoon icing sugar.

598 FRENCH DRESSING

For all tossed salads.

4 tablespoons olive or corn oil or mixture
$\frac{1}{2}$ level teaspoon *each* **salt, icing or caster sugar and dry mustard**
$\frac{1}{4}$ teaspoon Worcester sauce
2 tablespoons vinegar (wine for preference) or lemon juice

1. Put oil, salt, sugar, mustard and Worcester sauce into a basin. **2.** Beat until smooth. **3.** Gradually beat in vinegar or lemon juice. Continue beating until dressing thickens.

599 BLUE STILTON DRESSING

For all green and mixed salads.

Gradually beat French Dressing (No. 598) into 1 or 2 oz. finely-mashed Blue Stilton.

600 RAVIGOTTE

For cold meat salads.

1. Add to French Dressing (No. 598): 1 level tablespoon finely-grated onion, 1 level dessertspoon finely-chopped capers, 1 heaped tablespoon finely-chopped parsley and $\frac{1}{2}$ level teaspoon *each* finely-chopped fresh chervil and tarragon. **2.** Mix well.

BASIC MERINGUES 60

Whites of 2 standard eggs
$\frac{1}{4}$ lb. caster sugar
Pinch of cream of tartar (optional)
1 oz. granulated sugar

1. Brush large baking tray with salad oil. Cover with double thickness of greaseproof paper. Brush paper lightly with more oil. **2.** Put egg whites into clean dry bowl. Add cream of tartar, if used. Beat until stiff and peaky. **3.** Add half the caster sugar. **4.** Continue beating until meringue is shiny and stands in firm peaks. **5.** Add rest of caster sugar. Beat until meringue is very stiff and silky-looking and texture is fairly close. **6.** Gently fold in granulated sugar. **7.** Pipe or spoon 16 rounds or ovals on to prepared tray. **8.** Bake in centre of very cool oven (225°F. or Gas No. $\frac{1}{4}$) for $1\frac{1}{2}$ hours. **9.** Remove from oven. Carefully peel away from paper and gently press a small hole in base of each with thumb. **10.** Stand upside down on baking tray. Return to oven and dry out for further $\frac{3}{4}$ to 1 hour. **11.** Transfer to wire cooling rack. **16 Meringue Halves.**

●*If flavoured meringues are preferred, add flavouring essence to taste.*
●*If preferred, leave in oven for total cooking time of $2\frac{1}{2}$ hours (or until meringues are crisp and firm).*

COFFEE MERINGUES 60

1. Follow recipe and method for Basic Meringues (No. 601). **2.** Add 2 level teaspoons instant coffee powder with granulated sugar. **3.** Sandwich together with whipped cream or Coffee Butter Cream Frosting (No. 815). **8 Filled Meringues.**

HAZELNUT MERINGUES 60

1. Follow recipe and method for Basic Meringues (No. 601). **2.** Add 2 oz. very finely-chopped hazelnuts with granulated sugar. **3.** Sandwich together with Chocolate Butter Cream Frosting (No. 816). **8 Filled Meringues.**

ALMOND COFFEE KISSES 60

1. Follow recipe and method for Basic Meringues (No. 601). **2.** Add 2 oz. ground almonds with granulated sugar. **3.** Sandwich together with Coffee Butter Cream Frosting (No. 815). **8 Filled Coffee Kisses.**

05 LEMON OR ORANGE MERINGUES

1. Follow recipe and method for Basic Meringues (No. 601). **2.** Add $\frac{1}{2}$ level teaspoon very finely-grated lemon or orange peel with granulated sugar. **4.** Sandwich together with whipped cream or Lemon Butter Cream Frosting (No. 812) or Orange Butter Cream Frosting (No. 813). **8 Filled Meringues.**

06 CREAM MERINGUES

1. Follow recipe and method for Basic Meringues (No. 601). **2.** Sandwich together, in pairs, with $\frac{1}{4}$ pint fresh double cream, beaten until thick with tablespoon of milk. **8 Filled Meringues.**

07 CHOCOLATE CREAM MERINGUES

1. Follow recipe and method for Basic Meringues (No. 601). **2.** Add $1\frac{1}{2}$ level teaspoons chocolate-flavoured blancmange powder with granulated sugar. **3.** Sandwich together with whipped cream. **8 Filled Meringues.**

●*If preferred, omit chocolate blancmange powder. Add 1 oz. grated plain chocolate with granulated sugar.*

08 RASPBERRY OR STRAWBERRY CREAM MERINGUES

1. Follow recipe and method for Basic Meringues (No. 601). **2.** Flavour with raspberry or strawberry culinary flavouring or add $1\frac{1}{2}$ level teaspoons raspberry or strawberry blancmange powder with the granulated sugar. **3.** Sandwich together with whipped cream. **8 Filled Meringues.**

09 WALNUT CHOCOLATE FINGERS

1. Follow recipe and method for Basic Meringues (No. 601). **2.** Add 2 oz. very finely-chopped shelled walnut halves with granulated sugar. **3.** Pipe 20 × 3-in. lengths of mixture on to baking tray. **3.** Sandwich together with Chocolate Butter Cream Frosting (No. 816). **10 Filled Fingers.**

MERINGUE TOPPING   610

Whites of 2 standard eggs
2 to 3 oz. caster sugar
1 level tablespoon granulated sugar

1. Put egg whites into clean dry bowl. Beat until stiff and peaky (when bowl is turned upside down the whites should stay where they are). **2.** Gently fold in caster sugar with large metal spoon. **3.** Pile meringue over pie or pudding, etc., and sprinkle with granulated sugar.

BAKING

●*Quick cooking is essential if meringue is used as decoration on frozen or chilled desserts; therefore 'flash' bake dish towards top of hot oven (450°F. or Gas No. 8) until meringue just starts turning gold. (About 1 to 3 minutes but no longer).*

●*If meringue is on a pudding or pie that is made to be served cold later, it is important to dry out the meringue thoroughly, otherwise it will sag on standing and become wet and syrupy; therefore put dish into centre of very cool oven (225°F. or Gas No. $\frac{1}{4}$) and bake for $1\frac{1}{2}$ to 2 hours (or until meringue is firm, crisp and golden).*

●*For a hot pudding topped with meringue, bake in centre of cool oven (300°F. or Gas No. 2) for 20 to 30 minutes (or until pale gold).*

FRUIT & CREAM PAVLOVAS   611

1 recipe Basic Meringues (No. 601)
$\frac{1}{4}$ pint fresh double cream
1 tablespoon milk
Fresh or canned fruit

1. Cover 2 oiled baking trays with double thickness of greaseproof paper. Outline 3 × 3-in. rounds on each. **2.** Brush with oil. Cover each round with Meringue mixture, about $\frac{1}{4}$ in. thick. **3.** Put into centre of cool oven (275°F. or Gas No. 1) and bake for 35 to 45 minutes (or until Pavlovas are pale gold and crisp looking). Insides should be fairly soft. **4.** Carefully peel away from paper. Cool on wire rack. **5.** Before serving, whip cream and milk together until stiff. **6.** Spread two-thirds over Pavlovas. **7.** Cover with fresh raspberries, halved strawberries or well-drained canned mandarins or peach slices. **8.** Top each with a whirl of cream and serve straight away. **Serves 6.**

Cream Meringues (No. 606)

612 COCONUT PYRAMIDS

Whites of 2 standard eggs
5 oz. caster sugar
6 oz. desiccated coconut
10 glacé cherries, halved

1. Line 1 or 2 unbuttered baking trays with rice paper. **2.** Beat egg whites to stiff snow. **3.** Stir in sugar and coconut. Mix well. **4.** Place about 20 to 24 mounds of mixture on to trays. Shape into pyramids with fork. **5.** Bake in centre of cool oven (300°F. or Gas No. 2) for 20 minutes. Put half a cherry on top of each. **6.** Return to oven. Bake until pale gold (15 to 20 minutes). **7.** Remove from trays. **8.** Trim away surplus rice paper. **9.** Cool on wire rack. **10.** Store in airtight tin when cold. **20 to 24 Pyramids.**

GOLDEN COCONUT PYRAMIDS
6

2 standard eggs
½ lb. desiccated coconut
5 oz. caster sugar

1. Line 1 or 2 unbuttered baking trays with rice paper. **2.** Beat eggs well. Stir in coconut and sugar. **3.** Leave to stand for 20 minutes. **4.** Dip hands in cold water. Shape mixture into about 2 dozen Pyramids. **5.** Place on tray or trays. **6.** Put into centre of moderate oven (350°F. or Gas No. 4). Bake until pale gold (about 25 to 30 minutes). **7.** Remove Pyramids from trays and trim away surplus rice paper. **8.** Cool on wire rack. **9.** Store in airtight tin when cold. **About 24 Pyramids.**

613 MERINGUE BASKET

1 recipe Basic Meringues (No. 601)

1. Make up Meringue mixture as directed for Basic Meringues (No. 601). **2.** Lightly oil baking tray. Cover with 4 thicknesses of greaseproof paper. **3.** Outline 8-in. round on centre of paper, using cake tin or plate as guide. Brush lightly with oil. **4.** Spread Meringue mixture thickly over oiled round. **5.** Make shallow sides by spooning or piping small mounds of mixture all the way round edge. **6.** Put into centre of very cool oven (225°F. or Gas No. ¼). Bake until Basket is firm and set (2½ to 3 hours). **7.** Carefully peel away from paper. Stand upside down on baking tray. **8.** Return to oven for further 45 minutes to dry out thoroughly. **9.** Fill when cold (see Cold Desserts Section). **Serves 6.**

Batters

615 PANCAKE BATTER

¼ lb. plain or self-raising flour
Large pinch salt
1 standard egg
½ pint milk
1 tablespoon melted English or Welsh
butter

1. Sift flour and salt into bowl. **2.** Beat to smooth creamy batter with unbeaten egg, half the milk and melted butter. **3.** Stir in remaining milk and use as required.

● *It has for many years been accepted that batter is improved by standing; but modern research has shown that this is not so. Long beating of batter is unnecessary. The batter will rise satisfactorily if the egg and the first half of the milk are beaten in briskly for a short time.*

PANCAKES 616

Melted butter for frying
1 recipe Pancake Batter (No.615)

1. Lightly brush base of 8 or 9-in. frying pan with melted butter. Stand over medium heat. **2.** When pan and butter are hot, pour in 2 or 3 tablespoons of batter mixture (just enough to coat base of pan thinly and evenly). **3.** Fry until golden brown. Turn over with fish slice or spatula, or toss. **4.** Cook second side until golden and mottled. **5.** Repeat with rest of batter mixture. **8 Pancakes.**

● *To keep Pancakes warm as they are being made, stack one on top of the other on large plate. Stand over pan of gently-simmering water. Cover with large lid or second plate.*

● *To store cooked Pancakes, stack in airtight tin with greaseproof paper between each. Leave in a cold larder or refrigerator for 1 or 2 days. To re-heat, fry about ½ minute per side in pan lightly brushed with butter.*

SWEET PANCAKES

617 LEMON & APRICOT PANCAKES

1. Make Pancakes (No. 616). **2.** Spread with 5 or 6 tablespoons apricot jam, melted and warmed with 1 or 2 tablespoons lemon juice and 1 level teaspoon finely-grated lemon peel. **3.** Roll up. **Serves 4.**

618 SPICED APPLE PANCAKES

1. Make Pancakes (No.616). **2.** Spread with hot thick apple purée (made from about 1 lb. apples), flavoured with cinnamon and sweetened to taste with sugar. **3.** Roll up. **4.** Top each with dessertspoon of fresh double cream. **Serves 4.**

619 BANANA CREAM PANCAKES

1. Make Pancakes (No. 616). **2.** Spread with 4 large mashed bananas, combined with ¼ pint lightly-whipped fresh double cream, ½ level teaspoon nutmeg and sifted icing sugar to taste. **3.** Roll up. **Serves 4.**

LEMON OR ORANGE PANCAKES 620

1. Make Pancakes (No. 616). **2.** Sprinkle with caster sugar and either lemon or orange juice. **3.** Roll up by sliding nearest edge of Pancake between prongs of fork and turning fork over and over. **4.** Remove fork. Serve Pancakes as soon as possible after rolling. **5.** Accompany with wedges of lemon or orange. **Serves 4.**

RASPBERRY OR STRAWBERRY PANCAKES 621

1. Make Pancakes (No. 616). **2.** Spread with 5 or 6 tablespoons melted and warmed raspberry or strawberry jam. **3.** Roll up. **Serves 4.**

GOLDEN SYRUP & ORANGE PANCAKES 622

1. Make Pancakes (No. 616). **2.** Spread with 5 or 6 tablespoons golden syrup, melted and warmed, with 1 level teaspoon finely-grated orange peel. **3.** Roll up. **Serves 4.**

623 MANDARIN CREAM PANCAKES

1. Make Pancakes (No. 616). **2.** Spread with can of mandarin oranges (well drained), combined with $\frac{1}{4}$ pint stiffly-whipped fresh double cream. **3.** Roll up. **4.** Accompany with syrup from can of mandarins warmed through with 1 or 2 tablespoons sherry. **Serves 4.**

624 COTTAGE CHEESE & PINEAPPLE PANCAKES

1. Make Pancakes (No. 616). **2.** Spread with $\frac{1}{2}$ lb. cottage cheese combined with 4 or 5 tablespoons canned, drained and chopped pineapple and caster or sifted icing sugar to taste. **3.** Roll up. **4.** Sprinkle each with sifted icing sugar. **Serves 4.**

625 COCONUT & APRICOT PANCAKES

1. Make up Pancake Batter (No. 615). **2.** Stir in 2 level tablespoons desiccated coconut before making Pancakes (No. 616). **3.** Spread evenly with 3 or 4 tablespoons melted apricot jam. **4.** Fill with canned drained apricot halves. **5.** Roll up. **6.** Dust evenly with caster or sifted icing sugar. **7.** Top each with heaped tablespoon stiffly-whipped fresh double cream. **Serves 4.**

626 PARTY LAYER PANCAKES

6 tablespoons apricot jam
1 tablespoon lemon juice
8 freshly made Pancakes (No. 616)
1 recipe Meringue Topping (No. 610)
8 halved glacé cherries

1. Put jam and lemon juice into saucepan. Stand over low heat until warm. **2.** Place first Pancake on large heatproof plate. **3.** Spread with jam and lemon juice. Add second Pancake. Spread with more jam and lemon juice. **4.** Repeat with rest of Pancakes. **5.** Swirl Meringue mixture over the top. **6.** Stud with halved cherries. **7.** Flash bake in hot oven (450°F. or Gas No. 8) for 1 or 2 minutes (or until pale gold). **8.** Cut into wedges like a cake. Serve straight away. **Serves 8.**

COTTAGE CHEESE BLINTZES 627

1 recipe Pancake Batter (No. 615)
$\frac{3}{4}$ lb. cottage cheese
Yolk of 1 standard egg
4 level tablespoons caster sugar
1 teaspoon vanilla essence
About 2 oz. English or Welsh butter
1 level teaspoon cinnamon
1 carton (5 oz.) soured cream or natural yogurt

1. Cook 8 Pancakes on *one side only*. Turn out on to clean tea-towel. **2.** Mix cottage cheese well together with egg yolk, 2 tablespoons caster sugar and vanilla. **3.** Put equal amounts on to centres of *cooked* sides of Pancakes. **4.** Fold edges of Pancakes over filling, envelope style. **5.** Melt butter in large pan. Leave until hot and sizzling. **6.** Put in 4 Blintzes, with joins underneath. Fry on both sides until golden. **7.** Remove from pan. Drain on kitchen paper. Keep hot. **8.** Add more butter to pan if necessary. Fry remaining Blintzes until golden. **9.** Sprinkle with sugar and cinnamon. **10.** Serve straight away. **11.** Pass soured cream or yogurt separately. **Serves 4.**

COTTAGE CHEESE & RAISIN BLINTZES 62

1. Follow recipe and method for Cottage Cheese Blintzes (No. 627). **2.** Omit vanilla. **3.** Add 2 to 3 oz. seedless raisins and 1 level teaspoon finely-grated lemon or orange peel to cottage cheese with yolk and sugar. **Serves 4.**

COTTAGE CHEESE & STRAWBERRY BLINTZES 62

1. Follow recipe and method for Cottage Cheese Blintzes (No. 627). **2.** Instead of sprinkling fried Blintzes with sugar and cinnamon, arrange on warm serving platter and cover with 5 or 6 tablespoons melted and warmed strawberry jam. **Serves 4.**

630 COTTAGE CHEESE & BANANA BLINTZES

1. Follow recipe and method for Cottage Cheese Blintzes (No. 627). **2.** Add 3 medium-sized, mashed bananas to cottage cheese with yolk, sugar and vanilla. **Serves 4.**

631 COTTAGE CHEESE & PEACH BLINTZES

1. Follow recipe and method for Cottage Cheese Blintzes (No. 627). **2.** Add 4 or 5 heaped tablespoons canned peach slices (well drained) to cottage cheese with yolk and sugar. **Serves 4.**

632 CRÊPES SUZETTES

8 cooked Pancakes (No. 616)
$\frac{1}{4}$ lb. English or Welsh butter
1 oz. caster sugar
$\frac{1}{2}$ level teaspoon finely-grated lemon peel
$\frac{1}{2}$ level teaspoon finely-grated orange peel
4 tablespoons Cointreau, Curaçao or
   Grand Marnier
2 tablespoons brandy

1. Fold Pancakes like envelopes. **2.** Melt butter in pan. Add sugar, lemon and orange peel, and Cointreau, Curaçao or Grand Marnier. **3.** Bring to boil. Add Pancakes. **4.** Heat through, turning twice. **5.** Pour Brandy into pan. Put lighted match to sauce and allow it to flame. **6.** Serve Pancakes as soon as flames have subsided. **Serves 4.**

633 MOCK CRÊPES SUZETTES

8 cooked Pancakes (No. 616)
2 oz. English or Welsh butter
2 oz. caster sugar
Finely-grated peel and juice of 1 large
   orange
3 tablespoons sweet sherry or white wine

1. Fold Pancakes like envelopes. **2.** Melt butter in pan. Add sugar, orange peel and juice and sherry, or wine. **3.** Bring to boil. Add Pancakes. **4.** Heat through, turning twice. **5.** Serve straight away. **Serves 4.**

SAVOURY PANCAKES

BRITTANY PANCAKES 634

1. Make Pancakes (No. 616). **2.** Stuff with $\frac{1}{2}$ lb. cooked minced beef moistened with 1 or 2 tablespoons Gravy (No. 147), 1 tablespoon tomato ketchup and dash of Worcester sauce. **3.** Roll up. Arrange in heatproof dish. **4.** Coat with 1 can (10$\frac{1}{2}$-oz.) condensed cream soup (flavour to taste). **5.** Re-heat in centre of moderate oven (350°F. or Gas No. 4) for 20 minutes. **Serves 4.**

COUNTRY PANCAKES 635

1. Make Pancakes (No. 616). **2.** Fry $\frac{1}{4}$ lb. chopped mushrooms and stalks and 4 large skinned and chopped tomatoes in 1 oz. English or Welsh butter. Use to stuff Pancakes. **3.** Roll up. Arrange in heatproof dish. **4.** Coat with $\frac{1}{2}$ pint Cheese Coating Sauce (No. 116) combined with 1 carton (5 oz.) natural yogurt. **5.** Sprinkle with 1 oz. crumbled Lancashire cheese. Brown under hot grill. **6.** Serve straight away. **Serves 4.**

CREAMED SMOKED HADDOCK PANCAKES 636

1. Make Pancakes (No. 616). **2.** Combine 1 lb. flaked smoked haddock (cooked in milk) with 1 carton (5 oz.) soured cream or $\frac{1}{4}$ pint fresh double cream. Use to stuff Pancakes. **3.** Roll up. Arrange in heatproof dish. **4.** Coat with freshly-made Mock Hollandaise Sauce (No. 124). Sprinkle with 1 oz. crumbled Lancashire cheese. **5.** Brown under hot grill. **6.** Garnish with parsley and lemon wedges. **Serves 4.**

CREAMED CHICKEN PANCAKES 637

1. Make Pancakes (No. 616). **2.** Combine $\frac{3}{4}$ lb. cooked minced chicken with $\frac{1}{2}$ pint Béchamel Sauce (No. 110). **3.** Add 2 tablespoons dry sherry or white wine. Season well. Use to stuff Pancakes. **4.** Roll up. Transfer to heatproof dish. **5.** Coat with 2 oz. melted butter mixed with 2 tablespoons dry sherry or white wine. Cover dish with lid or aluminium foil. **6.** Re-heat just above centre of fairly hot oven (375°F. or Gas No. 5) for 15 to 20 minutes. **Serves 4.**

638 KIDNEY PANCAKES

1. Make Pancakes (No. 616). **2.** Fill with $\frac{3}{4}$ lb. cooked, chopped kidney, combined with $\frac{1}{4}$ pint Brown Sauce (No. 130). **3.** Roll up. Serve straight away. **Serves 4.**

639 MINIATURE PARTY PANCAKES

1. Follow recipe and method for Pancakes (No. 616) but pour only 1 tablespoon batter, for each Pancake, into lightly-buttered and heated small frying pan. **2.** Fry on both sides. **3.** Stack on clean tea-towel. Spread with cottage cheese. **4.** Roll up. Spear on to cocktail sticks. **About 25 pancakes.**

640 PARTY PANCAKE KEBABS

1. Make 25 Miniature Party Pancakes (No. 639). **2.** Wrap round cooked cocktail sausages, sections of grilled tomatoes, rolls of grilled bacon, whole grilled mushrooms and pieces of cooked kidney. **3.** Spear on to cocktail sticks. If liked, sticks can be pressed into a grapefruit or small green cabbage. **25 Kebabs.**

641 YORKSHIRE PUDDING

2 oz. English or Welsh butter or meat dripping
1 recipe Pancake Batter (No. 615)

1. Pre-heat oven to hot (425°F. or Gas No. 7). **2.** Put butter or dripping (or use mixture of both) into 10-in. × 12-in. baking tin. Heat in oven until faint haze just appears. **3.** Pour in batter. **4.** Bake just above centre of oven 30 minutes. **5.** Reduce temperature to fairly hot (400°F. or Gas No. 6). **6.** Bake for further 15 to 20 minutes. **Serves 6 to 8.**

642 SMALL YORKSHIRE PUDDING

1. Follow recipe and method for Yorkshire Pudding (No. 641). **2.** Use half quantity of Pancake Batter. **3.** Pour into 9-in. × 7-in. baking tin. **4.** Bake for same length of time as large Pudding. **Serves 3 to 4.**

PRAWN & LEMON PANCAKES — 64

1. Make Pancakes (No. 616). **2.** Fill with $\frac{1}{2}$ lb. peeled prawns, combined with $\frac{1}{4}$ pint Basic White Coating Sauce (No. 106). **3.** Roll up. Arrange in heatproof dish. **4.** Coat with Black Butter Sauce (No. 149). Cover with lid or aluminium foil. **5.** Re-heat in centre of moderate oven (350°F. or Gas No. 4) for 20 minutes. **6.** Garnish with lemon wedges. **Serves 4.**

HAM & CHEESE PANCAKES — 64

1. Make Pancakes (No. 616). **2.** Stuff with $\frac{1}{2}$ lb. chopped lean ham, combined with $\frac{1}{4}$ pint Mornay Sauce (No. 123). **3.** Roll up. Arrange in heatproof dish. **4.** Top each with pat of Devilled Butter (No. 186). Cover with lid or aluminium foil. **5.** Re-heat in centre of moderate oven (350°F. or Gas No. 4) for 20 minutes. **Serves 4.**

BACON & PARSLEY PANCAKES — 64

1. Make Pancakes (No. 616). **2.** Stuff with $\frac{3}{4}$ lb. chopped fried bacon combined with $\frac{1}{4}$ pint Parsley Coating Sauce (No. 107). **3.** Roll up. Arrange in heatproof dish. **4.** Top each with pat of Mustard Butter (No. 199). Cover with lid or aluminium foil. **5.** Re-heat in centre of moderate oven (350°F. or Gas No. 4) for 20 minutes **Serves 4.**

TUNA & CUCUMBER PANCAKES — 64

1. Make Pancakes (No. 616). **2.** Fill with 1 can (7 oz.) drained tuna, finely mashed with 4 tablespoons natural yogurt. **3.** Roll up. Arrange in heatproof dish. **4.** Coat with $\frac{1}{2}$ pint Cucumber Coating Sauce (No. 121). Sprinkle lightly with toasted breadcrumbs. **5.** Re-heat in centre of moderate oven (350°F. or Gas No. 4) for 20 minutes. **Serves 4.**

Right: Crêpes Suzettes (No. 632)

647 AMERICAN PANCAKES

1. Make Pancakes (No. 616). **2.** Stuff with hot, grilled bacon rashers, allowing 2 rashers per Pancake. **3.** Roll up. **4.** Top each with half a canned pineapple ring and sprig of watercress. **Serves 4.**

648 TOREADOR PANCAKES

1. Make Pancakes (No. 616). **2.** Chop 1 small onion. Fry in 1 oz. English or Welsh butter until golden. **3.** Add $\frac{1}{2}$ lb. chopped corned beef. Fry further 2 minutes. Use to stuff Pancakes. **4.** Roll up. Arrange in heatproof dish. **5.** Coat with 1 can condensed tomato soup. Sprinkle with crushed potato crisps or toasted breadcrumbs. **6.** Re-heat in centre of fairly hot oven (375°F. or Gas No. 5) for 15 to 20 minutes. **Serves 4.**

SAVOURY BATTER PUDDINGS

649 CORNED BEEF BATTER PUDDING

1. Follow recipe and method for Yorkshire Pudding (No. 641). **2.** After pouring batter into tin add $\frac{1}{2}$ to $\frac{3}{4}$ lb. corned beef, cut into 1-in. cubes. **3.** Bake as for Yorkshire Pudding. **Serves 4 to 6.**

650 BACON BATTER PUDDING

1. Follow recipe and method for Yorkshire Pudding (No. 641). **2.** After pouring batter into tin add $\frac{1}{2}$ to $\frac{3}{4}$ lb. chopped lean bacon. **3.** Bake as for Yorkshire Pudding. **Serves 4 to 6.**

651 MEAT BALL BATTER PUDDING

1. Follow recipe and method for Yorkshire Pudding (No. 641). **2.** After pouring batter into tin add 1 lb. lean minced beef, well seasoned and shaped into small balls. **3.** Bake as for Yorkshire Pudding. **Serves 4 to 6.**

TOAD-IN-THE-HOLE 65

1. Arrange 1 lb. pork sausages in 10-in. × 12-in. baking tin. **2.** Bake just above centre of hot oven (425°F. or Gas No. 7) for 10 minutes. **3.** Remove from oven. Pour in 1 recipe Pancake Batter (No. 615). **4.** Bake as for Yorkshire Pudding. **Serves 4 to 6.**

● *Most sausages can be cooked in their own fat. Other sausages however—especially thin or skinless ones—might need the addition of 1 to 2 oz. butter.*

SWEET BATTER PUDDINGS

APPLE BATTER PUDDING 65

1. Follow recipe and method for Yorkshire Pudding (No. 641). **2.** Add 1 lb. peeled, cored and thickly-sliced apples to hot butter in tin. **3.** Sprinkle with $\frac{1}{4}$ lb. caster sugar and 1 level teaspoon cinnamon. **4.** Pour in Pancake Batter. **5.** Bake as for Yorkshire Pudding. **Serves 4 to 6.**

RHUBARB BATTER PUDDING 65

1. Follow recipe and method for Yorkshire Pudding (No. 641). **2.** Add 1 lb. rhubarb, cut into 1-in. lengths, to hot butter in tin. **3.** Sprinkle with $\frac{1}{4}$ lb. caster sugar and 1 level teaspoon powdered ginger. **4.** Pour in Pancake Batter. **5.** Bake as for Yorkshire Pudding. **Serves 4 to 6.**

DRIED FRUIT BATTER PUDDING 65

1. Follow recipe and method for Yorkshire Pudding (No. 641). **2.** Add $\frac{1}{4}$ lb. mixed dried fruit to hot butter in tin. **3.** Sprinkle with 2 oz. caster sugar and 1 level teaspoon finely-grated lemon peel. **4.** Pour in Pancake Batter. **5.** Bake as for Yorkshire Pudding. **Serves 4 to 6.**

656 PLUM BATTER PUDDING

1. Follow recipe and method for Yorkshire Pudding (No. 641). **2.** Add 1 lb. halved and stoned cooking plums to hot butter in tin. **3.** Sprinkle with $\frac{1}{4}$ lb. caster sugar and 1 level teaspoon mixed spice. **4.** Pour in Pancake Batter. **5.** Bake as for Yorkshire Pudding. **Serves 4 to 6.**

657 POPOVERS

2 oz. plain flour
Pinch of salt
1 small egg
$\frac{1}{4}$ pint milk
$1\frac{1}{2}$ oz. English or Welsh melted butter

1. Pre-heat oven to hot (425°F. or Gas No. 7). **2.** Sift flour and salt into bowl. Beat to smooth creamy batter with unbeaten egg and milk. **3.** Pour a little melted butter into 12 deep bun tins. **4.** Heat in oven for 3 minutes. Spoon about 1 tablespoon batter into each. **5.** Bake for 20 minutes. **6.** Serve hot with any roast joint or with bacon or gammon. **Serves 4.**

658 FRUIT POPOVERS

1. Follow recipe and method for Popovers (No. 657). **2.** Add 6 level teaspoons currants to hot butter in tins before spooning in batter. **3.** Bake as for Popovers. Serve hot with syrup or honey and English or Welsh butter. **Serves 4.**

COATING & FRITTER BATTERS

659 COATING BATTER

For coating fish, meat and vegetables.

$\frac{1}{4}$ lb. plain or self-raising flour
$\frac{1}{4}$ level teaspoon salt
1 standard egg
1 tablespoon melted English or Welsh butter
$\frac{1}{4}$ pint milk

1. Sift flour and salt into bowl. **2.** Beat to smooth creamy batter with unbeaten egg, butter and milk. Use as required.

SWEET FRITTER BATTER 660

For coating fruit such as bananas and pineapple.

2 oz. plain flour
Pinch of salt
1 level teaspoon sifted icing sugar
4 tablespoons lukewarm water
1 dessertspoon melted English or Welsh butter
White of 1 standard egg

1. Sift flour and salt into bowl. Add sugar. **2.** Gradually mix to thick smooth batter with water and butter. **3.** Whisk egg white to stiff snow. **4.** Fold into flour mixture. Use as required.

CINNAMON FRITTER BATTER 661

1. Follow recipe and method for Sweet Fritter Batter (No. 660). **2.** Sift $\frac{1}{2}$ level teaspoon cinnamon with flour and salt.

ALMOND FRITTER BATTER 662

1. Follow recipe and method for Sweet Fritter Batter (No. 660). **2.** Add $\frac{1}{2}$ teaspoon almond essence with water and butter.

ORANGE OR LEMON FRITTER BATTER 663

1. Follow recipe and method for Sweet Fritter Batter (No. 660). **2.** Add $\frac{1}{2}$ level teaspoon finely-grated orange or lemon peel with water and butter.

SPICY FRITTER BATTER 664

1. Follow recipe and method for Sweet Fritter Batter (No. 660). **2.** Sift $\frac{1}{2}$ level teaspoon mixed spice with flour and salt.

665 SAVOURY FRITTER BATTER

For coating fish, meat, poultry and vegetables.

¼ lb. plain flour
½ level teaspoon salt
Shake of pepper
¼ pint lukewarm water
1 tablespoon melted English or Welsh
  butter
Whites of 2 standard eggs

1. Sift flour and salt into bowl. Add pepper.
2. Gradually mix to thick smooth batter with
water and butter. **3.** Whisk egg whites to stiff
snow. **4.** Fold into flour mixture. Use as required.

MUSTARD FRITTER BATTER 6

1. Follow recipe and method for Savoury Fritter
Batter (No. 665). **2.** Sift 1 level teaspoon dry
mustard with flour and salt.

CURRY FRITTER BATTER 6

1. Follow recipe and method for Savoury Fritter
Batter (No. 665). **2.** Sift 3 level teaspoons curry
powder with flour and salt.

Toreador Pancakes (No. 648)

Sugar & Spice Rings (No. 668)

Scone Mixtures

Freshly-baked scones should be pulled gently apart with fingers. Cutting spoils the texture and makes them doughy. As scones stale quickly it is preferable to make and eat them on the same day.

668 SUGAR & SPICE RINGS

½ lb. self-raising flour
¼ level teaspoon salt
1½ oz. English or Welsh butter
¼ pint milk
FILLING
1 oz. English or Welsh butter, melted
2 oz. caster sugar
1 level teaspoon cinnamon
1½ oz. currants

1. Sift flour and salt into bowl. **2.** Rub in butter finely. **3.** Add milk all at once. Mix to soft, but not sticky, dough with knife. **4.** Turn on to lightly-floured board. Knead quickly until smooth then roll into rectangle approximately 8 in. × 12 in. **5.** Brush with butter to within ½ in. of edges. **6.** Mix sugar with cinnamon and currants then sprinkle over butter. **7.** Moisten edges of dough lightly with water. Roll up like a Swiss roll, starting from one of the longer sides. **8.** Cut into 12 slices. Arrange, cut sides down, in 8-in., well-buttered round cake tin or fairly deep sandwich tin. **9.** Bake towards top of hot oven (425°F. or Gas No. 7) for 15 to 20 minutes (or until well risen and golden). **10.** Turn out on to wire cooling rack. Leave until lukewarm. **11.** Gently pull apart to separate rings. Serve as they are or with extra butter. **Serves 4 to 6.**

ALL-PURPOSE SCONES   669

½ lb. self-raising flour
¼ level teaspoon salt
2 oz. English or Welsh butter
¼ pint milk
Extra milk for brushing

1. Sift flour and salt into bowl. **2.** Rub in butter finely. **3.** Add milk all at once. Mix to soft, but not sticky, dough with knife. **4.** Turn on to lightly-floured board. Knead quickly until smooth. **5.** Roll out to about ½-in. thickness. **6.** Cut into 9 or 10 rounds with 2½-in. biscuit cutter. **7.** Transfer to buttered baking tray. Brush tops with milk. **8.** Bake towards top of hot oven (450°F. or Gas No. 8) for 7 to 10 minutes (or until well risen and golden brown). **9.** Cool on wire rack. Serve with butter or whipped cream and jam, or butter and cheese. **9 to 10 Scones.**

CHEESE SCONES   670

1. Follow recipe and method for All-Purpose Scones (No. 669). **2.** Sift 1 level teaspoon dry mustard and pinch of Cayenne pepper with flour and salt. **3.** Mix in 2 oz. very finely-grated English Cheddar cheese before adding milk. **9 to 10 Scones.**

671 HAM & PARSLEY SCONES

1. Follow recipe and method for All-Purpose Scones (No. 669). **2.** Sift ½ level teaspoon dry mustard with flour and salt. **3.** Mix in 1 oz. very finely-chopped ham and 1 level tablespoon very finely-chopped parsley before adding milk. **9 to 10 Scones.**

672 TEA SCONES

½ lb. self-raising flour
½ level teaspoon salt
2 oz. English or Welsh butter
1 oz. caster sugar
¼ pint milk
Extra milk for brushing

1. Sift flour and salt into bowl. **2.** Rub in butter finely. **3.** Add sugar. **4.** Add milk all at once. Mix to soft, but not sticky, dough with knife. **5.** Turn out on to lightly-floured board. Knead quickly until smooth. **6.** Roll out to about ½-in. thickness. Cut into 16 to 18 rounds with 1¾ to 2-in. fluted biscuit cutter. **7.** Transfer to buttered baking tray. Brush tops with milk. **8.** Bake towards top of hot oven (450°F. or Gas No. 8) for 7 to 10 minutes (or until well risen and golden). **9.** Cool on wire rack. **10.** Serve fresh with butter and whipped fresh double cream or clotted cream and jam. **16 to 18 Scones.**

673 SULTANA SCONES

1. Follow recipe and method for Tea Scones (No. 672). **2.** Add 1 to 2 oz. sultanas with sugar. **16 to 18 Scones.**

674 CURRANT SCONES

1. Follow recipe and method for Tea Scones (No. 672). **2.** Add 1 to 2 oz. currants with sugar. **16 to 18 Scones.**

675 DATE & WALNUT SCONES

1. Follow recipe and method for Tea Scones (No. 672). **2.** Add 1 oz. very finely-chopped dates and ½ oz. very finely-chopped shelled walnut halves with sugar. **16 to 18 Scones.**

SPICE SCONES 6

1. Follow recipe and method for Tea Scones (No. 672). **2.** Sift 1 level teaspoon mixed spice with flour and salt. **3.** Use 1 oz. soft brown sugar instead of caster. **4.** Serve warm. **16 to 18 Scones.**

LEMON & RAISIN SCONES 6

1. Follow recipe and method for Tea Scones (No. 672). **2.** Add ½ level teaspoon finely-grated lemon peel and 2 oz. seedless raisins with sugar. **16 to 18 Scones.**

ORANGE & CHERRY SCONES 6

1. Follow recipe and method for Tea Scones (No. 672). **2.** Add ½ level teaspoon finely-grated orange peel and 1½ oz. finely-chopped glacé cherries (which should be well washed and dried first). with sugar. **16 to 18 Scones.**

CINNAMON SCONES 6

1. Follow recipe and method for Tea Scones (No. 672). **2.** Sift 1 level teaspoon cinnamon with flour and salt. **16 to 18 Scones.**

SYRUP OR HONEY SCONES 6

1. Follow recipe and method for Tea Scones (No. 672). **2.** Mix to dough with 1 level tablespoon golden syrup or clear honey (slightly warmed) and 7 tablespoons milk. **3.** Serve warm. **16 to 18 Scones.**

SYRUP OR GINGER SCONES 6

1. Follow recipe and method for Syrup Scones (No. 680). **2.** Sift ½ level teaspoon ground ginger with flour and salt. **3.** Serve warm. **16 to 18 Scones.**

682 SOURED CREAM SCONES

½ lb. self-raising flour
½ level teaspoon salt
1½ oz. English or Welsh butter
4 tablespoons soured cream
4 tablespoons milk
Extra milk for brushing

1. Sift flour and salt into bowl. **2.** Rub in butter finely. **3.** Add cream and milk all at once. Mix to soft, but not sticky, dough with knife. **4.** Turn out on to lightly-floured board. Knead quickly until smooth. **5.** Roll out to about ½-in. thickness. **6.** Cut into 9 or 10 rounds with 2½-in. biscuit cutter. **7.** Transfer to buttered baking tray. Brush tops with milk. **8.** Bake towards top of hot oven (450°F. of Gas No. 8) for 7 to 10 minutes (or until well risen and golden brown). **9.** Cool on wire rack. Serve with butter and jam. **9 to 10 Scones.**

683 YOGURT SCONES

1. Follow recipe and method for Soured Cream Scones (No. 682). **2.** Use 4 tablespoons natural yogurt instead of soured cream. **9 to 10 Scones.**

684 BUTTERMILK SCONES

1. Follow recipe and method for Soured Cream Scones (No. 682). **2.** Use ¼ pint buttermilk instead of soured cream and milk. **9 to 10 Scones.**

685 DROPPED SCONES

½ lb. self-raising flour
¼ level teaspoon salt
1 level tablespoon caster sugar
1 standard egg
½ pint milk
1 or 2 oz. English or Welsh butter, melted

1. Sift flour and salt into bowl. **2.** Add sugar. **3.** Mix to smooth creamy batter with whole egg and half the milk. **4.** Stir in rest of milk. **5.** Brush large heavy frying pan with melted butter. Heat. **6.** Drop small rounds of scone mixture (about 12 in all), from dessertspoon, into pan. **7.** Cook until bubbles show on surface (2½ to 3 minutes). **8.** Carefully turn over with knife. Cook for further 2 minutes. **9.** Pile Scones in clean, folded tea towel to keep warm and moist. **10.** Serve straight away with butter and jam, golden syrup or honey. **Serves 4.**

DROPPED SCONES WITH SPICE 686

1. Follow recipe and method for Dropped Scones (No. 685). **2.** Sift 1 level teaspoon mixed spice with flour and salt. **3.** Use 1 level tablespoon soft brown sugar instead of caster. **Serves 4.**

DROPPED SCONES WITH HAM 687

½ lb. self-raising flour
¼ level teaspoon salt
1 level teaspoon dry mustard
2 oz. very finely-chopped lean ham
1 standard egg
½ pint milk
1 or 2 oz. English or Welsh butter, melted

1. Sift flour, salt and mustard into bowl. Add ham. **2.** Mix to smooth creamy batter with whole egg and half the milk. **3.** Stir in rest of milk. **4.** Brush large heavy frying pan with melted butter. Heat. **5.** Drop small rounds of scone mixture (about 12 in all), from dessertspoon, into pan. **6.** Cook until bubbles show on surface (2½ to 3 minutes). **7.** Carefully turn over with knife. Cook for further 2 minutes. **8.** Pile Scones in clean folded tea towel to keep warm. **9.** Serve straight away with butter and Wensleydale or Double Gloucester cheese. **Serves 4.**

WHOLEMEAL SCONES 688

¼ lb. wholemeal flour
¼ lb. plain flour
2 level teaspoons baking powder
½ level teaspoon salt
1½ oz. English or Welsh butter
¼ pint milk
Extra milk for brushing

1. Sift flours, baking powder and salt into bowl. **2.** Rub in butter finely. **3.** Add milk all at once. Mix to soft, but not sticky, dough with knife. **4.** Turn on to lightly-floured board. Knead quickly until smooth. **5.** Roll out to about ½-in. thickness. Cut into 9 or 10 rounds with 2½-in. biscuit cutter. **6.** Transfer to buttered baking tray. Brush tops with milk. **7.** Bake towards top of hot oven (450°F. or Gas No. 8) for 7 to 10 minutes (or until well risen and golden). **8.** Cool on wire rack. **9.** Serve with butter and cottage cheese. **9 or 10 Scones.**

689 RASPBERRY SHORTCAKES

1 recipe Tea Scones (No. 672)
Milk for brushing
2 to 3 oz. English or Welsh butter
½ lb. raspberries
2 oz. sifted icing sugar
4 tablespoons fresh double cream, whipped

1. Roll out Tea Scone dough to 1-in. thickness.
2. Cut into 4 rounds with 3-in. biscuit cutter.
3. Stand on buttered baking tray. Brush tops
with milk. **4.** Bake towards top of hot oven
(425°F. or Gas No. 7) for 15 to 20 minutes (or
until well risen and golden). **5.** Transfer to wire
cooling rack. Leave until lukewarm. **6.** Pull apart
gently with fingers and butter thickly. **7.**
Sandwich each together with whole raspberries
mixed with sugar. **8.** Put tablespoon of cream on
each. **9.** Serve warm. **Serves 4.**

690 STRAWBERRY SHORTCAKES

1. Follow recipe and method for Raspberry
Shortcakes (No. 689). **2.** Sandwich together with
½ lb. sliced strawberries mixed with 2 oz. sifted
icing sugar. **Serves 4.**

RING DOUGHNUTS 6

¾ lb. self-raising flour
¼ level teaspoon salt
½ level teaspoon cinnamon
½ level teaspoon mixed spice
¼ lb. English or Welsh butter
2 oz. caster sugar
1 standard egg
¼ pint milk
Deep fat or oil for frying
Extra caster sugar

1. Sift flour, salt, cinnamon and spice into bowl.
2. Rub in butter finely. **3.** Add caster sugar.
4. Beat egg with milk. Add, all at once, to dry
ingredients. **5.** Mix to soft, but not sticky, dough
with knife. **6.** Turn out on to lightly-floured
board. Knead quickly until smooth. **7.** Roll out to
½-in. thickness. **8.** Cut into rounds with 2-in.
biscuit cutter. Remove centres with 1-in. cutter.
Re-roll and cut into more rings. **9.** Fry, a few at a
time, in hot fat or oil for 2 to 3 minutes, turning
once. **10.** Remove from pan. Drain thoroughly on
soft kitchen paper. **11.** Toss in caster sugar.
Serve while still warm. **20 Doughnuts.**

Raspberry Shortcake (No. 689)

Biscuits

Brandy Snaps (No. 707)

2   PLAIN BISCUITS

½ lb. self-raising flour
Pinch of salt
5 oz. English or Welsh butter
¼ lb. caster or sifted icing sugar
Beaten egg to mix

1. Sift flour and salt into bowl. **2.** Rub in butter finely. **3.** Add sugar. **4.** Mix to very stiff dough with beaten egg. **5.** Turn out on to lightly-floured board. Knead gently until smooth. **6.** Put into polythene bag or wrap in aluminium foil. Chill 30 minutes. **7.** Roll out fairly thinly. Cut into about 30 rounds with 2-in. plain or fluted biscuit cutter. **8.** Transfer to buttered baking trays. Prick biscuits well with fork. **9.** Bake in centre of moderate oven (350°F. or Gas No. 4) for about 12 to 15 minutes (or until pale gold). **10.** Leave on trays for 2 to 3 minutes. Transfer to wire cooling rack. **11.** Store in airtight tin when cold. **About 30 Biscuits.**

3   WALNUT BISCUITS

1. Follow recipe and method for Plain Biscuits (No. 692). **2.** Add 1½ oz. very finely-chopped shelled walnut halves with sugar and ½ teaspoon vanilla essence with egg. **Cut into about 36 Biscuits.**

ALMOND BISCUITS   694

1. Follow recipe and method for Plain Biscuits (No. 692). **2.** Add 2 oz. ground almonds with sugar, and ½ teaspoon almond essence with egg. **Cut into 34 to 36 Biscuits.**

LEMON OR ORANGE BISCUITS   695

1. Follow recipe and method for Plain Biscuits (No. 692). **2.** Add 1 level teaspoon finely-grated lemon or orange peel with sugar. **Cut into about 30 Biscuits.**

CURRANT BISCUITS   696

1. Follow recipe and method for Plain Biscuits (No. 692). **2.** Add 2 oz. currants with sugar. **Cut into about 30 Biscuits.**

CHERRY BISCUITS   697

1. Follow recipe and method for Plain Biscuits (No. 692). **2.** Add 2 oz. very finely-chopped glacé cherries with sugar. **Cut into about 30 Biscuits.**

698 SPICE OR CINNAMON BISCUITS

1. Follow recipe and method for Plain Biscuits (No. 692). **2.** Sift 1½ level teaspoons mixed spice or cinnamon with flour and salt. **Cut into about 30 Biscuits.**

699 COCONUT BISCUITS

1. Follow recipe and method for Plain Biscuits (No. 692). **2.** Add 2 oz. desiccated coconut with sugar and ½ teaspoon vanilla essence with egg. **Cut into about 36 Biscuits.**

700 CHOCOLATE FLAKE BISCUITS

1. Follow recipe and method for Plain Biscuits (No. 692). **2.** Add 2 oz. grated plain chocolate with sugar. **Cut into about 36 Biscuits.**

701 JAM SANDWICH BISCUITS

1. Follow recipe and method for Plain Biscuits (No. 692). **2.** When Biscuits are cold, sandwich together with raspberry or apricot jam. **3.** Dust tops with sifted icing sugar. **About 15 Sandwich Biscuits.**

702 SUGAR-TOPPED BISCUITS

1. Follow recipe and method for any of the above biscuits. **2.** Before baking brush with lightly-beaten egg white and sprinkle with caster sugar. **30 to 36 Biscuits.**

703 CHOCOLATE DROPS

¼ lb. English or Welsh butter, softened
2 oz. caster sugar
½ teaspoon vanilla essence
3½ oz. plain flour
½ oz. cocoa powder

1. Cream butter with sugar and essence until light and fluffy. **2.** Stir in flour sifted with cocoa. **3.** Drop 18 to 20 teaspoons of mixture, well apart, on to buttered baking tray. **4.** Bake just above centre of fairly hot oven (375°F. or Gas No. 5) for 17 minutes. **5.** Leave on tray 1 or 2 minutes before transferring to wire cooling rack. **6.** Store in airtight tin when cold. **18 to 20 Drops.**

RICH SHORTBREAD 70

¼ lb. English or Welsh butter, softened
2 oz. caster sugar
5 oz. plain flour
1 oz. semolina
Extra caster sugar

1. Cream butter and sugar together until light and fluffy. **2.** Using fork, gradually stir in flour and semolina. **3.** Draw mixture together with finger tips. Press into lightly-buttered 7-in. sandwich tin. **4.** Prick well all over. Either pinch up edges with finger and thumb or ridge with prongs of fork. **5.** Bake in centre of moderate oven (325°F. or Gas No. 3) for about 40 minutes (or until colour of pale straw). **6.** Leave in tin for 5 minutes. **7.** Cut into 8 triangles. Dredge with extra caster sugar. **8.** Remove from tin when cold. **9.** Store in airtight tin. **8 Shortbreads.**

LEMON OR ORANGE SHORTBREAD 70

1. Follow recipe and method for Rich Shortbread (No. 704). **2.** Add 1 level teaspoon finely-grated lemon or orange peel with flour and semolina. **8 Shortbreads.**

ALMOND SHORTBREAD BISCUITS 70

¼ lb. English or Welsh butter, softened
2 oz. caster or sifted icing sugar
¼ lb. plain flour
2 oz. ground almonds
1 oz. semolina
A little beaten egg for brushing
Extra caster sugar

1. Cream butter and sugar together until light and fluffy. **2.** Using fork, gradually stir in flour, almonds and semolina. **3.** Draw together with fingertips. Turn on to lightly-floured board. **4.** Shape into ball. Either put into polythene bag or wrap in aluminium foil. Chill for at least 30 minutes. **5.** Roll out to ¼-in. thickness. Cut into approximately 18 rounds with 2-in. fluted biscuit cutter. **6.** Transfer to buttered trays and prick well with fork. Brush with egg. **7.** Bake in centre of moderate oven (325°F. or Gas No. 3) for 20 to 25 minutes (or until pale gold). **8.** Transfer to wire cooling rack. Dredge with caster sugar. **9.** Store in airtight tin when cold. **18 Biscuits.**

07 BRANDY SNAPS

2 oz. English or Welsh butter
2 oz. granulated sugar
2½ oz. golden syrup
2 oz. plain flour
1 level teaspoon ground ginger
2 teaspoons lemon juice
¼ pint fresh double cream

1. Put butter, sugar and syrup into pan. Stand over low heat until melted. **2.** Sift together flour and ginger. Add to melted mixture with lemon juice. **3.** Drop 4 teaspoons of mixture (well apart to allow for spreading) on to large buttered baking tray. **4.** Bake in centre of moderate oven (325°F. or Gas No. 3) for 8 minutes. **5.** Leave 1 minute. Lift off with palette knife. Roll quickly and loosely round buttered handle of wooden spoon. **6.** Leave until firm and slide off handle. **7.** Repeat with rest of mixture, making total of 16 Brandy Snaps. **8.** When cold, fill both ends of each with stiffly-whipped cream. **16 Brandy Snaps.**

8 FLORENTINES

3 oz. English or Welsh butter
4 tablespoons milk
¼ lb. sifted icing sugar
1½ oz. plain flour
3 oz. chopped mixed peel
2 oz. finely-chopped glacé cherries
3 oz. flaked almonds
1 teaspoon lemon juice
¼ lb. plain chocolate
¼ oz. extra English or Welsh butter

1. Cover 2 large baking trays with rice paper. **2.** Put butter, milk and sugar into saucepan. Stand over low heat until butter melts. **3.** Remove from heat. Stir in flour, peel, cherries, almonds and lemon juice. **4.** Leave on one side until completely cold. **5.** Spoon equal amounts of mixture (well apart to allow for spreading) on to baking trays. **6.** Bake just above centre of fairly hot oven (375°F. or Gas No. 5) for 10 minutes (or until pale gold). **7.** Leave until lukewarm. Carefully lift off trays and remove surplus rice paper round edges. **8.** Cool completely on wire cooling rack. **9.** Melt chocolate and extra butter in basin standing over saucepan of hot water. **10.** Put heaped teaspoonful on to rice paper side of each Florentine. **11.** Spread evenly with knife. **12.** Mark wavy lines with fork on each. Leave until chocolate hardens before serving. **13.** Store in airtight tin. **12 Florentines.**

VANILLA REFRIGERATOR BISCUITS 709

½ lb. plain flour
1 level teaspoon baking powder
¼ lb. English or Welsh butter
6 oz. caster sugar
1 level teaspoon vanilla essence
1 standard egg, beaten

1. Sift together flour and baking powder. **2.** Rub in butter finely. **3.** Add sugar. Mix to dough with vanilla and beaten egg. **4.** Shape into long sausage. Transfer to length of aluminium foil. **5.** Wrap foil round 'sausage' and twist ends. Work backwards and forwards to form evenly-shaped roll about 2-in. diameter. **6.** Refrigerate overnight.

SHAPING AND BAKING

Full quantity of mixture makes between 4 and 5 dozen Biscuits. For only a dozen or so, slice these very thinly from roll and stand (well apart to allow for spreading) on buttered baking tray. Bake in centre of fairly hot oven (375°F. or Gas No. 5) for 10 to 12 minutes (or until pale gold). Cool on wire rack. Store in airtight tin when cold. Remainder of roll can be returned to refrigerator and left – up to about a week – until more Biscuits are wanted.

CHOCOLATE REFRIGERATOR BISCUITS 710

1. Follow recipe and method for Vanilla Refrigerator Biscuits (No. 709). **2.** Add 2 oz. very finely-grated plain chocolate with sugar. **4 to 5 dozen Biscuits.**

NUT REFRIGERATOR BISCUITS 711

1. Follow recipe and method for Vanilla Refrigerator Biscuits (No. 709). **2.** Add 2 oz. very finely-chopped or ground walnuts or hazelnuts with sugar. **4 to 5 dozen Biscuits.**

SPICY REFRIGERATOR BISCUITS 712

1. Follow recipe and method for Vanilla Refrigerator Biscuits (No. 709). **2.** Omit vanilla. **3.** Sift 2 level teaspoons mixed spice with flour and baking powder. **4 to 5 dozen Biscuits.**

713 GINGER REFRIGERATOR BISCUITS

1. Follow recipe and method for Vanilla Refrigerator Biscuits (No. 709) **2.** Omit vanilla. **3** Sift 1½ level teaspoons ground ginger and ½ level teaspoon mixed spice with flour and baking powder. **4 to 5 dozen Biscuits.**

714 COCONUT REFRIGERATOR BISCUITS

1. Follow recipe and method for Vanilla Refrigerator Biscuits (No. 709). **2.** Add 2 oz. desiccated coconut with sugar. **4 to 5 dozen Biscuits.**

715 ORANGE OR LEMON REFRIGERATOR BISCUITS

1. Follow recipe and method for Vanilla Refrigerator Biscuits (No. 709). **2.** Omit vanilla. **3.** Add 2 level teaspoons finely-grated orange or lemon peel with sugar. **4 to 5 dozen Biscuits.**

716 RAISIN REFRIGERATOR BISCUITS

1. Follow recipe and method for Vanilla Refrigerator Biscuits (No. 709). **2.** Add 2 oz. very finely chopped, seedless raisins with sugar. **4 to 5 dozen Biscuits.**

717 BUTTER WHIRLS

6 oz. English or Welsh butter, softened
2 oz. sifted icing sugar
½ teaspoon vanilla essence
6 oz. plain flour
8 or 9 glacé cherries, halved

1. Cream butter with sugar and vanilla until light and fluffy. **2.** Stir in flour. **3.** Transfer mixture to forcing bag fitted with star-shaped meringue tube. **4.** Pipe 16 to 18 flat whirls on to buttered baking tray or trays. Put half a cherry on to each. **5.** Bake in centre of moderate oven (325°F. or Gas No. 3) for 20 minutes (or until pale gold). **6.** Leave on trays 5 minutes. Transfer to wire cooling rack. **7.** Store in airtight tin when cold. **16 to 18 Whirls.**

FLAPJACKS 71

¼ lb. English or Welsh butter
3 oz. golden syrup
3 oz. soft brown sugar
½ lb. rolled oats

1. Put butter, syrup and sugar into saucepan and stand over low heat until melted. **2.** Stir in oats and mix well. **3.** Spread into buttered Swiss roll tin, approximately 8 in. × 12 in., and smooth top with knife. **4.** Bake in centre of moderate oven (350°F. or Gas No. 4) for 30 minutes. **5.** Leave in tin 5 minutes, then cut into 24 fingers. **6.** Remove from tin when cold. **7.** Store in airtight tin. **24 Flapjacks.**

GINGER SNAPS 71

¼ lb. self-raising flour
1 level teaspoon ground ginger
¼ level teaspoon mixed spice
2 oz. English or Welsh butter
1½ oz. caster sugar
1 level tablespoon black treacle, melted
Milk to mix

1. Sift flour, ginger and spice into bowl. **2.** Rub in butter finely. **3.** Add sugar. Mix to very stiff paste with treacle and milk. **4.** Roll out very thinly and cut into 26 to 30 rounds with 2-in. biscuit cutter. **5.** Transfer to buttered baking trays. **6.** Bake just above centre of moderate oven (350°F. or Gas No. 4) for 10 minutes. **7.** Leave on trays for 1 or 2 minutes before transferring to wire cooling rack. **8.** Store in airtight tin when cold. **26 to 30 Ginger Snaps.**

COFFEE WALNUT COOKIES 7

¼ lb. English or Welsh butter, softened
2 oz. caster sugar
2 oz. finely-chopped walnuts
¼ lb. plain flour
2 level teaspoons instant coffee powder

1. Cream butter with sugar until light and fluffy. **2.** Add walnuts. Stir in flour sifted with coffee powder. **3.** Put 18 to 20 teaspoons of mixture, well apart, on to buttered baking tray. **4.** Bake just above centre of fairly hot oven (375°F. or Gas No. 5) for 15 to 20 minutes. **5.** Leave on tray 1 or 2 minutes before transferring to wire cooling rack. **6.** Store in airtight tin when cold. **18 to 20 Cookies.**

Sugar-Topped Biscuits (No. 702), Jam Sandwich Biscuits (No. 701), Butter Whirls (No. 717), Flapjacks (No. 718) and Ginger Nuts (No. 721)

21 GINGER NUTS

2½ oz. English or Welsh butter
3 oz. soft brown sugar
3 oz. golden syrup
½ lb. plain flour
½ level teaspoon mixed spice
1½ level teaspoons ground ginger
1 level teaspoon bicarbonate of soda
1 tablespoon warm water

1. Put butter, sugar and syrup into pan. Stand over low heat until melted. **2.** Sift flour, spice and ginger into bowl. **3.** Add melted butter mixture and bicarbonate of soda combined with water. **4.** Mix well and shape into approximately 24 small balls. **5.** Stand on buttered baking trays, allowing room between for spreading. **6.** Bake just above centre of moderate oven (325°F. or Gas No. 3) for 15 minutes. **7.** Leave on trays for 1 or 2 minutes before transferring to wire cooling rack. **8.** Store in airtight tin when cold. **24 Ginger Nuts.**

CHOCOLATE CHERRY COOKIES 722

¼ lb. English or Welsh butter, softened
2 oz. caster sugar
½ teaspoon vanilla essence
1 oz. finely-chopped glacé cherries
1 oz. finely-chopped plain chocolate
¼ lb. sifted plain flour

1. Cream butter with sugar and vanilla until light and fluffy. **2.** Add cherries and chocolate. Stir in flour. **3.** Put 18 to 20 teaspoons of mixture, well apart, on to buttered baking tray. **4.** Bake just above centre of fairly hot oven (375°F. or Gas No. 5) for 15 to 20 minutes. **5.** Leave on tray for 1 or 2 minutes before transferring to wire cooling rack. **6.** Store in airtight tin when cold. **18 to 20 Cookies.**

DATE COOKIES 723

1. Follow recipe and method for Chocolate Cherry Cookies (No. 722). **2.** Add 2 oz. very finely-chopped dates instead of chocolate and cherries. **18 to 20 Cookies.**

BISCUITS

724 ALMOND MACAROONS

Whites of 2 standard eggs
$\frac{1}{4}$ lb. ground almonds
$\frac{1}{2}$ lb. caster sugar
$\frac{1}{2}$ oz. ground rice
$\frac{1}{2}$ teaspoon vanilla essence
$\frac{1}{2}$ teaspoon almond essence
A little extra egg white
9 blanched and split almonds

1. Brush 1 or 2 baking trays with melted butter. Line with rice paper. **2.** Beat egg whites until foamy but not stiff. **3.** Add almonds, sugar, ground rice and essences. Beat well. **4.** Pipe or spoon 18 mounds of mixture, well apart, on to prepared tray or trays. Brush with egg white. **5.** Put half an almond on middle of each. **6.** Bake in centre of moderate oven (325°F. or Gas No. 3) for 20 to 25 minutes (or until pale gold). **7.** Leave on trays for 5 minutes. **8.** Carefully lift off and remove rice paper round edges of each. **9.** Cool on wire rack. **10.** Store in airtight tin when cold. **18 Macaroons.**

725 PEANUT CRISPS

2 oz. plain flour
$\frac{1}{4}$ level teaspoon bicarbonate of soda
2 oz. English or Welsh butter, softened
1 oz. caster sugar
2 oz. soft brown sugar
$\frac{1}{2}$ teaspoon vanilla essence
2 oz. peanut butter
1 standard egg

1. Sift together flour and bicarbonate of soda. **2.** Cream butter with sugars, vanilla and peanut butter until very light and fluffy. **3.** Beat in egg then stir in dry ingredients. **4.** Drop 2 dozen teaspoons of mixture, 1 in. apart, on to un-buttered baking trays. **5.** Bake in centre of moderate oven (350°F. or Gas No. 4) for 10 to 12 minutes. **6.** Leave on trays for 1 or 2 minutes. Transfer to wire cooling rack. **7.** Store in airtight tin when cold. **24 Crisps.**

BUTTER DIGESTIVE BISCUITS 72

3 oz. wholemeal flour
$\frac{1}{2}$ oz. plain flour
$\frac{1}{4}$ level teaspoon salt
$\frac{1}{2}$ level teaspoon baking powder
$\frac{1}{2}$ oz. oatmeal
$1\frac{1}{2}$ oz. English or Welsh butter
$1\frac{1}{2}$ oz. caster sugar
3 tablespoons milk

1. Sift flours, salt and baking powder into bowl. Add oatmeal. **2.** Rub in butter finely. Add sugar. **3.** Mix to stiff paste with milk. **4.** Turn out on to lightly-floured board. Knead well. **5.** Roll out thinly. Cut into 12 rounds with $2\frac{1}{2}$-in. fluted biscuit cutter. **6.** Transfer to buttered baking tray and prick well. **7.** Bake in centre of fairly hot oven (375°F. or Gas No. 5) for 15 to 20 minutes (or until light gold). **8.** Transfer to wire cooling rack. **9.** Store in airtight tin when cold. **12 Biscuits.**

TREACLE BITES 72

$\frac{1}{4}$ lb. self-raising flour, sifted
3 oz. rolled oats
1 oz. desiccated coconut
$\frac{1}{4}$ lb. English or Welsh butter
5 oz. caster sugar
3 level dessertspoons treacle
1 level teaspoon bicarbonate of soda
1 tablespoon milk

1. Combine flour with oats and coconut. **2.** Put butter, sugar and treacle into saucepan. Very slowly bring to boil, stirring all the time. **3.** Remove from heat. Add bicarbonate of soda dissolved in milk. **4.** Pour hot mixture on to dry ingredients. Mix thoroughly. Leave on one side for 30 minutes or until firm. **5.** Break off 24 pieces of mixture and roll into marbles. **6.** Transfer to buttered baking trays (leaving room between to allow for spreading). Bake in centre of moderate oven (350°F. or Gas No. 4) for 15 minutes. **7.** Leave on trays 1 or 2 minutes before transferring to wire cooling rack. Store in airtight tin when cold. **24 Treacle Bites.**

Large & Small Cakes

728 VICTORIA SANDWICH

$\frac{1}{4}$ lb. English or Welsh butter, softened
$\frac{1}{4}$ lb. caster sugar
2 standard eggs
$\frac{1}{4}$ lb. self-raising flour, sifted

1. Brush two 7-in. sandwich tins with melted butter. Line bases with rounds of greaseproof paper. Brush paper with more butter. **2.** Cream butter and sugar together until very pale in colour, light in texture and fluffy. **3.** Beat in whole eggs, one at a time, adding tablespoon of flour with each. **4.** Gently fold in remaining flour with metal spoon. **5.** Transfer to prepared tins and smooth tops with knife. **6.** Bake in centre of moderate oven (350°F. or Gas No. 4) for 25 to 30 minutes (or until well risen, golden brown and firm). **7.** Leave in tins for 2 to 3 minutes. Turn out on to wire cooling rack. **8.** Strip off paper and leave until cold. **About 6 portions.**

729 JAM SANDWICH

1. Follow recipe and method for Victoria Sandwich (No. 728). **2.** When cakes are cold, sandwich together with 2 or 3 level tablespoons jam. **3.** Dust top of cake with sifted icing sugar. **About 6 portions.**

730 JAM & CREAM SANDWICH

1. Follow recipe and method for Victoria Sandwich (No. 728). **2.** When cakes are cold, sandwich together with 2 to 3 tablespoons jam and 3 to 4 tablespoons fresh double cream, whipped until thick. **3.** Dust top of cake with sifted icing sugar. **About 6 portions.**

731 LEMON SANDWICH

1. Follow recipe and method for Victoria Sandwich (No. 728). **2.** Cream butter and sugar with 1 level teaspoon finely-grated lemon peel. **3.** When cakes are cold, sandwich together with either 4 tablespoons fresh double cream, whipped until thick, half a recipe Lemon Butter Cream Frosting (No. 812) or Lemon Velvet Frosting (No. 804). **4.** Dust top of cake with sifted icing sugar. **About 6 portions.**

ORANGE SANDWICH 732

1. Follow recipe and method for Victoria Sandwich (No. 728). **2.** Cream butter and sugar with 1 level teaspoon finely-grated orange peel. **3.** When cakes are cold, sandwich together with either 4 tablespoons fresh double cream, whipped until thick, half a recipe Orange Butter Cream Frosting (No. 813) or Orange Velvet Frosting (No. 803). **4.** Dust top of cake with sifted icing sugar. **About 6 portions.**

PINEAPPLE SANDWICH 733

1. Follow recipe and method for Victoria Sandwich (No. 728). **2.** When cakes are cold, sandwich together and cover top with double recipe Pineapple Velvet Frosting (No. 806). **3.** Decorate top with pieces of crystallized pineapple. **About 6 portions.**

WALNUT COFFEE SANDWICH 734

1. Follow recipe and method for Victoria Sandwich (No. 728). **2.** Stir 1 oz. very finely-chopped walnuts into mixture after beating in eggs. **3.** When cakes are cold, sandwich together with half a recipe Coffee Butter Cream Frosting (No. 815) or half a recipe Coffee Cream Frosting (No. 821). Dust top of cake with sifted icing sugar. **About 6 portions.**

CHOCOLATE SANDWICH 735

1. Follow recipe and method for Victoria Sandwich (No. 728). **2.** When cakes are cold, sandwich together with half a recipe Chocolate Butter Cream Frosting (No. 816). **3.** Dust top of cake with sifted icing sugar. **About 6 portions.**

FAIRY CAKES 736

1. Follow recipe and method for Victoria Sandwich (No. 728). **2.** Stir 2 oz. currants or sultanas into mixture after beating in eggs. **3.** Transfer equal amounts to 18 paper cases standing in 18 ungreased bun tins. **4.** Bake just above centre of fairly hot oven (375°F. or Gas No. 5) for 20 to 25 minutes (or until well risen and golden). Cool on wire rack. **18 Cakes.**

LARGE & SMALL CAKES

737 CHOCOLATE CHIP CAKES

1. Follow recipe and method for Fairy Cakes (No. 736). **2.** Stir in 2 oz. chopped plain chocolate instead of currants or sultanas. **18 Cakes.**

738 GENOESE SANDWICH

2 oz. English or Welsh butter
3 standard eggs
3 oz. caster sugar
3 oz. plain flour, sifted twice

1. Brush two 7-in. sandwich tins with melted butter. Line bases with rounds of greaseproof paper. Brush paper with more butter. Dust insides of tins lightly with sifted flour. **2.** Melt butter over low heat. Strain into clean basin through muslin. **3.** Put eggs into large bowl standing over saucepan of hand-hot water. Whisk for 2 minutes. **4.** Add sugar. Continue whisking for further 8 to 10 minutes (or until mixture is very light in colour, fairly thick in texture – consistency of softly-whipped cream – and at least double its original volume). **5.** Remove bowl from saucepan. Continue whisking for further 5 minutes until egg mixture is cool. **6.** With large metal spoon, gently fold in half of the melted and cooled butter and half of the flour. Repeat with rest of butter and flour. **7.** Transfer to prepared tins. Bake in centre of moderate oven (350°F. or Gas No. 4) for 25 to 30 minutes (when cakes should have shrunk slightly away from sides of tins and be golden brown on top). **8.** Leave in tins for 1 minute. Turn out on to folded tea-towel. (A wire cooling rack is inclined to sink into these very light cakes and leave deep lines). **9.** Carefully peel away paper. Sandwich together as for Victoria Sandwich cakes (No. 728). **About 6 portions.**

739 GENOESE CAKE

1. Follow recipe and method for Genoese Sandwich (No. 738). **2.** Transfer mixture to buttered and paper-lined 7-in. deep cake tin. **3.** Bake in centre of moderate oven (350°F. or Gas No. 4) for 40 to 45 minutes (or until wooden cocktail stick, inserted into centre, comes out clean). **4.** Leave until cold. Slice into 1 or 2 layers. Sandwich together and cover top with filling and frosting to taste. (See Fillings and Frostings section). **Serves 6 to 8.**

CHOCOLATE LAYER CAKE 7

¼ lb. self-raising flour
2 level tablespoons cocoa powder
¼ lb. English or Welsh butter
¼ lb. caster sugar
1 oz. golden syrup
½ teaspoon vanilla essence
2 standard eggs
2 dessertspoons milk

1. Brush 8-in. deep sandwich tin with melted butter and cover base with round of greaseproof paper. Brush paper with more butter. **2.** Sift flour twice with cocoa. **3.** Cream butter, sugar, syrup and essence together until very pale in colour, light in texture and fluffy. **4.** Beat in whole eggs, one at a time, adding tablespoon of sifted dry ingredients with each. **5.** Fold in milk and remaining dry ingredients with metal spoon. **6.** Transfer to prepared tin and smooth top with a knife. **7.** Bake in centre of moderate oven (350°F. or Gas No. 4) for 35 to 40 minutes (or until wooden cocktail stick, inserted into centre of cake, comes out clean). **8.** Turn out on to wire rack, strip off paper and leave until cold. **9.** Cut cake into 2 or 3 layers. **10.** Fill and cover top with either ½ pint fresh double cream, whipped until thick, Caramel Cream Frosting (No. 814), Whipped Cream Frosting with Nuts (No. 820) or Vanilla Butter Cream Frosting (No. 810). **6 to 8 portions.**

LIME & CHOCOLATE 7 LAYER CAKE

1. Follow recipe and method for Chocolate Layer Cake (No. 740). **2.** When cake is cold, cut into 2 layers. **3.** Sandwich together and cover top with double recipe Lime Velvet Frosting (No. 805). **4.** Decorate with small leaves cut from angelica. **6 to 8 portions.**

MOCHA LAYER CAKE 74

1. Follow recipe and method for Chocolate Layer Cake (No. 740). **2.** When cake is cold, cut into 2 layers. **3.** Sandwich together with Coffee Velvet Frosting (No. 808). **4.** Decorate with 1 or 2 level tablespoons grated plain chocolate and 8 halved glacé cherries. **6 to 8 portions.**

150

Chocolate Layer Cake (No. 740) with double cream filling and topping

743 FRESH FRUIT SANDWICH

1. Follow recipe and method for Victoria Sandwich (No. 728). **2.** When cakes are cold, sandwich together with Whipped Cream Frosting (No. 819) or Whipped Cream Frosting with Rum, Sherry or Brandy (No. 823). **3.** Spread more Frosting thickly over top. Then cover with 4 to 6 oz. halved fresh strawberries or whole raspberries or loganberries. **4.** Brush fruit with 1 or 2 tablespoons melted redcurrant jelly or apricot jam. **5.** Pipe small whirls or rosettes with remaining Frosting round top edge of cake. **6.** Chill lightly before serving. **6 to 8 portions.**

744 MIXED FRUIT SANDWICH

1. Follow recipe and method for Fresh Fruit Sandwich (No. 743). **2.** Instead of strawberries, raspberries or loganberries, cover top of cake with rings or lines of well-drained canned peach slices; halved and de-seeded black or green grapes and drained and halved canned red cherries. **6 to 8 portions.**

745 SMALL SEED CAKES

1. Follow recipe and method for Victoria Sandwich (No. 728). **2.** Stir 2 level teaspoons caraway seeds into mixture after beating in eggs. **3.** Transfer equal amounts to 18 paper cases standing in 18 ungreased bun tins. **4.** Bake just above centre of fairly hot oven (375°F. or Gas No. 5) for 20 to 25 minutes (or until well risen and golden). **5.** Cool on wire rack. **18 Cakes.**

BUTTERFLY CAKES 746

1. Follow recipe and method for Victoria Sandwich (No. 728). **2.** Transfer equal amounts of mixture to 18 well-buttered bun tins. **3.** Bake just above centre of fairly hot oven (375°F. or Gas No. 5) for 20 to 25 minutes (or until well risen and golden). **4.** Cool on wire rack. **5.** To make Butterflies cut a slice off the top of each cake. Cut slices in halves (for wings). **6.** Pipe 3 lines of Butter Cream Frosting (No. 809 onwards) to taste on top of each cake. **7.** Put halved slices into cream at an angle to form wings. **8.** Dust lightly with sifted icing sugar. **18 Cakes.**

SMALL ICED CAKES 747

1. Follow recipe and method for Victoria Sandwich (No. 728). **2.** Transfer equal amounts of mixture to 18 paper cases standing in 18 ungreased bun tins. **3.** Bake just above centre of fairly hot oven (375°F. or Gas No. 5) for 20 to 25 minutes (or until well risen and golden). **4.** Cool on wire rack. **5.** When completely cold cover tops with either a Velvet Frosting, Butter Cream Frosting or Glacé Icing to taste (see Fillings & Frostings Section). **6.** Decorate with halved glacé cherries, pieces of angelica, chocolate buttons, grated chocolate, whole hazelnuts, pieces of shelled walnut halves or halved and toasted almonds. **18 Cakes.**

151

748 MADELEINES

1. Follow recipe and method for Victoria Sandwich (No. 728). **2.** Transfer equal amounts of mixture to 12 to 14 well-buttered Dariole moulds. **3.** Bake just above centre of moderate oven (350°F. or Gas No. 4) 20 to 25 minutes (or until well risen and golden). **4.** Turn out and cool on wire rack. **5.** When completely cold, trim slice off wide part of each so that Madeleines stand upright without toppling. **6.** Brush with melted apricot jam, roll in desiccated coconut then put $\frac{1}{2}$ glacé cherry and 2 leaves cut from angelica on top of each. **12 to 14 Madeleines.**

749 SPONGE SANDWICH

3 standard eggs
3 oz. caster sugar
3 oz. self-raising flour, sifted twice

1. Brush two 7-in. sandwich tins with melted butter. Line bases with rounds of greaseproof paper. Brush paper with more butter. Dust sides of tins with sifted plain flour. **2.** Put eggs into large bowl standing over saucepan of hand-hot water. **3.** Whisk for 2 minutes. **4.** Add sugar. Continue whisking further 8 to 10 minutes (or until mixture is very light in colour, thick in texture — consistency of softly-whipped cream — and at least double its original volume). **5.** Remove bowl from saucepan. Continue whisking further 5 minutes (or until egg mixture is cool). **6.** Gently fold in flour with large metal spoon. **7.** Transfer to prepared tins. Bake in centre of moderate oven (350°F. or Gas No. 4) for 20 minutes (or until well risen and golden). **8.** Turn out on to sheet of sugared greaseproof paper resting on folded tea-towel. Carefully peel off lining paper. Leave until completely cold. **About 6 portions.**

750 DEEP SPONGE CAKE

1. Follow recipe and method for Sponge Sandwich (No. 749) but use plain flour instead of self-raising. **2.** Transfer mixture to buttered and paper-lined 7-in. deep cake tin. **3.** Bake in centre of moderate oven (350°F. or Gas No. 4) for 40 to 45 minutes (or until wooden cocktail stick, inserted into centre, comes out clean). **4.** Leave until cold. Slice into 1 or 2 layers. **5.** Sandwich together and cover top with Filling and Frosting to taste. (See Fillings and Frostings section). **6 to 8 portions.**

JAM SPONGE SANDWICH 7

1. Follow recipe and method for Sponge Sandwich (No. 749). **2.** When cakes are cold, sandwich together with 2 or 3 tablespoons jam. **3.** Dust top of cake with caster sugar. **About 6 portions.**

JAM & CREAM SPONGE SANDWICH 7

1. Follow recipe and method for Sponge Sandwich (No. 749). **2.** When cakes are cold, sandwich together with 2 or 3 tablespoons jam and 4 tablespoons double cream, whipped until thick. **3.** Dust top of cake with caster sugar. **About 6 portions.**

SWISS ROLL 7

1. Follow recipe and method for Sponge Sandwich (No. 749). **2.** Transfer mixture to buttered and paper-lined, 12-in. × 8-in. Swiss roll tin. **3.** Bake towards top of fairly hot oven (400°F. or Gas No. 6) for 10 to 12 minutes (or until well risen and firm). **4.** Turn out on to sheet of sugared greaseproof paper resting on folded tea-towel. Carefully peel off paper. **5.** Cut away crisp edges with sharp knife. Spread quickly with 4 level tablespoons warm jam. **6.** Roll up tightly and hold in position for 1 minute. Cool on wire rack. **8 to 10 slices.**

CHOCOLATE SWISS ROLL 7

1. Follow recipe and method for Swiss roll (No. 753). **2.** When making up sponge mixture, use $2\frac{1}{2}$ oz. self-raising flour sifted twice with $\frac{1}{2}$ oz. cocoa powder. **6 to 8 slices.**

CREAM-FILLED SWISS ROLL 7

1. Follow recipe and method for Swiss Roll (No. 753) or Chocolate Swiss Roll (No. 754). **2.** After trimming away crisp edges, roll up loosely with paper inside to prevent sticking. Cover with damp tea-towel and leave until completely cold. **3.** Unroll carefully, remove paper and fill with $\frac{1}{4}$ pint fresh double cream, whipped until thick. **4.** Roll up again and hold in position for about 1 minute. **8 to 10 slices.**

756 COFFEE HAZELNUT GÂTEAU

3 Victoria Sandwich Cakes (1½ × recipe No. 728)
Double recipe Coffee Butter Cream Frosting (No. 815)
2 oz. finely-chopped nuts
About 1 extra oz. whole hazelnuts

1. Sandwich Cakes together with Frosting. **2.** Cover top and sides smoothly with more Frosting. **3.** Press chopped hazelnuts against sides. **4.** With remaining Frosting, pipe lines in trellis design over top of Cake. Decorate top and lower edges with small piped whirls or rosettes. **5.** Decorate top with hazelnuts. **6.** Chill lightly before serving. **8 to 10 portions.**

757 CARAMEL & ALMOND GÂTEAU

1 Genoese Cake (No. 739) or
Deep Sponge Cake (No. 750)
1 recipe Caramel Cream Frosting (No. 814)
2 to 3 oz. flaked and toasted almonds
12 blanched and toasted almonds

1. Cut Cake into 2 layers. **2.** Sandwich together with Frosting. **3.** Spread more Frosting round sides. Cover with flaked almonds. **4.** Swirl rest of Frosting over top of Cake. Decorate with whole almonds. **5.** Chill lightly before serving. **About 8 portions.**

758 RICH BUTTER CAKE

½ lb. English or Welsh butter, softened
½ lb. caster sugar
4 large or 5 standard eggs
½ lb. plain flour, sifted

1. Brush 7-in. round cake tin with melted butter. Line base and sides with greaseproof paper. Brush paper with more butter. **2.** Cream butter with sugar until light and fluffy. Beat in whole eggs, one at a time, adding tablespoon of flour with each. **3.** Gently fold in rest of flour with large metal spoon. **4.** Transfer to prepared tin and smooth top with knife. **5.** Bake in centre of moderate oven (325°F. or Gas No. 3) for 1¾ to 2 hours (or until wooden cocktail stick, inserted into centre of cake, comes out clean). **6.** Leave in tin for 5 minutes. Turn out on to wire cooling rack. **7.** Carefully peel off paper when cake is cold. **8.** Store cake in an airtight tin. **8 to 10 portions.**

MADEIRA CAKE 759

1. Follow recipe and method for Rich Butter Cake (No. 758). **2.** Cream butter and sugar with finely-grated peel of 1 medium-sized lemon. **3.** Before baking cake arrange 2 strips of candied citron or lemon peel on top of mixture. **8 to 10 portions.**

ORANGE CAKE 760

1. Follow recipe and method for Rich Butter Cake (No. 758). **2.** Cream butter and sugar with 2 level teaspoons finely-grated orange peel. **8 to 10 portions.**

FROSTED WALNUT CAKE 761

1. Follow recipe and method for Rich Butter Cake (No. 758). **2.** Stir in 2 oz. very finely-chopped shelled walnut halves after beating in eggs. **3.** When cake is cold, cut into 2 layers. Sandwich together with American Boiled Frosting (No. 818). **4.** Quickly swirl rest of Frosting over top and sides. Decorate with 1 or 2 oz. shelled walnut halves. **8 to 10 portions.**

DUNDEE CAKE 762

1. Follow recipe and method for Rich Butter Cake (No. 758). **2.** Cream butter and sugar with finely-grated peel of 1 small orange. **3.** After beating in eggs, stir in 2 oz. ground almonds, ¼ lb. *each,* currants, sultanas and seedless raisins and 2 oz. chopped mixed peel. **4.** Before baking cake, cover top of mixture with 1 or 2 oz. blanched and split almonds. **5.** Bake in centre of cool oven (300°F. or Gas. No. 2) for 2½ to 3 hours (or until wooden cocktail stick, inserted into centre, comes out clean). **8 to 10 portions.**

GINGER CAKE 763

1. Follow recipe and method for Rich Butter Cake (No. 758). **2.** Sift flour with 1 level teaspoon ground ginger. **3.** Add 3 oz. chopped preserved ginger after beating in eggs. **8 to 10 portions.**

764 COCONUT CAKE

1. Follow recipe and method for Rich Butter Cake (No. 758). **2.** Cream butter and sugar with 1 level teaspoon vanilla essence. **3.** After beating in eggs stir in 2 oz. desiccated coconut and 2 tablespoonsful milk. **8 to 10 portions.**

765 CURRANT CAKE

1. Follow recipe and method for Rich Butter Cake (No. 758). **2.** Cream butter and sugar with 1 level teaspoon finely-grated lemon peel. **3.** After beating in eggs stir in 6 oz. currants. **8 to 10 portions.**

766 SULTANA CAKE

1. Follow recipe and method for Rich Butter Cake (No. 758). **2.** Cream butter and sugar with 1 level teaspoon finely-grated lemon peel and ½ teaspoon vanilla essence. **3.** After beating in eggs stir in 6 oz. sultanas. **8 to 10 portions.**

767 SEED CAKE

1. Follow recipe and method for Rich Butter Cake (No. 758). **2.** After beating in eggs stir in 3 level teaspoons caraway seeds. **8 to 10 portions.**

768 ALMOND & RAISIN CAKE

1. Follow recipe and method for Rich Butter Cake (No. 758). **2.** Cream butter and sugar with ½ teaspoon almond essence. **3.** After beating in eggs stir in 2 oz. ground almonds and ¼ lb. seedless raisins. **8 to 10 portions.**

769 GENOESE SLAB

1. Follow recipe and method for Genoese Sandwich (No. 738). **2.** Transfer mixture to buttered and paper-lined 12-in. × 8-in. Swiss roll tin. **3.** Bake in centre of moderate oven (350°F. or Gas No. 4) for 15 to 20 minutes (or until well risen and firm). **4.** When cold, cut into 2 to 3 dozen fingers or squares and serve plain. **Serves 6 to 8.**

GENOA CAKE 7

1. Follow recipe and method for Rich Butter Cake (No. 758). **2.** Cream butter and sugar with 1 level teaspoon finely-grated lemon peel. **3.** After beating in eggs, stir in ¼ lb. *each*, currants, sultanas and chopped mixed peel, 2 oz. finely-chopped glacé cherries and 1 oz. finely-chopped almonds. **4.** Before baking cake, cover top of mixture with 1 or 2 oz. blanched and split almonds. **5.** Bake in centre of cool oven (300°F. or Gas No. 2) for 2½ to 3 hours (or until wooden cocktail stick, inserted into centre of cake, comes out clean). **8 to 10 portions.**

RICH FRUIT CAKE 7

½ lb. plain flour
1 level teaspoon mixed spice
½ level teaspoon cinnamon
½ level teaspoon grated nutmeg
1 level teaspoon cocoa powder
6 oz. English or Welsh butter
6 oz. soft brown sugar
1 level tablespoon black treacle
1 level teaspoon *each* finely-grated orange and lemon peel
4 standard eggs
1¼ lb. mixed dried fruit (currants, sultanas and seedless raisins)
¼ lb. chopped mixed peel
2 oz. chopped, shelled walnut halves or blanched almonds
2 oz. chopped dates
2 oz. chopped glacé cherries
2 dessertspoons milk

1. Brush 8-in. round or 7-in. square cake tin with melted butter. Line base and sides with double thickness of greaseproof paper. Brush paper with more butter. **2.** Sift flour with spice, cinnamon, grated nutmeg and cocoa. **3.** Cream butter with sugar, treacle and lemon and orange peel. **4.** Beat in whole eggs, one at a time, adding tablespoon of sifted dry ingredients with each. **5.** Stir in currants, sultanas, raisins, chopped peel, nuts, dates and cherries. **6.** Fold in dry ingredients alternately with milk. **7.** Transfer to prepared tin and smooth top with knife. **8.** Bake in centre of cool oven (300°F. or Gas No. 2) for 4 to 4½ hours (or until fine knitting needle, inserted into centre of cake, comes out clean). **9.** Leave in tin for 15 minutes. Turn out on to wire cooling rack. **10.** When completely cold, wrap in aluminium foil and store in airtight tin until needed. **20 to 30 portions.**

72 GENOESE PASTRIES

1. Follow recipe and method for Genoese Slab (No. 769). **2.** When cold, cut into fancy shapes with biscuit cutters. Turn into Pastries by spreading sides of each with Butter Cream Frostings and covering with Glacé Icings (see Fillings & Frostings Section). **3.** When each Pastry has set, pipe small rosettes of Butter Cream Frosting along edges. **4.** Decorate with nuts, glacé cherries, and pieces of angelica. **Makes 24 to 30 assorted-shaped pastries.**

73 FAMILY FRUIT CAKE

½ lb. self-raising flour
¼ lb. English or Welsh butter
¼ lb. caster sugar
¼ lb. mixed dried fruits (currants, sultanas or seedless raisins)
1 level teaspoon finely-grated lemon peel
1 standard egg
5 tablespoons milk

1. Brush 6-in. round cake tin or 1-lb. loaf tin with melted butter. Line base and sides with greaseproof paper. Brush paper with more butter. **2.** Sift flour into bowl. **3.** Rub in butter finely. **4.** Add sugar, fruit and lemon peel. **5.** Mix to batter with egg and milk. **6.** Stir with metal spoon until evenly combined. Do not beat. **7.** Transfer to prepared tin. **8.** Bake in centre of moderate oven (350°F. or Gas No. 4) for 1¼ to 1½ hours (or until wooden cocktail stick, inserted into centre, comes out clean). **9.** Leave in tin for 5 minutes. Turn out on to wire cooling rack. **10.** Peel off paper. Store cake in airtight tin when cold. **6 to 8 portions.**

74 DATE & WALNUT CAKE

1. Follow recipe and method for Family Fruit Cake (No. 773). **2.** Sift 1 level teaspoon mixed spice with flour. **3.** Add 3 oz. finely-chopped dates and 1 oz. finely-chopped walnuts instead of mixed fruit. **4.** Omit lemon peel. **6 to 8 portions.**

75 SULTANA & ORANGE CAKE

1. Follow recipe and method for Family Fruit Cake (No. 773). **2.** Use ¼ lb. sultanas instead of mixed fruit, and orange peel instead of lemon. **6 to 8 portions.**

Genoese Pastries (No. 772)

155

776 FARMHOUSE CAKE

1. Follow recipe and method for Family Fruit Cake (No. 773). **2.** Add 2 oz. chopped mixed peel with fruit. **6 to 8 portions.**

777 CHERRY & GINGER CAKE

1. Follow recipe and method for Family Fruit Cake (No. 773). **2.** Use 2 oz. *each,* finely-chopped glacé cherries and finely-chopped preserved ginger instead of mixed fruit. **6 to 8 portions.**

778 COCONUT & LEMON CAKE

1. Follow recipe and method for Family Fruit Cake (No. 773). **2.** Omit fruit. **3.** Add 2 oz. desiccated coconut with sugar. **4.** Increase lemon peel to 2 level teaspoons. **6 to 8 portions.**

779 PLAIN FAMILY CAKE

1. Follow recipe and method for Family Fruit Cake (No. 773). **2.** Omit fruit. **3.** If preferred, lemon peel can also be omitted and, instead, $\frac{1}{2}$ teaspoon vanilla essence added with egg and milk. **6 to 8 portions.**

780 CHOCOLATE WALNUT GÂTEAU

1 Genoese Cake (No. 739) or Deep Sponge Cake (No. 750)
Double recipe Chocolate Butter Cream Frosting (No. 816)
2 oz. finely-chopped walnuts
1 recipe Chocolate Glacé Icing (No. 829)
$\frac{1}{2}$ to 1 extra oz. shelled walnut halves

1. Cut cake into 3 layers. **2.** Sandwich together and cover sides with Frosting. **3.** Press chopped walnuts against sides. **4.** Spread Chocolate Glacé Icing over top and leave Cake undisturbed until icing has set. **5.** Pipe rosettes or small whirls of remaining Frosting round top and lower edges of Cake. **6.** Decorate with walnut halves. **7.** Chill lightly before serving. **About 8 portions.**

ICED CHRISTMAS CAKE 78

1 Rich Fruit Cake (No. 771)
4 level tablespoons warmed and melted apricot jam
1 recipe Almond Paste (No. 832)
1 recipe Royal Icing (No. 827)

1. Brush top and sides of Cake with melted jam. **2.** Turn Almond Paste on to sugared surface (either sifted icing or caster). Roll out about half into 8-in. round or 7-in. square. Use to cover top of Cake. **3.** Roll out rest of Paste into strip — same depth as Cake — and wrap round sides. **4.** Press edges and joins well together with fingers dipped in caster sugar. **5.** When Almond Paste has set (overnight) wrap Cake loosely in aluminium foil. Leave at least 1 week before icing. **6.** To ice Cake, stand on suitable silver board. **7.** Spread Royal Icing thickly and evenly over top and sides. **8.** Flick Icing upwards with back of teaspoon so that it stands in soft peaks. **9.** Decorate with Christmas ornaments. Leave Cake undisturbed overnight while Icing hardens. **20 to 30 portions.**

ROCK CAKES 78

$\frac{1}{2}$ lb. self-raising flour
$\frac{1}{4}$ lb. English or Welsh butter
3 oz. caster sugar
$\frac{1}{4}$ lb. mixed dried fruit
1 standard egg, beaten
1 or 2 dessertspoons milk

1. Sift flour into bowl. **2.** Rub in butter finely. **3.** Add sugar and fruit. **4.** Mix to very stiff batter with beaten egg and milk. **5.** Place 10 heaped dessertspoons of mixture, in rocky mounds, on well-buttered baking tray (allow room between each as they spread slightly). **6.** Bake just above centre of fairly hot oven (400°F. or Gas No. 6) for 15 to 20 minutes. **7.** Cool on wire rack. **10 Cakes.**

DATE & LEMON CAKES 78

1. Follow recipe and method for Rock Cakes (No. 782). **2.** Use $\frac{1}{4}$ lb. finely-chopped dates instead of mixed dried fruit. **3.** Add 1 level teaspoon finely-grated lemon peel with dates. **10 Cakes.**

784 CHERRY CAKES

1. Follow recipe and method for Rock Cakes (No. 782). **2.** Use 3 oz. chopped glacé cherries instead of dried fruit. **10 Cakes.**

785 WALNUT & ORANGE CAKES

1. Follow recipe and method for Rock Cakes (No. 782). **2.** Add 2 to 3 oz. chopped, shelled walnut halves and 1 level teaspoon finely-grated orange peel with sugar. **10 Cakes.**

786 SPICE & RAISIN CAKES

1. Follow recipe and method for Rock Cakes (No. 782). **2.** Sift 1 level teaspoon mixed spice with flour. **3.** Add ¼ lb. seedless raisins instead of mixed dried fruit. **10 Cakes.**

787 CHOCOLATE CAKES

1. Follow recipe and method for Rock Cakes (No. 782). **2.** Sift 7 oz. self-raising flour with 1 oz. cocoa powder. **3.** Omit fruit. **4.** Add 1 teaspoon vanilla essence with egg and milk. **10 Cakes.**

788 ALMOND SLICES

1 recipe Short Crust Pastry (No. 88)
2 level tablespoons raspberry or apricot jam
¼ lb. caster sugar
¼ lb. sifted icing sugar
6 oz. ground almonds
1 standard egg
White of one standard egg
½ teaspoon almond essence
About 2 dozen blanched and split almonds

1. Roll out Pastry into 10-in. × 6-in. rectangle. **2.** Transfer to buttered baking tray. **3.** Pinch up long edges of Pastry between finger and thumb to form raised border. **4.** Cover base with jam. **5.** Combine sugars with almonds. **6.** Mix to paste with whole egg, egg white and almond essence. **7.** Cover jam with almond mixture, spreading it evenly with knife. **8.** Decorate with split almonds. **9.** Bake just above centre of fairly hot oven (400°F. or Gas No. 6) for 25 minutes. **10.** Cool on wire rack. **11.** Cut into 14 slices when cold. **14 Almond Slices.**

PARKIN 789

6 oz. plain flour
½ level teaspoon salt
1 level teaspoon *each,* mixed spice, cinnamon and ground ginger
1 level teaspoon bicarbonate of soda
10 oz. medium oatmeal
6 oz. black treacle
5 oz. English or Welsh butter
¼ lb. soft brown sugar
¼ pint milk
1 standard egg, beaten

1. Brush 7-in. square cake tin with melted butter. Line base and sides with greaseproof paper. Brush paper with more butter. **2.** Sift flour, salt, spice, cinnamon, ground ginger and bicarbonate of soda into bowl. Add oatmeal. Make a well in centre. **3.** Put treacle, butter, sugar and milk into saucepan. Stir over low heat until butter has melted. **4.** Pour into well and add egg. Stir mixture briskly, without beating, until smooth and evenly combined. **5.** Transfer to prepared tin. Bake in centre of moderate oven (350°F. or Gas No. 4) for 1 hour (or until wooden cocktail stick, inserted into centre, comes out clean). **6.** Cool Parkin on wire rack. Store, without removing paper, in an airtight tin about 1 week before cutting. **12 to 14 portions.**

ECCLES CAKES 790

½ oz. English or Welsh butter
1 oz. currants
1 oz. chopped mixed peel
1 level dessertspoon soft brown sugar
¼ level teaspoon mixed spice
½ recipe Flaky Pastry (No. 99)
Milk for brushing
Extra caster sugar

1. Melt butter in saucepan. **2.** Stir in currants, peel, sugar and spice. Mix well. **3.** Roll out Pastry to just under ¼-in. thickness. **4.** Cut into 8 rounds with 3-in. biscuit cutter. **5.** Put heaped teaspoon of fruit mixture on to centre of each. **6.** Moisten edges of Pastry with water. **7.** With fingertips, draw up edges of each round so that they meet in the centre, completely enclosing filling. **8.** Press well together to seal. Turn each cake over. **9.** Roll to about ½-in. thickness. **10.** Make 3 slits in top of each with sharp knife. **11.** Brush with milk. Sprinkle thickly with caster sugar. **12.** Bake just above centre of hot oven (425°F. or Gas No. 7) for 20 minutes. **13.** Cool on wire rack. **8 Cakes.**

791 MARMALADE CAKE

½ lb. plain flour
Pinch of salt
3 level teaspoons baking powder
¼ lb. English or Welsh butter
2 oz. caster sugar
½ level teaspoon finely-grated orange peel
2 standard eggs, beaten
3 level tablespoons orange marmalade
2 to 3 tablespoons milk

1. Brush 6-in. round cake tin or 1-lb. loaf tin with melted butter. Line base and sides with greaseproof paper. Brush paper with more butter. **2.** Sift flour, salt and baking powder into bowl. **3.** Rub in butter finely. **4.** Add sugar and orange peel. **5.** Mix to fairly soft batter with eggs, marmalade and milk. **6.** Transfer to prepared tin. Bake in centre of moderate oven (350°F. or Gas No. 4) for 1¼ to 1½ hours (or until wooden cocktail stick, inserted into centre, comes out clean). **7.** Leave in tin for 5 minutes. Turn out on to wire cooling rack. **8.** Peel off paper. Store cake in airtight tin when cold. **6 to 8 portions.**

792 MARMALADE & WALNUT CAKE

1. Follow recipe and method for Marmalade Cake (No. 791). **2.** Add 2 oz. finely-chopped shelled walnut halves with sugar. **6 to 8 portions.**

LEMON & ALMOND RING   7

¼ lb. English or Welsh butter
¼ lb. caster sugar
1 level teaspoon finely-grated lemon peel
2 standard eggs
¼ lb. self-raising flour, sifted
1½ to 2 oz. blanched and finely-chopped almonds
1 recipe Lemon Glacé Icing (No. 825)

DECORATION
Small leaves cut from angelica

1. Brush base and sides of 1½-pint ring tin with melted butter. **2.** Cream butter with sugar and lemon peel until light and fluffy. **3.** Beat in whole eggs, one at a time, adding tablespoon of sifted flour with each. **4.** Stir in almonds. **5.** Fold in remaining flour with metal spoon. **6.** Transfer to prepared tin. Bake in centre of moderate oven (350°F. or Gas No. 4) for 35 to 40 minutes (or until wooden cocktail stick, inserted into centre of cake, comes out clean). **7.** Leave in tin for 2 or 3 minutes. Turn out on to wire cooling rack. **8.** When cake is cold pour Icing over top and allow to run down sides. **9.** Leave undisturbed until Icing has set. Decorate with angelica. **About 8 portions.**

COFFEE HAZELNUT RING   7

1. Follow recipe and method for Lemon and Almond Ring (No. 793). **2.** Use hazelnuts instead of almonds. **3.** Coat Ring with Coffee Glacé Icing (No. 826) instead of Lemon. **4.** When Icing is set decorate with about 1 dozen whole hazelnuts. **About 8 portions.**

Cherry Cake (No. 796)

5 CREAM HORNS

1 recipe Flaky Pastry (No. 99)
Milk for brushing
Caster sugar
12 level teaspoons raspberry or
    strawberry jam
$\frac{1}{2}$ pint fresh double cream
Sifted icing sugar

1. Brush 12 Cream Horn tins with melted butter. **2.** Roll out pastry thinly. Cut into 12 × 1-in. strips, each about 12 in . long. **3.** Moisten one side of each strip with water. **4.** Starting at pointed end of each tin, wind pastry strip round. Make sure moistened side faces inwards and that the strip overlaps by about $\frac{1}{4}$ in. **5.** Transfer to damp baking tray. Leave for 30 minutes. **6.** Bake just above centre of hot oven (450°F. or Gas No. 8) for 10 minutes. **7.** Remove from oven Brush with milk and sprinkle with caster sugar. **8.** Return to oven. Bake for further 7 to 10 minutes. **9.** Transfer to wire cooling rack. Cool for about 5 minutes. **10.** Carefully remove tins. Leave Horns until completely cold. **11.** Put teaspoon of jam into each. Fill with cream, whipped until thick and sweetened to taste with icing sugar. **12 Cream Horns.**

6 CHERRY CAKE

$\frac{1}{4}$ lb. glacé cherries
$\frac{1}{2}$ lb. self-raising flour
2 oz. semolina
5 oz. English or Welsh butter
$\frac{1}{4}$ lb. caster sugar
1 level teaspoon finely-grated lemon peel
$\frac{1}{2}$ teaspoon vanilla essence
2 standard eggs, well beaten
2 to 3 tablespoons milk

1. Brush 7-in. round cake tin with melted butter. Line base and sides with greaseproof paper. Brush paper with more butter. **2.** Cut cherries into quarters. **3.** Wash thoroughly to remove syrup. **4.** Dry well. Mix with 1 tablespoon of measured flour. **5.** Sift rest of flour and semolina into bowl. **6.** Rub in butter finely. **7.** Add sugar, lemon peel and cherries. **8.** Mix to stiff batter with vanilla, eggs and milk. **9.** Stir briskly, without beating, until well mixed. Transfer to prepared tin. **10.** Bake in centre of moderate oven (350°F. or Gas No. 4) for 1 hour (or until wooden cocktail stick, inserted into centre of cake, comes out clean). **11.** Leave in tin 5 minutes. Turn out on to wire cooling rack. **12.** Peel away paper. Store in airtight tin when cold. **About 8 portions.**

From the top: Cream Slices (No. 801) with Glacé Icing (No. 824), Chocolate Éclairs (No. 798) with Chocolate Glacé Icing (No. 829) and Cream Horns (No. 795)

797 GINGERBREAD

6 oz. plain flour
2 level teaspoons ground ginger
1 level teaspoon mixed spice
½ level teaspoon bicarbonate of soda
¼ lb. golden syrup
1 oz. English or Welsh butter
1 oz. soft brown sugar
1 standard egg, beaten
1 level tablespoon black treacle
2 tablespoons milk

1. Brush 6-in. square cake tin with melted butter. Line base and sides with greaseproof paper. Brush with more butter. **2.** Sift flour, ginger, spice and bicarbonate of soda into bowl. Make a well in centre. **3.** Put syrup, butter and brown sugar into saucepan. Stir over low heat until butter has melted. **4.** Pour into well with egg, treacle and milk. **5.** Stir briskly, without beating, until well combined. **6.** Transfer to prepared tin. Bake in centre of moderate oven (350°F. or Gas No. 4) for 1 hour (or until wooden cocktail stick, inserted into centre, comes out clean). **7.** Turn out on to wire cooling rack. Remove paper when gingerbread is cold. **10 to 12 portions.**

798 CHOCOLATE ÉCLAIRS

1 recipe Choux Pastry (No. 102)
½ pint fresh double cream
2 tablespoons milk
Sifted icing sugar
1 recipe Chocolate Glacé Icing (No. 829)

1. Fit forcing bag with ½-in. plain tube. **2.** Fill bag with pastry. Pipe 12 × 4-in. lengths on to buttered baking tray. **3.** Put into centre of fairly hot oven (400°F. or Gas No. 6) and bake for 10 minutes. **4.** Reduce temperature to moderate (350°F. or Gas No. 4). Bake for further 20 or 25 minutes (or until Éclairs are well puffed and golden). **5.** Remove from oven and make slit in side of each. **6.** Return to oven for further 5 minutes to dry out. **7.** Cool on wire rack. **8.** When completely cold cut each Éclair through along one side. Fill with cream, whipped until thick with milk and sweetened to taste with icing sugar. **9.** Cover tops with Icing. Leave until Icing has set. **12 Éclairs.**

799 COFFEE ÉCLAIRS

1. Follow recipe and method for Chocolate Éclairs (No. 798). **2.** Cover tops with Coffee Glacé Icing (No. 826) instead of chocolate. **12 Éclairs.**

CHOCOLATE CREAM PUFFS 80

1. Follow recipe and method for Chocolate Éclairs (No. 798). **2.** Pipe or spoon 16 to 18 equal amounts of mixture, well apart, on to buttered tray. **3.** Bake, fill and ice as for Éclairs. **16 to 18 Puffs.**

CREAM SLICES 80

1 recipe Flaky Pastry (No. 99) or
  Puff Pastry (No. 96)
½ pint fresh double cream
6 level tablespoons jam
Glacé Icing (No. 824)

1. Roll out pastry into 16-in. × 4-in. strip. **2.** Cut into eight 4-in. × 2-in. pieces. **3.** Transfer to damp baking tray. Leave for 30 minutes. **4.** Bake towards top of hot oven (450°F. or Gas No. 8) for 15 to 20 minutes (or until well risen, puffy and golden). **5.** Transfer to wire cooling rack. **6.** When completely cold, split in half. Sandwich together with cream, whipped until thick, and jam. **7.** Cover tops with Icing. Leave until Icing has set. **8 Cream Slices.**

CHEESECAKE 80

¼ lb. digestive biscuits
½ level teaspoon cinnamon
1½ oz. English or Welsh butter, melted
¾ lb. cottage cheese
Yolks and whites of 3 standard eggs
¼ lb. caster sugar
2 level tablespoons custard powder or
  cornflour
1 level teaspoon finely-grated lemon peel
4 tablespoons fresh double cream

1. Crush biscuits. Mix with cinnamon and melted butter. **2.** Use to cover base of 6-in. loose-bottomed buttered round cake tin. **3.** Rub cottage cheese through sieve. **4.** Add egg yolks, 3 oz. sugar, custard powder or cornflour, lemon peel and double cream. Mix well. **5.** Beat egg whites to stiff snow. Gently fold in rest of sugar. **6.** Fold into cheese mixture with large metal spoon. Pour into tin. Bake in centre of cool oven (300°F. or Gas No. 2) for 1 hour. **7.** Turn off heat and open oven door. Leave cake in oven for further 30 minutes. **8.** Gently remove from tin when cold. **About 8 portions.**

Fillings & Frostings

803 ORANGE VELVET FROSTING

3 dessertspoons melted English or Welsh butter
3 dessertspoons orange squash
6 oz. sifted icing sugar

1. Combine butter and squash. **2.** Gradually stir in icing sugar. **3.** Beat until icing is fairly thick and creamy, and stiff enough to spread. **Sufficient to fill or cover top of 7 to 8-in. cake.**

804 LEMON VELVET FROSTING

1. Follow recipe and method for Orange Velvet Frosting (No. 803). **2.** Use lemon squash instead of orange. **Sufficient to fill or cover top of 7 to 8-in. cake.**

805 LIME VELVET FROSTING

1. Follow recipe and method for Orange Velvet Frosting (No. 803). **2.** Use 3 dessertspoons lime cordial instead of orange squash. **Sufficient to fill or cover top of 7 to 8-in. cake.**

806 PINEAPPLE VELVET FROSTING

1. Follow recipe and method for Orange Velvet Frosting (No. 803). **2.** Use 3 dessertspoons pineapple juice instead of orange squash. **Sufficient to fill or cover top of 7 to 8-in. cake.**

807 GRAPEFRUIT VELVET FROSTING

1. Follow recipe and method for Orange Velvet Frosting (No. 803). **2.** Use 3 dessertspoons grapefruit juice instead of orange squash. **Sufficient to fill or cover top of 7 to 8-in. cake.**

808 COFFEE VELVET FROSTING

1. Follow recipe and method for Orange Velvet Frosting (No. 803). **2.** Use 3 dessertspoons liquid coffee essence instead of orange squash. **Sufficient to fill or cover top of 7 to 8-in. cake.**

BASIC BUTTER CREAM FROSTING 809

$\frac{1}{4}$ lb. English or Welsh butter
$\frac{1}{2}$ lb. sifted icing sugar
3 dessertspoons cold milk
Red or green food colouring (optional)

1. Beat butter until soft. **2.** Gradually beat in sugar alternatively with milk. **3.** Continue beating until Frosting is light and fluffy. **4.** If liked, colour pale pink or green with colouring. **Sufficient to fill and cover top of 2-layer, 7-in. sandwich cake.**

VANILLA BUTTER CREAM FROSTING 810

1. Follow recipe and method for Basic Butter Cream Frosting (No. 809). **2.** Add $\frac{1}{2}$ to 1 teaspoon vanilla essence with milk. **3.** If liked, colour pale pink or green. **Sufficient to fill and cover top of 2-layer, 7-in. sandwich cake.**

ALMOND BUTTER CREAM FROSTING 811

1. Follow recipe and method for Basic Butter Cream Frosting (No. 809). **2.** Add $\frac{1}{2}$ to 1 teaspoon almond essence with milk. **3.** If liked, colour pale pink or green. **Sufficient to fill and cover top of 2-layer, 7-in. sandwich cake.**

LEMON BUTTER CREAM FROSTING 812

1. Follow recipe and method for Basic Butter Cream Frosting (No. 809). **2.** Beat 1 level teaspoon finely-grated lemon peel with butter before adding sugar and milk. **3.** If liked, colour pale yellow with yellow food colouring. **Sufficient to fill and cover top of 2-layer, 7-in. sandwich cake.**

ORANGE BUTTER CREAM FROSTING 813

1. Follow recipe and method for Basic Butter Cream Frosting (No. 809). **2.** Beat 1 level teaspoon finely-grated orange peel with butter before adding sugar and milk. **3.** If liked, colour pale orange with orange food colouring. **Sufficient to fill and cover top of 2-layer, 7-in. sandwich cake.**

Method of rolling up Cream-Filled Swiss Roll (No. 755)

814 CARAMEL CREAM FROSTING

1 oz. caster sugar
1 dessertspoon water
½ pint fresh double cream, chilled

1. Put sugar and water into saucepan and stand over low heat until sugar dissolves. **2.** Bring to boil. Cover pan and boil half a minute. **3.** Uncover. Continue to boil steadily until syrup turns a light caramel colour. **4.** Remove from heat. Quickly stir in 2 tablespoons of measured cream. **5.** Leave until cold. Add rest of cream and whip until thick. **Sufficient to fill and cover top of 3 × 8-in. sandwich cakes or fill and thickly cover top and sides of 2-layer, 7-in. sandwich cake.**

815 COFFEE BUTTER CREAM FROSTING

1. Follow recipe and method for Basic Butter Cream Frosting (No. 809). **2.** Sift 3 to 4 level teaspoons instant coffee powder with icing sugar. **Sufficient to fill and cover top of 2-layer, 7-in. sandwich cake.**

CHOCOLATE BUTTER CREAM FROSTING 816

1. Follow recipe and method for Basic Butter Cream Frosting (No. 809). **2.** Beat in 2 oz. melted and cooled plain chocolate with sugar and only 1 dessertspoon milk. **Sufficient to fill and cover top of 2-layer, 7-in. sandwich cake.**

COFFEE FUDGE FROSTING 81

2 oz. English or Welsh butter
¼ lb. soft brown sugar
3 tablespoons liquid coffee essence
1 tablespoon fresh single cream
1 lb. sifted icing sugar

1. Put butter, sugar, coffee essence and cream into saucepan. **2.** Stand over low heat, stirring, until butter melts and sugar dissolves. **3.** Bring to boil. Boil briskly for 3 minutes only. **4.** Remove from heat. Gradually stir in icing sugar. **5.** Beat until smooth. Continue beating further 5 minutes (or until Frosting has cooled and is stiff enough to spread). **Sufficient to fill and cover top and sides of 2-layer, 7-in. sandwich cake.**

818 AMERICAN BOILED FROSTING

This Frosting is soft inside and crisp outside.

1 lb. granulated sugar
¼ pint water
Whites of 2 standard eggs
Pinch of cream of tartar
1 teaspoon vanilla essence

1. Put sugar and water into saucepan. Stir over low heat until sugar dissolves. **2.** Bring to boil. Cover pan and boil 1 minute. **3.** Uncover. Continue to boil fairly briskly, without stirring, for further 5 minutes (or until small quantity of mixture, dropped into cup of very cold water, forms soft ball when gently rolled between finger and thumb). Temperature on sugar thermometer, if used, should be 238°F. **4.** Meanwhile, beat egg whites and cream of tartar to a very stiff snow. **5.** When sugar and water have boiled for required amount of time, pour on to egg whites in slow, steady stream, beating all the time. **6.** Add vanilla. Continue beating until Frosting is cool and thick enough to spread. **7.** Quickly use to fill cake (it is important to work quickly: Frosting hardens rapidly when once it has cooled). Swirl remainder over top and sides. **Sufficient to fill and cover top and sides of 3 × 7-in. sandwich cakes or 1 deep 7 to 8-in. cake, cut into 2 layers.**

819 WHIPPED CREAM FROSTING

¼ pint fresh double cream
1 tablespoon milk
1 level tablespoon caster sugar

1. Whip cream and milk together until thick. **2.** Gently stir in caster sugar. **Sufficient to fill thickly and cover top of 2-layer, 7-in. sandwich cake.**

820 WHIPPED CREAM FROSTING WITH NUTS

1. Follow recipe and method for Whipped Cream Frosting (No. 819). **2.** After adding caster sugar, stir in 1 level tablespoon very finely-chopped shelled walnut halves, hazelnuts or toasted almonds. **Sufficient to fill thickly and cover top of 2-layer, 7-in. sandwich cake.**

821 COFFEE CREAM FROSTING

1. Follow recipe and method for Whipped Cream Frosting (No. 819). **2.** Add 1 level teaspoon instant coffee powder with caster sugar. **Sufficient to fill thickly and cover top of 2-layer, 7-in. sandwich cake.**

822 VANILLA CREAM FROSTING

1. Follow recipe and method for Whipped Cream Frosting (No. 819). **2.** Whip cream and milk with ½ teaspoon vanilla essence. **Sufficient to fill thickly and cover top of 2-layer, 7-in. sandwich cake.**

823 WHIPPED CREAM WITH RUM, SHERRY OR BRANDY

1. Follow recipe and method for Whipped Cream Frosting (No. 819). **2.** After adding caster sugar, stir in 1 or 2 teaspoons rum, sherry or brandy. **Sufficient to fill thickly and cover top of 2-layer, 7-in. sandwich cake.**

824 GLACÉ ICING

½ lb. sifted icing sugar
3 dessertspoons hot water

1. Put sugar into bowl. Gradually add water. **2.** Stir briskly until smooth and thick enough to coat back of spoon without running off. **3.** If too thick, add a little more water; if too thin, stir in more sifted icing sugar. If liked, colour to taste with food colouring. **4.** Use straight away. **Sufficient to cover top of 7 to 8-in. cake.**

● *Do not disturb cake until Icing has set, or cracks will form.*

825 ORANGE OR LEMON GLACÉ ICING

1. Follow recipe and method for Glacé Icing (No. 824). **2.** Add 1 level teaspoon very finely-grated orange or lemon peel to sifted sugar. **3.** Mix with 3 dessertspoons strained and warmed orange or lemon juice instead of water. If liked, colour with orange or lemon food colouring. **Sufficient to cover top of 7 to 8-in. cake.**

826 COFFEE GLACÉ ICING

1. Follow recipe and method for Glacé Icing (No. 824). **2.** Dissolve 2 level teaspoons instant coffee powder in hot water before adding to sugar. **Sufficient to cover top of 7 to 8-in. cake.**

827 ROYAL ICING

Whites of 2 standard eggs
1 lb. sifted icing sugar
$\frac{1}{2}$ teaspoon lemon juice
2 to 3 drops glycerine

1. Beat egg whites until foamy. **2.** Gradually beat in icing sugar, lemon juice and glycerine (glycerine prevents icing from becoming too hard to cut). **3.** Continue beating hard a good 5 to 7 minutes (or until icing is snowy-white and firm enough to stand in straight points when spoon is lifted out of bowl). **4.** If too stiff, add a little more egg white or lemon juice. If too soft, beat in a little more sifted icing sugar. **5.** If coloured icing is required, beat in a few drops of food colouring. **Sufficient to cover top and sides of 7 to 8-in. cake.**

● *It is best to use Royal Icing as soon as it is made because it sets and hardens fairly quickly. If this is not possible, keep the Icing covered with a cloth wrung out in cold water until ready for use.*

828 ROYAL ICING FOR PIPING

1. Follow recipe and method for Royal Icing (No. 827). **2.** Omit glycerine. **3.** Make up $\frac{1}{4}$ to $\frac{1}{2}$ quantity only.

829 CHOCOLATE GLACÉ ICING

2 oz. plain chocolate
$\frac{1}{2}$ oz. English or Welsh butter
4 dessertspoons warm water
$\frac{1}{2}$ teaspoon vanilla essence
$\frac{1}{4}$ lb. sifted icing sugar

1. Break up chocolate and put, with butter and water, into basin standing over saucepan of hot water. **2.** Leave until melted, stirring once or twice. **3.** Add vanilla. Gradually beat in icing sugar. **4.** Use straight away. **Sufficient to cover top of 7 to 8-in. cake.**

MOCHA GLACÉ ICING 830

1. Follow recipe and method for Chocolate Glacé Icing (No. 829). **2.** Add 2 level teaspoons instant coffee powder to chocolate, butter and water in basin. **Sufficient to cover top of 7 to 8-in. cake.**

COCOA GLACÉ ICING 83

2 level tablespoons sifted cocoa powder
4 dessertspoons boiling water
$\frac{1}{2}$ oz. English or Welsh butter, melted
$\frac{1}{2}$ lb. sifted icing sugar

1. Mix cocoa to smooth paste with boiling water. **2.** Add butter. **3.** Gradually stir in icing sugar. **4.** Use straight away. **Sufficient to cover top of 7 to 8-in. cake.**

ALMOND PASTE 83

$\frac{1}{2}$ lb. ground almonds
$\frac{1}{2}$ lb. sifted icing sugar
$\frac{1}{2}$ lb. caster sugar
Yolks of 2 standard eggs
1 teaspoon lemon juice
$\frac{1}{2}$ teaspoon each vanilla and almond
  essences

1. Combine almonds with both sugars. **2.** Mix to fairly stiff paste with remaining ingredients. **3.** Turn out on to board or table covered with sifted icing sugar. Knead lightly with fingertips until smooth, crack-free and pliable. **Sufficient to cover top and sides of 8 to 9-in. rich fruit cake fairly thickly.**

Yeast Recipes

WHITE BREAD

1 lb. plain flour
2 level teaspoons salt
$\frac{1}{2}$ oz. English or Welsh butter
$\frac{1}{2}$ oz. fresh yeast
$\frac{1}{2}$ pint warm water
FOR BRUSHING
Milk or beaten egg

1. Sift flour and salt into bowl. **2.** Rub in butter. **3.** Mix yeast to smooth and creamy liquid with a little of the warm water. Blend in rest of water. **4.** Add all at once to dry ingredients. Mix to firm dough, adding more flour if needed, until dough leaves sides of bowl clean. **5.** Turn out on to lightly-floured board. Knead thoroughly 10 minutes. **6.** Cover and leave to rise until dough doubles in size. **7.** Turn out on to lightly-floured board and knead until firm. **8.** Shape to fit 1-lb. loaf tin. Brush tin with melted butter then put in dough. **9.** Cover and leave to rise until dough doubles in size and reaches top of tin. **10.** Brush with milk or beaten egg and milk. Bake in centre of hot oven (450°F. or Gas No. 8) 30 to 40 minutes (or until loaf shrinks slightly from sides of tin and crust is golden brown). **11.** Cool on wire rack. **1 Loaf.**

834 WHITE BREAD ROLLS

1. Follow recipe and method for White Bread (No. 833). **2.** After first rising, divide dough into 12 equal-sized pieces and shape into round rolls, miniature plaits and tiny cottage loaves. **3.** Put on to buttered baking tray, cover and leave to rise until double in size. **4.** Brush with milk or beaten egg and milk. Bake towards top of hot oven (450°F. or Gas No. 8) 20 to 25 minutes (or until brown and crisp). **5.** Cool on wire rack. **12 Rolls.**

835 MILK LOAF

1 lb. plain flour
1 level teaspoon sugar
$\frac{1}{2}$ oz. fresh yeast or 1 level teaspoon dried yeast
$\frac{1}{4}$ pint + 4 tablespoons lukewarm milk
1 level teaspoon salt
2 oz. English or Welsh butter
1 standard egg, beaten
Extra milk for brushing

1. Put one third of flour into large bowl. Add sugar, yeast (fresh or dried) and milk. Mix well. Leave in warm place for 20 minutes (or until frothy). **2.** Meanwhile, sift rest of flour and salt into bowl. Rub in butter then add, with beaten egg, to yeast mixture. Mix well. **3.** Turn out on to lightly-floured board. Knead for 10 minutes (or until dough loses its stickiness). **4.** Cover and leave to rise until double in size. **5.** Turn out on to floured board. Knead lightly. **6.** Shape to fit 1-lb. loaf tin. Brush tin with melted butter. Put in dough. **7.** Cover and leave to rise until dough doubles in size and reaches top of tin. **8.** Brush with milk. Bake in centre of fairly hot oven (375°F. or Gas No. 5) for 45 to 50 minutes (or until loaf shrinks slightly from sides of tin and crust is golden brown). **9.** Cool on wire rack. **1 Milk Loaf.**

DRIED YEAST

This can be used instead of fresh. Allow 2 level teaspoons dried for every $\frac{1}{2}$ oz. fresh yeast recommended in a recipe. To reconstitute, dissolve a teaspoon of sugar in a little of the measured liquid — which should be warm. Sprinkle yeast on top. Leave in a warm place for 10 to 15 minutes, or until frothy. Add to dry ingredients with rest of warm liquid.

FLOUR

For best results (especially for breadmaking) use a strong plain flour. It absorbs more water, resulting in larger volume and lighter texture.

COVERING

To prevent a skin forming on the dough, cover with buttered polythene, or put bowl or tin or tins inside a buttered polythene bag.

RISING

For a quick rise, leave dough for about $\frac{1}{2}$ an hour in a warm place. For a slow rise, leave dough 1 to $1\frac{1}{2}$ hours on the kitchen table. For an overnight rise, leave dough up to 12 hours in a cold larder. For a very slow rise, leave dough in the refrigerator for 24 hours but allow to reach room temperature before shaping.

SURPLUS DOUGH

Put into a polythene bag, tie loosely and leave in the refrigerator up to 2 days. Allow to soften in a warm place for 15 to 20 minutes before shaping into loaves or rolls etc.

836 QUICK BROWN BREAD

½ lb. brown flour
½ lb. plain white flour
2 level teaspoons salt
2 level teaspoons granulated sugar
½ oz. English or Welsh butter
½ oz. fresh yeast
¼ pint lukewarm water
¼ pint lukewarm milk
Salted water
1 or 2 tablespoons cracked wheat or
crushed cornflakes

1. Sift flours, salt and sugar into bowl. **2.** Rub in butter finely. **3.** Mix yeast to smooth and creamy liquid with a little of the warm water. Blend in rest of water and milk. **4.** Add all at once to dry ingredients. Mix to fairly soft dough that leaves sides of bowl clean. **5.** Turn out on to floured board. Knead 10 minutes (or until smooth and elastic.) **6.** Cut into 2 and shape each to fit a 1-lb. loaf tin. **7.** Brush tins with melted butter. Put in dough. **8.** Brush tops of loaves with salted water. Sprinkle with cracked wheat (if available) or crushed cornflakes. **9.** Cover and leave to rise until loaves have doubled in size and spring back when pressed lightly with floured finger. **10.** Put into centre of hot oven (450°F. or Gas No. 8). Bake 30 to 40 minutes. **11.** Turn out and cool on wire rack. **2 Loaves.**

837 CRUSTY BROWN ROLLS

1. Follow recipe and method for Quick Brown Bread (No. 836) but divide dough into 12 equal-sized pieces after kneading. **2.** Roll into balls. Place 1 in. apart on lightly buttered and floured baking tray. **3.** Brush tops with salted water. Sprinkle with cracked wheat (if available) or crushed cornflakes. **4.** Cover and leave to rise until rolls have doubled in size. Bake towards top of hot oven (450°F. or Gas No. 8) 20 to 30 minutes. **5.** Cool on wire rack. **12 Rolls.**

HOT CROSS BUNS 83

1 lb. plain flour
2 oz. caster sugar
1 oz. fresh yeast or 1 level tablespoon dried
yeast
¼ pint lukewarm milk
4 tablespoons lukewarm water
1 level teaspoon salt
1 level teaspoon mixed spice
½ level teaspoon cinnamon
¼ lb. currants
2 oz. chopped mixed peel
2 oz. English or Welsh butter, melted and
cooled
1 standard egg, beaten

GLAZE
2 oz. granulated sugar
3 tablespoons milk

1. Sift 4 oz. flour into bowl. Add 1 teaspoon sugar. **2.** Blend yeast with milk and water. Add to sifted flour and sugar. **3.** Mix well and leave 20 to 30 minutes (or until frothy). **4.** Meanwhile sift remaining flour, salt and spices into another bowl. Add rest of sugar, currants and peel. Toss lightly together. **5.** Add to yeast mixture with butter and beaten egg. Mix to fairly soft dough that leaves sides of bowl clean. **6.** Turn out on to floured board and knead 5 minutes (or until dough is smooth and no longer sticky). **7.** Cover and leave to rise until double in size. **8.** Turn out on to floured board. Knead lightly and divide into 12 equal-sized pieces. **9.** Shape each into round bun. Stand well apart on lightly-buttered and floured baking tray. **10.** Cover and leave to rise 30 minutes (or until dough feels springy when pressed lightly with floured finger). **11.** Cut a cross on top of each with sharp knife. Bake just above centre of hot oven (425°F. or Gas No. 7) 20 to 25 minutes. **12.** Transfer to wire rack. Brush twice with glaze, made by dissolving sugar in milk and boiling for 2 minutes. **12 Hot Cross Buns.**

838 POPPY SEED PLAITS

1. Follow recipe and method for Milk Loaf (No. 835). **2.** After dough has risen for first time, turn out on to floured board, knead lightly and cut in half. **3.** Cut each half into 3 pieces. **4.** Shape each piece into long thin roll and plait together (two plaited loaves). **5.** Stand on buttered and floured baking tray. Brush with a little beaten egg. Sprinkle with 5 to 6 level teaspoons poppy seeds. **6.** Cover and leave to rise until double in size. **7.** Put into centre of fairly hot oven (375°F. or Gas No. 5). Bake for 45 to 50 minutes (or until bases of loaves sound hollow when tapped and tops and sides are lightly brown). **8.** Cool on wire rack. **2 Loaves.**

Yorkshire Tea Cakes (No. 841)

40 WHOLEMEAL BREAD

3 lb. wholemeal flour
2 level teaspoons salt
2 level teaspoons caster sugar
1 oz. English or Welsh butter
2 oz. fresh yeast
1 pint lukewarm water
½ pint lukewarm milk
Salted water

1. Sift flour, salt and sugar into bowl and rub in butter. **2.** Mix yeast to smooth and creamy liquid with a little of the warm water. **3.** Mix dry ingredients with yeast liquid, milk, and sufficient of remaining water to make firm dough that leaves sides of bowl clean. **4.** Turn out on to lightly-floured board. Knead thoroughly 10 minutes (or until dough is smooth and elastic and no longer sticky). **5.** Cover and leave until double in size. **6.** Turn out on to floured board. Knead well and cut in half. **7.** Shape each piece to fit 2-lb. loaf tin. Brush tins with melted butter then put in dough. **8.** Brush top of loaves with salted water. Cover and leave to rise until dough reaches tops of tins. **9.** Bake in centre of hot oven (450°F. or Gas No. 8) 40 to 45 minutes (or until loaves shrink slightly from sides of tins). **10.** Turn out and cool on wire rack. **2 Loaves.**

YORKSHIRE TEA CAKES 841

1 lb. plain flour
1 level teaspoon salt
1 oz. English or Welsh butter
1 oz. caster sugar
2 oz. currants
½ oz. fresh yeast
½ pint lukewarm milk

FOR BRUSHING
Extra milk

1. Sift flour and salt into bowl and rub in butter. **2.** Add sugar and currants. Toss lightly together. **3.** Blend yeast with milk. Add all at once to dry ingredients. **4.** Mix to firm dough, adding little extra flour if necessary, until dough leaves sides of bowl clean. **5.** Turn out on to lightly-floured board. Knead 10 minutes (or until dough is smooth and elastic). **6.** Cover and leave to rise until double in size. **7.** Turn out on to lightly-floured board. Knead well and divide into 6 equal-sized pieces. **8.** Roll each out into 6-in. round. Transfer to buttered baking tray. **9.** Brush tops with milk. Cover and leave to rise until almost double in size. **10.** Bake just above centre of fairly hot oven (400°F. or Gas No. 6) 20 minutes. **11.** Cool on wire rack. **12.** To serve, split open and spread thickly with English or Welsh butter. The Tea Cakes can also be split and toasted before being buttered. **6 Tea Cakes.**

842 BABAS

1 oz. fresh yeast or 1 level tablespoon dried yeast
6 tablespoons lukewarm milk
½ lb. plain flour
½ level teaspoon salt
1 oz. caster sugar
4 standard eggs, beaten
¼ lb. English or Welsh butter, softened
¼ lb. currants

SYRUP
4 level tablespoons golden syrup
4 tablespoons water
2 tablespoons rum

GLAZE
3 level tablespoons apricot jam
2 tablespoons water

DECORATION
½ pint fresh double cream

1. Mix yeast with milk and 2 oz. flour. Leave 20 to 30 minutes or until frothy. **2.** Combine with rest of flour, salt, sugar, beaten eggs, butter and currants. Beat thoroughly for 5 minutes. **3.** Brush 16 Dariole moulds with melted butter and half fill with mixture. **4.** Cover and leave to rise until moulds are two-thirds full. **5.** Bake towards top of fairly hot oven (400°F. or Gas No. 6) 15 to 20 minutes. **6.** Cool 5 minutes. Turn out of moulds then transfer to wire rack with large plate underneath. **7.** Warm golden syrup, water and rum together. Pour sufficient over Babas to soak them well. **8.** Heat jam slowly with water. Strain. Brush thickly over Babas then leave until cold. **9.** Transfer to serving dish. Top each with a mound of cream, whipped until thick. **Serves 8.**

843 PLAIN SAVARIN

1. Follow recipe and method for Babas (No. 842) but omit currants. **2.** Instead of using Dariole moulds, half-fill one well-buttered 8-in. ring mould or two 6-in. moulds with mixture. **3.** After mixture has risen, bake towards top of fairly hot oven (400°F. or Gas No. 6) 20 minutes. **4.** Turn out on to dish and prick with skewer. **5.** Soak with hot syrup made by dissolving 6 tablespoons granulated sugar in ¼-pint water and 2 or 3 tablespoons rum or white wine. **6.** Serve hot. **Serves 8.**

MALT LOAVES 844

3 oz. malt extract
2 level tablespoons black treacle
1 oz. English or Welsh butter
1 lb. plain flour
1 level teaspoon salt
½ lb. sultanas
1 oz. fresh yeast
¼ pint plus 3 tablespoons lukewarm water
Clear honey

1. Put malt extract, treacle and butter into pan. Heat through gently. Leave to cool. **2.** Sift flour and salt into bowl. Add sultanas and toss lightly together. **3.** Mix yeast to smooth and creamy liquid with a little of the water. Blend in rest of water. **4.** Add to dry ingredients with cooled malt mixture. Work to soft dough that leaves sides of bowl clean. **5.** Turn out on to lightly-floured board. Knead until dough is smooth and elastic. **6.** Cut into 2 equal-sized pieces. Shape each to fit 1-lb. loaf tin. **7.** Brush tins with melted butter and put in dough. Cover and leave to rise until loaves double in size. **8.** Put into centre of fairly hot oven (400°F. or Gas No. 6). Bake 40 to 45 minutes. **9.** Turn out on to wire rack. Glaze tops of hot loaves with wet brush dipped in honey. **10.** Leave until cold before cutting. **2 Malt Loaves.**

MUFFINS 84

1 lb. plain flour
1 level teaspoon salt
1 oz. fresh yeast
¼ pint lukewarm milk
6 tablespoons lukewarm water
1 standard egg, beaten
1 oz. English or Welsh butter, melted

1. Sift flour and salt into bowl. **2.** Mix yeast to smooth and creamy liquid with a little milk. Blend in rest of milk and water. **3.** Add to dry ingredients with beaten egg and melted butter. Mix to fairly soft dough. **4.** Turn out on to well-floured board. Knead 10 minutes (or until dough is smooth and no longer sticky). **5.** Cover and leave to rise until double in size. **6.** Turn out on to floured board. Knead lightly and roll out to ½-in. thickness. **7.** Cut into 12 rounds with 3½-in. biscuit cutter. Transfer to well-floured baking tray. Dust with flour. **8.** Cover and leave to rise until double in size. **9.** Bake towards top of hot oven (450°F. or Gas No. 8) 5 minutes. **10.** Remove from oven. Turn over and bake further 5 minutes. **11.** To serve, toast on both sides, pull apart with fingers, butter thickly and put together again. Serve hot. **12 Muffins.**

46 DOUGHNUTS

½ lb. plain flour
½ level teaspoon caster sugar
½ oz. fresh yeast or 2 level teaspoons dried
  yeast
6 tablespoons lukewarm milk
¼ level teaspoon salt
½ oz. English or Welsh butter, melted and
  cooled
1 standard egg, beaten
4 teaspoons red jam
Deep fat or oil for frying
4 level tablespoons caster sugar mixed
  with 1 level teaspoon cinnamon

1. Sift 2 oz. flour into bowl then add sugar and yeast blended with milk. **2.** Mix well and leave 20 to 30 minutes or until frothy. **3.** Meanwhile, sift remaining flour and salt together and add to yeast mixture with butter and beaten egg. **4.** Mix to fairly soft dough that leaves sides of bowl clean. **5.** Turn out on to floured board and knead 5 minutes (or until dough is smooth and no longer sticky). **6.** Cover and leave to rise until double in size. **7.** Turn out on to floured board. knead lightly and divide into 8 equal-sized pieces. **8.** Shape into balls. Cover and leave to rise 30 minutes (or until dough feels springy when pressed lightly with floured finger). **9.** Press a hole in each ball with finger. Put in about ½ teaspoon of jam. **10.** Pinch up edges of dough so that jam is completely enclosed. Deep fry Doughnuts in hot fat or oil for 4 minutes. **11.** Drain thoroughly on soft kitchen paper. Roll in sugar and cinnamon. **8 Doughnuts.**

● *For luxury touch, split doughnuts halfway down and fill with fresh double cream, whipped.*

BATH BUNS 848

1 lb. plain flour
1 oz. caster sugar
1 oz. fresh yeast or 1 level tablespoon dried
  yeast
¼ pint lukewarm milk
4 tablespoons lukewarm water
1 level teaspoon salt
6 oz. sultanas
2 oz. chopped mixed peel
2 oz. English or Welsh butter, melted and
  cooled
1 standard egg, beaten

FOR BRUSHING
Beaten egg mixed with a little water
Coarsely-crushed cube sugar

1. Sift ¼ lb. flour into bowl. Add 1 teaspoon sugar. **2.** Blend yeast with milk and water. Add to sifted flour and sugar. **3.** Mix well and leave 20 to 30 minutes (or until frothy). **4.** Meanwhile, sift remaining flour and salt into another bowl. Add rest of sugar, sultanas and peel. Toss lightly together. **5.** Add to yeast mixture with butter and beaten egg. Mix to fairly soft dough that leaves sides of bowl clean. **6.** Turn out on to floured board and knead 5 minutes (or until dough is smooth and no longer sticky). **7.** Cover and leave to rise until double in size. **8.** Turn out on to floured board. knead lightly. **9.** Put 14 tablespoons of dough on to lightly-buttered and floured baking tray. **10.** Cover and leave to rise 30 minutes (or until dough feels springy when pressed lightly with floured finger). **11.** Brush with egg and water, sprinkle with crushed sugar and bake just above centre of hot oven (425°F. or Gas No. 7) 20 to 25 minutes. **12.** Cool on wire rack. **14 Bath Buns.**

47 BRIOCHES

½ lb. plain flour
½ level teaspoon salt
½ oz. caster sugar
½ oz. fresh yeast
3 dessertspoons lukewarm water
2 standard eggs, beaten
2 oz. English or Welsh butter, melted and
  cooled

FOR BRUSHING
Little extra beaten egg

1. Sift flour, salt and sugar into bowl. **2.** Mix yeast to smooth and creamy liquid with water. **3.** Add to dry ingredients with beaten eggs and butter. **4.** Mix to soft dough. Turn on to floured board and knead 5 minutes (or until dough is smooth and no longer sticky). **5.** Cover and leave to rise until double in size. **6.** Turn out on to floured board. Knead lightly. **7.** Divide three quarters of the dough into 12 equal-sized pieces. **8.** Shape into balls. Put into well-buttered deep bun tins or into 3-in. fluted Brioche tins. Press a deep hole in centre of each. **9.** Divide remaining dough into 12 pieces. Roll into small balls and stand on top of holes. **10.** Cover and leave to rise in warm place for about 1 hour (or until Brioches are light and well risen). **11.** Brush gently with beaten egg. Bake in centre of hot oven (450°F. or Gas No. 8) 10 minutes. **12.** Transfer to wire rack. Serve warm with butter. **12 Brioches.**

849 CURRANT BREAD

1 lb. plain flour
1 level teaspoon salt
1 oz. English or Welsh butter
1 oz. caster sugar
$\frac{1}{4}$ lb. currants
1 oz. fresh yeast
$\frac{1}{4}$ pint lukewarm water
$\frac{1}{4}$ pint lukewarm milk
Clear honey or golden syrup

1. Sift flour and salt into bowl and rub in butter. Add sugar and currants and toss lightly together. 2. Mix yeast to smooth and creamy liquid with a little of the warm water. Blend in rest of water and milk. 3. Add all at once to dry ingredients. Mix to firm dough, adding little extra flour if necessary, until dough leaves sides of bowl clean. 4. Turn out on to lightly-floured board. Knead 10 minutes (or until dough is smooth and elastic). 5. Cut into 2 equal-sized pieces. Shape each to fit a 1-lb. loaf tin. 6. Brush tins with melted butter and put in dough. 7. Cover and leave to rise until dough reaches tops of tins. 8. Put into centre of hot oven (425°F. or Gas No. 7). Bake 40 to 45 minutes. 9. Turn out on to wire rack. Glaze tops of hot loaves by brushing with wet brush dipped in clear honey or golden syrup. 10. Leave until cold before cutting. 2 Loaves.

850 SCOTTISH BAP OR FLAT LOAF

1 lb. plain flour
1 level teaspoon salt
2 oz. English or Welsh butter
$\frac{1}{2}$ oz. fresh yeast
$\frac{1}{4}$ pint lukewarm water
$\frac{1}{4}$ pint lukewarm milk

1. Sift flour and salt into bowl. Rub in butter. 2. Mix yeast to smooth and creamy liquid with a little of the warm water. Blend in rest of water and milk. 3. Add all at once to dry ingredients. Mix to firm dough, adding a little extra flour if necessary, until dough leaves sides of bowl clean. 4. Turn out on to lightly-floured board. Knead 10 minutes (or until smooth and elastic). 5. Cover and leave to rise until dough doubles in size. 6. Turn out on to floured board. Knead lightly and shape into ball. 7. Roll out to $\frac{3}{4}$-in. thick round, transfer to lightly-buttered and floured baking tray and dredge with plain flour. 8. Cover and leave to rise until double in size. 9. Lightly dent top of Bap in 3 places with fingers (to prevent blistering). 10. Bake just above centre of fairly hot oven (400°F. or Gas No. 6) for 20 to 25 minutes. 11. Cool on wire rack. 1 Bap.

SMALL BAPS OR FLAT LOAVES   85

1. Follow recipe and method for Scottish Bap (No. 850). 2. After first rising, divide dough into 10 equal-sized pieces. Roll each into $\frac{1}{2}$-in. thick ovals. 3. Transfer to lightly-buttered and floured baking tray. Dredge with flour. 4. Cover and leave to rise until double in size. 5. Make 3 shallow dents in top of each. Bake just above centre of fairly hot oven (400°F. or Gas No. 6) 15 to 20 minutes. 6. Cool on wire rack. 10 Small Baps.

CORNISH SPLITS   85

1 lb. plain flour
2 oz. caster sugar
1 oz. fresh yeast or 1 level tablespoon dried yeast
$\frac{1}{4}$ pint lukewarm milk
$\frac{1}{4}$ pint lukewarm water
1 level teaspoon salt
2 oz. English or Welsh butter, melted and cooled

1. Sift $\frac{1}{4}$ lb. flour into bowl. Add 1 teaspoon sugar. 2. Blend yeast with milk and water. Add to sifted flour and sugar. 3. Mix well and leave 20 to 30 minutes (or until frothy). 4. Meanwhile, sift remaining flour and salt into another bowl. Add rest of sugar. 5. Add to yeast mixture with butter. Mix to fairly soft dough that leaves sides of bowl clean. 6. Turn out on to floured board. Knead 5 minutes (or until dough is smooth and no longer sticky). 7. Cover and leave to rise until double in size. 8. Turn out on to floured board. Knead lightly and divide into 14 equal-sized pieces. 9. Shape each into round bun. Stand well apart on lightly-buttered and floured baking tray. 10. Cover and leave to rise 30 minutes (or until dough feels springy when pressed lightly with floured finger). 11. Bake just above centre of hot oven (425°F. or Gas No. 7) 20 to 25 minutes. 12. Cool on wire rack. 13. When cold, split open and fill with jam and either fresh whipped or clotted cream. 14 Splits.

Right: Quick Brown Bread (No. 836) Crusty Brown Rolls (No. 837), Poppy Seed Plaits (No. 838), Currant Bread (No. 849) Malt Loaves (844) and Scottish Bap or Flat Loaf (No. 850)

Cold Puddings

853 ORANGE & STRAWBERRY CHANTILLY

3 large oranges
¾ lb. strawberries
2 to 3 tablespoons sweet white wine (or brandy)
½ pint fresh double cream
2 tablespoons milk
2 oz. sifted icing sugar
White of 1 standard egg

1. Put oranges into large bowl, cover with boiling water and leave 10 minutes. (This makes the skin and pith easier to remove.) **2.** Drain oranges, peel and chill. **3.** Halve strawberries and put into shallow serving dish. **4.** Slice oranges thinly, arrange on top of strawberries, sprinkle with the wine or brandy. Chill at least 1 hour. **5.** Just before serving, whip cream and milk together until thick. Stir in sugar and egg white, beaten to a stiff snow. **6.** Pile over fruit mixture and serve straight away. **Serves 4 to 6.**

854 GOOSEBERRY WHIP

½ lb. gooseberries
5 dessertspoons water
1 to 2 oz. granulated sugar
2 level teaspoons gelatine
4 tablespoons boiling water
½ level teaspoon finely-grated lemon peel
4 tablespoons fresh double cream
1 dessertspoon milk
White of 1 standard egg
Green food colouring

DECORATION
4 tablespoons fresh double cream, whipped
Leaves cut from angelica

1. Top and tail gooseberries. Put into pan with 5 dessertspoons water. **2.** Bring slowly to the boil. Cover pan with lid and simmer until fruit is soft. **3.** Remove from heat. Sweeten to taste with sugar. Either rub through sieve or liquidise. **4.** Shower gelatine into 4 tablespoons boiling water and stir briskly until dissolved. **5.** Add to gooseberry mixture with lemon peel. Leave in the cold until just beginning to thicken and set. **6.** Whip cream and milk together until lightly stiff. Gradually stir in fruit mixture then gently fold in egg white, beaten to stiff snow. **7.** Tint pale green with colouring. Turn into large serving bowl and chill until firm and set. **8.** Just before serving, decorate with whipped cream and angelica. **Serves 4.**

RICH FRUIT FOOL 85

1 lb. either gooseberries, apples, black or redcurrants, rhubarb, blackberries or raspberries
3 tablespoons water
3 to 6 oz. caster sugar to sweeten, depending on sharpness of fruit
½ pint fresh double cream
2 tablespoons milk
Red or green food colouring

DECORATION
4 tablespoons fresh double cream, whipped
About 1 oz. finely-chopped, shelled walnut halves or finely-chopped toasted almonds

1. Prepare fruit according to type. Put into pan with the water. **2.** Bring slowly to the boil, cover with lid and simmer until fruit is soft. **3.** Remove from heat. Add sugar to taste. Either rub through sieve or liquidise. Leave until completely cold. **4.** Whip cream and milk together until lightly stiff then gradually fold in the fruit purée. **5.** If Fool is pale (which it will be if made from apples or gooseberries) tint pale pink or green. **6.** Transfer to 4 sundae glasses and chill. **7.** Before serving, whip cream until thick, pipe whirls on top of each Fool, then sprinkle with nuts. **Serves 4.**

CUSTARD CREAM FRUIT FOOL 85

1. Follow recipe and method for Rich Fruit Fool (No. 855) but use half the cream and milk and ¼ pint cold custard. **2.** Mix the custard with the fruit purée then fold into the whipped cream and milk. **Serves 4.**

CUSTARD FRUIT FOOL 85

Follow recipe and method for Rich Fruit Fool (No. 855) but instead of cream and milk, combine ½ pint fairly thick cold custard with the fruit purée. **Serves 4.**

58 SUMMER PUDDING

6 large slices stale bread
$\frac{1}{4}$ lb. granulated sugar
5 tablespoons water
1$\frac{1}{2}$ lb. soft summer fruits (either rhubarb, raspberries, strawberries, gooseberries, stoned cherries, black or redcurrants, or mixture of fruits)
$\frac{1}{4}$ pint fresh double cream
1 tablespoon milk

1. Remove crusts from bread. Cut slices into neat fingers. 2. Put sugar and water into pan and heat slowly until sugar melts, stirring. 3. Add fruit and simmer gently for about 7 to 10 minutes (gooseberries, blackcurrants may take a few minutes longer). 4. Line base and sides of 2-pint pudding basin with bread fingers. Add half the hot fruit mixture. Cover with more bread fingers. 5. Pour in rest of fruit mixture and top with remaining bread fingers. 6. Cover with saucer or plate. Put a heavy weight on top. 7. Refrigerate or leave in cold pantry overnight. 8. Turn out on to plate. Serve with the cream, whipped with the milk until lightly stiff. **Serves 4 to 6.**

9 FROSTED FRUIT MOULD

1 lemon-flavoured jelly
5 tablespoons boiling water
$\frac{1}{4}$ pint fairly thick apricot purée, made from stewed or canned fruit
2 level teaspoons finely-grated lemon peel
1 carton (5 oz.) natural yogurt
DECORATION
16 black grapes, in pairs
White of 1 small egg, lightly beaten
2 to 3 level tablespoons caster sugar

1. Put jelly and 5 tablespoons boiling water into a saucepan and stand over very low heat until jelly dissolves. 2. Pour into a measuring jug and make up to $\frac{1}{2}$ pint with cold water. Stir in the fruit purée and lemon peel. 3. Leave until cold but still liquid, then gradually beat into the yogurt. 4. When evenly combined, transfer to 1-pint fancy mould, first rinsed with cold water. 5. Chill for at least 2 hours. 6. Before serving, frost grapes by dipping in the beaten egg white then tossing in the caster sugar. 7. Turn mould out on to a plate and surround with grapes. **Serves 4.**

LEMON MILK JELLY   860

4 level teaspoons gelatine
3 tablespoons boiling water
2 oz. caster sugar
1 level teaspoon finely-grated lemon peel
1 pint milk
Yellow food colouring

1. Shower gelatine into boiling water and stir briskly until dissolved. 2. Put sugar, lemon peel and milk into saucepan. Stand over very low heat until sugar dissolves. 3. When gelatine and milk are both lukewarm, combine by pouring milk gently on to the gelatine. 4. Stir well and tint pale yellow with colouring. 5. Pour into a 1$\frac{1}{4}$ to 1$\frac{1}{2}$-pint mould, first rinsed with cold water. 6. Leave in cool until set. Turn out on to a serving plate. **Serves 4.**

ORANGE MILK JELLY   861

1. Follow recipe and method for Lemon Milk Jelly (No. 860) but use grated orange peel instead of lemon peel. 2. Colour pale orange with orange food colouring. **Serves 4.**

CHOCOLATE MILK JELLY   862

1. Follow recipe and method for Lemon Milk Jelly (No. 860) but omit lemon peel and colouring. 2. Dissolve 2 oz. plain chocolate with the sugar in the milk. 3. Stir in 1 teaspoon vanilla essence. **Serves 4.**

COFFEE MILK JELLY   863

1. Follow recipe and method for Lemon Milk Jelly (No. 860) but omit lemon peel and colouring. 2. Instead, add 2 to 3 level teaspoons instant coffee powder to the milk. **Serves 4.**

VANILLA MILK JELLY   864

1. Follow recipe and method for Lemon Milk Jelly (No. 860) but use 1 or 2 teaspoons vanilla essence instead of lemon peel. 2. Colour pale pink or green with red or green food colouring. **Serves 4.**

4 canned peach halves
$\frac{1}{4}$ lb. strawberries
1 oz. sifted icing sugar
$\frac{1}{4}$ pint fresh double cream
1 tablespoon milk
12 blanched and toasted almonds

1. Drain peach halves thoroughly and put on to 4 individual plates, cut sides uppermost. **2.** Slice strawberries, mix with icing sugar then spoon equal amounts into peach cavities. **3.** Whip cream and milk together until thick. Pipe whirls over each peach half. **4.** Decorate with whole almonds. Chill at least $\frac{1}{2}$ an hour before serving. **Serves 4.**

6 oz. cooking apples, weighed after
  peeling and coring
1 clove
$\frac{1}{4}$ level teaspoon mixed spice
$\frac{1}{2}$ level teaspoon finely-grated lemon peel
5 dessertspoons water
1 to 1$\frac{1}{2}$ oz. granulated sugar
2 level teaspoons gelatine
4 tablespoons boiling water
4 tablespoons fresh double cream
1 dessertspoon milk
White of one standard egg
Red food colouring

DECORATION
4 tablespoons fresh double cream,
  whipped
8 glacé cherries

1. Slice apples thinly and put into a saucepan with the clove, spice, lemon peel and 5 dessert-spoons water. **2.** Bring slowly to the boil, cover pan with lid and simmer until fruit is soft. **3.** Remove from heat. Sweeten to taste with sugar. Either rub through sieve or liquidise. **4.** Shower gelatine into 4 tablespoons boiling water and stir briskly until dissolved. **5.** Add to apple mixture and leave in cold until just beginning to thicken and set. **6.** Whip cream and milk together until lightly stiff. Gradually stir in fruit mixture then gently fold in egg white, beaten to a stiff snow. **7.** Tint pale pink. Turn into serving bowl and chill until firm and set. **8.** Just before serving, decorate with whipped cream and whole cherries. **Serves 4.**

Peaches Mistral (No. 865)

867 PINEAPPLE ROMANOFF

1 large fresh pineapple
3 tablespoons Curaçao
½ lb. fresh strawberries
½ pint fresh double cream
3 oz. sifted icing sugar
Finely-grated peel and juice of ½ a lemon

1. Cut pineapple in half lengthwise, cutting through leafy crown as well. (Each half should have own crown.) **2.** Remove and discard core. Gently scoop out flesh and cut into neat cubes. **3.** Put pineapple cubes into a bowl, mix with the Curaçao and chill for at least 2 hours. **4.** About 1 hour before serving, slice all but 4 strawberries. Whip the cream thick then stir in sugar, grated lemon peel and juice, pineapple cubes and juices and sliced strawberries. **5.** Mix well, spoon into pineapple halves and chill at least ½ an hour. **6.** Just before serving, decorate with remaining 4 whole strawberries. **Serves 4.**

868 RASPBERRY CREAM RING

1 lemon-flavoured jelly
5 tablespoons boiling water
¾ pint milk
Finely-grated peel and juice of 1 large lemon
1 level tablespoon caster sugar
1½ oz. semolina
½ pint fresh double cream
Whites of 2 standard eggs

DECORATION
½ to ¾ lb. fresh raspberries

1. Put jelly and 5 tablespoons boiling water into a saucepan. Stand over very low heat until jelly dissolves. **2.** Pour into measuring jug and make up to ½ pint with cold water. Leave on one side. **3.** Put milk, grated lemon peel and sugar into a saucepan. Heat to lukewarm. **4.** Sprinkle in semolina and cook slowly, stirring, until mixture comes to the boil and thickens. **5.** Simmer gently for 3 minutes. Remove from heat then stir in the melted jelly and lemon juice. **6.** Leave in cold until just beginning to thicken and set. **7.** Whip cream until lightly stiff. Beat egg whites to stiff snow. **8.** Fold cream and beaten egg whites alternately into cooled jelly and semolina mixture. Transfer to 2-pint ring mould, first rinsed with cold water. **9.** Chill until firm and set. Turn out on to plate and fill centre with raspberries. **Serves 4.**

ORANGE SNOW CREAMS 869

1 orange-flavoured jelly
5 tablespoons boiling water
¼ pint fresh double cream
Whites of 2 standard eggs

DECORATION
Fresh mint leaves or glacé cherries

1. Put jelly and 5 tablespoons boiling water into a saucepan. Stand over a very low heat until jelly dissolves. **2.** Pour into a measuring jug and make up to ¾ pint with cold water. Leave in cool place until just beginning to thicken and set. **3.** Whip cream until lightly stiff. Beat egg whites to stiff snow. **4.** Turn jelly into large bowl and whisk until foamy. Fold in whipped cream alternately with beaten egg whites. **5.** When smooth and well blended, transfer to 4 sundae glasses and chill until firm. **6.** Just before serving, decorate with mint leaves or halved glacé cherries. **Serves 4.**

PEACH SHERBET 870

3 level teaspoons gelatine
6 tablespoons boiling water
1 level tablespoon granulated sugar
¼ pint peach purée, made from canned peaches
1 tablespoon lemon juice
Whites of 2 standard eggs

DECORATION
¼ pint fresh double cream, whipped
Cinnamon or blanched and chopped pistachio nuts or chopped almonds or toasted coconut

1. Shower gelatine into boiling water and stir until dissolved. **2.** Add sugar. Stir in peach purée and lemon juice. **3.** When cold and just beginning to thicken and set, fold in egg whites, beaten to stiff snow. **4.** Pile into 4 sundae glasses and chill until set. **5.** Just before serving, decorate each with whipped cream. Dust cream with cinnamon or sprinkle with nuts or coconut. **Serves 4.**

APRICOT SHERBET 871

1. Follow recipe and method for Peach Sherbet (No. 870) but use apricot purée instead of peach. **2.** Decorate with cream and sprinkle with chopped nuts, coconut or chopped glacé cherries. **Serves 4.**

872 POTS-AU-CHOCOLAT

3 oz. plain chocolate
1 oz. English or Welsh butter
Yolks and whites of 3 standard eggs
1 tablespoon warm water
¼ pint fresh double cream

1. Break up chocolate and put into basin standing over saucepan of hot water. Add butter and leave until both have melted, stirring once or twice. **2.** Beat in egg yolks. When mixture is smooth, remove from heat and stir in warm water. **3.** Beat egg whites to stiff snow and gently fold into chocolate mixture. **4.** Transfer to 4 individual dishes or sundae glasses and chill. **5.** Just before serving, decorate each with the cream, whipped until lightly stiff. **Serves 4.**

873 POTS-AU-CHOCOLAT WITH COFFEE

Follow recipe and method for Pots-au-Chocolat (No. 872) but add 2 level teaspoons instant coffee powder with the butter. **Serves 4.**

874 POTS-AU-CHOCOLAT WITH SHERRY, BRANDY OR RUM

Follow recipe and method for Pots-au-Chocolat (No. 872) but omit water. Use instead 1 tablespoon lukewarm sherry, brandy or rum. **Serves 4.**

875 BLANCMANGE

3 level tablespoons cornflour
1 pint milk
1½ oz. caster sugar
1 teaspoon vanilla essence
½ oz. English or Welsh butter

1. Mix cornflour to smooth paste with a little of the cold milk. **2.** Warm remainder, combine with cornflour paste, then return to pan. **3.** Cook, stirring, until mixture comes to boil and thickens. Reduce heat to low and simmer 3 minutes. **4.** Remove from heat and stir in remaining ingredients. **5.** Pour into 1-pint mould, first rinsed with cold water, then cool. **6.** Refrigerate until cold and firm. Turn out on to plate. **7.** Serve with stewed or canned fruit. **Serves 4.**

LEMON BLANCMANGE 87

Follow recipe and method for Blancmange (No. 875) but add 1 level teaspoon finely-grated lemon peel and a few drops of yellow colouring to the milk while it is warming. **Serves 4.**

ORANGE BLANCMANGE 87

Follow recipe and method for Blancmange (No. 875) but add 1 level teaspoon finely-grated orange peel and a few drops of orange colouring to the milk while it is warming. **Serves 4.**

COFFEE BLANCMANGE 87

Follow recipe and method for Blancmange (No. 875) but add 2 to 3 level teaspoons instant coffee powder to the milk while it is warming. **Serves 4.**

HONEY BLANCMANGE 87

Follow recipe and method for Blancmange (No. 875) but use 1 tablespoon honey instead of the sugar. **Serves 4.**

EXTRA CREAMY BLANCMANGE 8

Follow recipe and method for Blancmange (No. 875) but use either 1 pint Channel Island milk or ½ pint of your usual milk and ½ pint fresh single cream. **Serves 4.**

JUNKET 8

1 pint Pasteurised (or Channel Island) milk
1 level dessertspoon caster sugar
1 teaspoon essence of rennet

1. Put milk and sugar into saucepan and warm to blood heat. The temperature should be no more than 98°. (To test this, dip the tip of the little finger in the milk. It should strike neither hot nor cold but should feel comfortably warm.) **2.** Pour milk into serving dish, stir in rennet and leave for 1½ to 2 hours. **3.** After junket has set, it can be refrigerated and served very cold. **Serves 4 to 6.**

882 FRESH LEMON JUNKET

1. Follow recipe and method for Junket (No. 881) but stir in 1 level teaspoon finely-grated lemon peel with the sugar. **2.** Colour pale yellow with food colouring before adding rennet. **Serves 4 to 6.**

883 FRESH ORANGE JUNKET

1. Follow recipe and method for Junket (No. 881) but stir in 1 level teaspoon finely-grated orange peel with the sugar. **2.** Colour pale orange with food colouring before adding rennet. **Serves 4 to 6.**

884 COFFEE JUNKET

Follow recipe and method for Junket (No. 881) but stir in 2 level teaspoons instant coffee powder with the sugar. **Serves 4 to 6.**

885 CRÈME CAFÉ

¼ pint strong black coffee
3 level teaspoons gelatine
¾ pint milk
2 oz. semolina
3 oz. caster sugar
Yolks and whites of 2 standard eggs
¼ pint fresh double cream

DECORATION
About 2 oz. grated plain chocolate

1. Bring coffee just up to boil, remove from heat and add gelatine. Stir briskly until dissolved. Leave to cool. **2.** Put milk into pan, heat to luke-warm, then sprinkle in the semolina. Cook, stirring all the time, until the mixture comes to boil and thickens. **3.** Lower heat and simmer for 3 minutes. **4.** Remove from heat and beat in sugar, egg yolks and dissolved gelatine and coffee. Leave in the cool until just beginning to thicken and set. **5.** Beat cream until lightly stiff. Whisk egg whites to stiff snow. **6.** Fold cream and beaten whites alternately into semolina mixture. When evenly combined, transfer to serving dish. **7.** Chill until lightly set. Just before serving, sprinkle with grated chocolate. **Serves 4 to 6.**

CRÈME ORANGE 886

1. Follow recipe and method for Crème Café (No. 885) but use ¼ pint fresh orange juice instead of the coffee. **2.** Beat in 1 level teaspoon finely-grated orange peel with the sugar. **Serves 4 to 6.**

VANILLA HONEYCOMB MOULD 887

4 level teaspoons gelatine
4 tablespoons boiling water
Yolks and whites of 2 standard eggs
2 oz. caster sugar
1 pint milk
1 teaspoon vanilla essence

1. Shower gelatine into boiling water and stir until dissolved. **2.** Beat egg yolks and sugar together until thick. Transfer to double saucepan (or basin standing over saucepan of simmering water). **3.** Add milk. Cook, stirring, until custard thickens and coats back of spoon thinly. (Do not boil or mixture will curdle.) **4.** Remove from heat and add vanilla and dissolved gelatine. **5.** Whisk egg whites to stiff snow and fold into custard mixture. **6.** Pour into 1½ to 2-pint mould, first rinsed with cold water. **7.** Chill until firm and set. Turn out on to plate. **Serves 4 to 6.**

● *If separate layers are preferred, bring mixture just up to boil after egg whites have been added and pour into the mould straight away. Cool and chill.*

LEMON HONEYCOMB MOULD 888

Follow recipe and method for Vanilla Honeycomb Mould (No. 887) but use 1 level teaspoon finely-grated lemon peel instead of vanilla. **Serves 4 to 6.**

ORANGE HONEYCOMB MOULD 889

Follow recipe and method for Vanilla Honeycomb Mould (No. 887) but use 1 level teaspoon finely-grated orange peel instead of vanilla. **Serves 4 to 6.**

890 CRÈME BRULÉE ('BURNT' CREAM)

Yolks of 4 standard eggs
½ pint fresh double cream
3 level tablespoons sifted icing sugar
1 teaspoon vanilla essence
Caster sugar

1. Beat egg yolks thoroughly. **2.** Heat cream until hot in double saucepan (or basin standing over saucepan of simmering water). **3.** Pour hot cream on to yolks, beating all the time. **4.** Return mixture to saucepan or basin. Add icing sugar and vanilla. **5.** Cook without boiling, stirring all the time, until mixture thickens and coats back of spoon heavily. **6.** Remove from heat, pour into 1-pint buttered baking dish and chill overnight. **7.** About 1 hour before serving, sprinkle ¼-in. thick layer of caster sugar over the top. **8.** Stand under hot grill and leave until sugar starts to turn deep gold and caramelise. **9.** Remove from heat and chill again. **10.** Can be accompanied with cold stewed apricots or gooseberries. **Serves 4.**

891 CRÈME CARAMEL

2 oz. granulated sugar
2 tablespoons cold water
1 dessertspoon boiling water
3 large eggs
½ pint milk
1 oz. caster sugar
½ teaspoon vanilla essence
¼ pint fresh single cream

1. Brush 1-pint heatproof dish with melted butter. **2.** Put granulated sugar and water into a small heavy-based pan. Stand over low heat and stir until sugar dissolves. **3.** Bring to boil, then boil more briskly—without stirring—until syrup turns a deep gold. Remove from heat and stir in boiling water. Pour into heatproof dish. **4.** Tilt dish quickly so that base is completely covered with caramel. **5.** Beat eggs and milk well together. Add sugar and vanilla and mix well. **6.** Strain into dish (any sugar remaining in strainer should be rubbed through). Stand dish in roasting tin containing enough cold water to come halfway up the sides of the dish. **7.** Put into centre of moderate oven (325°F. or Gas No. 3) and cook for ¾ to 1 hour. **8.** Remove from oven and cool. **9.** Turn out on to serving dish when completely cold. Chill lightly before serving. **10.** Serve single cream separately. **Serves 4.**

SMALL CRÈMES CARAMEL 89

1. Follow recipe and method for Crème Caramel (No. 891). Very carefully spoon equal amounts of hot caramel into 4 individual, well-buttered metal moulds. **2.** Strain in custard mixture then bake for ½ an hour. **3.** Leave until completely cold before unmoulding. **Serves 4.**

STRAWBERRY CHOUX RING 89

1 recipe Choux Pastry (No. 102)
½ pint fresh double cream
2 tablespoons milk
1 level teaspoon vanilla essence
¼ lb. sifted icing sugar
¾ lb. fresh strawberries, sliced

1. Using a forcing bag and ½-in. plain icing tube, pipe a thick 7-in. ring on a buttered baking tray. **2.** Put into centre of fairly hot oven (400°F or Gas No. 6) and bake 15 minutes. **3.** Reduce temperature to moderate (350°F or Gas No. 4). Bake further 30 minutes (or until well puffed and golden). **4.** Cool on wire rack. **5.** About 1 hour before serving, cut ring in half horizontally. Beat cream and milk together until thick. Gently stir in vanilla, 3 oz. icing sugar and sliced strawberries. **6.** Pile mixture into bottom half of ring. Replace top and dredge with remaining icing sugar. **7.** Chill and serve. **Serves 5 to 6.**

TRIFLE ALEXANDRA 89

Stale sponge or Madeira cake
1 medium-sized can peach halves
¼ pint fresh double cream
1 tablespoon milk
1 level tablespoon sifted icing sugar
White of 1 standard egg
¼ lb. fresh or frozen strawberries
Extra sifted icing sugar

1. Line base of fairly small serving dish with cake. Moisten with 4 to 5 tablespoons syrup from peaches. **2.** Arrange peach halves on top. **3.** Whip cream and milk together until thick. Stir in sugar then fold in egg white, beaten to a stiff snow. **4.** Pile over peaches and chill. **5.** Just before serving, crush strawberries finely, sweeten to taste with icing sugar and trickle gently over the cream. **Serves 4 to 5.**

95 CHARLOTTE MOCHA

4 level teaspoons gelatine
4 tablespoons boiling water
Yolks and whites of 2 standard eggs
2 level tablespoons caster sugar
½ pint milk
¼lb. plain chocolate
¼ pint strong black coffee
About 20 Boudoir biscuits

DECORATION
¼ pint fresh double cream, whipped

1. Shower gelatine into boiling water. Stir briskly until dissolved. **2.** Put egg yolks and sugar into double saucepan (or basin standing over pan of simmering water). Beat until very thick and pale in colour. **3.** Heat milk to lukewarm. Combine with beaten yolks and sugar. Cook, stirring, until custard thickens slightly. **4.** Remove from heat, add dissolved gelatine and mix well. **5.** Cover base of 6-in. soufflé dish, Charlotte mould or cake tin with 5 tablespoons custard. Chill. **6.** Break up chocolate and put into basin standing over pan of hot water. Leave until melted, stirring once or twice. **7.** Add coffee. Mix thoroughly and combine with remaining custard. Fold in egg whites, whipped until stiff. **8.** Arrange biscuits close together round sides of dish, mould or cake tin. Fill with custard mixture. **9.** Chill until firm and set. **10.** Just before serving, trim biscuits level with filling then turn out on to a plate. **11.** Decorate with whipped cream. **Serves 5 to 6.**

96 CHOCOLATE APRICOT TRIFLE

1 cream-filled chocolate Swiss roll
1 medium-sized can apricot halves
2 tablespoons orange squash or brandy
¼ pint fresh double cream
1 tablespoon milk
2 level tablespoons sifted icing sugar
White of 1 standard egg

DECORATION
2 oz. grated plain chocolate

1. Cut Swiss roll into about 10 slices. Arrange over base of shallow serving dish, overlapping if necessary. **2.** Moisten with 4 tablespoons syrup from apricots mixed with squash or brandy. Arrange apricots on top. **3.** Whip cream and milk together until thick. Stir in sugar then fold in the egg white, beaten to a stiff snow. **4.** Pile over apricots and chill. **5.** Just before serving, sprinkle with grated chocolate. **Serves 4 to 6.**

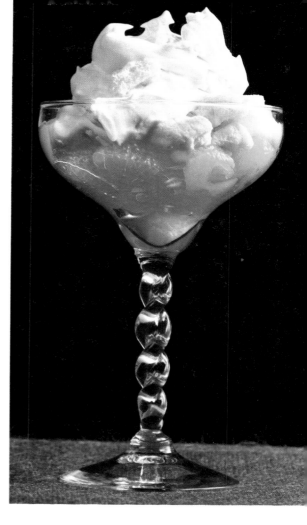

Crème Monte Carlo (No. 897)

CRÈME MONTE CARLO 897

1 can mandarin oranges
½ pint fresh double cream
2 tablespoons milk
2 level tablespoons sifted icing sugar
1 level teaspoon finely-grated tangerine peel (optional)
6 meringue halves, bought or home made

1. Reserve 8 mandarin segments for decoration. **2.** Divide remainder, with syrup, between 4 sundae glasses. **3.** Whip cream and milk together until mixture stands in soft peaks then stir in sugar and tangerine peel if used. **4.** Break up meringues into small pieces and fold into cream mixture. **5.** Pile over fruit in glasses. Decorate each with 2 mandarin segments. **6.** Chill well before serving. **Serves 4.**

COLD PUDDINGS

898 BERRY FLAN

. . . with a layer of French Custard Filling underneath the fruit to prevent the pastry from becoming wet and soggy.

1 recipe Sweet Flan Pastry (No. 98)
Yolk of 1 standard egg
1 oz. caster sugar
½ oz. flour
½ teaspoon vanilla essence
¼ pint milk
1 lb. raspberries, strawberries or loganberries
2 tablespoons redcurrant jelly
¼ pint fresh double cream
1 tablespoon milk
1 level tablespoon sifted icing sugar
2 teaspoons orange juice or sherry

1. Roll out pastry. Use it to line a 6 to 7-in. fluted flan ring resting on lightly-buttered baking tray. Prick well all over. Line with aluminium foil (to prevent pastry rising as it cooks). Bake just above centre of hot oven (425°F. or Gas No. 7) for 15 minutes. **2.** Remove foil. Return flan to oven. Bake further 15 minutes (or until crisp and golden). Remove and cool. **3.** Beat egg yolk and sugar together until thick and light. Stir in flour and vanilla and gradually blend in milk. **4.** Pour into small saucepan and cook, stirring, until mixture comes to boil and thickens. Simmer 3 minutes. Remove from heat and cool. **5.** When completely cold, spread over base of flan case, cover with berries and brush with melted redcurrant jelly. **6.** Beat cream and milk together until thick. Stir in sugar and either orange juice or sherry. **7.** Pipe or spoon mixture over fruit filling. Chill for a good ½ hour before serving. **Serves 6.**

899 PEACH OR APRICOT FLAN

1. Follow recipe and method for Berry Flan (No. 898) but use well-drained peach slices or apricot halves instead of berry fruit. **2.** Brush with melted apricot jam instead of redcurrant jelly. **Serves 6.**

900 FRESH GRAPE FLAN

1. Follow recipe and method for Berry Flan (No. 898) but cover filling with alternate rows of halved and seeded black and green grapes instead of berry fruit. **2.** Brush with melted apricot jam instead of redcurrant jelly. **Serves 6.**

GLAZED APPLE FLAN 901

1. Follow recipe and method for Berry Flan (No. 898) but cover filling with thin slices of peeled apple, poached in syrup (made from ¼ lb. granulated sugar and 4 tablespoons water) and then drained. **2.** Sprinkle apples with caster sugar. **3.** Put under hot grill until sugar just starts turning golden. **4.** Chill before decorating with cream mixture. **Serves 6.**

LOGANBERRY MERINGUE BASKET 902

1 Meringue Basket (No. 613)
½ pint double cream
3 tablespoons milk
1 dessertspoon Grand Marnier or Cointreau
3 to 4 oz. sifted icing sugar
1 lb. fresh loganberries

1. Put Meringue Basket on serving dish. **2.** Whip cream and milk together until thick. Gently stir in liqueur, sugar to taste and half of the loganberries. **3.** Pile into Basket and stud top with remaining berries. **4.** Chill thoroughly before serving. **Serves 4 to 6.**

STRAWBERRY OR RASPBERRY MERINGUE BASKET 903

1. Follow recipe and method for Loganberry Meringue Basket (No. 902), but use strawberries or raspberries instead of the loganberries. **2.** Cut half the strawberries into slices or use half of the whole raspberries and stir into the cream. Stud the top with whole berries. **Serves 4 to 6.**

FRUIT SALAD MERINGUE BASKET 904

1. Follow recipe and method for Loganberry Meringue Basket (No. 902) but omit berry fruit. **2.** Pile cream into Basket. Cover top with rings of sliced bananas (first dipped in lemon juice to prevent browning), cubes of pineapple, halved black and green grapes (with seeds removed), halved and pitted canned red cherries, drained canned peach slices and drained mandarin oranges. **4.** Brush fruit with melted apricot jam just before serving. **Serves 4 to 6.**

905 LEMON MERINGUE PIE

Short Crust Pastry, made with 6 oz. flour (No. 88)
2 level tablespoons cornflour
2 oz. caster sugar
Finely-grated peel and juice of 2 large lemons
¼ pint water
Yolks of 2 standard eggs
½ oz. English or Welsh butter
1 recipe Meringue Topping (No. 610)

1. Roll out pastry. Use it to line a 7 to 8-in. fluted flan ring resting on lightly-buttered baking tray. Prick well all over, line with aluminium foil (to prevent pastry rising as it cooks). Bake just above centre of a hot oven (425°F. or Gas No. 7) for 15 minutes. **2.** Remove foil. Return flan to oven. Bake further 15 minutes (or until crisp and golden). Remove from oven. **3.** To make filling, put cornflour, sugar and lemon peel into a basin. Mix to smooth paste with a little of the cold water. **4.** Heat rest of water with the lemon juice. Combine with paste then return to pan. **5.** Cook, stirring, until mixture comes to boil and thickens. Simmer 3 minutes. **6.** Beat in yolks and butter. Cook gently further minute then pour into flan case. **7.** Pile meringue on top. Bake as directed for Meringue Topping (No. 610). **8.** Serve very cold. **Serves 4 to 6.**

906 PEAR CONDÉ

1 pint milk
1 oz. caster sugar
3 oz. washed pudding rice
Strip of lemon peel
¼ pint fresh double cream
8 canned pear halves
4 to 5 level tablespoons apricot jam

DECORATION
8 glacé cherries
16 leaves cut from angelica

1. Put milk, sugar, rice and lemon peel into double saucepan. Cook very slowly, stirring occasionally, until rice is tender and swollen and most of milk has been absorbed (this should take from 1½ to 2 hours). **2.** Remove strip of lemon peel. Spread rice into shallow serving dish. **3.** Leave until cold and then chill. **4.** Just before serving, whip cream until thick. Arrange pear halves, cut side down, on chilled rice then brush with melted apricot jam. **5.** Decorate with the whipped cream, halved cherries and angelica. **Serves 4.**

PEACH CONDÉ 907

Follow recipe and method for Pear Condé (No. 906) but use 8 canned peach halves instead of the pears. **Serves 4.**

OEUFS À LA NEIGE (SNOW EGGS) 908

Yolks and whites of 3 standard eggs
¼ lb. caster sugar
¾ pint milk
1 teaspoon vanilla essence or ½ level teaspoon finely-grated lemon peel

1. Beat egg whites to a stiff snow. **2.** Add 2 oz. sugar and continue beating until mixture is shiny and stands in firm peaks. **3.** Put milk into saucepan. Heat slowly until bubbles just start appearing (it must never boil). **4.** Reduce heat and drop small mounds of egg white mixture, from a tablespoon, into the milk. **5.** Poach gently for 4 minutes turning once. **6.** Lift out carefully with draining spoon and stand on clean, folded tea-towel. **7.** Pour warm milk on to egg yolks and whisk lightly. **8.** Transfer to a double saucepan (or basin standing over saucepan of simmering water). Add remaining sugar and cook, stirring all the time, until custard thickens. Do not allow to boil. **9.** Remove from heat, add vanilla or lemon peel, and cool. **10.** Pour into serving dish, arrange poached meringues on the top and chill. **Serves 4.**

BANANA SNOW 909

6 medium-sized bananas
3 tablespoons lemon juice
2 cartons (10 oz.) natural or banana yogurt
4 level tablespoons caster sugar
¼ pint fresh double cream
Whites of 2 standard eggs

DECORATION
About 1 oz. grated plain chocolate

1. Mash bananas to a purée with the lemon juice. Stir in yogurt and sugar and mix well. **2.** Whip cream until lightly stiff. Beat egg whites to stiff snow. **3.** Fold cream and beaten whites alternately into banana mixture. Pile into a serving dish. **4.** Chill thoroughly. Just before serving, sprinkle with grated chocolate. **Serves 4 to 6.**

910 BASIC CREAM MOULD

3 tablespoons water
1 level tablespoon granulated sugar
3 level teaspoons gelatine
½ pint fresh double cream
½ pint sweetened cold custard (made
  with custard powder)
1 teaspoon vanilla essence

1. Put water, sugar and gelatine into a saucepan. Stand over a low heat and stir until sugar and gelatine have dissolved. Leave on one side until cool. **2.** Whip cream until lightly stiff. Remove skin from custard, whisk until completely smooth, then whisk in cooled gelatine mixture and vanilla. **3.** Fold in whipped cream then leave in the cool until mixture just begins to thicken and set, stirring occasionally. **4.** Transfer to 1½-pint mould, first rinsed with cold water. Chill until firm and set. **5.** Turn out on to plate and serve with stewed or canned fruit. **Serves 4 to 5.**

911 COFFEE CREAM MOULD

Follow recipe and method for Basic Cream Mould (No. 910) but stir 2 to 3 level teaspoons instant coffee powder into hot gelatine mixture and omit vanilla. **Serves 4 to 5.**

912 CHOCOLATE CREAM MOULD

Follow recipe and method for Basic Cream Mould (No. 910) but melt 3 oz. plain, grated chocolate in the water with the sugar and gelatine. **Serves 4 to 5.**

CHERRY CREAM MOULD 91

1. Follow recipe and method for Basic Cream Mould (No. 910) but use almond essence instead of vanilla. **2.** Just before moulding, stir in 2 to 3 oz. finely-chopped glacé cherries. **Serves 4 to 5.**

BASIC FRUIT & 91
CREAM MOULD

4 tablespoons water
1 level tablespoon granulated sugar
3 level teaspoons gelatine
¼ pint fresh double cream
¼ pint sweetened, cold custard (made
  from custard powder)
¼ pint sweetened gooseberry purée,
  made from canned or stewed fruit
Green food colouring

DECORATION
Whole gooseberries

1. Put water, sugar and gelatine into saucepan. Stand over low heat and stir until sugar and gelatine have dissolved. Leave on one side until cool. **2.** Whip cream until lightly stiff. Remove skin from custard, whisk until completely smooth, then whisk in fruit purée and cooled gelatine mixture. **3.** Fold in whipped cream and colour pale green. Leave in cool until just beginning to thicken and set. **4.** Transfer to 1½-pint mould, first rinsed with cold water, and chill until firm. **5.** Turn out on to a plate. Decorate lower edge of mould with a border of whole gooseberries. **Serves 4 to 6.**

Cherry Cream Mould (No. 913)

PROFITEROLES

1 recipe Choux Pastry (No. 102)
½ pint fresh double cream
2 tablespoons milk
3 to 4 level tablespoons sifted icing sugar
Quick Chocolate Sauce (No. 176)

1. Pipe or spoon 20 equal amounts of Choux Pastry — well apart — on large buttered baking tray. Put into centre of fairly hot oven (400°F. or Gas No. 6). Bake 10 minutes. **2.** Reduce temperature to moderate (350°F. or Gas No. 4). Bake a further 25 minutes (or until golden and well puffed). **3.** Remove from oven. Make a small slit in the side of each. Return to oven (with heat switched off) for a further 5 minutes for puffs to dry out. Cool on a wire rack. **4.** About 1 hour before serving, whip cream and milk together until thick. Stir in sugar. **5.** Halve puffs and fill with the cream. Pile in a pyramid shape in shallow serving dish. **6.** Pour over lukewarm Quick Chocolate Sauce. Chill a good ½ hour before serving. **Serves 4.**

ALMOND & APRICOT FLAN

Short Crust Pastry made with ¼ lb. flour (No. 88)
2 level tablespoons apricot jam
3 oz. English or Welsh butter
3 oz. caster sugar
1 large egg
1 oz. cake crumbs (from plain cake)
2 oz. ground almonds
1 oz. self-raising flour
1 tablespoon milk
1 medium-sized can apricot halves

DECORATION
¼ pint fresh double cream, whipped
6 glacé cherries

1. Roll out pastry. Use it to line a 6 to 7-in. fluted flan ring resting on lightly-buttered baking tray. **2.** Spread base with jam. **3.** Cream butter with sugar until light and fluffy, then beat in whole egg. **4.** Stir in cake crumbs and almonds. Fold in flour alternately with milk. **5.** Transfer to pastry case and smooth top with a knife. **6.** Bake just above centre of a hot oven (425°F. or Gas No. 7) for 15 minutes. Reduce temperature to moderate (350°F. or Gas No. 4) and bake a further 30 minutes. **7.** Remove flan ring and cool flan. **8.** Just before serving, cover top of cold flan with well-drained apricot halves. Decorate with whipped cream and halved cherries. **Serves 4 to 6.**

Profiteroles (No. 915) with Quick Chocolate Sauce (No. 176)

CHOCOLATE HAZELNUT FLAN
917

1. Follow recipe and method for Almond and Apricot Flan (No. 916) but use raspberry jam instead of apricot and ground hazelnuts instead of almonds. **2.** Cover top of cold flan with ¼ pint fresh double cream, whipped until stiff with 1 tablespoon milk and sweetened to taste with sifted icing sugar. **3.** Decorate by sprinkling grated plain chocolate thickly over the top. **Serves 4 to 6.**

918 GÂTEAU ST. HONORÉ

1 recipe Sweet Flan Pastry (No. 98)
1 recipe Choux Pastry (No. 102)
½ pint fresh double cream
2 tablespoons milk
4 level tablespoons sifted icing sugar
4 level tablespoons apricot jam
10 glacé cherries

1. Pre-heat oven to hot (425°F or Gas No. 7).
2. Roll out Sweet Flan Pastry into a round 7½ to 8 in. across. Stand on a buttered baking tray. Prick all over with a fork. Moisten ½-in. wide band round the edge with cold water. 3. With a forcing bag and ½-in. plain icing tube, pipe fairly thin circle of Choux Pastry on top of moistened edge. 4. Pipe rest of Choux Pastry into 10 small mounds on second buttered baking tray. 5. Stand Sweet Flan round towards top of oven; the tray of small Choux mounds in the centre. 6. Bake for 15 minutes. Reduce temperature to fairly hot (375°F or Gas No. 5) then reverse position of trays and bake a further 20 minutes. 7. Remove both trays from oven. Transfer pastry round and baked puffs to cooling rack. Make small slits in both the Choux ring and puffs to allow steam to escape. 8. When pastry is completely cold, whip cream and milk together until thick. Stir in the sugar. Halve puffs and fill with whipped cream. Pile remaining cream into centre of pastry round. 9. Brush Choux ring heavily with melted apricot jam and stand filled puffs on top. 10. Brush puffs with rest of melted jam. Top each with a whole cherry. 11. Chill ½ an hour before serving. **Serves 8 to 10.**

919 STRAWBERRY MOUSSE

¾ lb. strawberries
1 tablespoon orange juice (or sherry, Cointreau or Grand Marnier)
2 to 3 oz. sifted icing sugar
½ pint fresh double cream
Whites of 2 standard eggs

DECORATION
12 extra strawberries

1. Either crush strawberries finely or rub through a sieve or liquidise. 2. Add orange juice or alternative, then sweeten to taste with icing sugar. 3. Whip cream until lightly stiff. Beat egg whites to stiff snow. 4. Fold cream and beaten whites alternately into fruit mixture. Pile into 4 sundae glasses. 5. Chill well. Just before serving, decorate each with whole strawberries. **Serves 4.**

RASPBERRY MOUSSE 9:

Follow recipe and method for Strawberry Mousse (No. 919) but use ¾ lb. fresh raspberries instead of the strawberries. **Serves 4.**

ORANGE CHIFFON PIE 9

Short Crust Pastry made with 6 oz. flour (No. 88)
1 orange flavour jelly
¼ pint boiling water
Yolks and whites of 2 standard eggs
3 oz. caster sugar

DECORATION
¼ pint fresh double cream, whipped
2 to 3 oz. green or black grapes

1. Roll out pastry. Use it to line a 7 to 8-in. fluted flan ring resting on lightly buttered baking tray. Prick well all over. Line with aluminium foil (to prevent pastry rising as it cooks). Bake just above centre of hot oven (425°F. or Gas No. 7) for 15 minutes. 2. Remove foil and return flan to oven. Bake further 15 minutes (or until crisp and golden). Remove from oven and cool. 3. To make filling, put jelly and water into saucepan. Stand over very low heat until jelly dissolves, stirring all the time. 4. Remove from heat. Leave in cool until just beginning to thicken and set. 5. Beat egg yolks and sugar together until very thick and pale in colour. Gradually whisk in cooled jelly. 6. Beat egg whites to stiff snow. Gently fold in jelly and egg yolk mixture. 7. Pile into baked pastry case and chill. 8. Before serving, decorate with whipped cream and halved and seeded grapes. **Serves 4 to 6.**

SYLLABUB 92

¼ pint white wine
2 tablespoons lemon juice
2 level teaspoons finely-grated lemon peel
3 oz. caster sugar
½ pint fresh double cream

1. Put wine, lemon juice, peel and sugar into bowl. Leave for minimum of 3 hours. 2. Add cream and whip until mixture stands in soft peaks. 3. Transfer to 6 sundae glasses. Leave in a cool place for several hours before serving. **Serves 6.**

Hot Puddings

3 BREAD & BUTTER PUDDING

6 thin slices white bread
About 2 oz. English or Welsh butter
2 oz. currants or sultanas (or mixture)
1½ oz. caster sugar
2 large eggs
1 pint milk

1. Remove crusts from bread. Spread slices thickly with butter. Cut into fingers or small squares. **2.** Put half fingers or squares into 2-pint buttered heatproof dish. **3.** Sprinkle with all the fruit and half the sugar. **4.** Top with remaining bread fingers or squares, buttered sides uppermost. Sprinkle with rest of sugar. **5.** Beat eggs and milk well together. Strain into dish over bread. **6.** Leave to stand ½ an hour (so that bread absorbs some of the liquid). Bake in centre of moderate oven (325°F. or Gas No. 3) for ¾ to 1 hour (or until Pudding is set and the top is crisp and golden). **Serves 4.**

4 SEMOLINA PUDDING

1 pint milk
1½ oz. semolina
1 oz. caster sugar
½ oz. English or Welsh butter

1. Put milk into pan and heat to lukewarm. **2.** Sprinkle in semolina. Cook slowly, stirring, until mixture comes to boil and thickens. **3.** Add sugar and butter. Cook very gently further 5 to 7 minutes, stirring often. **Serves 4.**

● *Alternative, turn the Pudding into 1-pint buttered heatproof dish as soon as it has come to the boil and thickened. Sprinkle with nutmeg and bake in centre of moderate oven (325°F. or Gas No. 3) for 30 minutes.*

● *To make Semolina Pudding with egg, cook Pudding gently for 5 minutes only, after adding sugar and butter. Cool 7 to 10 minutes. Stir in 1 standard egg, well beaten. Re-heat gently, **without boiling**, further 2 to 3 minutes.*

25 SAGO PUDDING

1. Follow recipe and method for Semolina Pudding (No. 924).. **2.** Use Sago instead of semolina. **Serves 4.**

LEMON SEMOLINA (OR SAGO) PUDDING 926

1. Follow recipe and method for Semolina Pudding (No. 924) or Sago Pudding (No. 925). **2.** Add 1 level teaspoon finely-grated lemon peel with sugar. **Serves 4.**

ORANGE SEMOLINA (OR SAGO) PUDDING 927

1. Follow recipe and method for Semolina Pudding (No. 924) or Sago Pudding (No. 925). **2.** Add 1 level teaspoon finely-grated orange peel with the sugar. **Serves 4.**

CHOCOLATE SEMOLINA (OR SAGO) PUDDING 928

1. Follow recipe and method for Semolina Pudding (No. 924) or Sago Pudding (No. 925). **2.** Melt 1 oz. grated plain chocolate in the milk while it is warming. **Serves 4.**

FRUIT SEMOLINA (OR SAGO) PUDDING 929

1. Follow recipe and method for Semolina Pudding (No. 924) or Sago Pudding (No. 925). **2.** Add 2 oz. seedless raisins with the sugar. **Serves 4.**

CABINET PUDDING 930

6 trifle sponge cakes
2 oz. glacé cherries
1 oz. caster sugar
2 large eggs
1 pint milk
1 teaspoon vanilla essence

1. Cut each cake into 6 cubes. **2.** Chop cherries coarsely. Put cake cubes and cherries into basin. Add sugar and toss lightly together to mix. **3.** Beat eggs, milk and vanilla well together. Gently stir into cake cube mixture. **4.** Leave to stand for 30 minutes. Turn into 1½-pint well-buttered pudding basin. Cover securely with buttered greaseproof paper or buttered aluminium foil. **5.** Steam very gently for 1 hour. Turn out carefully on to warm plate. Accompany with fresh double cream. **Serves 4.**

931 BAKED RICE PUDDING

2 oz. pudding rice (or flaked rice)
1 pint milk
1 oz. caster sugar
1 strip of lemon peel
Grated nutmeg
½ oz. English or Welsh butter

1. Wash rice and drain well. Put into 1½-pint, buttered heatproof dish and stir in milk. **2.** Leave rice to soak and soften for 30 minutes. Add sugar and lemon peel and stir well. **3.** Sprinkle top with grated nutmeg. Dot with butter. **4.** Put into centre of cool oven (300°F. or Gas No. 2) and bake 2 to 2½ hours. Stir in skin 2 or 3 times during first hour of cooking to increase creaminess. **Serves 4.**

● *To make a Rice Pudding with egg, remove Pudding from oven after 1½ or 2 hours. Cool for 10 minutes. Stir in 1 standard egg well beaten, and return to oven. Continue to bake for recommended cooking time.*

932 BAKED BARLEY PUDDING

1. Follow recipe and method for Baked Rice Pudding (No. 931). **2.** Instead of the rice use 2 oz. washed barley. **Serves 4.**

933 BAKED TAPIOCA PUDDING

1. Follow recipe and method for Baked Rice Pudding (No. 931). **2.** Instead of the rice use 2 oz. washed tapioca. **Serves 4.**

934 BAKED MACARONI PUDDING

1. Follow recipe and method for Baked Rice Pudding (No. 931). **2.** Instead of the rice use 2 oz. broken and washed macaroni. **Serves 4.**

935 VANILLA RICE PUDDING (OR BARLEY, TAPIOCA OR MACARONI)

1. Follow recipe and method for Baked Rice Pudding (No. 931) or for Baked Barley Pudding (No. 932), Baked Tapioca Pudding (No. 933) or Baked Macaroni Pudding (No. 934). **2.** Add ½ teaspoon vanilla with the sugar instead of strip of lemon peel. **Serves 4.**

LEMON RICE PUDDING (OR BARLEY, TAPIOCA OR MACARONI) 93

1. Follow recipe and method for Baked Rice Pudding (No. 931) or for Baked Barley Pudding (No. 932), Baked Tapioca Pudding (No. 933) or Baked Macaroni Pudding (No. 934). **2.** Add 1 level teaspoon finely-grated lemon peel with the sugar instead of strip of lemon peel. **Serves 4.**

ORANGE RICE PUDDING (OR BARLEY, TAPIOCA OR MACARONI) 93

1. Follow recipe and method for Baked Rice Pudding (No. 931) or for Baked Barley Pudding (No. 932), Baked Tapioca Pudding (No. 933) or Baked Macaroni Pudding (No. 934). **2.** Add 1 level teaspoon finely-grated orange peel with sugar. **Serves 4.**

CHOCOLATE RICE PUDDING (OR BARLEY, TAPIOCA OR MACARONI) 93

1. Follow recipe and method for Baked Rice Pudding (No. 931) or for Baked Barley Pudding (No. 932), Baked Tapioca Pudding (No. 933) or Baked Macaroni Pudding (No. 934). **2.** Melt 1½ to 2 oz. grated plain chocolate in the milk before stirring into the rice. **3.** Omit strip of lemon peel and nutmeg. **4.** If liked, add ½ teaspoon vanilla essence with the sugar. **Serves 4.**

FRUIT RICE PUDDING (OR BARLEY, TAPIOCA OR MACARONI) 93

1. Follow recipe and method for Baked Rice Pudding (No. 931) or for Baked Barley Pudding (No. 932), Baked Tapioca Pudding (No. 933) or Baked Macaroni Pudding (No. 934). **2.** Add 2 oz. seedless raisins with the sugar. **Serves 4.**

6 oz. self-raising flour
Pinch of salt
3 oz. English or Welsh butter
3 oz. caster sugar
1 large beaten egg
5 to 6 tablespoons cold milk for mixing

1. Sift flour and salt into bowl. **2.** Rub in butter finely. **3.** Add sugar. Mix to fairly soft consistency with egg and milk. **4.** Stir briskly until well combined. Transfer to $1\frac{1}{2}$ to 2-pint buttered pudding basin. **5.** Cover securely with buttered greaseproof paper or aluminium foil. Steam steadily for $1\frac{1}{2}$ to 2 hours (or until Pudding is well risen and firm). **6.** Turn out on to warm plate. Serve with fresh double cream or sweet sauce to taste (see Sauce Section). **Serves 4.**

● *To bake Pudding:* Turn mixture into $1\frac{1}{2}$ to 2-pint buttered pie dish. Put into centre of fairly hot oven (375°F. or Gas No. 5) and bake 15 minutes. Reduce temperature to moderate (325°F. or Gas No. 3) and bake a further 35 to 40 minutes (or until wooden cocktail stick inserted into centre of Pudding comes out clean). Remove from oven and turn out on to warm plate.

·1 CHOCOLATE PUDDING

1. Follow recipe and method for Plain Family Pudding (No. 940) but use 5 oz. self-raising flour only. **2.** Sift into bowl with the salt *plus* $\frac{1}{2}$ oz. cornflour and $\frac{1}{2}$ oz. cocoa powder. **Serves 4.**

·2 COCONUT PUDDING

1. Follow recipe and method for Plain Family Pudding (No. 940) but add $1\frac{1}{2}$ to 2 oz. desiccated coconut with the sugar. **2.** Add 1 teaspoon vanilla essence with egg and milk. **Serves 4.**

·3 DATE & WALNUT PUDDING

1. Follow recipe and method for Plain Family Pudding (No. 940). **2.** Add 2 oz. chopped dates and 1 oz. finely-chopped walnuts with sugar. **Serves 4.**

Baked Rice Pudding (No. 931)

944 BAKED EGG CUSTARD

3 large eggs or yolks of 4 standard eggs
1 pint milk
1 oz. caster sugar
Grated nutmeg

1. Beat whole eggs or egg yolks with milk. Strain into 1½-pint buttered heatproof dish then stir in sugar. **2.** Sprinkle top lightly with nutmeg. Stand in roasting tin containing enough water to come about half way up the sides of the dish. **3.** Bake in centre of moderate oven (325°F. or Gas No. 3) for 45 minutes to 1 hour (or until firm). **Serves 4.**

945 COCONUT EGG CUSTARD

1. Follow recipe and method for Baked Egg Custard (No. 944). **2.** Add 2 level tablespoons desiccated coconut with sugar. **Serves 4.**

946 LEMON EGG CUSTARD

1. Follow recipe and method for Baked Egg Custard (No. 944). **2.** Add 1 level teaspoon finely-grated lemon peel with sugar. **Serves 4.**

947 ORANGE EGG CUSTARD

1. Follow recipe and method for Baked Egg Custard (No. 944). **2.** Add 1 level teaspoon finely-grated orange peel with sugar. **Serves 4.**

948 APPLE CHARLOTTE

1 lb. cooking apples
¼ lb. caster sugar
¼ lb. fresh white breadcrumbs
Finely-grated peel of 1 medium-sized lemon
3 oz. English or Welsh butter, melted

1. Peel, core and slice apples. **2.** Combine sugar, breadcrumbs and lemon peel. **3.** Fill buttered 2-pint heatproof dish with alternate layers of breadcrumb mixture and apples. Begin and end with breadcrumb mixture and sprinkle melted butter between layers. **4.** Put into centre of fairly hot oven (375°F. or Gas No. 5). Bake for 45 minutes to 1 hour (or until apples are tender and top is golden brown). **5.** Serve with fresh double cream, soured cream or custard. **Serves 4.**

SPONGE PUDDING 9

¼ lb. self-raising flour
Pinch of salt
¼ lb. English or Welsh butter
¼ lb. caster sugar
2 large eggs
2 tablespoons cold milk

1. Sift flour and salt into bowl. **2.** Cream butter and sugar until light and fluffy. Beat in eggs, singly, adding tablespoon of flour with each. **3.** Fold in remaining flour alternately with milk. Transfer to buttered 1½-pint pudding basin. **4.** Cover securely with buttered greaseproof paper or aluminium foil. Steam steadily 1½ to 2 hours (or until well risen and firm). **5.** Turn out on to warm plate. Serve with fresh double cream or sweet sauce to taste (see Sauce Section). **Serves 4.**

● *To bake Pudding: Turn mixture into 1½ to 2-pint buttered pie dish. Bake in centre of moderate oven (350°F. or Gas No. 4) for ¾ to 1 hour (or until wooden cocktail stick, inserted into centre, comes out clean).*

CHOCOLATE SPONGE PUDDING 95

1. Follow recipe and method for Sponge Pudding (No. 949) but use 3 oz. self-raising flour only. **2.** Sift into bowl with salt *plus* ½ oz. cornflour and ½ oz. cocoa powder. **3.** Cream butter and sugar with ½ teaspoon vanilla essence. **Serves 4.**

FRUIT SPONGE PUDDING 95

1. Follow recipe and method for Sponge Pudding (No. 949). **2.** Stir in 2 oz. currants, sultanas or seedless raisins (or mixture) after beating in eggs. **Serves 4.**

JAM SPONGE PUDDING 95

1. Follow recipe and method for Sponge Pudding (No. 949). **2.** Put 2 level tablespoons jam into bottom of buttered basin before adding Pudding mixture. **Serves 4.**

3 FRESH FRUIT SUET PUDDING

1½ lb. cooking apples, rhubarb, plums, damsons, blackberries, gooseberries, black or redcurrants or mixture of fruits
1 recipe Suet Crust Pastry (No. 97)
2 level dessertspoons fresh white breadcrumbs
4 to 5 oz. granulated or soft brown sugar
1 tablespoon water

1. Prepare fruit according to type. **2.** Roll out two-thirds of Pastry and use to line buttered 2-pint pudding basin: **3.** Fill with alternate layers of breadcrumbs, sugar and fruit, beginning and ending with breadcrumbs. **4.** Pour in water. **5.** Moisten edges of lining Pastry with water. Cover with lid rolled from rest of Pastry. **6.** Press edges of lining and Pastry lid well together to seal. **7.** Cover securely with buttered greaseproof paper or aluminium foil. Steam steadily for 2½ to 3 hours. **8.** Serve from basin, with clean table napkin round it. **Serves 4.**

4 FRUIT PIE

2 lb. apples, rhubarb, gooseberries, plums, damsons, fresh apricots, cooking cherries, blackberries or mixture of fruits
6 to 8 oz. granulated sugar, depending on sharpness of fruit
1 recipe Short Crust (No. 88), Rough Puff (No. 94) or Flaky Pastry (No. 99)
Beaten egg or milk for brushing

1. Prepare fruit according to type. **2.** Fill 2-pint pie dish with alternate layers of fruit and sugar. Begin and end with fruit. Dome fruit in centre so that it supports pastry. **3.** Roll out Pastry. Cut into oval or round 1½ in. wider than top of dish. **4.** Moisten edges of dish with water. Line with strip of Pastry cut from trimmings. **5.** Moisten strip with water then cover with Pastry lid, pressing edges well together to seal. **6.** Flake edges by cutting lightly with back of knife then 'ridge' with fork all way round. **7.** Brush with beaten egg or milk. Make 2 slits in top to allow steam to escape. **8.** Bake just above centre of hot oven (425°F. or Gas No. 7) for 15 minutes. Reduce temperature to moderate (350°F. or Gas No. 4). Bake further 30 to 45 minutes. **9.** Remove from oven. Sprinkle top lightly with caster sugar. **10.** Serve with fresh single or double cream, soured cream, natural yogurt or custard. **Serves 4 to 6.**

DOUBLE CRUST FRUIT PIE 955

1 lb. apples, rhubarb, gooseberries, plums, damsons, fresh apricots, cooking cherries, blackberries or mixture of fruits
4 to 5 oz. granulated sugar
1 recipe Short Crust Pastry (No. 88)
Beaten egg or milk for brushing

1. Prepare fruit according to type. **2.** Cut Pastry into 2 equal pieces. **3.** Roll out half and use to line 8-in. lightly-buttered flat heatproof plate (or shallow heatproof pie plate). Cover Pastry – to within 1 in. of edges – with alternate layers of fruit and sugar, beginning and ending with fruit. **4.** Moisten edges of Pastry with water. Cover with lid, rolled and shaped from rest of Pastry. **5.** Press edges well together to seal. **6.** Flake edges by cutting lightly with back of knife then 'ridge' with fork all round. **7.** Brush with beaten egg or milk. Make 2 slits in top to allow steam to escape then stand Pie on baking tray. **8.** Bake just above centre of hot oven (425°F. or Gas No. 7) for 20 minutes. Reduce heat to moderate (350°F. or Gas No. 4). Bake further 30 to 45 minutes. **9.** Remove from oven. Sprinkle top lightly with caster sugar. **10.** Serve with fresh single or double cream, soured cream, natural yogurt, ice cream or custard. **Serves 4 to 5.**

FRUIT CRUMBLE 956

1 lb. either cooking apples, rhubarb, goose-berries, damsons, plums, blackberries or red or blackcurrants
4 to 6 oz. granulated sugar, depending on sharpness of fruit

CRUMBLE TOPPING

6 oz. plain flour
3 oz. English or Welsh butter
2 to 3 oz. caster sugar

1. Prepare fruit according to type. Put into 1½ to 2-pint heatproof dish in layers with granulated sugar. **2.** Sift flour into bowl and rub in butter finely. Add sugar, then toss ingredients lightly together to mix. **3.** Sprinkle Crumble thickly and evenly over fruit. Press down lightly with palm of hand then smooth top with knife. **4.** Put into centre of fairly hot oven (375°F. or Gas No. 5) and bake 15 minutes. **5.** Reduce temperature to moderate (350°F. or Gas No. 4). Bake further 45 minutes or until top is lightly brown. **6.** Serve with fresh double cream, soured cream or custard. **Serves 4.**

Coffee Fudge Cream Pie (No. 959)

4 medium-sized cooking apples
1½ oz. granulated sugar
¼ level teaspoon finely-grated lemon peel
or 1 level teaspoon cinnamon
1 recipe Short Crust Pastry (No. 88) or
Rich Short Crust Pastry (No. 89)
Milk for brushing
Sifted icing sugar

1. Peel apples thinly. Remove cores two-thirds of the way down each apple. (If cut right through, filling will fall out and make pastry soggy). **2.** Mix sugar with lemon peel or cinnamon. Put equal amounts into apple cavities. **3.** Cut Pastry into 4 pieces. Roll each out into circle about 1½ in. larger all the way round than the apples. **4.** Place apples on centre of each Pastry round. Moisten edges with water. Wrap Pastry closely round each apple, pressing joins well together to seal. **5.** Stand on lightly-buttered baking tray with joins underneath. Brush with milk. Make a slit in top of each to allow steam to escape. **6.** Bake in centre of hot oven (425°F. or Gas No. 7) for 15 minutes. Reduce temperature to moderate (350°F. or Gas No. 4). Bake further 30 minutes. **7.** Remove from oven, dredge with sifted icing sugar and serve with fresh single or double cream, soured cream, natural yogurt or custard. **Serves 4.**

PINEAPPLE & LEMON UPSIDE-DOWN PUDDING

BASE
2 oz. English or Welsh butter
2 oz. soft brown sugar
1 medium-sized can pineapple rings

PUDDING MIXTURE
½ lb. self-raising flour
¼ level teaspoon salt
¼ lb. English or Welsh butter
¼ lb. caster sugar
Finely-grated peel of 1 medium-sized lemon
2 large eggs
4 to 5 tablespoons cold milk to mix

1. For base, melt butter and stir in sugar. Use to cover bottom of 2-pint buttered pie dish. Arrange pineapple rings – well drained – over base and sides. **2.** For pudding, sift flour and salt into bowl and rub in butter finely. **3.** Add sugar and lemon peel. Toss ingredients lightly together. Mix to fairly soft batter with eggs and milk. **4.** Transfer to prepared dish and bake in centre of fairly hot oven (375°F. or Gas No. 5) for 30 minutes. Reduce temperature to moderate (350°F. or Gas No. 4). Bake further 35 to 45 minutes (or until wooden cocktail stick, inserted into centre of pudding, comes out clean). **5.** Leave in dish 5 minutes. Turn out on to warm plate. **6.** Serve with fresh double cream or with pineapple syrup from can, warmed through gently. **Serves 4 to 6.**

9 COFFEE FUDGE CREAM PIE

Short Crust Pastry (No. 88) made with
  6 oz. flour
2 level tablespoons apricot jam
3 oz. English or Welsh butter
3 oz. caster sugar
1 standard egg
1½ oz. finely-chopped shelled walnut halves
¼ lb. sifted self-raising flour
2 dessertspoons liquid coffee essence
1 dessertspoon cold milk
1 carton (5 oz.) soured cream

1. Roll out Pastry. Use to line 8-in. plain or fluted
flan ring resting on lightly-buttered baking tray.
2. Spread base with apricot jam. **3.** Cream butter
and sugar together until light and fluffy. Beat in
egg and walnuts. **4.** Fold in flour alternately with
coffee essence and milk. Transfer to pastry case.
5. Smooth top with knife. Put into centre of hot
oven (425°F. or Gas No. 7) and bake 15 minutes.
6. Reduce temperature to moderate (325°F. or
Gas No. 3). Bake further 25 to 30 minutes (or
until wooden cocktail stick, inserted into centre,
comes out clean). **7.** Remove from oven. Cover
top with soured cream then return to oven for
further 2 minutes. **Serves 4 to 6.**

STEAMED SUET PUDDING 960

¼ lb. plain flour
¼ level teaspoon salt
1½ level teaspoons baking powder
¼ lb. fresh white breadcrumbs
3 oz. caster sugar
3 oz. finely-shredded suet (beef for
  preference)
1 large egg, beaten
6 to 8 tablespoons cold milk to mix

1. Sift flour, salt and baking powder into bowl.
2. Add breadcrumbs, sugar and suet. Mix to soft
batter with beaten egg and milk. **3.** Turn into
buttered 2-pint pudding basin and cover securely
with buttered greaseproof paper or aluminium
foil. Steam steadily for 2½ to 3 hours. **4.** Turn out
on to warm plate. Serve with sweet sauce to
taste (see Sauce Section). **Serves 4.**

FAIR LADY PUDDING 961

1. Follow recipe and method for Steamed Suet
Pudding (No. 960). **2.** Add finely-grated peel of
1 medium-sized orange or lemon with sugar.
Serves 4.

Pineapple & Lemon Upside-Down Pudding (No. 958)

962 FOUR-FRUIT PUDDING

1. Follow recipe and method for Steamed Suet Pudding (No. 960). **2.** Add 1 oz. *each* dates, figs and prunes – all chopped – and 1 oz. mixed chopped peel with sugar. **Serves 4.**

963 COLLEGE PUDDING

1. Follow recipe and method for Steamed Suet Pudding (No. 960). **2.** Sift 1 level teaspoon mixed spice with flour. **3.** Add ¼ lb. mixed dried fruit with sugar (use ½ caster sugar and ½ soft brown). **Serves 4.**

964 MARMALADE PUDDING

1. Follow recipe and method for Steamed Suet Pudding (No. 960). **2.** Put 2 level tablespoons marmalade into bottom of buttered basin before adding pudding mixture. **Serves 4.**

965 SYRUP OR TREACLE PUDDING

1. Follow recipe and method for Steamed Suet Pudding (No. 960). **2.** Put 2 level tablespoons golden syrup or treacle into bottom of buttered basin before adding pudding mixture. **Serves 4.**

966 SPOTTED DICK

1. Follow recipe and method for Steamed Suet Pudding (No. 960). **2.** Add 3 oz. currants and 1 oz. mixed chopped peel with sugar. **Serves 4.**

CHRISTMAS PUDDING 9

¼ lb. plain flour
½ level teaspoon mixed spice
¼ level teaspoon grated nutmeg
¼ lb. fresh white breadcrumbs
10 oz. finely-shredded suet (beef for preference)
½ lb. soft brown sugar
¾ lb. *each* seedless raisins and sultanas
2 oz. mixed chopped peel
2 oz. shelled walnut halves or blanched almonds
Finely-grated peel of 1 small orange
4 large eggs, beaten
½ wine glass brandy or dry sherry
½ teaspoon almond essence
¼ pint milk

1. Sift flour, spice and nutmeg into large bowl. Add breadcrumbs, suet, sugar, raisins, sultanas, peel, finely-chopped walnuts or almonds and grated orange peel. **2.** Toss well together. **3.** Combine with beaten eggs, brandy or sherry, almond essence and milk. Mix well. **4.** Leave overnight in cool. Divide between two buttered 2-pint basins. **5.** Cover securely with buttered greaseproof paper or aluminium foil. Steam steadily for 6 hours, replenishing water as it boils away. **6.** Cool 15 minutes in basins. Turn out and leave until completely cold. **7.** Wrap in aluminium foil. Store in cool dry cupboard until needed. **8.** To serve, unwrap Pudding or Puddings, return to buttered basin or basins, cover and steam a further 2 hours. Turn out on to warm dish. Serve with sweet sauce to taste (see Sauce Section) or fresh double cream. **Each Pudding serves 6 to 7.**

● *If preferred, puddings may be stored in the basins in which they are cooked.*

967 BAKED BANANA SPONGE

3 oz. self-raising flour
Pinch of salt
3 oz. English or Welsh butter
3 oz. caster sugar
½ level teaspoon finely-grated lemon peel
2 small eggs
2 small bananas

1. Sift flour and salt into bowl. **2.** Cream butter, sugar and lemon peel until light and fluffy. Beat in eggs, singly, adding tablespoon of flour with each. **3.** Slice in bananas (slices should be about ½ in. thick). Mix well, then gently fold in remaining flour. **4.** Transfer to well-buttered 1 lb. loaf tin. Bake in centre of moderate oven (350°F. or Gas No. 4) for 20 minutes. Reduce temperature (325°F. or Gas No. 3) and bake further 20 to 25 minutes (or until wooden cocktail stick, inserted into centre, comes out clean). **5.** Turn out on to warm dish and serve with fresh single cream or custard. **Serves 4.**

69 EVE'S OR APPLE PUDDING

1 lb. cooking apples
3 to 4 oz. caster sugar
1 recipe Sponge Pudding (No. 949)

1. Peel, core and thinly slice apples. Arrange, in layers, in 2½-pint buttered pie dish, sprinkling sugar between layers. **2.** Cover with Sponge Pudding mixture. **3.** Bake in centre of moderate oven (350°F. or Gas No. 4) for 1 to 1¼ hours (or until wooden cocktail stick, inserted into centre of sponge mixture, comes out clean). Accompany with fresh double cream. **Serves 4 to 5.**

● *If preferred, gooseberries, rhubarb, apple mixed with blackberries, plums or damsons may be used instead of apples.*

70 ROLY-POLY PUDDING

1 recipe Suet Crust Pastry (No. 97)
3 to 4 level tablespoons golden syrup, treacle, marmalade or jam
1 level teaspoon finely-grated lemon peel

1. Roll out Pastry into 10-in. × 8-in. rectangle. **2.** Spread with syrup, treacle, marmalade or jam to within 1 in. of edges. Sprinkle with lemon peel. **3.** Moisten edges of Pastry with cold water. Roll up loosely like Swiss roll, starting from one of the shorter sides. **4.** Press edges and join underneath well together to seal. Wrap loosely in buttered aluminium foil. **5.** Twist ends of foil so that they stay closed. Steam Pudding for 2½ to 3 hours. **5.** Unwrap and serve with sweet sauce to taste (see Sauce Section). **Serves 4.**

71 APPLE FRITTERS

3 medium-sized cooking apples
1 recipe Sweet Fritter Batter (No. 660)
Deep fat or oil for frying
Sifted icing sugar

1. Peel and core apples. Cut each into ¼-in. thick rings. **2.** Coat with Fritter Batter. Fry in deep hot fat or oil for 2 to 3 minutes (or until golden). **3.** Remove from pan and drain on soft kitchen paper. Dredge thickly with sifted icing sugar. Accompany with fresh single cream, soured cream or natural yogurt. **Serves 4.**

BAKED APPLES WITH SYRUP & LEMON 972

4 Bramley apples (or other cooking apples)
1 level tablespoon golden syrup
½ level teaspoon finely-grated lemon peel
1 oz. English or Welsh butter
3 tablespoons warm water

1. Wash apples and wipe dry. Remove cores two-thirds of the way down each. **2.** With sharp knife, score line round each apple, about a third of the way down from top. **3.** Stand apples in heatproof dish. **4.** Mix syrup and lemon peel well together. Spoon equal amounts into apple cavities. **5.** Top each with large knob of butter. Pour the warm water into dish. **6.** Bake just above centre of moderate oven (350°F. or Gas No. 4) for 45 minutes to 1 hour (or until apples puff up and are tender). Baste at least twice while apples are cooking. Serve with fresh single or double cream, soured cream, natural yogurt or custard. **Serves 4.**

TREACLE TART 973

Short Crust Pastry (No. 88) made with 6 oz. flour
2 level tablespoons fresh white breadcrumbs
2 level tablespoons black treacle
1 level tablespoon golden syrup
½ level teaspoon finely-grated lemon peel
1 dessertspoon lemon juice

1. Roll out Pastry. Use to line 8-in. heatproof buttered plate. Trim surplus from edges. **2.** Mix breadcrumbs with treacle, syrup, lemon peel and juice. Spread over Pastry to within 1 in. of edges. Moisten edges with cold water. **3.** Cut remaining Pastry into thin strips. Arrange in criss-cross design over treacle filling. **4.** Press strips well on to Pastry edges and put plate on to baking tray. Bake just above centre of fairly hot oven (400°F. or Gas No. 6) for 30 minutes (or until Pastry is golden). Serve with fresh single or double cream, soured cream, natural yogurt or custard. **Serves 4.**

SYRUP TART 974

Follow recipe and method for Treacle Tart (No. 973) but instead of treacle and syrup use 3 level tablespoons syrup. **Serves 4.**

975 JAM TART

1. Follow recipe and method for Treacle Tart (No. 973) but instead of treacle and syrup use 3 level tablespoons jam. **2.** Omit lemon peel and juice. **Serves 4.**

976 MINCE TART

1 recipe Short Crust (No. 88) or Rich Short Crust Pastry (No. 89)
1 lb. mincemeat
Beaten egg
Sifted icing sugar

1. Cut Pastry into 2 equal portions. **2.** Roll out one half. Use to line 7 to 8-in. flat heatproof plate, lightly-buttered. **3.** Spread mincemeat over Pastry to within $\frac{1}{2}$ in. of edges. Moisten edges of Pastry with water. **4.** Cover with lid, rolled and shaped from rest of Pastry. Press edges well together to seal. **5.** Flake edges by cutting lightly with the back of a knife. 'Ridge' with fork all way round. **6.** Brush with beaten egg and stand plate on baking tray. Bake just above centre of hot oven (425°F. or Gas No. 7) for 15 minutes. **7.** Reduce temperature to fairly hot (400°F. or Gas No. 6). Bake further 30 minutes. **8.** Remove from oven, dredge thickly with icing sugar and serve warm with fresh single or double cream or custard. **Serves 6.**

977 QUEEN OF PUDDINGS

3 oz. fresh white breadcrumbs
1 oz. caster sugar
1 level teaspoon finely-grated lemon peel
$\frac{3}{4}$ pint cold milk
1 oz. English or Welsh butter
Yolks of 2 standard eggs
2 level tablespoons warmed raspberry jam
1 recipe Meringue Topping (No. 610)

1. Put breadcrumbs, sugar and lemon peel into basin. Toss lightly together to mix. **2.** Pour milk into pan. Add butter and heat gently until butter melts. **3.** Pour on to breadcrumb mixture. Stir well and leave to stand for 30 minutes. Beat in egg yolks. **4.** Spread into $1\frac{1}{2}$-pint buttered heatproof dish. **5.** Put into centre of moderate oven (325°F. or Gas No. 3) and bake 30 minutes (or until firm and set). **6.** Remove from oven and spread with jam. Cover with whirls of Meringue. **7.** Return to oven and bake further 30 to 40 minutes (or until Meringue is pale gold). Accompany with fresh double cream. **Serves 4.**

APPLE TURNOVERS

1 recipe Rough Puff (No. 94), Flaky (No. 99), Cream Cheese Pastry (No. 101) or Milk 'Puff' Pastry (No. 100)
$\frac{1}{2}$ lb. cooking apples
2 oz. caster sugar
A little lightly beaten egg white
Extra caster sugar

1. Roll out Pastry and cut into six 4-in. squares. **2.** Peel, core and thinly slice apples. Mix with sugar. Put equal amounts on to centres of each square. **3.** Moisten edges of Pastry with cold water. Fold each in half to form a triangle, completely enclosing fruit. **4.** Press edges well together to seal. Flake by cutting lightly with back of knife then 'ridge' with fork. **5.** Transfer Turnovers to buttered baking tray. Brush with egg white and sprinkle with sugar. **6.** Bake towards top of hot oven (425°F. or Gas No. 7) for 20 minutes. Reduce temperature to moderate (350°F. or Gas No. 4). Bake further 20 minutes. **7.** Serve with fresh single or double cream or custard. **Serves 6.**

APPLE & BLACKBERRY TURNOVERS

1. Follow recipe and method for Apple Turnovers (No. 978). **2.** Use 6 oz. cooking apples and 2 oz. blackberries. **Serves 6.**

MINCE PIES

1 recipe Short Crust (No. 88) or Rich Short Crust Pastry (No. 89)
$\frac{3}{4}$ lb. mincemeat
Beaten egg for brushing
Sifted icing sugar

1. Roll out Pastry. From it cut 12 rounds with $3\frac{1}{2}$-in. plain or fluted biscuit cutter and 12 rounds with $2\frac{1}{2}$-in. biscuit cutter. **2.** Use larger rounds to line 12 deep bun tins. **3.** Put equal amounts of mincemeat into each. Top with remaining rounds. Brush with beaten egg. **4.** Bake in centre of hot oven (425°F. or Gas No. 7) for 20 to 25 minutes (or until golden brown). **5.** Remove from tins and dredge thickly with sifted icing sugar. **6.** Serve warm with lightly-whipped fresh double cream or custard. **Serves 4 to 6.**

Apple & Blackberry Turnover (No. 979)

1 recipe Short Crust Pastry (No. 88)
½ lb. jam
Milk for brushing
Caster sugar

1. Roll out Pastry into 10-in. × 8-in. rectangle
2. Spread with jam to within ½ in. of edges
Moisten edges with cold water. **3.** Roll up like
Swiss roll, starting from one of the longer sides.
Press edges well together to seal. **4.** Transfer to
buttered baking tray, with join underneath.
Brush with milk. Sprinkle with caster sugar.
5. Bake just above centre of hot oven, (425°F. or
Gas No. 7) for 20 minutes. Lower heat to fairly
hot (375°F. or Gas No. 5). Bake further 20
minutes. **6** Serve with fresh single or double
cream, natural yogurt or custard. **Serves 4.**

APPLE AMBER   983

1 lb. cooking apples
1 tablespoon water
1 oz. English or Welsh butter
2 to 3 oz. caster sugar
3 level tablespoons stale cake crumbs
  (plain cake is best)
1 level teaspoon cinnamon
Yolks of 2 standard eggs
Meringue Topping (No. 610)

1. Peel, core and slice apples. Put into pan with
water and butter. **2.** Cook until soft and pulpy.
Beat until smooth. **3.** Add sugar, cake crumbs,
cinnamon and egg yolks. Mix well. **4.** Transfer to
1-pint heatproof dish and top with Meringue.
5. Put into centre of cool oven (300°F. or
Gas No. 2). Bake 30 minutes (or until Meringue
is light gold). Accompany with fresh double
cream. **Serves 4.**

Short Crust Pastry (No. 88) made with
6 oz. flour
1 level tablespoon fresh white breadcrumbs
½ pint lukewarm milk
2 standard eggs
Yolk of one standard egg
1 oz. caster sugar
Grated nutmeg

1. Roll out Pastry. Use to line 8 to 9-in. heatproof
buttered pie plate. **2.** Sprinkle base of Pastry
with breadcrumbs. Stand plate on baking tray.
3. Beat milk with eggs, egg yolk and sugar.
Strain into Pastry-lined pie plate. **4.** Sprinkle top
with nutmeg. Put into centre of fairly hot oven
(400°F. or Gas No. 6). **5.** Bake 15 minutes.
Reduce temperature to moderate (325°F. or
Gas No. 3). Bake further 30 to 45 minutes (or
until custard is set). **6.** Serve warm. **Serves 4 to 6.**

Frozen Desserts

DAIRY CREAM ICE

½ pint fresh double cream
2 tablespoons milk
5 level tablespoons sifted icing sugar
1 teaspoon vanilla essence

1. Turn refrigerator to coldest setting at least 1 hour before making Cream Ice. **2.** Pour cream and milk into well-chilled bowl and beat both together until lightly stiff. **3.** Stir in icing sugar and essence. Pour into ice cube tray. **4.** Put tray in freezing compartment of refrigerator. Freeze for 45 minutes or until Cream Ice has frozen about ½ in. round sides of tray. **5.** Pour into chilled bowl, break up with fork and stir gently until smooth. **6.** Return to washed and dried tray. Freeze 2 hours or until firm. **Serves 4.**

985 ALMOND DAIRY CREAM ICE

1. Follow recipe and method for Dairy Cream Ice (No. 984) but add 1 teaspoon almond essence instead of vanilla. **2.** Before second freezing, stir in 1 oz. toasted, finely-chopped almonds. **Serves 4.**

986 COFFEE DAIRY CREAM ICE

Follow recipe and method for Dairy Cream Ice (No. 984) but add 2 to 3 level teaspoons instant coffee powder mixed with 1 dessert-spoon hot water (then left to get cold) instead of vanilla. **Serves 4.**

987 PISTACHIO DAIRY CREAM ICE

1. Follow recipe and method for Dairy Cream Ice (No. 984) but omit vanilla. **2.** Stir in 1 oz. very finely-chopped blanched Pistachio nuts before second freezing. **3.** Cream Ice can be tinted pale green with food colouring. **Serves 4.**

988 CHOCOLATE CHIP DAIRY CREAM ICE

Follow recipe and method for Dairy Cream Ice (No. 984) but stir in 2 oz. coarsely-grated plain chocolate before second freezing. **Serves 4.**

PRESERVED GINGER DAIRY CREAM ICE

1. Follow recipe and method for Dairy Cream Ice (No. 984) but reduce sugar by 1 tablespoon and omit vanilla. **2.** Before second freezing, stir in 1 to 1½ oz. very finely-chopped preserved ginger and 1 tablespoon ginger syrup. **Serves 4.**

CHOCOLATE DAIRY CREAM ICE

1. Follow recipe and method for Dairy Cream Ice (No. 984). **2.** While mixture is freezing for first time, mix 2 level tablespoons cocoa powder to a smooth paste with 3 tablespoons boiling water. **3.** Leave until cold then beat into Cream Ice before second freezing. **Serves 4.**

CHOCOLATE BRANDY DAIRY CREAM ICE

Follow recipe and method for Chocolate Dairy Cream Ice (No. 990) but stir in 3 teaspoons brandy with cocoa mixture. **Serves 4.**

CHOCOLATE HAZELNUT DAIRY CREAM ICE

Follow recipe and method for Chocolate Dairy Cream Ice (No. 990) but stir in 1½ oz. very finely-chopped hazelnuts with cocoa mixture. **Serves 4.**

CHOCOLATE RUM DAIRY CREAM ICE

Follow recipe and method for Chocolate Dairy Cream Ice (No. 990) but stir in 2 teaspoons rum with cocoa mixture. **Serves 4.**

MARASCHINO DAIRY CREAM ICE

1. Follow recipe and method for Dairy Cream Ice (No. 984) but reduce sugar by 1 tablespoon and omit vanilla. **2.** Before second freezing, stir in 2 to 3 tablespoons coarsely-chopped Mara-schino-flavoured cherries and 1 tablespoon Maraschino-flavoured syrup. **Serves 4.**

5 ORANGE DAIRY CREAM ICE

1. Follow recipe and method for Dairy Cream Ice (No. 984) but reduce sugar by 1 tablespoon and omit vanilla. **2.** Before second freezing, add 1 level teaspoon finely-grated orange peel and 1 tablespoon Cointreau. **Serves 4.**

6 LEMON DAIRY CREAM ICE

1. Follow recipe and method for Dairy Cream Ice (No. 984) but omit vanilla. **2.** Before second freezing, stir in 2 level teaspoons finely-grated lemon peel. **Serves 4.**

7 LEMON CREAM SNOW

1. Follow recipe and method for Dairy Cream Ice (No. 984) but omit vanilla. **2.** Before second freezing, fold in 1 stiffly-beaten white of standard egg and 2 level teaspoons finely-grated lemon peel. **Serves 4.**

8 PRALINE DAIRY CREAM ICE

1. Follow recipe and method for Dairy Cream Ice (No. 984) but omit vanilla. **2.** Before second freezing, stir in 2 oz. finely-crushed nut brittle. **Serves 4.**

9 PEACH DAIRY CREAM ICE

1. Follow recipe and method for Dairy Cream Ice (No. 984) but reduce sugar by 2 tablespoons and omit vanilla. **2.** Before second freezing, stir in 2 tablespoons rose hip syrup, 1 level teaspoon finely-grated lemon peel and 4 drained, coarsely-chopped, canned peach halves. **Serves 4.**

00 APRICOT DAIRY CREAM ICE

1. Follow recipe and method for Dairy Cream Ice (No. 984) but reduce sugar by 2 tablespoons and omit vanilla. **2.** Before second freezing, stir in 2 tablespoons rose hip syrup, 1 level teaspoon finely-grated orange peel and 8 drained, coarsely-chopped, canned apricot halves. **Serves 4.**

TUTTI-FRUTTI DAIRY CREAM ICE 1001

1. Follow recipe and method for Dairy Cream Ice (No. 984). **2.** Before second freezing, stir in 2 drained and finely-chopped, canned pine-apple rings, 2 tablespoons drained and coarsely-chopped, canned mandarin oranges and 1 small sliced banana. **Serves 4.**

STRAWBERRY OR 1002 RASPBERRY DAIRY CREAM ICE

1. Follow recipe and method for Dairy Cream Ice (No. 984). **2.** Before second freezing, stir in 3 to 4 oz. sliced strawberries or the same amount of whole raspberries. **Serves 4.**

FRENCH CUSTARD 1003 ICE CREAM

$\frac{1}{2}$ **pint fresh single cream**
2 large beaten eggs
3 level tablespoons granulated sugar
2 teaspoons vanilla essence

1. Turn refrigerator to coldest setting at least 1 hour before making Ice Cream. **2.** Put cream, eggs and sugar into double saucepan (or basin standing over saucepan of gently simmering water). **3.** Cook, stirring all the time, until custard is thick enough to coat thinly the back of the spoon. Do not allow to boil. **4.** Pour into a bowl, stir in vanilla and leave until cold. **5.** Pour into ice cube tray and transfer to freezing compartment of refrigerator. **6.** Freeze for 1 hour or until Ice Cream has frozen about $\frac{1}{2}$ in. round sides of tray. **7.** Turn into a chilled bowl and whisk until smooth. **8.** Return to washed and dried tray and freeze $1\frac{1}{2}$ to 2 hours or until firm. **Serves 4.**

FRENCH CUSTARD 1004 DAIRY ICE

1. Follow recipe and method for French Custard Ice Cream (No.1003) but increase sugar by 1 level tablespoon and vanilla by 1 teaspoon. **2.** After beating Ice Cream until smooth, fold in $\frac{1}{4}$ pint very cold, fresh double cream, whipped until lightly stiff. **3.** Return to tray, or trays, depending on size, and freeze for $1\frac{1}{2}$ to 2 hours or until firm. **Serves 4 to 6.**

1005 RICH CHOCOLATE CREAM ICE

2 oz. plain chocolate
1 standard egg
1 oz. icing or caster sugar
2 teaspoons vanilla essence
$\frac{1}{4}$ pint fresh double cream

1. Turn refrigerator to coldest setting at least 1 hour before making Cream Ice. **2.** Break up chocolate. Melt in basin standing over a saucepan of hot water. Cool. **3.** Put egg and sugar into a double saucepan (or basin standing over saucepan of hot water). Whisk until thick and creamy. **4.** Remove from heat. Continue whisking until mixture is cool. **5.** Stir in cooled chocolate and vanilla. Fold in cream, beaten until lightly stiff. **6.** Pour into ice cube tray. Put into freezing compartment of refrigerator and freeze for 45 minutes (or until Cream Ice has frozen $\frac{1}{2}$ in. round sides of tray). **7.** Turn into chilled bowl, break up with a fork then stir until smooth. **8.** Return to washed and dried tray. Freeze for 1$\frac{1}{2}$ to 2 hours or until firm. **Serves 4.**

ITALIAN CREAM ICE 100

Yolks of 2 standard eggs
2 oz. sifted icing sugar
1 dessertspoon vanilla essence
$\frac{1}{2}$ pint fresh double cream
2 tablespoons milk

1. Turn refrigerator to coldest setting at least 1 hour before making Cream Ice. **2.** Put egg yolks and sugar into a double saucepan (or basin standing over saucepan of gently simmering water). Beat until thick and creamy. **3.** Remove from heat. Continue beating until cool, then stir in vanilla. **4.** Pour cream and milk into chilled bowl and beat until lightly stiff. **5.** Gently fold in beaten yolks and sugar then transfer to 1 or 2 ice cube trays, depending on size. Put into freezing compartment of refrigerator. **6.** Freeze for 45 minutes (or until Cream Ice has frozen about $\frac{1}{2}$ in. round sides of tray). **7.** Turn into chilled bowl, break up gently with a fork then stir until smooth. **8.** Return to washed and dried tray, or trays. Freeze for 1$\frac{1}{2}$ to 2 hours or until firm. **Serves 4.**

Ice Cream Gâteau (No. 1009)

Left to right: Raspberry Dairy Cream Ice (No. 1002), Chestnut Cream Sundae (No. 1021) and Chocolate Dairy Cream Ice (No. 990)

1007 CRUSHED FRUIT ICE CREAM

¼ pint fresh double cream
3 tablespoons sweetened fruit purée
  (made from choice of strawberries
  raspberries, canned peaches or canned
  apricots)
2 level tablespoons sifted icing sugar
2 level tablespoons sliced strawberries,
  whole raspberries or coarsely-chopped
  peaches or apricots

1. Turn refrigerator to coldest setting at least 1 hour before making Ice Cream. **2.** Whip cream and fruit purée until thick. **3.** Stir in sugar then pour into ice cube tray. **4.** Put into freezing compartment of refrigerator. Freeze for 45 minutes (or until Ice Cream has frozen about ½ in. round sides of tray). **5.** Turn into a chilled bowl, break up gently with a fork and stir until smooth. **6.** Add pieces of fruit. Mix well. Return to washed and dried tray. **7.** Freeze for 1½ to 2 hours or until firm. **Serves 4.**

ICE CREAM GÂTEAU 1009

½ pint fresh double cream
4 tablespoons milk
2 to 3 level tablespoons sifted icing sugar
2 Victoria Sandwich Cakes (No. 728)
2 tablespoons sweet sherry
2 tablespoons apricot jam
1 recipe Dairy Cream Ice (No. 984),
  Maraschino Dairy Cream Ice (No. 994)
  or Rich Chocolate Cream Ice (No. 1005)

DECORATION
Fresh berry fruits (strawberries or
  raspberries) or pieces of glacé fruits

1. Put cream and milk into a bowl and whip until thick. **2.** Sweeten with the icing sugar. **3.** Sprinkle each sandwich cake with sherry then spread with apricot jam. **4.** Sandwich together with table-spoons of Cream Ice and stand on a serving dish. **5.** Quickly swirl whipped cream over top and sides with a knife then decorate with fruit. **6.** Serve immediately. **Serves 6.**

1008 BANANA SPLITS

¼ pint fresh double cream
4 large bananas
1 recipe French Custard Ice Cream
  (No. 1003)
1 oz. finely-chopped shelled walnut halves
4 glacé cherries
Hot Chocolate Sauce (No. 177) or
    Hot Fudge Sauce (No. 155)

1. Whip cream until lightly stiff. **2.** Split bananas lengthwise and quickly sandwich together with dessertspoons of the Ice Cream. **3.** Stand on 4 individual plates then top with the whipped cream. **4.** Sprinkle with nuts and put whole cherry in centre of each. **5.** Serve straight away. Serve Chocolate or Fudge Sauce separately. **Serves 4.**

FROZEN DESSERTS

1010 FROZEN RASPBERRY MOUSSE

¼ pint sweetened raspberry purée, made from fresh, frozen or canned fruit
1 dessertspoon lemon juice
1 to 3 oz. sifted icing sugar, depending on sharpness of fruit
¼ pint fresh double cream
1 tablespoon milk
Whites of 2 standard eggs

1. Turn refrigerator control to coldest setting at least 1 hour before making Mousse. **2.** Put purée into basin. Add lemon juice and sugar to taste. (Freezing tends to reduce sweetness so it is better to over-sweeten). **3.** Whip cream and milk together until lightly stiff. Beat egg whites to stiff snow. **4.** Fold cream and egg whites alternately into fruit mixture. Transfer to 1 or 2 ice cube trays. **5.** Put into freezing compartment of refrigerator and freeze until firm. **6.** To serve, spoon into small glass dishes. **Serves 4.**

1011 FROZEN STRAWBERRY MOUSSE

Follow recipe and method for Frozen Raspberry Mousse (No. 1010) but use strawberry purée instead of the raspberry. **Serves 4.**

1012 OMELETTE SOUFFLÉ SURPRISE (BAKED ALASKA)

1 × 7-in. single layer sponge or sandwich cake (at least 1 day old)
1 or 2 tablespoons brandy or sherry
Meringue Topping, made with 3 egg whites (No. 610)
1 recipe Dairy Cream Ice (No. 984), French Custard Dairy Ice (No. 1004) or Italian Cream Ice (No. 1006)
Pieces of glacé fruits (optional)

1. Put cake on to a heatproof plate and moisten with brandy or sherry. **2.** Make Meringue Topping. **3.** Put tablespoons of Cream Ice in mound on top of cake. **4.** Swirl Meringue completely over cake and Cream Ice or pipe it over with a large star-shaped tube and forcing bag. **5.** Stud with fruits (if used) then flash bake (for directions see No. 610). **6.** Serve straight away. **Serves 4 to 6.**

TANGY FRUIT SORBET 101

6 oz. granulated sugar
6 mint leaves or ½ teaspoon dried mint
Juice of 1 small lemon
Finely-grated peel and strained juice of 1 medium-sized orange
4 tablespoons rose hip syrup
White of 1 standard egg
1 oz. caster sugar
DECORATION
Mint leaves or fresh strawberries or raspberries

1. Turn refrigerator to coldest setting at least 1 hour before making Sorbet. **2.** Put granulated sugar, ¼ pint water and mint into a pan. **3.** Stand pan over low heat and stir until sugar dissolves. **4.** Remove from heat and strain. Stir in ½ pint water, lemon juice, orange peel, orange juice and rose hip syrup. **5.** Mix well. Pour into 2 ice cube trays. **6.** Put into freezing compartment of refrigerator. Freeze for 1 hour or until mixture has half frozen. **7.** Beat egg white to stiff snow. Add caster sugar. Continue whisking until white is very stiff and shiny. **8.** Pour fruit mixture into chilled bowl. Whisk until smooth. Gently stir in beaten egg white. Return to washed and dried ice cube trays. Chill 45 minutes and re-whisk. **9.** Pour back into trays. Freeze 1½ to 2 hours or until firm. **10.** Spoon into small dishes and top with more mint leaves or fresh strawberries or raspberries. **11.** Serve straight away. **Serves 6.**

MIDSUMMER GLORIES 101

½ pint strawberry or raspberry jelly, already set
¼ pint fresh double cream
1 recipe Dairy Cream Ice (No. 984), French Custard Dairy Ice (No. 1004) or Italian Cream Ice (No. 1006)
1 medium-sized can peach slices
½ lb. fresh strawberries (small for preference) or raspberries
4 glacé cherries

1. Turn jelly out on to a sheet of damp greaseproof paper and chop coarsely with knife dipped in and out of cold water. **2.** Whip cream until stiff. **3.** Quickly fill tall glasses with alternate layers of jelly, Cream Ice and fruit. **4.** Put 1 or 2 tablespoons of cream on to each. Top with a whole cherry. **5.** Serve straight away. **Serves 4.**

1015 FRUIT COCKTAIL & STRAWBERRY SUNDAE

1. Divide a medium-sized can of fruit cocktail between 4 to 6 sundae glasses. **2.** Sprinkle with Kirsch, if liked. **3.** Top with scoops of Strawberry Dairy Cream Ice (No. 1002). **Serves 4 to 6.**

1016 MANDARIN & LEMON SUNDAE

1. Mix a can of mandarin oranges with sweet sherry or Grand Marnier to taste and reserve 4 to 6 segments for decoration. **2.** Divide fruit between 4 to 6 sundae glasses. Top with scoops of Lemon Dairy Cream Ice (No. 996). **3.** Put heaped tablespoon of lightly-whipped fresh double cream on to each. **4.** Decorate with mandarins and fresh mint leaves if available. **Serves 4 to 6.**

1017 PINEAPPLE & LEMON SUNDAE

1. Soak 1 medium-sized can of pineapple cubes in Maraschino-flavoured syrup. **2.** Divide between 4 to 6 sundae glasses. Top each with scoop of Lemon Dairy Cream Ice (No. 996). **Serves 4 to 6.**

1018 COFFEE CREAM SUNDAE

1. Scoop Coffee Dairy Cream Ice (No. 986), into 6 sundae glasses. **2.** Top with lightly-whipped fresh double cream, flavoured to taste with liquid coffee essence or Tia Maria liqueur. **Serves 6.**

1019 CHERRY CREAM SUNDAE

1. Scoop Dairy Cream Ice (No. 984), French Custard Dairy Ice (No. 1004) or Italian Cream Ice (No. 1006) into 6 sundae glasses. **2.** Add stewed red cherries to each then decorate with lightly-whipped, fresh double cream. **3.** Top each with 2 whole raspberries. **Serves 6.**

PINEAPPLE & STRAWBERRY SUNDAE 1020

1. Put 1 pineapple ring into 4 or 6 sundae glasses. **2.** Top with scoops of Dairy Cream Ice (No. 984), French Custard Dairy Ice (No. 1004) or Italian Cream Ice (No. 1006). **3.** Decorate with whipped fresh double cream and whole strawberries. **Serves 4 to 6.**

CHESTNUT CREAM SUNDAE 1021

1. Scoop French Custard Ice Cream (No. 1003) into 4 sundae glasses. **2.** Pipe canned chestnut purée over top of each to resemble vermicelli. **3.** Put mound of lightly-whipped, fresh double cream on to the centre of each. **4.** Top with 2 Maraschino-flavoured cherries. **Serves 4.**

PINEAPPLE & COFFEE SUNDAE 1022

1. Soak 1 medium-sized can of pineapple cubes in a little rum. **2.** Divide between 4 to 6 sundae glasses then top with scoops of Coffee Dairy Cream Ice (No. 986). **3.** Pipe stiffly-whipped, fresh double cream over each. **4.** Sprinkle *lightly* with ground coffee. **Serves 4 to 6.**

REDCURRANT SUNDAE 1023

1. Put scoops of Dairy Cream Ice (No. 984), French Custard Dairy Ice (No. 1004) or Italian Cream Ice (No. 1006) into 4 to 6 sundae glasses. **2.** Cover with fresh redcurrants (removed from stems). **3.** Top with softly-whipped fresh double cream. **Serves 4 to 6.**

PEACH MELBA 1024

1. Put scoops of French Custard Ice Cream (No.1003) into 4 sundae glasses. **2.** Top each with canned peach half. **3.** Spoon over raspberry purée made by crushing 6 to 8 oz. fresh raspberries with sifted icing sugar to taste. **4.** If fresh peaches are preferred, skin them, cut in half and poach gently in a syrup made by dissolving 4 oz. granulated sugar in 4 tablespoons water. **Serves 4.**

Frozen Crunch Flan (No. 1025)

FROZEN CRUNCH FLAN   1025

½ lb. plain chocolate digestive biscuits
3 oz. English or Welsh butter
¼ pint fresh double cream
1 recipe Almond Dairy Cream Ice (No. 985)
   or Preserved Ginger Dairy Cream Ice
   (No. 989)

DECORATION
Peach slices and glacé cherries

1. To make flan case, crush biscuits finely.
2. Melt butter in pan and stir in the crumbs.
3. Stand 7-in. plain flan ring on a baking tray.
Press crumbs thickly and evenly over base and
sides. **4.** Refrigerate until firm. **5.** Just before
serving, whip cream until lightly stiff. **6.** Remove
flan from refrigerator, gently lift off ring and
transfer case to serving plate. **7.** Fill with tablespoons of the Cream Ice then cover with the
whipped cream. **8.** Decorate with peach slices
(well drained) and cherries. **9.** Serve straight
away. **Serves 6.**

CANTELOUPE CUPS   1026

2 small Cantaloupe melons
1 recipe Lemon Cream Snow (No.997)
¼ pint fresh double cream
¼ lb. whole strawberries

1. Chill melons for at least 1 hour before using.
2. Cut each in half, remove pips and put on to
4 plates. **3.** Fill cavities with scoops of Lemon
Cream Snow. Decorate with stiffly-whipped
cream and strawberries. **4.** Serve straight away.
Serves 4.

TUTTI-FRUTTI BASKET   1027

¼ pint fresh double cream
1 tablespoon milk
1 recipe Tutti-Frutti Dairy Cream Ice
   (No. 1001)
1 Meringue Basket (No. 613)
Hot Chocolate Sauce (No. 177)

1. Whip cream and milk together until thick.
2. Spoon Tutti-Frutti Dairy Cream Ice neatly into
Meringue Basket **3.** Quickly pipe trellis of cream
over the top. **4.** Serve straight away. **5.** Serve
Hot Chocolate Sauce separately. **Serves 4 to 6.**

Dishes from Abroad

ITALY

028 GNOCCHI

1 pint milk
¼ lb. semolina
1 level teaspoon salt
2 oz. English or Welsh butter
3 oz. very finely-grated English Cheddar
  cheese
¼ level teaspoon grated nutmeg
1 level teaspoon made mustard
1 large egg, beaten

1. Pour milk into saucepan and sprinkle in semolina and salt. **2.** Cook over medium heat, stirring, until mixture comes to boil and thickens. **3.** Simmer 1 minute and remove from heat. **4.** Beat in 1 oz. butter, half the cheese, nutmeg, mustard and beaten egg. **5.** Mix thoroughly. Return to heat and cook further minute, stirring. **6.** Transfer mixture to oiled Swiss roll tin (about 8 in. × 12 in.) spreading it about ¼-in. thick. **7.** Leave in cool several hours until firm and set. **8.** Cut into 1½-in. squares. Lift out of tin and arrange, in layers, in fairly shallow, buttered heatproof dish (about 1-pint size). **9.** Sprinkle top with remaining cheese. Dot with rest of butter. Re-heat towards top of hot oven (425°F. or Gas No. 7) about 15 minutes (or until brown). **10.** Serve as a main course with tossed green salad or as side dish with lamb. **Serves 4.**

029 RISOTTO MILANESE

1 small onion
2 oz. English or Welsh butter
¾ lb. long grain rice
1½ pints hot chicken stock or water
Salt and pepper to taste
1 extra oz. English or Welsh butter

ACCOMPANIMENT
3 oz. finely-grated English Cheddar
  cheese

1. Chop onion very finely. Fry gently in butter until pale gold. **2.** Add rice. Fry further minute, turning it over all the time. **3.** Gradually pour in hot stock or water. **4.** Cover pan. Simmer for 20 to 30 minutes (or until rice grains have swollen and absorbed most of the liquid). Stir frequently with fork. **5.** Season to taste with salt and pepper. Add extra butter and 1 oz. cheese. **6.** Stir gently with fork until both have melted. **7.** Serve Risotto while still very hot. Pass remaining cheese separately. **Serves 4.**

Pizza Neapolitan (No. 1032)

ITALY (continued)

1030 SPAGHETTI BOLOGNESE

1 medium-sized onion
1½ oz. English or Welsh butter
1 dessertspoon olive or corn oil
½ lb. lean minced beef
1 garlic clove (optional)
¼ lb. mushrooms
½ pint water
1 bay leaf
1 small can (5 oz.) tomato purée
2 level teaspoons sugar
½ level teaspoon basil or mixed herbs
Salt and pepper to taste
¾ lb. spaghetti

ACCOMPANIMENT
3 to 4 oz. finely-grated English Cheddar
  cheese

1. Chop onion finely. Fry slowly in butter and oil until pale gold. **2.** Add beef. Fry further 3 to 4 minutes, breaking it up and stirring all the time. **3.** Chop garlic (if used). Wash mushrooms and stalks. **4.** Add to saucepan with water, bay leaf, purée, sugar, basil or mixed herbs and salt and pepper to taste. **5.** Bring slowly to boil, stirring. Cover pan and lower heat. **6.** Simmer gently for 30 minutes and uncover. **7.** Continue to cook for further 20 to 30 minutes (or until sauce is thick and creamy and about half the liquid has evaporated). Stir frequently. **8.** Meanwhile, cook spaghetti in boiling salted water until tender (about 20 minutes), stirring often to prevent sticking. **9.** Drain well. Transfer equal amounts to 4 warm serving plates. **10.** Pour sauce over each. Serve straight away. **11.** Pass cheese separately. **Serves 4.**

1031 SPAGHETTI NEAPOLITAN

¾ lb. spaghetti
1 recipe freshly-made Tomato Sauce
  (No. 144)

ACCOMPANIMENT
3 to 4 oz. finely-grated English Cheddar
  cheese

1. Cook spaghetti in boiling salted water until tender (about 20 minutes), stirring often to prevent sticking. **2.** Drain well. Transfer equal amounts to 4 warm serving plates. **3.** Pour Tomato Sauce over each. Serve straight away. **4.** Pass cheese separately. **Serves 4.**

PIZZA NEAPOLITAN

DOUGH BASE
½ lb. plain flour
1 level teaspoon salt
½ oz. English or Welsh butter
¼ oz. fresh yeast or 1 level teaspoon dried
  yeast
4 tablespoons lukewarm water
4 tablespoons lukewarm milk
¼ level teaspoon sugar (only if using dried
  yeast)
About 1 extra oz. English or Welsh butter,
  melted

FILLING
½ lb. grated English Cheddar cheese
¼ lb. grated Caerphilly cheese
1 lb. skinned and sliced tomatoes
1 level teaspoon marjoram, basil or thyme
Salt and pepper
Anchovy fillets
Black olives

1. Sift flour and salt into bowl. **2.** Rub in butter. **3.** Blend yeast to smooth cream with water. Stir in milk. If using dried yeast, dissolve sugar in water and sprinkle yeast on top. Leave 10 to 15 minutes (or until frothy). Stir in milk. **4.** Mix dry ingredients to dough with yeast liquid, adding extra flour if needed, until dough leaves sides of bowl clean. **5.** Turn out and knead thoroughly 5 to 10 minutes (or until dough feels smooth and elastic). **6.** Cover and leave until doubled in size. **7.** Turn out on to floured board. Roll into long strip. Brush with melted butter and roll up like Swiss roll. Repeat 3 times. **8.** Divide dough into 4 equal-sized pieces. Shape each into 6-in. round. **9.** Place on large buttered baking tray. **10.** Cover with alternate layers of cheese and tomatoes, sprinkling herbs and salt and pepper between layers. **11.** Finish with layer of cheese. Decorate tops with lattice of anchovy fillets. **12.** Stud with olives. Leave in cool for ½ an hour. **13.** Bake towards top of hot oven (450°F. or Gas No. 8) for 25 to 30 minutes. **14.** Serve hot or cold. **Serves 4.**

1. Follow recipe and method for Pizza Neapolitan (No. 1032). **2.** Instead of garnishing with anchovies and olives, use 2 oz. sliced mushrooms, lightly fried in a little English or Welsh butter, 2 oz. ham cut into strips and 2 small skinned tomatoes, cut into wedges. **Serves 4.**

GERMANY

034 SWEET-SOUR RED CABBAGE

1 medium-sized red cabbage (2 to 2½ lb.)
2 oz. English or Welsh butter
3 level tablespoons soft brown sugar
1 level teaspoon caraway seeds
3 cloves
1 lb. cooking apples
1 level tablespoon cornflour
4 tablespoons vinegar
½ pint water
Salt and pepper to taste

1. Wash cabbage and cut into fine shreds. **2.** Melt butter in large saucepan. Add cabbage and fry briskly 5 minutes, shaking pan frequently. **3.** Stir in sugar, caraway seeds and cloves. Leave over low heat. **4.** Peel, core and chop apples. Add to pan. **5.** Mix cornflour to thin paste with vinegar. Add water and pour over cabbage. **6.** Cook, stirring, until mixture comes to boil and thickens. Season to taste. **7.** Reduce heat. Cover pan and simmer very slowly for 1½ hours. **8.** Stir occasionally. Serve hot with any meat or poultry dish. **Serves 4 to 6.**

CANADA

035 BAKED HALIBUT ROYAL

2 tablespoons lemon juice
½ level teaspoon salt
½ level teaspoon paprika
4 halibut steaks (each about 6 oz.)
1 small chopped onion
2 oz. English or Welsh butter
½ small green pepper, cut into strips

ACCOMPANIMENT
1 recipe Hot Tartare Sauce (No. 125)
4 lemon wedges

1. Combine lemon juice, salt and paprika. Pour into shallow heatproof dish. **2.** Add halibut. Leave to marinate for 1 hour, turning steaks over after 30 minutes. **3.** Fry onion slowly in butter until soft but not brown. **4.** Top halibut with pepper strips. **5.** Sprinkle with onion and remaining butter from pan. Bake, uncovered, towards top of hot oven (425°F. or Gas No. 7) for 15 minutes (or until fish flakes easily with fork). **6.** Pass Tartare Sauce and lemon wedges separately. **Serves 4.**

HOLLAND

BUTTERCAKE   1036

½ lb. English or Welsh butter
½ lb. soft brown sugar
1 level teaspoon finely-grated lemon peel
1 standard egg
½ lb. plain flour
2 oz. blanched and chopped almonds

1. Cream butter, sugar and lemon peel until light and fluffy. **2.** Beat in egg. Gently fold in flour. **3.** Spread into Swiss roll tin (approximately 8 in. × 12 in.) and scatter almonds over top. **4.** Bake in centre of moderate oven (350°F. or Gas No. 4) for 45 to 50 minutes (or until golden). **5.** Remove from oven. Cool slightly and cut into squares or fingers. **6.** Store in an airtight tin when cold. **About 24 pieces.**

GREECE

MOUSSAKA   1037

2 medium-sized aubergines
Salt
3 oz. English or Welsh butter
1 tablespoon olive or corn oil
2 large onions
¾ lb. cooked minced lamb or beef
2 level tablespoons fresh white
  breadcrumbs
¼ pint water
1 level tablespoon tomato purée
Seasoning to taste
1 standard egg, beaten
1 recipe freshly-made Cheese Coating
  Sauce (No. 116)
2 oz. grated English Cheddar cheese

1. Cut aubergines into ¼-in. thick slices. Sprinkle with salt and leave ½ an hour. Drain thoroughly. Fry quickly in butter and oil until golden on both sides. **2.** Remove from pan and leave on one side. **3.** Slice onions thinly. Fry in remaining butter and oil until pale gold. Remove from heat. **4.** Combine meat with breadcrumbs, water and tomato purée. Season to taste. **5.** Line base of oblong or square heatproof dish with half the fried aubergine slices. **6.** Cover with meat mixture and onions. Arrange remaining aubergine slices attractively on the top **7.** Gradually beat egg into Cheese Sauce. Pour into dish over aubergine slices. **8.** Sprinkle with cheese. Bake, uncovered, in centre of moderate oven (350°F. or Gas No. 4) for 45 minutes to 1 hour. **Serves 4.**

Bornholm Herrings (No. 1042)

SPAIN

4 small joints roasting chicken
2 oz. English or Welsh butter
1 tablespoon olive oil
1 small onion
1 garlic clove
$\frac{1}{2}$ lb. long grain rice
$\frac{1}{2}$ level teaspoon saffron strands
1 pint warm chicken stock or water
1 bay leaf
6 oz. cooked peas
$\frac{1}{4}$ lb. peeled prawns
$\frac{1}{4}$ lb. cooked lobster meat (optional)
8 cooked and shelled mussels
1 canned or bottled pimento, cut into
   strips

1. Skin chicken joints. Fry in butter and oil until light brown and crisp. 2. Transfer to plate. 3. Chop onion and garlic. Add to remaining butter in pan. Fry slowly until pale gold. 4. Add rice and fry further minute. 5. Mix saffron with chicken stock or water. Pour into pan. 6. Add bay leaf, bring to boil and cover pan. 7. Simmer slowly for 10 minutes. Transfer to large heatproof dish, about 3 in. deep. 8. Stand chicken joints on top. Cover with lid or aluminium foil and cook just above centre of moderate oven (350°F. or Gas No.4) for 30 minutes. 9. Uncover and arrange peas, prawns, lobster meat, mussels and strips of pimento attractively over rice and chicken. 10. Return to oven and cook, uncovered, for 10 to 15 minutes (or until chicken is tender and rice grains have absorbed all the liquid). 11. Serve straight away. **Serves 4.**

MEXICO

$\frac{1}{2}$ lb. haricot or red kidney beans, soaked
   overnight
2 medium-sized onions
2 garlic cloves
2 oz. English or Welsh butter
1 dessertspoon olive or corn oil
1 lb. lean minced beef
$\frac{1}{2}$ lb. skinned tomatoes
1 medium-sized green pepper
$1\frac{1}{2}$ level tablespoons chilli powder
$\frac{1}{4}$ level teaspoon salt
1 level teaspoon caraway seeds
$\frac{1}{4}$ pint water
1 level tablespoon flour
4 tablespoons fresh single cream

1. Drain beans. Cook in boiling salted water until almost tender. Strain and keep on one side. 2. Chop onion and garlic finely. Fry gently in butter and oil until gold. 3. Add meat and fry 5 minutes (or until brown), breaking it up with fork and turning it over all the time. 4. Chop tomatoes and green pepper (remove and discard seeds of pepper first). Add to pan with beans, chilli powder, salt, caraway seeds and half the quantity of water. 5. Cover and cook over very low heat for 45 minutes to 1 hour (or until beans are soft), stirring occasionally. 6. Combine flour with rest of water. Pour into pan. 7. Cook and stir until mixture thickens. Remove from heat and stir in cream. 8. Serve straight away. **Serves 4.**

● *This is a very fiery dish! To make it milder, halve or even quarter quantity of chilli powder.*

FRANCE

1040 QUICHE LORRAINE

Short Crust Pastry made with 6 oz. flour
(No. 88)
¼ lb. streaky bacon
¼ pint milk
¼ pint fresh single cream
3 standard eggs, beaten
Large pinch grated nutmeg
Pepper and salt to taste

1. Roll out Pastry. Use to line 8-in. flan ring resting on lightly-buttered baking tray. 2. Cut bacon into strips. Fry lightly in its own fat until soft but not crisp. 3. Drain thoroughly on soft kitchen paper. Use to line base of pastry case. 4. Heat milk and cream to just below boiling point. Combine with beaten eggs. 5. Season with grated nutmeg and salt and pepper to taste. Pour into pastry case. 6. Bake in centre of fairly hot oven (400°F. or Gas No. 6) for 10 minutes. Reduce temperature to moderate (325°F. or Gas No. 3). Bake for further 35 to 45 minutes (or until filling is set). 7. Serve hot. **Serves 4 to 5.**

1041 PIPÉRADE

¾ lb. onions
3 oz. English or Welsh butter
1 dessertspoon olive oil
3 medium-sized green peppers
1 lb. skinned tomatoes
¼ level teaspoon marjoram or basil
Salt and freshly-milled pepper to taste
6 standard eggs
4 tablespoons fresh double cream
4 gammon rashers, freshly grilled

1. Chop onion. Fry gently in butter and oil until soft but not brown. 2. Meanwhile, remove seeds and inside fibres from green peppers and discard. Cut peppers into strips and add to pan. Cook slowly with onion until soft. 3. Chop tomatoes. Add to pan with marjoram or basil and salt and pepper to taste. Cover and simmer for 20 minutes. 4. Beat eggs lightly with cream. Pour over vegetable mixture. 5. Cook slowly, stirring, until eggs are lightly scrambled. 6. Transfer to warm serving dish and top with gammon. **Serves 4.**

Right: Pipérade (No. 1041)

DENMARK

BORNHOLM HERRINGS 1042

2 rollmops or pickled herrings
2 cartons (½ pint) natural yogurt
¼ to ½ level teaspoon salt
Shake of pepper
2 level teaspoons finely-grated onion
Large pinch grated nutmeg

GARNISH
Paprika and snipped chives

1. Cut each rollmop or pickled herring into 8 pieces. 2. Arrange in shallow serving dish. 3. Combine yogurt with salt, pepper, onion and nutmeg. Pour over the fish. 4. Chill. 5. Just before serving, sprinkle with paprika and chives. 6. Accompany with brown bread and butter. **Serves 4.**

SWITZERLAND

MUSELLI OR SWISS BREAKFAST 1043

½ lb. rolled oats
2 large eating apples
Juice of 1 lemon
2 level tablespoons chopped hazelnuts
2 to 3 oz. caster sugar
¾ pint milk

1. Put oats into large bowl. 2. Grate unpeeled apples fairly coarsely. Combine with lemon juice. 3. Add to oats with nuts, sugar and milk. 4. Stir well, and cover. Leave to stand in the cool 30 minutes before serving. **Serves 4.**

Sandwiches & Sandwich Fillings

Use fresh, but not very new, bread. Make sure that the slices are not too thick.

Allow 6 oz. softened and well-creamed English or Welsh butter for every 2 dozen large bread slices.

Make sure that the butter completely covers the bread slices. It acts as a waterproof barrier, preventing moisture from fillings seeping through into the bread and making it soggy.

Prepare all fillings beforehand and check to see that they are really well seasoned. If using soft fillings, such as chopped hard-boiled eggs combined with natural yogurt, have something crisp – lettuce or chopped celery for example – to go with it. Contrast of texture adds interest.

Half a pound of sliced meat, cheese or smoked fish will fill about 8 sandwiches.

Number of sandwiches to allow per person will depend on appetite and type of fillings used. As a general guide, allow $1\frac{1}{2}$ to 2 full rounds or 8 to 10 small sandwiches for each person. A round is two slices of bread.

If sandwiches are made in advance at night for a packed lunch the next day wrap them in aluminium foil or in a polythene bag and keep in a cold larder or refrigerator overnight.

Crust removal is a matter of choice. Large sandwiches keep better if the crusts are left on. Dainty afternoon sandwiches, made from very thin bread, look more attractive and less clumsy if the crusts are removed.

BASIC SANDWICHES

1044 CHEESE APPLE & LEEK SANDWICH

12 large slices brown bread
English or Welsh butter
6 oz. thinly-sliced Derby or Wensleydale cheese
3 level tablespoons grated unpeeled eating apple
3 level tablespoons chopped raw leek
4 to 5 tablespoons natural yogurt

1. Spread bread thickly with butter. 2. Sandwich slices together, in pairs, with cheese followed by apple and leek, well mixed with yogurt. 3. Cut each sandwich into 2 or 4 pieces. Serves 4.

LETTUCE, BEEF & HORSERADISH SANDWICH   104

12 large slices white or brown bread
English or Welsh butter
6 large slices beef or corned beef
Shredded lettuce
4 tablespoons natural yogurt
$\frac{1}{2}$ to 1 level teaspoon grated horseradish

1. Spread bread thickly with butter. 2. Sandwich slices together, in pairs, with beef or corned beef and lettuce followed by yogurt mixed with horseradish. 3. Cut each sandwich into 2 or 4 pieces. Serves 4.

1045 CRESS, CHEESE & CARROT SANDWICH

12 large slices brown bread
English or Welsh butter
Mustard and cress
6 oz. thinly-sliced Double Gloucester cheese
6 level tablespoons grated carrot
4 tablespoons soured cream or natural yogurt

1. Spread bread thickly with butter. 2. Sandwich slices together, in pairs, with mustard and cress and cheese, followed by grated carrot mixed with soured cream or yogurt. 3. Cut each sandwich into 2 or 4 pieces. Serves 4.

WATERCRESS & CREAMED FISH SANDWICH   104

12 large slices brown bread
English or Welsh butter
About 6 tablespoons chopped watercress
6 oz. flaked white fish, cooked
2 oz. peeled prawns
$\frac{1}{2}$ level teaspoon finely-grated lemon peel
4 to 5 tablespoons salad cream

1. Spread bread thickly with butter. 2. Sandwich slices together, in pairs, with watercress followed by fish, prawns and lemon peel mixed with salad cream. 3. Cut each sandwich into 2 or 4 pieces. Serves 4.

48 LETTUCE, COTTAGE CHEESE & PINEAPPLE SANDWICH

12 large slices white or brown bread
English or Welsh butter
Shredded lettuce
$\frac{1}{2}$ lb. cottage cheese
4 level tablespoons chopped canned pineapple

1. Spread bread thickly with butter. **2.** Sandwich slices together, in pairs, with lettuce followed by cottage cheese mixed with pineapple. **3.** Cut each sandwich into 2 or 4 pieces. **Serves 4.**

49 CHEESE & CELERY SANDWICH

12 large slices brown bread
English or Welsh butter
6 oz. thinly-sliced Cheshire cheese
3 level tablespoons chopped celery
4 tablespoons fresh double cream

1. Spread bread thickly with butter. **2.** Sandwich slices together, in pairs, with cheese followed by celery well mixed with double cream. **3.** Cut each sandwich into 2 or 4 pieces. **Serves 4.**

50 STILTON, LETTUCE & HAM SANDWICH

12 large slices white or brown bread
English or Welsh butter
6 oz. Blue Stilton cheese
6 slices lean ham (approximately 6 oz.)
Shredded lettuce

1. Spread bread thickly with butter. **2.** Sandwich slices together, in pairs, with cheese, ham and shredded lettuce. **3.** Cut each sandwich into 2 or 4 pieces. **Serves 4.**

51 PORK & APPLE SANDWICH

12 large slices white or brown bread
English or Welsh butter
6 large slices cold roast pork
1 large unpeeled and grated eating apple
4 tablespoons natural yogurt

1. Spread bread thickly with butter. **2.** Sandwich slices together, in pairs, with slices of pork followed by apple mixed with yogurt. **3.** Cut each sandwich into 2 or 4 pieces. **Serves 4.**

CHEESE, ONION & TOMATO SANDWICH 1052

12 large slices white bread
English or Welsh butter
6 oz. sliced English Cheddar cheese
1 medium-sized thinly-sliced raw onion
4 large tomatoes, skinned if preferred, and sliced

1. Spread bread thickly with butter. **2.** Sandwich slices together, in pairs, with cheese, raw onion rings and slices of tomato. **3.** Cut each sandwich into 2 or 4 pieces. **Serves 4.**

CREAM CHEESE, GHERKIN & TOMATO SANDWICH 1053

12 large slices brown bread
English or Welsh butter
4 to 6 oz. cream cheese
3 to 4 level tablespoons finely-chopped gherkins
4 large tomatoes, skinned if preferred, and sliced

1. Spread bread thickly with butter. **2.** Sandwich together, in pairs, with cream cheese, gherkins and slices of tomato. **3.** Cut each Sandwich into 2 or 4 pieces. **Serves 4.**

BACON & BANANA SANDWICH 1054

12 large slices white or brown bread
English or Welsh butter
3 medium-sized mashed bananas
12 rashers grilled bacon

1. Spread bread thickly with butter. **2.** Sandwich slices together, in pairs, with mashed bananas and bacon rashers. **3.** Cut each sandwich into 2 or 4 pieces. **Serves 4.**

SMOKED ROE & CUCUMBER SANDWICH 1055

12 large slices brown bread
English or Welsh butter
Smoked cod's roe
Cucumber slices, peeled if preferred

1. Spread bread thickly with butter. **2.** Sandwich slices together, in pairs, with a thin spread of cod's roe and slices of cucumber. **3.** Cut each sandwich into 2 or 4 pieces. **Serves 4.**

Afternoon Tea Sandwiches (No. 1058) filled with chopped egg, egg and pâté, Pin Wheel Sandwiches (No. 1059) filled with cream cheese and smoked salmon, and Asparagus Rolls (No. 1062)

1056 TOMATO, CRESS & SARDINE SANDWICH

12 slices white or brown bread
English or Welsh butter
4 large tomatoes, skinned if preferred, and sliced
Mustard and cress
1 can drained sardines
4 tablespoons natural yogurt
2 teaspoons lemon juice

1. Spread bread thickly with butter. **2.** Sandwich slices together, in pairs, with tomato slices and mustard and cress followed by sardines, mashed with yogurt and lemon juice. **3.** Cut each sandwich into 2 or 4 pieces. **Serves 4.**

1057 SALMON & LETTUCE SANDWICH

12 large slices white or brown bread
English or Welsh butter
Shredded lettuce
1 can (approximately ½ lb.) red salmon
1 level teaspoon finely-grated lemon peel
2 level teaspoons finely-grated onion
3 to 4 tablespoons natural yogurt

1. Spread bread thickly with butter. **2.** Sandwich slices together, in pairs, with lettuce followed by well-drained salmon mashed with lemon peel, grated onion and yogurt. **3.** Cut each sandwich into 2 or 4 pieces. **Serves 4.**

AFTERNOON TEA SANDWICHES   10

1. Spread very thin slices of white or brown bread with well-creamed English or Welsh butter. **2.** Sandwich together with choice of finely-chopped hard-boiled egg mixed with salad cream, thin slices of peeled cucumber, smoked salmon, well-seasoned cream cheese or fish or meat paste. **3.** Remove crusts and cut each sandwich into 4 squares or triangles. **4.** Arrange attractively on serving plate. **5.** Sprinkle with mustard and cress. **Allow 8 to 10 squares or triangles per person.**

PIN WHEEL SANDWICHES   10

1. Remove crusts from very thin, very fresh, slices of white or brown bread. **2.** Stand on damp tea towel (this helps to prevent bread from cracking). **3.** Spread with well-creamed English or Welsh butter. **4.** Cover with choice of well-seasoned cream cheese, smoked cod's roe, smoked salmon, soft liver sausage, pâté or fish or meat paste. **5.** Roll up and hold in place with wooden cocktail sticks. **6.** Stand on plate or small serving tray. **7.** Cover with aluminium foil or sheet of polythene. **8.** Chill thoroughly. **9.** Just before serving, remove sticks and cut each roll into thin slices. **Allow about 8 to 12 Pin Wheels per person.**

060 LETTUCE, CHEESE & WALNUT SANDWICH

12 large slices white or brown bread
English or Welsh butter
Shredded lettuce
6 to 8 oz. grated Leicester cheese
1 oz. finely-chopped shelled walnut halves
3 tablespoons natural yogurt

1. Spread bread thickly with butter. **2.** Sandwich slices together, in pairs, with lettuce followed by cheese well mixed with walnuts and yogurt. **3.** Cut each sandwich into 2 or 4 pieces. **Serves 4.**

061 AVOCADO & ONION SANDWICH

12 slices white or brown bread
English or Welsh butter
1 large thinly-sliced onion
1 medium-sized avocado pear
1 tablespoon lemon juice
2 tablespoons fresh double cream
½ level teaspoon paprika

1. Spread bread thickly with butter. **2.** Sandwich slices together, in pairs, with onion rings followed by avocado pulp, finely mashed with lemon juice, cream and paprika. **3.** Cut each sandwich into 2 or 4 pieces. **Serves 4.**

062 ASPARAGUS ROLLS

1. Remove crusts from very thin, very fresh, slices of white or brown bread. **2.** Stand on damp tea towel (this helps to prevent bread from cracking). **3.** Spread with well-creamed English or Welsh butter. **4.** Put 2 asparagus tips, with points facing outwards, on to each slice. **5.** Roll up and hold in place with wooden cocktail sticks. **6.** Stand on plate or small tray. **7.** Cover with aluminium foil or sheet of polythene. **8.** Chill thoroughly. **9.** Remove sticks just before serving. **Allow 2 to 3 per person.**

Right (from the top): Prawn & Mayonnaise Open Sandwich (No. 1066), Liver Sausage & Potato Salad Open Sandwich (No. 1070), and Scrambled Egg & Salmon Open Sandwich (No. 1071)

1063 TONGUE & CUCUMBER SANDWICH

12 large slices white or brown bread
English or Welsh butter
6 large slices tongue
4 level tablespoons cucumber, peeled if preferred, and chopped
4 to 5 tablespoons fresh double or soured cream

1. Spread bread thickly with butter. **2.** Sandwich slices together, in pairs, with tongue followed by cucumber mixed with cream. **3.** Cut each sandwich into 2 or 4 pieces. **Serves 4.**

There are four pointers to success when making these.

1. *Whether you are using white, brown, rye bread or pumpernickel, make sure the slices are covered thickly with English or Welsh butter.*

2. *See that the butter comes right to the edges of every slice.*

3. *Be generous with toppings and garnishes.*

4. *Provide knives and forks.*

1064 FRIED SANDWICHES

4 large slices white bread
English or Welsh butter
3 to 4 oz. English Cheddar Cheese or sliced cooked meat or 2 sliced hard-boiled eggs
Ketchup or pickles
1 standard egg
4 tablespoons milk
2 extra oz. English or Welsh butter
2 teaspoons olive or corn oil

1. Spread bread with butter. **2.** Sandwich slices together, in pairs, with choice of cheese, meat or eggs and ketchup or pickles to taste. **3.** Press firmly together and cut each sandwich into 2 triangles or squares. **4.** Soak a few minutes in egg beaten with milk. **5.** Fry in hot butter and oil until golden brown on both sides. **6.** Drain on soft kitchen paper. **7.** Serve straight away. **Serves 2.**

1065 EGG & CREAMED SALAD SANDWICH

12 large slices white or brown bread
English or Welsh butter
4 large sliced hard-boiled eggs
4 level tablespoons grated cabbage
2 level tablespoons grated carrot
4 chopped spring onions
4 tablespoons fresh double cream

1. Spread bread thickly with butter. **2.** Sandwich slices together, in pairs, with slices of egg followed by cabbage, carrot and onions mixed with cream. **3.** Cut each sandwich into 2 or 4 pieces. **Serves 4.**

PRAWN & MAYONNAISE OPEN SANDWICH 106

1. Cover slice of buttered bread with lettuce leaves. **2.** Arrange mound of peeled prawns or shrimps in centre. **3.** Top with heaped tablespoon Mayonnaise (No. 577). **4.** Sprinkle lightly with paprika. **5.** Garnish with parsley. **Serves 1.**

EGG & TOMATO OPEN SANDWICH 106

1. Arrange slices of tomatoes, skinned if preferred, down one edge of buttered bread slice. **2.** Arrange hard-boiled egg slices down the other edge of slice. **3.** Cover centre join with spoons of Mayonnaise (No. 577). **4.** Sprinkle with chopped chives. **Serves 1.**

BOILED BEEF & CARROT OPEN SANDWICH 106

1. Cover slice of buttered bread with slices of boiled beef. **2.** Put a mound of natural yogurt in centre. **3.** Surround with ring of cooked carrot slices. **4.** Top with half a pickled onion. **Serves 1.**

ROLLMOP & YOGURT OPEN SANDWICH 106

1. Stand crisp lettuce leaf on corner of buttered bread slice. **2.** Cover rest of slice with large pieces of rollmop. **3.** Put heaped dessertspoon natural yogurt in centre. **4.** Sprinkle with paprika. **5.** Garnish with slices of pickled cucumber. **Serves 1.**

DANISH-STYLE
OPEN SANDWICHES

1070 LIVER SAUSAGE & POTATO SALAD OPEN SANDWICH

1. Cover slice of buttered bread with rounds of liver sausage. **2.** Arrange a cross of potato salad on top. **3.** Sprinkle lightly with paprika. **4.** Garnish with one gherkin. **Serves 1.**

1071 SCRAMBLED EGG & SALMON OPEN SANDWICH

1. Cover slice of buttered bread with lettuce leaves or watercress. **2.** Top with 1 or 2 cold scrambled eggs and strips of smoked salmon. **3.** Garnish with 1 or 2 black olives. **Serves 1.**

1072 HAM, CHEESE & PINEAPPLE OPEN SANDWICH

1. Cover slice of buttered bread with large slice of ham. **2.** Top with 1 canned pineapple ring, well drained. **3.** Fill centre with mound of cottage cheese. **4.** Garnish with strips of red or green pepper. **Serves 1.**

1073 LETTUCE & TONGUE OPEN SANDWICH

1. Cover slice of buttered bread with shredded lettuce. **2.** Top with slice of tongue. **3.** Arrange line of skinned tomato slices down centre. **4.** Sprinkle with chopped parsley. **5.** Garnish by piping with Mustard Butter (No.199). **Serves 1.**

1074 CAVIARE, EGG YOLK & ONION OPEN SANDWICH

1. Cover slice of buttered bread with lettuce leaves. **2.** Top with ring of caviare or Danish-style caviare (Lump fish). **3.** Fill centre with raw egg yolk. **4.** Sprinkle with finely-grated onion. **Serves 1.**

PORK & ORANGE OPEN SANDWICH 1075

1. Cover slice of buttered bread with crisp lettuce leaves. **2.** Top with slices of cold roast pork. **3.** Put heaped teaspoon of Yogurt Curry Dressing (No. 569) in centre. **4.** Garnish with slice of orange, shaped into twist, and watercress. **Serves 1.**

SALAMI & CHEESE OPEN SANDWICH 1076

1. Cover slice of buttered bread with crisp lettuce leaves. **2.** Top with ring of salami slices. **3.** Fill centre with cottage cheese. **4.** Garnish with wedge of tomato. **Serves 1.**

CHEESE & LEEK OPEN SANDWICH 1077

1. Cover slice of buttered bread with skinned tomato slices. **2.** Top with slices of Caerphilly cheese. **3.** Put heaped teaspoon of Soured Cream with Tomato Dressing (No. 554) in centre. **4.** Garnish with rings of raw leek. **Serves 1.**

CHEESE, PEACH & OLIVE OPEN SANDWICH 1078

1. Cover slice of buttered bread with crisp lettuce leaves. **2.** Top with layer of cottage cheese. **3.** Stand line of well-drained peach slices down centre. **4.** Garnish with black olives. **Serves 1.**

CHEESE & DATE OPEN SANDWICH 1079

1. Cover slice of buttered bread with crisp lettuce leaves or watercress. **2.** Top with slice of Cheshire cheese. **3.** Put heaped teaspoon of Soured Cream with Dates Dressing (No. 559) in centre. **4.** Garnish with orange slice, shaped into twist. **Serves 1.**

213

Toasted Bacon & Mushroom Sandwich (No. 1081)

TOASTED SANDWICHES

1080 TOASTED BEEF & TOMATO SANDWICH

8 large slices white or brown bread
English or Welsh butter
4 to 6 oz. cold roast beef, sliced
Made mustard
4 medium-sized sliced tomatoes

GARNISH
Watercress or parsley

1. Spread bread thickly with butter. **2.** Sandwich together, in pairs, with beef, spread with mustard and covered with tomato slices. **3.** Toast each sandwich lightly on both sides. **4.** Press down firmly and cut into 2 triangles. **5.** Garnish with watercress or parsley. **6.** Serve straight away. **Serves 3 to 4.**

1081 TOASTED BACON & MUSHROOM SANDWICH

1. Follow recipe and method for Toasted Beef and Tomato Sandwich (No. 1080). **2.** Fill sandwiches with ½ lb. grilled bacon rashers and ¼ lb. sliced and fried or grilled mushrooms. **Serves 4.**

TOASTED CHEESE & PICKLE SANDWICH 108

1. Follow recipe and method for Toasted Beef and Tomato Sandwich (No.1080). **2.** Fill each with slices of English Cheddar cheese (4 to 6 oz.) and mustard pickle. **Serves 4.**

TOASTED EGG & HADDOCK 108 SANDWICH

8 large slices white or brown bread
English or Welsh butter
4 large eggs
¼ lb. cooked flaked smoked haddock
2 tablespoons milk
½ extra oz. English or Welsh butter
1 level tablespoon finely-chopped parsley
Seasoning to taste

GARNISH
Watercress or parsley

1. Spread bread thickly with butter. **2.** Scramble eggs lightly with smoked haddock, milk, ½ oz. butter, parsley and seasoning to taste. **3.** Sandwich buttered bread slices together, in pairs, with egg mixture. **4.** Toast each sandwich ightly on both sides. **5.** Press down firmly and cut into 2 triangles. **6.** Garnish with watercress or parsley. **7.** Serve straight away. **Serves 3 to 4.**

214

CLUB SANDWICHES

These are hearty-sized tasty sandwiches made from 3 slices white or brown bread layered with a variety of fillings. They are very useful for a quick lunch or supper.

84 HAWAIIAN CLUB SANDWICH

3 large slices freshly-made white or brown
  toast
English or Welsh butter
4 small crisp lettuce leaves
1 large canned pineapple ring, well drained
About 2 oz. sliced Derby cheese
Mild mustard

GARNISH
2 stuffed olives or gherkins

1. Spread first slice of toast with English or Welsh butter. **2.** Cover with lettuce leaves and pineapple ring. **3.** Top with second slice of toast. **4.** Spread with more butter. **5.** Cover with cheese. Spread cheese with a little mild mustard. **6.** Butter third slice of toast. Put on top of cheese, buttered side down. **7.** Cut into 2 triangles. **8.** Garnish with olives or gherkins speared on to cocktail sticks. **Serves 1.**

SAUSAGE & CHUTNEY CLUB SANDWICH · 1085

1. Follow recipe and method for Hawaiian Club Sandwich (No.1084). **2.** For first layer, use crisp lettuce leaves topped with slices of cold cooked pork sausages. **3.** For second layer, use 2 or 3 slices of Wensleydale cheese covered with sweet pickle or chutney. **Serves 1.**

EGG & CHEESE CLUB SANDWICH · 1086

1. Follow recipe and method for Hawaiian Club Sandwich (No.1084). **2.** For first layer, use crisp lettuce leaves topped with slices of hard-boiled egg and hot Mornay Sauce (No. 123). **3.** For second layer, use 2 slices of Caerphilly cheese covered with skinned tomato slices. **Serves 1.**

HAM CLUB SANDWICH · 1087

1. Follow recipe and method for Hawaiian Club Sandwich (No.1084). **2.** For first layer, use crisp lettuce leaves topped with about 2 tablespoons cottage cheese. **3.** For second layer, use slices of ham covered with thin raw onion rings. **Serves 1.**

Ham Club Sandwich (No. 1087)

Lunch & Supper Dishes

1088 SAVOURY CHEESE & ONION CASSEROLE

6 large slices white bread
6 oz. grated Double Gloucester cheese
3 standard eggs
¼ level teaspoon salt
½ small onion, finely grated
¾ pint lukewarm milk
Shake of pepper

1. Trim crusts off bread. Cut each slice into 2 triangles. **2.** Arrange half the triangles over base of fairly shallow buttered 1½ to 2-pint heatproof dish. **3.** Sprinkle bread layer with ¼ lb. cheese. Cover with remaining bread triangles. **4.** Beat eggs with salt, onion, warm milk and pepper. Pour into dish over bread and cheese. **5.** Leave to stand for 30 minutes. **6.** Sprinkle with rest of cheese. **7.** Bake in centre of moderate oven (350°F. or Gas No. 4) for 50 minutes to 1 hour (or until well browned). **8.** Serve straight away. **Serves 4.**

1089 CHEESE & SULTANA PIE

½ pint Basic White Coating Sauce (No.106)
¼ lb. finely-grated Derby or English Cheddar cheese
1 standard egg, beaten
6 oz. sultanas
1 recipe Short Crust Pastry (No. 88)
Milk for brushing

1. Warm sauce, add cheese and stir until melted. **2.** Remove from heat and cool to lukewarm. Beat in egg and sultanas. **3.** Cut Pastry into 2 equal-sized pieces. **4.** Roll out one half and use to line 8-in. buttered heatproof pie plate. **5.** Fill with cheese mixture. Moisten edges of pastry with cold water. **6.** Cover with lid rolled from rest of pastry. **7.** Press pastry edges well together to seal. Make 2 slits in top with knife. **8.** Transfer pie to baking tray and brush with milk. **9.** Bake towards top of fairly hot oven (400°F. or Gas No. 6) for 40 minutes. **10.** Serve hot or cold. **Serves 4.**

1090 CHEESE & SAUSAGE PIE

1. Follow recipe and method for Cheese and Sultana Pie (No.1089). **2.** Use 6 oz. thinly-sliced, cooked pork sausages instead of sultanas. **Serves 4.**

CORNED BEEF & VEGETABLE TARTS 109

Short Crust Pastry (No. 88) made with 6 oz. flour
¼ lb. corned beef
2 oz. cooked diced potato
2 oz. cooked peas
½ oz. butter
½ oz. flour
4 tablespoons milk
1 standard egg, beaten
Seasoning to taste

1. Roll out Pastry. Cut into 12 rounds with 3-in. biscuit cutter. **2.** Use to line 12 lightly-buttered bun tins. **3.** Chop corned beef. Combine with potatoes and peas. **4.** Melt butter in pan. Stir in flour and cook 2 minutes without browning. Gradually blend in milk. **5.** Cook, stirring, until mixture comes to boil and thickens. **6.** Remove from heat. Stir in beef, potatoes, peas and beaten egg. **7.** Season to taste with salt and pepper. **8.** Spoon equal amounts into pastry-lined tins. **9.** Bake just above centre of hot oven (425°F. or Gas No. 7) for 10 minutes. **10.** Reduce temperature to fairly hot (375°F. or Gas No. 5) and bake for further 12 to 15 minutes. **11.** Remove from tins. Serve hot or cold. **Serves 4.**

FLAKY CHEESE & ONION PASTIES 109

1 recipe Flaky Pastry (No. 99)
6 oz. finely-grated Wensleydale cheese
1 level tablespoon finely-grated onion
Beaten egg to bind
Salt and pepper to taste
Milk for brushing

1. Roll out Pastry into 16-in. × 8-in. rectangle. **2.** Cut into eight 4-in. squares. **3.** Combine cheese with onion. Bind fairly stiffly with egg. Season to taste with salt and pepper. **4.** Put equal amounts of cheese mixture on to centres of Pastry squares. **5.** Moisten edges of Pastry with water. Fold squares in half to form triangles. **6.** Press edges well together to seal. Flake by cutting with back of knife. **7.** Make 2 or 3 snips across top of each Pasty with scissors. Transfer to damp baking tray. **8.** Leave for 30 minutes. **9.** Brush with milk. Bake towards top of hot oven (450°F. or Gas No. 8) for 10 minutes. **10.** Reduce temperature to fairly hot (400°F. or Gas No. 6). Bake further 10 to 15 minutes (or until well puffed and brown). **11.** Serve hot. **Serves 4.**

093 CHEESE & PARSLEY PUDDING

Yolks and whites of 2 standard eggs
½ pint lukewarm milk
3 oz. grated Derby or Cheshire cheese
2 oz. fresh white breadcrumbs
½ level teaspoon dry mustard
½ level teaspoon salt
2 level tablespoons finely-chopped parsley

GARNISH
Watercress

1. Beat egg yolks with milk and cheese. **2.** Combine crumbs with mustard, salt and parsley. **3.** Gradually stir in warm milk mixture and mix well. **4.** Leave to stand 30 minutes. Fold in egg whites, beaten to stiff snow. **5.** Transfer to 1-pint buttered heatproof dish. Bake towards top of fairly hot oven (400°F. or Gas No. 6) for 25 to 30 minutes (or until golden). **6.** Garnish with watercress. **Serves 4.**

094 CHEESE & HAM PUDDING

1. Follow recipe and method for Cheese and Parsley Pudding (No.1093). **2.** Add 1 or 2 oz. finely-chopped ham instead of parsley. **Serves 4.**

095 CORNED BEEF PIE

6 oz. corned beef
2 oz. fresh white breadcrumbs
2 oz. finely-grated Caerphilly cheese
2 level tablespoons finely-chopped parsley
2 level teaspoons finely-grated onion
½ teaspoon Worcester sauce
3 tablespoons milk
¼ level teaspoon salt
Shake of pepper
1 recipe Short Crust Pastry (No. 88)
Milk for brushing

1. Chop beef. Combine with breadcrumbs, cheese, parsley, onion, Worcester sauce, milk, salt and pepper. **2.** Cut Pastry into 2 equal-sized pieces. **3.** Roll out one half and use to line 8-in. buttered heatproof plate. **4.** Pile filling in centre. Moisten edges of Pastry with water. **5.** Cover with rest of Pastry, rolled into lid. **6.** Press edges well together to seal. Ridge with fork or press into flutes. **7.** Brush with milk. **8.** Bake towards top of fairly hot oven (400°F. or Gas No. 6) for 45 minutes. **9.** Serve hot or cold. **Serves 4 to 6.**

PILCHARDS AU GRATIN 1096

4 large slices white or brown bread
8 canned pilchards (1-lb. can)
1 tablespoon lemon juice
1 level tablespoon finely-grated onion
1 level tablespoon finely-chopped parsley
6 oz. finely-grated English Cheddar cheese

GARNISH
Parsley sprigs

1. Toast bread on one side only. **2.** Moisten untoasted sides with a little pilchard liquor. **3.** Place 2 pilchards on top of each slice. Sprinkle with lemon juice, onion and parsley. **4.** Cover thickly with grated cheese. Brown under hot grill. **5.** Garnish with parsley. Serve straight away. **Serves 4.**

CHEESE & WALNUT BUNS 1097

6 oz. self-raising flour
¼ level teaspoon baking powder
¼ level teaspoon salt
½ level teaspoon dry mustard
3 oz. English or Welsh butter
1½ oz. very finely-grated Derby cheese
1 oz. finely-chopped shelled walnut halves
1 standard egg, beaten
5 to 6 tablespoons cold milk

1. Sift flour, baking powder, salt and mustard into bowl. **2.** Rub in butter finely. **3.** Add cheese and walnuts. Toss lightly together. **4.** Mix to fairly soft batter with egg and milk, stirring briskly. **5.** Transfer to 12 well-buttered bun tins. **6.** Bake just above centre of fairly hot oven (400°F. or Gas No. 6) for 20 minutes (or until well risen and golden). **7.** Serve hot with English or Welsh butter. **Serves 4.**

CHEESE & HAM BUNS 1098

1. Follow recipe and method for Cheese and Walnut Buns (No.1097). **2.** Use 1 oz. finely-chopped ham instead of walnuts. **Serves 4.**

CHEESE & RAISIN BUNS 1099

1. Follow recipe and method for Cheese and Walnut Buns (No.1097). **2.** Use 1 oz. chopped seedless raisins instead of walnuts. **Serves 4.**

Welsh Rarebit (No. 1101)

1100 CHEESE & PRAWN BUNS

1. Follow recipe and method for Cheese and Walnut Buns (No.1097). **2.** Use 2 oz. finely-chopped peeled prawns instead of walnuts. **Serves 4.**

1101 WELSH RAREBIT

4 large slices white or brown bread
1 oz. English or Welsh butter, softened
1 level teaspoon made mustard
¼ level teaspoon salt
Shake Cayenne pepper
¼ teaspoon Worcester sauce
6 oz. crumbled Lancashire or grated
English Cheddar cheese
2 tablespoons milk

1. Toast bread on one side only. **2.** Cream butter well. Stir in mustard, salt, Cayenne pepper, Worcester sauce, cheese and milk. **3.** Spread equal amounts thickly over untoasted sides of bread. **4.** Brown under hot grill. **Serves 4.**

1102 BUCK RAREBIT

1. Follow recipe and method for Welsh Rarebit (No.1101). **2.** Serve each with poached egg on top. **Serves 4.**

BACON RAREBIT 1103

1. Follow recipe and method for Welsh Rarebit (No.1101). **2.** Serve each with 2 slices grilled or fried streaky bacon on top. **Serves 4.**

TOMATO RAREBIT 1104

1. Follow recipe and method for Welsh Rarebit (No.1101). **2.** Serve each with 2 or 3 grilled or fried tomato slices on top. **Serves 4.**

CHEESE, EGG & 1105
NOODLE RING

6 oz. flat noodles
½ pint Basic White Coating Sauce (No.106)
½ lb. finely-grated English Cheddar cheese
½ lb. cooked sliced green beans or peas
Salt and pepper to taste
4 large hard-boiled eggs
1 level tablespoon finely-chopped parsley

1. Cook noodles in boiling salted water until tender. **2.** Drain and arrange in ring on warm serving dish. Keep hot. **3.** Warm sauce and stir in 6 oz. cheese and beans or peas. Season to taste. **4.** Halve eggs, add to sauce and heat through gently. **5.** Pour into noodle ring. **6.** Sprinkle with remaining cheese mixed with parsley. **7.** Serve straight away. **Serves 4.**

106 CHEESE ROLL PUFFS

2 oz. luncheon meat
1 large hard-boiled egg
1 small celery stalk
2 tablespoons sweet pickle
4 tablespoons fresh double cream
Salt and pepper to taste
4 large soft rolls
6 oz. grated Wensleydale cheese
1 standard egg, beaten
1 level teaspoon made mustard

1. Chop luncheon meat, egg and celery. **2.** Combine with pickle and 2 tablespoons cream. Season to taste with salt and pepper. **3.** Cut rolls in half. Spread with meat mixture. **4.** Arrange on lightly-buttered baking tray. **5.** Mix cheese with beaten egg, rest of cream and mustard. **6.** Spoon over roll halves. Bake just above centre of fairly hot oven (400°F. or Gas No. 6) for 10 to 15 minutes (or until golden and fluffy). **7.** Serve straight away. **Serves 4.**

107 MACARONI CHEESE

3 oz. broken macaroni
¾ oz. English or Welsh Butter
¾ oz. flour
½ level teaspoon dry mustard
½ pint milk
6 oz. crumbled Lancashire or grated
  English Cheddar cheese
Salt and pepper to taste

GARNISH
Parsley

1. Cook macaroni in about 2 pints boiling salted water until tender (15 to 20 minutes). **2.** After 10 minutes, melt butter in saucepan, add flour and mustard and cook slowly for 2 minutes. Stir often and do not allow mixture to brown. **3.** Gradually blend in milk. Cook, stirring until sauce comes to boil and thickens. **4.** Simmer for 2 minutes and remove from heat. **5.** Stir in ¼ lb. cheese. Season to taste with salt and pepper. **6.** Drain macaroni, add to sauce and mix well. **7.** Transfer to 1½-pint buttered heatproof dish. **8.** Sprinkle rest of cheese on top and brown under hot grill. **9.** Garnish with parsley. **Serves 4.**

●*If Macaroni Cheese is prepared in advance, re-heat towards top of fairly hot oven (400°F. or Gas No. 6) 15 to 20 minutes.*

Cheese, Egg & Noodle Ring (No. 1105) with Basic White Coating Sauce (No. 106)

1108 MACARONI CHEESE WITH BACON

1. Follow recipe and method for Macaroni Cheese (No.1107). **2.** Add $\frac{1}{4}$ lb. chopped and lightly-fried bacon to sauce with macaroni. **Serves 4.**

1109 MACARONI CHEESE WITH SMOKED HADDOCK

1. Follow recipe and method for Macaroni Cheese (No.1107). **2.** Add $\frac{1}{4}$ lb. cooked and flaked smoked haddock to sauce with macaroni. **Serves 4.**

1110 CREAMED ROES ON TOAST

$\frac{3}{4}$ lb. soft herring roes
$\frac{1}{4}$ pint milk
3 level teaspoons flour
2 extra dessertspoons milk
Salt and pepper
4 slices hot buttered toast
GARNISH
Paprika
4 lemon wedges
Parsley

1. Rinse roes in cold water. **2.** Put into saucepan. Add $\frac{1}{4}$ pint milk. **3.** Cover pan and simmer for 7 minutes. **4.** Mash with fork. Stir in flour blended with extra milk. **5.** Cook, stirring, until mixture comes to boil and thickens. Simmer gently for 5 minutes. **6.** Season to taste with salt and pepper. **7.** Transfer equal amounts to buttered toast. **8.** Sprinkle with paprika. Garnish with lemon and parsley. **Serves 4.**

CREAMED CORN & HAM SCRAMBLE 111

6 standard eggs
4 tablespoons fresh single cream
$\frac{1}{2}$ oz. English or Welsh butter
1 can sweetcorn kernels (about $\frac{1}{2}$ lb.)
$\frac{1}{4}$ lb. finely-chopped lean ham
Large pinch of grated nutmeg
Seasoning to taste
4 slices hot buttered toast
GARNISH
1 level tablespoon finely-chopped parsley

1. Beat eggs and cream well together. **2.** Pour into frying pan. Add butter, drained sweetcorn, ham, grated nutmeg and salt and pepper to taste. **3.** Scramble over low heat until creamy. **4.** Pile equal amounts on to buttered toast and sprinkle with parsley. **Serves 4.**

CHEESE & CRAB RAMEKINS 111

4 large hard-boiled eggs
$\frac{1}{4}$ pint Cheese Coating Sauce (No. 116)
$\frac{1}{4}$ lb. cooked crab meat
1 oz. English or Welsh butter
1 oz. grated Leicester cheese
GARNISH
Watercress
ACCOMPANIMENT
4 slices hot buttered toast

1. Chop eggs coarsely. **2.** Add to sauce with crab meat and butter. **3.** Heat through gently. Do not allow to boil. **4.** Transfer equal amounts to 4 buttered Ramekin dishes or individual heatproof dishes. **5.** Sprinkle tops with cheese. Brown under hot grill. Garnish with watercress. **6.** Serve at once with hot buttered toast. **Serves 4.**

Vegetarian Dishes

113 MARROW CHEESE

1 medium-sized marrow
2 large onions
$\frac{1}{4}$ lb. crumbled Lancashire cheese
$\frac{1}{2}$ pint Basic White Coating Sauce
 (No. 106)
2 level tablespoons toasted breadcrumbs
1 oz. English or Welsh butter

1. Peel marrow. Cut into 1-in. thick slices.
2. Remove centres. Cut rings into cubes. **3.**
Steam over boiling water until just tender. **4.** Peel
onions, cut into rings and cook in boiling salted
water until soft. Drain. **5.** Arrange half steamed
marrow over base of 2 to 2$\frac{1}{2}$-pint buttered heatproof dish. **6.** Cover with onions. Sprinkle with
3 oz. of cheese. Top with rest of marrow. **7.** Coat
with Sauce. Sprinkle with remaining cheese and
breadcrumbs. **8.** Dot with butter. Re-heat towards
top of hot oven (425°F. or Gas No. 7) for 15
minutes (or until top is light brown). Serve with
baked jacket potatoes and English or Welsh
butter. **Serves 4.**

114 POTATO CHEESE & PARSLEY PIE

1$\frac{1}{2}$ lb. potatoes
4 tablespoons milk
1 standard egg, beaten
1 level teaspoon dry mustard
6 oz. Double Gloucester cheese, grated
3 level tablespoons finely-chopped
 parsley
$\frac{1}{2}$ level teaspoon yeast extract
Seasoning to taste

1. Cook potatoes in boiling salted water until
tender. **2.** Drain. **3.** Mash finely with milk, egg,
mustard, $\frac{1}{4}$ lb. cheese, parsley and yeast extract.
4. Season to taste with salt and pepper. **5.** Transfer
to buttered 2-pint heatproof dish. **6.** Sprinkle
remaining cheese over top. **7.** Re-heat towards
top of hot oven (425°F. or Gas No. 7) for 15
minutes (or until top is light brown). Serve with
baked tomatoes. **Serves 4.**

115 POTATO CHEESE & ONION PIE

1. Follow recipe and method for Potato Cheese
and Parsley Pie (No. 1114). **2.** Add 1 medium-
sized finely-chopped boiled onion with parsley.
Serves 4.

VEGETABLE CURRY WITH CHEESE   1116

$\frac{1}{2}$ medium-sized cauliflower
$\frac{1}{2}$ lb. carrots
$\frac{1}{2}$ lb. potatoes
4 large celery stalks
1 recipe Curry Sauce (No. 141)
$\frac{3}{4}$ lb. freshly-boiled rice (about 6 oz. raw)

ACCOMPANIMENT
6 oz. grated Derby or crumbled
 Lancashire cheese

1. Divide cauliflower into florets. Slice carrots and
potatoes thinly. Chop celery. **2.** Cook all
vegetables in boiling salted water until tender.
Drain. **3.** Add to Curry Sauce. Heat through
gently. **4.** Cover base of warm serving dish with
rice. **5.** Arrange curried vegetables on top.
6. Pass cheese separately. **Serves 4.**

HARICOT BEAN & CHEESE CURRY   1117

1. Follow recipe and method for Vegetable Curry
with Cheese (No. 1116). **2.** Instead of vegetables,
add $\frac{3}{4}$ lb. haricot beans, soaked overnight and
cooked in boiling salted water until tender.
Serves 4.

PARSNIP CAKES   1118

1 lb. parsnips
2 oz. fresh brown breadcrumbs
1 level tablespoon fine oatmeal
1 level teaspoon grated onion
Salt and pepper to taste
Milk to bind

COATING
Beaten egg
About 1 oz. toasted breadcrumbs
2 oz. English or Welsh butter
1 dessertspoon olive or corn oil

1. Cook parsnips in boiling salted water until
tender. Drain. **2.** Mash finely. Combine with
breadcrumbs, oatmeal and onion. **3.** Season to
taste with salt and pepper. Bind with milk.
4. Leave until cold. Shape into 8 cakes. **5.** Coat
with beaten egg and crumbs. **6.** Fry in hot butter
and oil until crisp and golden, allowing 2 to 3
minutes per side. **7.** Drain on soft kitchen paper.
8. Serve hot with Parsley Coating Sauce
(No. 107) and a green vegetable. **Serves 4.**

Nut & Macaroni Curry (No. 1125) with Curry Sauce (No. 141)

1119 ALMOND RISSOLES

¼ lb. ground almonds
6 oz. fresh white breadcrumbs
1 small onion, finely grated
3 level tablespoons finely-chopped
  parsley
½ level teaspoon mixed herbs
1 standard egg, beaten
1 oz. English or Welsh butter, melted
Seasoning to taste
Cold milk to mix

COATING
1 small egg, beaten
About 1 oz. toasted breadcrumbs
2 oz. English or Welsh butter
1 dessertspoon olive or corn oil

1. Put almonds and breadcrumbs into bowl.
2. Finely grate onion and add to breadcrumb
mixture with parsley and herbs. **3.** Work in egg
and butter. Season to taste with salt and pepper.
4. Mix to stiff paste with milk. Shape into 8
rissoles. **5.** Coat with beaten egg and crumbs.
6. Fry in hot butter and oil until crisp and golden,
allowing about 4 to 5 minutes per side. **7.** Drain
on soft kitchen paper and serve hot with mixed
vegetables or cold with salad. **Serves 4.**

1120 HAZELNUT RISSOLES

1. Follow recipe and method for Almond Rissoles
(No.1119). **2.** Use ground hazelnuts instead of
almonds, and fresh brown breadcrumbs instead
of white. **Serves 4.**

CASHEW NUT RISSOLES   112

1. Follow recipe and method for Almond Rissoles
(No1119). **2.** Use ground cashew nuts instead of
almonds. **3.** Add 1 level teaspoon finely-grated
lemon peel with mixed herbs. **Serves 4.**

CHEESE & NOODLE   112
HOT POT

½ lb. flat noodles
1 medium-sized onion
1 oz. English or Welsh butter
½ pint Basic White Coating Sauce
  (No. 106)
2 level tablespoons tomato purée
2 oz. chopped hazelnuts
½ lb. cottage cheese
Seasoning to taste
2 oz. crumbled Lancashire cheese

GARNISH
1 sliced tomato
Parsley

1. Cook noodles in boiling salted water until
tender. Drain. **2.** Chop onion. Fry gently in butter
until golden. **3.** Stir cooked noodles and fried
onion into Sauce. **4.** Add purée, hazelnuts and
cottage cheese. **5.** Mix thoroughly. Season to
taste with salt and pepper. **6.** Transfer to 2-pint
buttered heatproof dish and sprinkle with cheese.
7. Re-heat just above centre of fairly hot oven
(375°F. or Gas No. 5) for 20 to 25 minutes (or
until top is golden). **8.** Garnish with tomato
slices and parsley. **9.** Serve with a green
vegetable. **Serves 4.**

123 CHEESE & RICE HOT POT

1. Follow recipe and method for Cheese and Noodle Hot Pot (No.1122). **2.** Use ½ to ¾ lb. rice instead of noodles. **Serves 4.**

124 EGG & MUSHROOM SAVOURY

½ lb. mushrooms
2 tablespoons milk
6 standard eggs
2 level tablespoons finely-chopped parsley
½ level teaspoon salt
2 large skinned tomatoes
3 oz. crumbled Lancashire cheese

1. Peel mushrooms. Arrange in frying pan and pour in milk. **2.** Bring just up to boil. Remove from heat. **3.** Transfer mushrooms to 1-pint buttered heatproof dish. **4.** Beat eggs with mushroom liquor. **5.** Add parsley and salt. **6.** Scramble lightly until creamy. **7.** Spoon over mushrooms. Top with slices of tomato. **8.** Sprinkle thickly with crumbled cheese. **9.** Brown under hot grill. **10.** Serve with fried potatoes. **Serves 4.**

125 NUT & MACARONI CURRY

¾ lb. broken macaroni
6 oz. cashew nuts
1 recipe Curry Sauce (No. 141)
ACCOMPANIMENTS
½ fresh cucumber, peeled and sliced
4 large sliced tomatoes
Finely-chopped parsley
½ bunch watercress

1. Cook macaroni in boiling salted water until tender. **2.** Drain. Add, with nuts, to Curry Sauce. Heat through gently. **3.** Pile on to warm plates. **4.** Accompany with separate bowls of cucumber slices, sliced tomatoes sprinkled with parsley and watercress. **Serves 4.**

Right: Egg & Mushroom Savoury (No. 1124)

1126 EGG & MACARONI CURRY

1. Follow recipe and method for Nut and Macaroni Curry (No.1125). **2.** Add 4 large chopped hard-boiled eggs instead of nuts. **Serves 4.**

1127 GLOUCESTER PIE

8 slices bread (day old for preference)
English or Welsh butter
¼ lb. Double Gloucester cheese
½ lb. skinned tomatoes
¼ pint milk
1 standard egg
1 level teaspoon made mustard
¼ level teaspoon salt
Shake of pepper
1 extra oz. English or Welsh butter

1. Cut crusts from slices of bread. Butter slices thickly. **2.** Sandwich together, in pairs, with thinly-sliced cheese and slices of tomato. **3.** Cut each sandwich into 4 triangles. Arrange in buttered shallow heatproof dish. **4.** Beat milk with egg, mustard and salt and pepper to taste. **5.** Pour into dish over sandwiches. **6.** Leave to stand for ½ an hour (or until bread has absorbed all the liquid). Dot top with pieces of extra butter. **7.** Bake just above centre of fairly hot oven (375°F. or Gas No. 5) for 25 to 30 minutes (or until top is crisp and golden). **8.** Serve with a green vegetable or green salad. **Serves 4.**

1128 PEANUT MINCE

1 large onion
¼ lb. mushrooms
1 medium-sized celery stalk
1 large carrot
1½ oz. English or Welsh butter
½ level teaspoon yeast extract
½ lb. coarsely-chopped peanuts
¼ pint milk
¼ pint water
4 heaped tablespoons rolled oats
Seasoning to taste
2 level tablespoons finely-chopped parsley

1. Chop onion, mushrooms and celery. **2.** Grate carrot. **3.** Fry gently in butter until pale gold. Stir in yeast extract, peanuts, milk and water. **4.** Slowly bring to boil. Cover pan. Simmer gently until vegetables are tender. **5.** Add oats. Continue to simmer, uncovered, until mince is thick. Stir frequently. **6.** Season to taste with salt and pepper. Add parsley. **7.** Serve with creamy mashed potato and green vegetable. **Serves 4.**

COTTAGE CHEESE & PARSLEY TART 1129

Short Crust Pastry made with 6 oz. flour (No. 88)
1 large onion
1 oz. English or Welsh butter
1 lb. cottage cheese
4 level tablespoons finely-chopped parsley
2 standard eggs, beaten
Seasoning to taste
GARNISH
Watercress
Grated carrot

1. Roll out Pastry. Use to line 8-in. plain flan ring resting on lightly-buttered baking tray. **2.** Chop onion finely. Fry gently in butter until golden. **3.** Rub cottage cheese through fine sieve. Combine with fried onion, parsley and beaten eggs. **4.** Season to taste with salt and pepper. Beat well. Pour into Pastry case. **5.** Bake just above centre of fairly hot oven (375°F. or Gas No. 5) for 15 minutes. **6.** Reduce temperature to moderate (325°F. or Gas No. 3). Continue to bake further 45 minutes (or until filling is set and top is golden). **7.** Carefully lift off flan ring. Transfer tart to warm serving dish. **8.** Garnish with watercress and mounds of grated carrot. **Serves 4 to 5.**

COTTAGE CHEESE & WALNUT TART 1130

1. Follow recipe and method for Cottage Cheese and Parsley Tart (No.1129). **2.** Add only 1 level tablespoon parsley and 2 oz. finely-chopped shelled walnut halves. **Serves 4 to 5.**

PARSNIP ROAST 113

1½ lb. parsnips
2 oz. English or Welsh butter
4 tablespoons fresh double cream
3 oz. grated English Cheddar cheese
Salt and pepper to taste

1. Slice parsnips. Cook in boiling salted water until tender. Drain. **2.** Mash finely. Beat in butter, cream and 2 oz. cheese. **3.** Season well to taste with salt and pepper. **4.** Transfer to 1½-pint buttered heatproof dish. **5.** Cover with remaining cheese. **6.** Brown towards top of hot oven (425°F. or Gas No. 7) for 10 to 15 minutes (or until top is golden). **7.** Serve with a crisp green salad and baked jacket potatoes. **Serves 4.**

Confectionery

1132 MILK FUDGE

½ pint milk
1¾ lb. granulated sugar
¼ lb. English or Welsh butter
2 teaspoons vanilla essence

1. Pour milk into pan. Bring slowly to boil. **2.** Add sugar and butter. **3.** Heat slowly, stirring all the time, until sugar dissolves and butter melts. **4.** Bring to boil. Cover pan with lid. Boil for 2 minutes. **5.** Uncover. Continue to boil steadily, stirring occasionally, for further 10 to 15 minutes (or until a little of the mixture, dropped into cup of cold water, forms soft ball when rolled gently between finger and thumb). Temperature on sugar thermometer, if used, should be 238°F. to 240°F. **6.** Remove from heat. Stir in vanilla. Leave mixture to cool 5 minutes. **7.** Beat Fudge until it just begins to lose its gloss and is thick and creamy. **8.** Transfer to buttered 7-in. square tin. **9.** Mark into squares when cool. Cut up with sharp knife when firm and set. **10.** Store in airtight tin. **About 50 pieces.**

1133 CHERRY FUDGE

1. Follow recipe and method for Milk Fudge (No. 1132). **2.** Add 2 oz. chopped glacé cherries with vanilla. **About 50 pieces.**

1134 CHOCOLATE FUDGE

1. Follow recipe and method for Milk Fudge (No. 1132). **2.** Melt ¼ lb. grated plain chocolate in milk before adding sugar and butter. **About 50 pieces.**

1135 COCONUT FUDGE

1. Follow recipe and method for Milk Fudge (No. 1132). **2.** Add 3 level tablespoons desiccated coconut with vanilla. **About 50 pieces.**

1136 FRUIT & NUT FUDGE

1. Follow recipe and method for Milk Fudge (No. 1132). **2.** Add 1 oz. currants and 1 oz. blanched and chopped almonds with vanilla. **About 50 pieces.**

WALNUT FUDGE 1137

1. Follow recipe and method for Milk Fudge (No. 1132). **2.** Add 2 oz. finely-chopped shelled walnut halves with vanilla. **About 50 pieces.**

UNCOOKED CHOCOLATE 1138 CREAM FUDGE

¼ lb. plain chocolate
2 oz. English or Welsh butter
3 tablespoons fresh single cream
1 teaspoon vanilla essence
1 lb. icing sugar, sifted

1. Break up chocolate. Put, with butter, in basin standing over saucepan of hot water. **2.** Leave until both have melted, stirring once or twice. **3.** Remove basin from pan of water. Stir in cream and vanilla. **4.** Gradually work in icing sugar. Mix well. **5.** Transfer to buttered 8-in. square tin. **6.** Leave in the cool until firm and set. **Cut into 60 squares.**

UNCOOKED MOCHA 1139 CREAM FUDGE

1. Follow recipe and method for Uncooked Chocolate Cream Fudge (No. 1138). **2.** Add 4 level teaspoons instant coffee powder to chocolate and butter in basin. **About 60 squares.**

MARSHMALLOW 1140 RAISIN FUDGE

¼ lb. icing sugar
2 oz. seedless raisins
¼ lb. marshmallows
2 tablespoons milk
2 oz. granulated sugar
2 oz. English or Welsh butter

1. Sift icing sugar into bowl. Add raisins. **2.** Slowly melt marshmallows in 1 tablespoon milk. Remove from heat. Leave on one side. **3.** Pour rest of milk into pan. Add sugar and butter. **4.** Heat slowly, stirring all the time, until sugar dissolves and butter melts. **5.** Bring to boil. Boil briskly 5 minutes only. Remove from heat. **6.** Add melted marshmallows and milk. Gradually stir in icing sugar and raisins. **7.** Mix well. Spread into buttered 6 in. square tin. **8.** Leave until firm and set. **Cut into 36 squares.**

Milk Fudge (No. 1132), Cherry Fudge (No. 1133), Chocolate Cream Truffles (No. 1142) and Chocolate Rum Truffles (No. 1145)

1141 MARSHMALLOW ALMOND FUDGE

1. Follow recipe and method for Marshmallow Raisin Fudge (No. 1140). **2.** Add 2 oz. blanched, toasted and chopped almonds instead of raisins. **About 36 squares.**

1142 CHOCOLATE CREAM TRUFFLES

2 oz. plain chocolate
3 dessertspoons fresh double cream
1 teaspoon vanilla essence
$\frac{1}{2}$ lb. icing sugar, sifted
Chocolate vermicelli

1. Break up chocolate. Put into basin standing over saucepan of hot water. **2.** Leave until melted, stirring once or twice. **3.** Add cream and essence. Gradually stir in icing sugar. **4.** Mix well. Transfer mixture to plate. Leave in cool until firm enough to handle (about 1½ hours). **5.** Roll equal amounts of mixture into 18 balls. Toss in chocolate vermicelli. **6.** Transfer to fluted paper sweet cases. **18 Truffles.**

COFFEE CREAMS 11.

1 lb. icing sugar
4 level teaspoons instant coffee powder
2 oz. melted English or Welsh butter
2 tablespoons lukewarm milk
Extra sifted icing sugar

1. Sift icing sugar into bowl with coffee. **2.** Combine melted butter with milk. Gradually stir into icing sugar. **3.** Mix well. Turn out on to board, dusted with sifted icing sugar. **4.** Knead until smooth. Roll equal amounts of mixture into 40 balls. **5.** Flatten slightly. **6.** Transfer to fluted paper sweet cases. **7.** Leave in the cool until firm. **About 40 Creams.**

PEPPERMINT WAFERS 11.

1. Follow recipe and method for Coffee Creams (No. 1143). **2.** Omit coffee powder. Add 1 teaspoon peppermint essence to icing sugar with melted butter and milk. **3.** Turn out on to board dusted with sifted icing sugar. Roll out to about $\frac{1}{8}$-in. thickness. **4.** Cut into about 30 rounds with 1½-in. plain biscuit cutter. Leave in the cool until firm. **About 30 Wafers.**

226

1145 CHOCOLATE RUM TRUFFLES

¼ lb. plain chocolate
2 oz. English or Welsh butter
1 tablespoon rum
Yolks of 2 standard eggs
1 oz. ground almonds
1 oz. stale cake crumbs
½ lb. icing sugar, sifted
Drinking chocolate

1. Break up chocolate and put, with butter, into basin standing over saucepan of hot water. **2.** Leave until both have melted, stirring occasionally. **3.** Add rum and egg yolks. Mix in well. **4.** Work in remaining ingredients (except drinking chocolate). Transfer mixture to plate. Leave in the cool until firm (about 1½ hours). **5.** Roll equal amounts of mixture into 36 balls. Toss in drinking chocolate. **6.** Transfer to fluted paper sweet cases. **36 Truffles.**

1146 CHOCOLATE SHERRY TRUFFLES

1. Follow recipe and method for Chocolate Rum Truffles (No. 1145). **2.** Use sherry instead of rum. **36 Truffles.**

1147 CHOCOLATE WHISKY TRUFFLES

1. Follow recipe and method for Chocolate Rum Truffles (No. 1145). **2.** Use whisky instead of rum. **36 Truffles.**

CHOCOLATE ORANGE TRUFFLES 1148

1. Follow recipe and method for Chocolate Rum Truffles (No. 1145). **2.** Omit rum and add finely-grated peel of 1 small orange and 1 tablespoon orange juice with almonds, cake crumbs and icing sugar. **36 Truffles.**

COCONUT ICE 1149

¼ pint milk
¼ pint water
2 lb. granulated sugar
1 oz. English or Welsh butter
½ lb. desiccated coconut
1 teaspoon vanilla essence
Red food colouring

1. Pour milk and water into saucepan. Bring to boil. **2.** Add sugar and butter. Heat slowly, stirring, until sugar dissolves and butter melts. **3.** Bring to boil. Cover pan. Boil gently for 2 minutes. **4.** Uncover. Continue to boil, stirring occasionally for 7 to 10 minutes (or until a little of the mixture, dropped into cup of cold water, forms soft ball when rolled gently between finger and thumb). Temperature on sugar thermometer, if used, should be 238°F. to 240°F. **5.** Remove from heat. Add coconut and vanilla. **6.** Beat briskly until mixture is thick and creamy-looking. **7.** Pour half into buttered 8-in. square tin. **8.** Quickly colour remainder pale pink with food colouring. **9.** Spread over white layer. **10.** Leave in the cool until firm and set. **Cut into about 60 pieces.**

Coconut Ice (No. 1149)

1150 CHOCOLATE COCONUT ICE

1. Follow recipe and method for Coconut Ice (No. 1149). **2.** Instead of colouring second layer pale pink, beat in 1 level teaspoon cocoa powder. **About 60 pieces.**

1151 EVERTON TOFFEE

4 tablespoons water
¼ lb. English or Welsh butter
¾ lb. Demerara sugar
2 level tablespoons golden syrup
1 level tablespoon black treacle

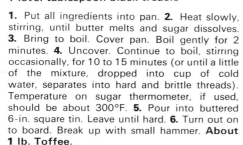

1. Put all ingredients into pan. **2.** Heat slowly, stirring, until butter melts and sugar dissolves. **3.** Bring to boil. Cover pan. Boil gently for 2 minutes. **4.** Uncover. Continue to boil, stirring occasionally, for 10 to 15 minutes (or until a little of the mixture, dropped into cup of cold water, separates into hard and brittle threads). Temperature on sugar thermometer, if used, should be about 300°F. **5.** Pour into buttered 6-in. square tin. Leave until hard. **6.** Turn out on to board. Break up with small hammer. **About 1 lb. Toffee.**

1152 HONEYCOMB

3 level tablespoons clear honey
5 level tablespoons granulated sugar
4 tablespoons water
½ oz. English or Welsh butter
½ teaspoon vinegar
½ level teaspoon bicarbonate of soda

1. Put honey, sugar, water, butter and vinegar into saucepan. **2.** Heat slowly, stirring, until sugar dissolves and butter melts. **3.** Bring to boil. Cover pan. Boil gently for 2 minutes. **4.** Uncover. Continue to boil, without stirring, for about 5 minutes (or until a little of the mixture, dropped into cup of cold water, separates into hard and brittle threads). Temperature on sugar thermometer, if used, should be about 300°F. **5.** Draw pan away from heat. Stir in bicarbonate of soda (mixture will rise in pan). **6.** Pour into small buttered tin. Break up when set. **7.** As Honeycomb does not keep well and very quickly gets sticky it should be made and eaten on the same day. **About ½ lb. Honeycomb.**

SYRUP TOFFEE 1153

5 tablespoons water
¼ lb. golden syrup
2 teaspoons vinegar
1 lb. granulated sugar
2 oz. English or Welsh butter

1. Pour water and syrup into saucepan. Bring to boil. **2.** Add vinegar, sugar and butter. Heat slowly, stirring, until sugar dissolves and butter melts. **3.** Bring to boil. Cover pan. Boil gently for 2 minutes. **4.** Uncover. Continue to boil, stirring occasionally, for 12 to 15 minutes (or until a little of the mixture, dropped into cup of cold water, forms very hard ball when rolled between finger and thumb). Temperature on sugar thermometer, if used, should be 280°F. to 290°F. **5.** Pour into buttered 6-in. square tin. Leave until hard. **6.** Turn out on to board. Break up with small hammer. **About 1¼ lb. Toffee.**

NUT TOFFEE 1154

1. Follow recipe and method for Syrup Toffee (No. 1153). **2.** Cover base of buttered tin with ¼ lb. blanched almonds or ¼ lb. sliced Brazils before pouring in Toffee. **About 1½ lb. Toffee.**

BUTTERSCOTCH 1155

¼ pint water
1 lb. Demerara sugar
2 oz. English or Welsh butter

1. Pour water into pan and bring to boil. **2.** Add sugar and butter. Heat slowly, stirring, until sugar dissolves and butter melts. **3.** Bring to boil. Cover pan. Boil gently for 2 minutes. **4.** Uncover. Continue to boil, without stirring, for about 12 minutes (or until a little of the mixture, dropped into cup of cold water, separates into hard brittle threads). Temperature on sugar thermometer, if used, should be about 300°F. **5.** Pour into buttered 6-in. square tin. **6.** Mark into squares or bars when almost set with buttered knife. **7.** Break up when hard and wrap in waxed paper. **About 1 lb. Butterscotch.**

Hot & Cold Drinks

COLD DRINKS

1156 YOGURT FRUIT CUP

1 carton (5 oz.) pineapple fruit yogurt
½ pint pineapple juice

1. Whisk yogurt and pineapple juice well together. **2.** Chill before serving. **Serves 2.**

1157 YOGURT STRAWBERRY COOLER

1 carton (5 oz.) strawberry fruit yogurt
½ pint chilled milk
A few crushed strawberries

1. Whisk yogurt and milk well together. **2.** Pour into 2 glasses. **3.** Top with crushed berries. **Serves 2.**

1158 RASPBERRY CRUSH

¼ pint raspberry purée (made from fresh, frozen or canned fruit)
1 pint chilled milk
Sifted icing sugar
4 tablespoons French Custard Dairy Ice (No. 1004)

1. Whisk purée and milk well together. **2.** Sweeten to taste with icing sugar. **3.** Chill thoroughly. **4.** Before serving pour into 4 glasses. **5.** Add tablespoon of Dairy Ice to each. **Serves 4.**

1159 STRAWBERRY CRUSH

1. Follow recipe and method for Raspberry Crush (No. 1158). **2.** Use strawberry purée instead of raspberry. **Serves 4.**

1160 APRICOT CRUSH

1. Follow recipe and method for Raspberry Crush (No. 1158). **2.** Use apricot purée instead of raspberry, and Lemon Dairy Cream Ice (No. 996) or Orange Dairy Cream Ice (No. 995) instead of French Custard Dairy Ice. **Serves 4.**

MINTED ORANGE CUPS   1161

4 unpeeled slices of orange
¼ pint fresh orange juice
1 pint chilled milk
2 tablespoons fresh double cream, whipped
Fresh mint leaves

1. Slit each orange slice from centre to outside edge. Slot over rims of 4 tumblers. **2.** Whisk orange juice and milk well together. **3.** Pour into glasses. **4.** Top each with whipped cream and mint leaves. **Serves 4.**

CHOCOLATE PEPPERMINT   1162 SIZZLERS

3 oz. grated plain chocolate
3 level dessertspoons caster sugar
1½ pints milk
1 teaspoon peppermint essence
2 tablespoons fresh double cream, whipped
Mint leaves

1. Slowly melt chocolate and sugar in ½ pint milk. **2.** Stir in rest of milk with peppermint essence. Chill. **3.** Just before serving pour into 4 glasses. **4.** Top each with cream and mint leaves. **Serves 4.**

CHOCOLATE GINGER   1163 FRAPPÉ

Crushed ice
2 heaped tablespoons drinking chocolate
3 tablespoons boiling water
1½ pints chilled milk
2 tablespoons ginger wine
2 tablespoons fresh double cream, whipped

1. Cover base of 4 tumblers with crushed ice. **2.** Mix drinking chocolate to smooth liquid with water. **3.** Whisk in milk and ginger wine. **4.** Pour into glasses. **5.** Top each with cream. **6.** Serve straight away. **Serves 4.**

229

1 pint chilled milk
3 standard eggs
4 level tablespoons sifted icing sugar
1 level teaspoon finely-grated lemon peel
6 tablespoons fresh orange juice
1 or 2 tablespoons sherry or brandy
 (optional)
Crushed ice
Nutmeg

1. Whisk milk and eggs well together. **2.** Whisk in sugar, lemon peel, orange juice and sherry or brandy if used. **3.** Cover base of 4 tumblers with crushed ice. **4.** Fill with milk mixture. **5.** Sprinkle each with nutmeg and serve straight away. **Serves 4.**

MALTED HONEY WHIP   116

$\frac{1}{8}$ pint chilled milk
1 level tablespoon clear honey
2 rounded tablespoons Dairy Cream
 Ice (No. 984) or bought vanilla dairy
 ice cream
1 standard egg
1 heaped teaspoon plain Horlicks

1. Put all ingredients into bowl. Beat well with rotary whisk until frothy. **2.** Pour into glasses and serve. **Serves 2.**

CHILLED CHOCOLATE   11
CREAM

2 heaped tablespoons drinking chocolate
3 tablespoons boiling water
1½ pints chilled milk
1 teaspoon vanilla essence
2 tablespoons fresh double cream,
 whipped
4 level tablespoons grated milk chocolate

1. Mix drinking chocolate to smooth liquid with water. **2.** Whisk in milk and vanilla. **3.** Pour into 4 tumblers. **4.** Top each with cream and sprinkle with chocolate. **Serves 4.**

Left: Chocolate Marshmallow Floats (No. 1177)
Right: front, left to right — Silk On The Rocks (No. 1176), Raspberry Crush (No. 1158) and Milk & Orange Nog (No. 1164); back — Chilled Chocolate Cream (No. 1166)

1167 CHILLED MOCHA CREAM

1. Follow recipe and method for Chilled Chocolate Cream (No. 1166). **2.** Mix 3 to 4 level teaspoons instant coffee powder with drinking chocolate before adding water. **Serves 4.**

1168 CHOCOLATE SHAKE

2 heaped tablespoons drinking chocolate
3 tablespoons boiling water
1½ pints chilled milk
4 heaped tablespoons bought vanilla
dairy ice cream

1. Mix drinking chocolate to smooth liquid with water. **2.** Whisk in milk and 2 tablespoons ice cream. **3.** Divide remaining ice cream equally between 4 tumblers. **4.** Fill with milk mixture. **5.** Serve straight away. **Serves 4.**

1169 MOCHA SHAKE

1. Follow recipe and method for Chocolate Shake (No. 1168). **2.** Mix 3 to 4 level teaspoons instant coffee powder with drinking chocolate before adding water. **Serves 4.**

1170 ROSE HIP SHAKE

4 to 5 tablespoons rose hip syrup
1½ pints chilled milk
3 heaped tablespoons bought vanilla
dairy ice cream, softened

1. Stir rose hip syrup into milk. **2.** Whisk in softened ice cream. **3.** Pour into 4 tumblers. **4.** Serve straight away. **Serves 4.**

1171 BANANA ROSE HIP SHAKE

2 medium-sized bananas
4 tablespoons rose hip syrup
1¼ pints chilled milk
3 heaped tablespoons bought vanilla
dairy ice cream, softened
Nutmeg

1. Mash bananas finely. **2.** Whisk in rose hip syrup, milk and ice cream. **3.** Pour into 4 tumblers. **4.** Sprinkle tops lightly with nutmeg. **5.** Serve straight away. **Serves 4.**

TROPICAL FRUIT SHAKE 117

2 medium-sized bananas
Finely-grated peel and juice of 1
medium-sized orange
4 tablespoons pineapple juice
1 pint milk
4 heaped tablespoons bought vanilla
dairy ice cream

1. Mash bananas finely. Whisk in orange and pineapple juice and milk. **2.** Divide ice cream between 4 tumblers. **3.** Fill with milk mixture. **4.** Sprinkle tops lightly with orange peel. **5.** Serve straight away. **Serves 4.**

ICED COFFEE 117

½ pint freshly-made double strength
black coffee
¾ pint milk
Sugar to taste

1. Combine coffee with milk. **2.** Sweeten to taste. Chill. **3.** Pour into 3 or 4 tumblers just before serving. **Serves 3 to 4.**

VIENNESE COFFEE 117

1. Follow recipe and method for Iced Coffee (No. 1173). **2.** Top each with swirl of lightly-whipped fresh double cream. **3.** If liked, sprinkle with drinking chocolate or grated plain chocolate. **Serves 3 to 4.**

MILK SHAKE FLOAT 117

⅓ pint chilled milk
2 rounded tablespoons bought vanilla
dairy ice cream
2 tablespoons milk shake syrup (flavour
to taste)

1. Whisk milk, 1 tablespoon ice cream and syrup well together. **2.** Pour into glass. **3.** Float remaining ice cream on top. **Serves 1.**

SILK ON THE ROCKS 117

Crushed ice
¾ pint chilled milk
Whisky

1. Half-fill 4 tumblers with crushed ice. **2.** Two-thirds fill with milk. **3.** Top up with whisky to taste. **4.** Sip through straw. **Serves 4.**

HOT DRINKS

177 CHOCOLATE MARSHMALLOW FLOATS

1¼ pints milk
2 heaped tablespoons drinking chocolate
8 marshmallows

1. Bring milk just up to boil. **2.** Remove from heat and whisk in drinking chocolate. **3.** Pour into 4 cups. **4.** Float 2 marshmallows on top of each **Serves 4.**

178 MOCHA MARSHMALLOW FLOATS

1. Follow recipe and method for Chocolate Marshmallow Floats (No.1177). **2.** Add 3 level teaspoons instant coffee powder with drinking chocolate. **Serves 4.**

179 HOT EGG & MILK NOG

Yolks and whites of 2 standard eggs
2 level tablespoons caster sugar
1 pint milk
Nutmeg

1. Whisk egg yolks and sugar together until very thick and pale in colour. **2.** Beat egg whites to stiff snow. **3.** Bring milk just up to boil and whisk into yolks and sugar. **4.** Quickly stir in beaten whites. **5.** Transfer to 3 tumblers. **6.** Sprinkle lightly with nutmeg. **7.** Serve straight away. **Serves 3.**

180 HOT SHERRY, BRANDY OR RUM NOG

1. Follow recipe and method for Hot Egg and Milk Nog (No.1179). **2.** Add 1 or 2 tablespoons sherry, brandy or rum with the hot milk. **Serves 3.**

181 HOT ORANGE OR LEMON NOG

1. Follow recipe and method for Hot Egg and Milk Nog (No.1179). **2.** Heat milk with 1 level teaspoon finely-grated orange or lemon peel. **Serves 3.**

CHOCOLATE CREAM NOG 1182

Yolks and whites of 2 standard eggs
1 level tablespoon caster sugar
2 oz. grated plain chocolate
½ pint milk
½ pint fresh single cream

1. Whisk egg yolks and sugar together until very thick and pale in colour. **2.** Beat egg whites to stiff snow. **3.** Put chocolate and milk into saucepan. Stand over low heat until chocolate has melted. **4.** Add cream and bring just up to boil. **5.** Whisk gently into egg yolk mixture. **6.** Quickly stir in beaten whites. **7.** Pour into 4 or 5 cups or glasses. **8.** Serve straight away. **Serves 4 or 5.**

WINTER MILK PUNCH 1183

2 pints milk
1 oz. ground almonds
¼ lb. granulated sugar
1 level teaspoon finely-grated orange peel
1 level teaspoon finely-grated lemon peel
Whites of 2 standard eggs
4 tablespoons rum
6 tablespoons brandy

1. Pour milk into large pan. **2.** Add almonds, sugar and grated peel. **3.** Bring just up to boil and remove from heat. **4.** Beat egg whites to stiff snow. **5.** Add to hot milk mixture with rum and brandy. **6.** Whisk gently until Punch is frothy. **7.** Ladle into 8 cups. **8.** Serve straight away. **Serves 8.**

ALMOND FLIP 1184

White of 1 standard egg
1 oz. ground almonds
1 oz. sifted icing sugar
½ teaspoon almond essence
1 pint milk
Cinnamon

1. Beat egg white to stiff snow. **2.** Fold in almonds, sugar and essence. **3.** Bring milk just up to boil. Gently whisk into egg white mixture. **4.** Pour into 3 cups. Sprinkle tops lightly with cinnamon. **5.** Serve straight away. **Serves 3.**

Irish Coffee (No. 1186)

JAMAICAN CHOCOLATE 1185

¼ pint water
1 pint milk
2 heaped tablespoons drinking chocolate
2 tablespoons rum
2 to 3 tablespoons fresh double cream

1. Bring water and milk just up to boil. **2.** Remove from heat. Whisk in drinking chocolate. **3.** Add rum. Pour into 4 cups. **4.** Float cream on the top of each by pouring it into cups over back of teaspoon. **Serves 4.**

IRISH COFFEE 1186

3 dessertspoons Irish whiskey
3 cubes sugar or 2 teaspoons brown sugar
Freshly-made strong coffee
Fresh double cream

1. Warm a stemmed goblet or medium-sized coffee cup with hot water. Quickly wipe dry. **2.** Pour in whiskey, add sugar and fill with coffee to within 1 in. of rim. **3.** Stir briskly to dissolve sugar. **4.** Top up with cream, by pouring it into goblet or cup over back of teaspoon. **5.** Serve straight away. **Serves 1.**

SCOTCH COFFEE 1187

1. Follow recipe and method for Irish Coffee (No. 1186). **2.** Use Scotch whisky instead of Irish whiskey. **Serves 1.**

RUSSIAN COFFEE 1188

1. Follow recipe and method for Irish Coffee (No. 1186). **2.** Use vodka instead of whiskey. **Serves 1.**

FRENCH COFFEE 1189

1. Follow recipe and method for Irish Coffee (No. 1186). **2.** Use brandy instead of whiskey. **Serves 1.**

JAMAICAN COFFEE 1190

1. Follow recipe and method for Irish Coffee (No. 1186). **2.** Use rum instead of whiskey. **Serves 1.**

Milk Posset (No. 1192)

191 SPANISH COFFEE

1. Follow recipe and method for Irish Coffee (No. 1186). **2.** Use sherry instead of whiskey. **Serves 1.**

192 MILK POSSET

¾ pint milk
2 level tablespoons golden syrup
Grated Nutmeg

1. Bring milk just up to boil. Stir in syrup. **2.** Pour into 2 cups or glasses. **3.** Sprinkle lightly with nutmeg. **Serves 2.**

193 DUTCH CHOCOLATE CUPS

½ pint milk
¼ pint fresh single cream
¼ pint water
3 heaped tablespoons drinking chocolate
¼ bottle Advocaat
Cinnamon

1. Pour milk, cream and water into pan. Bring just up to boil. **2.** Remove from heat. **3.** Whisk in drinking chocolate and Advocaat. **4.** Pour into 4 cups. **5.** Sprinkle lightly with cinnamon **Serves 4.**

HOT SPICED MILK   1194

1¼ pints milk
2 level tablespoons black treacle
2 tablespoons fresh double cream
Cinnamon

1. Bring milk and treacle just up to boil, stirring all the time. **2.** Pour into 4 cups. **3.** Float cream on each by pouring it into cups over back of teaspoon. **4.** Sprinkle lightly with cinnamon. **5.** Serve straight away. **Serves 4.**

HOT COFFEE FOAM   1195

Yolks and whites of 2 standard eggs
1 level tablespoon caster sugar
2 tablespoons Tia Maria (coffee liqueur)
½ pint hot strong black coffee
½ pint hot milk
Grated nutmeg

1. Beat egg yolks and sugar together until very thick and pale colour. Gently whisk in Tia Maria, coffee and milk. **2.** Beat egg whites to stiff snow. **3.** Put equal amounts into 4 cups. **4.** Pour hot coffee liquid into cups over egg whites. **5.** Sprinkle each lightly with nutmeg. **6.** Serve straight away. **Serves 4.**

Preserves

Fruit for jam making should be in good condition; either under-ripe or only just ripe and dry. Fruit that is over-ripe and on the point of turning mouldy will, in all probability, be lacking in acid and pectin. Jam made from it may not set properly. All fruit should be cleaned and picked over thoroughly.

If possible, choose a roomy saucepan – it should be no more than half-full when once the sugar has been added – and one that is also strong and heavy based to prevent the jam from sticking and burning.

Do not use a metal spoon for stirring. It will get over-heated and be uncomfortable to hold. A wooden spoon is the most suitable choice.

Removing scum while the jam is cooking is wasteful: a good deal of jam gets skimmed off with it. Better to wait until boiling has finished and then remove with a metal spoon any scum

that remains on the surface. The addition of a small piece of English or Welsh butter (about ½ oz.) often disperses scum completely.

To test for setting, pour a little jam on to a cold saucer and leave for 1 minute. If a skin forms on top and wrinkles when touched, the jam has reached setting point. (About 220°F. on sugar thermometer).

Allow the jam to cool off slightly before pouring into dry warm jars. To prevent strawberries or other whole fruits from rising in the jars, wait until a skin forms on the jam in the saucepan before potting.

Make sure that jam reaches brims of jars as it shrinks slightly on cooling.

Cover jam either while it is still very hot or completely cold. Store in a dry, cool and airy cupboard away from strong sunlight.

1196 BLACKCURRANT JAM

2½ lb. stemmed and washed blackcurrants
1½ pints water
3 lb. granulated sugar
½ oz. English or Welsh butter

1. Put blackcurrants into saucepan and add water. **2.** Bring to boil, cover pan and reduce heat. **3.** Simmer gently until fruit is tender (about 45 minutes). **4.** Add sugar and stir until dissolved. Bring to boil. Boil briskly for 5 to 10 minutes (or until setting point is reached). **5.** Draw pan away from heat. Stir in butter to disperse scum. **6.** Pot and cover. **About 5 lb. jam.**

1197 GOOSEBERRY JAM

1. Follow recipe and method for Blackcurrant Jam (No.1196). **2.** Use gooseberries instead of blackcurrants. Boil for 10 to 15 minutes (or until setting point is reached). **About 5 lb. Jam.**

1198 DAMSON JAM

1. Follow recipe and method for Blackcurrant Jam (No. 1196). **2.** Use damsons instead of blackcurrants. **3.** Boil for 10 to 15 minutes after adding sugar (or until setting point is reached). **4.** Remove stones with perforated spoon as they rise to surface. **About 5 lb. Jam.**

STRAWBERRY JAM 1199

3½ lb. strawberries
Juice of 1 large lemon
3 lb. granulated sugar
½ oz. English or Welsh butter

1. Put strawberries, lemon juice and sugar into pan. **2.** Heat slowly, stirring all the time, until sugar dissolves. **3.** Bring to boil. Boil briskly for 10 to 15 minutes (or until setting point is reached). **4.** Draw pan away from heat. Stir in butter to disperse scum. **5.** Leave Jam to cool off in pan until skin forms on surface. **6.** Stir gently, pot and cover. **About 5 lb. Jam.**

DRIED APRICOT JAM 1200

1 lb. dried apricots
3 pints water
3 lb. granulated sugar
3 oz. blanched and split almonds
Juice of 1 large lemon
½ oz. English or Welsh butter

1. Snip apricots into smallish pieces with kitchen scissors. Cover with cold water and leave to soak overnight. **2.** Drain, put into pan and add 3 pints water. **3.** Bring to boil, lower heat and cover pan. Simmer gently about 45 minutes (or until fruit is tender). **4.** Add sugar, almonds and lemon juice. Heat slowly, stirring all the time, until sugar dissolves. **5.** Bring to boil. Boil briskly until setting point is reached. **6.** Draw pan away from heat. Stir in butter to disperse scum. **7.** Pot and cover. **About 5 lb. Jam.**

1201 PLUM JAM

3 lb. washed plums
$\frac{3}{4}$ pint water
3 lb. granulated sugar
$\frac{1}{2}$ oz. English or Welsh butter

1. Put plums into saucepan and add water.
2. Bring to boil, cover pan and reduce heat.
3. Simmer gently until fruit is tender (10 to 20 minutes). **4.** Add sugar and stir until dissolved.
5. Bring jam to boil. Boil briskly for 10 to 15 minutes (or until setting point is reached). Remove stones with perforated spoon as they rise to surface. **6.** Draw pan away from heat. Stir in butter to disperse scum. **7.** Pot and cover. **About 5 lb. Jam.**

1202 GREENGAGE JAM

1. Follow recipe and method for Plum Jam (No.1201). **2.** Use greengages instead of plums. **About 5 lb. Jam.**

1203 RASPBERRY JAM

3 lb. raspberries
3 lb. granulated sugar
$\frac{1}{2}$ oz. English or Welsh butter

1. Put fruit into saucepan and crush finely with back of wooden spoon. **2.** Simmer gently for 5 minutes. **3.** Add sugar and stir until dissolved.
4. Bring to boil. Boil briskly for 5 to 7 minutes (or until setting point is reached). **5.** Draw pan away from heat. Stir in butter to disperse scum. **6.** Pot and cover. **About 5 lb. Jam.**

1204 LOGANBERRY JAM

1. Follow recipe and method for Raspberry Jam (No.1203). **2.** Use loganberries instead of raspberries. **About 5 lb. Jam.**

1205 RASPBERRY & LOGANBERY JAM

1. Follow recipe and method for Raspberry Jam (No.1203). **2.** Use half loganberries and half raspberries instead of all raspberries. **About 5 lb. Jam.**

MARROW & GINGER JAM 1206

3 lb. marrow (after peeling and removing seeds)
Finely-grated peel and juice of 2 large lemons
$1\frac{1}{2}$ oz. root ginger
3 lb. granulated sugar
$\frac{1}{2}$ oz. English or Welsh butter

1. Cut marrow into small cubes and steam gently for 20 minutes. **2.** Turn into bowl and add lemon peel and juice, ginger (tied in muslin bag) and sugar. **3.** Cover bowl and leave to stand 24 hours.
4. Transfer to large saucepan and heat slowly, stirring all the time, until sugar dissolves. **5.** Bring to boil. Boil steadily for 30 to 45 minutes (or until marrow is almost transparent and syrup is thick). **6.** Draw pan away from heat. Stir in butter to disperse scum. **7.** Remove ginger. Pot and cover Jam. **About 5 lb. Jam.**

● *This Jam never sets firmly and will always be syrupy.*

LEMON CURD 1207

$\frac{1}{4}$ lb. English or Welsh butter
$\frac{1}{2}$ lb. granulated sugar
3 standard eggs   1 standard yolk, beaten together
3 medium-sized lemons

1. Melt butter in double saucepan (or basin standing over saucepan of gently-simmering water). **2.** Add sugar, eggs and extra yolk, and finely-grated peel and juice of lemons. **3.** Cook gently without boiling until Curd thickens sufficiently to coat back of spoon. (This is important because if over-heated the mixture may curdle and separate.) **4.** Pour into clean, dry and warm jars and cover as for Jam. **About $1\frac{1}{4}$ lb. Curd.**

● *Store in a very cool place and do not keep longer than 2 weeks.*

ORANGE CURD 1208

1. Follow recipe and method for Lemon Curd (No.1207). **2.** Instead of all lemons, use 2 medium-sized oranges and 1 medium-sized lemon. **About $1\frac{1}{4}$ lb. Curd.**

PRESERVES

1209 APPLE & BLACKBERRY JAM

1½ lb. apples (after peeling and coring)
1½ lb. blackberries
½ pint water
3 lb. granulated sugar
½ oz. English or Welsh butter

1. Slice apples thinly and put into saucepan with blackberries. **2.** Pour in water. **3.** Bring to boil, reduce heat and cover pan. **4.** Simmer gently for 10 to 15 minutes, crushing fruit against sides of pan until it is soft and pulpy. **5.** Add sugar and heat slowly, stirring all the time, until sugar dissolves. **6.** Bring to boil. Boil briskly for 10 to 15 minutes (or until setting point is reached). **7.** Draw pan away from heat. Stir in butter to disperse scum. **8.** Pot and cover. **About 5 lb. Jam.**

1210 RASPBERRY & REDCURRANT JAM

1. Follow recipe and method for Apple and Blackberry Jam (No.1209). **2.** Use 1½ lb. *each*, raspberries and stemmed redcurrants instead of apples and blackberries. **3.** Cook fruit in ¼ pint water only. **About 5 lb. Jam.**

1211 RASPBERRY & RHUBARB JAM

1. Follow recipe and method for Apple and Blackberry Jam (No.1209). **2.** Use 1½ lb. *each*, raspberries and trimmed rhubarb (cut into 2-in. lengths) instead of apples and blackberries. **3.** Cook fruit in ¼ pint water only. **About 5 lb. Jam.**

1212 GOOSEBERRY & REDCURRANT JAM

1. Follow· recipe and method for Apple and Blackberry Jam (No.1209). **2.** Use 1½ lb. *each*, gooseberries and stemmed redcurrants instead of apples and blackberries. **3.** Cook fruit in ¼ pint water only. **About 5 lb. Jam.**

MIXED FRUIT JAM 121

1. Follow recipe and method for Apple and Blackberry Jam (No.1209). **2.** Use 3 lb. mixed soft fruit (such as raspberries, strawberries, gooseberries, rhubarb, redcurrants, and logan-berries) instead of apples and blackberries. **3.** Cook fruit in ¼ pint water only. **About 5 lb. Jam.**

THICK ORANGE MARMALADE 121

1½ lb. Seville (or bitter) oranges
3 pints water
Juice of 1 lemon
3 lb. granulated sugar
½ oz. English or Welsh butter

1. Scrub oranges well. **2.** Put, without slicing, into large saucepan. **3.** Pour in water and bring to boil. **4.** Reduce heat and cover pan. Simmer very gently for 1½ to 2 hours (or until skins of fruit are soft and can be pierced easily with fork or skewer). **5.** Lift oranges out of pan. Cool slightly and chop coarsely. **6.** Collect pips and tie in muslin bag. **7.** Return chopped oranges to pan with lemon juice and bag of pips. **8.** Add sugar and heat slowly, stirring all the time, until sugar dissolves. **9.** Bring to boil. Boil steadily until setting point is reached. **10.** Draw pan away from heat. Stir in butter to disperse scum. **11.** Leave Marmalade in saucepan until skin forms on surface. **12.** Stir gently, pot and cover. **About 5 lb. Marmalade.**

SWEET ORANGE MARMALADE 121

1. Follow recipe and method for Thick Orange Marmalade (No.1214). **2.** Use 1½ lb. sweet oranges and juice of 3 medium-sized lemons. **About 5 lb. Marmalade.**

GRAPEFRUIT & ORANGE MARMALADE 121

1. Follow recipe and method for Thick Orange Marmalade (No.1214). **2.** Use 1 lb. grapefruit, ½ lb. sweet oranges and juice of 3 medium-sized lemons. **About 5 lb. Marmalade.**

238

COLD SWEET SOUFFLÉS

217 LEMON SOUFFLÉ

3 level teaspoons gelatine
2 tablespoons boiling water
Yolks and whites of 2 large eggs
2 oz. caster sugar
Finely-grated peel and juice of 1
  medium-sized lemon
¼ pint fresh double cream

DECORATION
About 1½ oz. finely-chopped, shelled
  walnut halves or blanched and toasted
  almonds
4 tablespoons fresh double cream,
  whipped
Leaves of angelica or crystallised violet
  petals

1. Prepare dish first. Put 4-in. strip of folded greaseproof paper round 1-pint soufflé dish, making sure paper stands 1½ to 2 in. above edge of dish. Tie on securely. Brush inside of strip with salad oil. **2.** Shower gelatine into boiling water and stir briskly until dissolved. **3.** Whisk egg yolks and sugar together until very thick and pale. Gently whisk in dissolved gelatine, lemon peel and juice. **4.** Leave in cold until just beginning to thicken and set. **5.** Whisk cream until lightly stiff. Beat egg whites to stiff snow. **6.** Gently fold lemon mixture into cream. Fold in beaten whites. **7.** Pour into prepared soufflé dish (mixture should reach almost to top of paper). Chill until firm and set. **8.** Just before serving, remove paper carefully. Gently press chopped nuts against sides of Soufflé **9.** Decorate top with whipped cream and either angelica or crystallised violets. **Serves 4 to 5.**

218 ORANGE SOUFFLÉ

1. Follow recipe and method for Lemon Soufflé (No.1217) but instead of the lemon use finely-grated peel and juice of 1 small orange. **2.** Press chopped walnuts or almonds against the sides. **3.** Decorate with whipped cream and small pieces of glacé cherries. **Serves 4 to 5.**

Cold Lemon Soufflé (No. 1217)

1219 CHOCOLATE SOUFFLÉ

3 level teaspoons gelatine
2 tablespoons boiling water
2 oz. plain chocolate
1 tablespoon milk
1 teaspoon vanilla essence
Yolks and whites of 2 large eggs
2 oz. caster sugar
$\frac{1}{4}$ pint fresh double cream
DECORATION
About 1$\frac{1}{2}$ oz. finely-chopped shelled
  walnut halves, blanched toasted almonds
  or hazelnuts
4 tablespoons fresh double cream,
  whipped
Chocolate buttons or small pieces
  preserved ginger

1. Prepare dish as for Cold Lemon Soufflé (No.1217). **2.** Shower gelatine into boiling water and stir briskly until dissolved. **3.** Break up chocolate and put into basin standing over pan of hot water. Leave until melted, stirring once or twice. Blend in milk and vanilla. **4.** Beat egg yolks and sugar together until very thick and pale. Whisk in dissolved gelatine and melted chocolate and milk. Leave in cool until just beginning to thicken and set. **5.** Whip cream until lightly stiff. Beat egg whites to a stiff snow. **6.** Gently fold chocolate mixture into cream. Fold in beaten whites. **7.** Pour into prepared soufflé dish (mixture should reach almost to top of paper). Chill until firm and set. **8.** Just before serving, remove paper carefully. Gently press chopped nuts against sides of Soufflé. **9.** Decorate top with whipped cream and either chocolate buttons or ginger. **Serves 4 to 5.**

1220 COFFEE SOUFFLÉ

1. Follow recipe and method for Chocolate Soufflé (No. 1219) but omit chocolate and vanilla. **2.** Warm tablespoon of milk. Stir in 2 to 3 level teaspoons instant coffee powder. Whisk into beaten yolks and sugar with dissolved gelatine. **3.** Press chopped walnuts against sides of Soufflé. **4.** Decorate with whipped cream and shelled walnut halves. **Serves 4 to 5.**

MOCHA SOUFFLÉ 1221

1. Follow recipe and method for Chocolate Soufflé (No.1219) but add 2 to 3 level teaspoons instant coffee powder to the chocolate in the basin. **2.** Press chopped hazelnuts against sides of Soufflé. **3.** Decorate top with whipped cream and whole hazelnuts. **Serves 4 to 5.**

STRAWBERRY SOUFFLÉ 1222

3 level teaspoons gelatine
2 tablespoons boiling water
$\frac{1}{4}$ pint strawberry purée (made from
  canned, frozen or fresh berries)
2 teaspoons lemon juice
1 to 3 oz. sifted icing sugar
$\frac{1}{4}$ pint fresh double cream
Whites of 2 large eggs

DECORATION
4 tablespoons fresh double cream,
  whipped
Small whole strawberries

1. Prepare dish as for Cold Lemon Soufflé (No.1217). **2.** Shower gelatine into boiling water and stir until dissolved. **3.** Combine strawberry purée with lemon juice. Stir in dissolved gelatine. **4.** Sweeten to taste with icing sugar. Leave in the cool until just beginning to thicken and set. **5.** Whip cream until lightly stiff. Beat egg whites to stiff snow. **6.** Gently fold fruit mixture into cream. Lastly, fold in beaten egg whites. **7.** Pour into prepared soufflé dish (mixture should reach almost to top of paper). Chill until firm and set. **8.** Just before serving, remove paper carefully. Decorate top with whipped cream and whole berries. **Serves 4 to 5.**

RASPBERRY SOUFFLÉ 1223

1. Follow recipe and method for Strawberry Soufflé (No.1222). **2.** Use $\frac{1}{4}$ pint raspberry purée instead of the strawberry. **3.** Decorate top with whipped cream and whole raspberries. **Serves 4 to 5.**

LOGANBERRY SOUFFLÉ 1224

1. Follow recipe and method for Strawberry Soufflé (No.1222). **2.** Use $\frac{1}{4}$ pint loganberry purée instead of the strawberry. **3.** Decorate top with whipped cream and whole loganberries. **Serves 4 to 5.**

HOT SWEET SOUFFLÉS

25 VANILLA SOUFFLÉ

2 oz. English or Welsh butter
2 oz. plain flour
½ pint lukewarm milk
2 oz. caster sugar
1 teaspoon vanilla essence
Yolks of 3 large eggs
Whites of 3 or 4 large eggs

1. Melt butter in saucepan and add flour. Cook 2 minutes without browning, stirring all the time. **2.** Gradually whisk in warm milk (with a whisk, not a spoon). Continue whisking gently until sauce comes to boil and thickens. **3.** Simmer about 2 minutes. Sauce should be very thick and leave sides of pan clean. **4.** Remove from heat and cool slightly. Beat in sugar, vanilla and egg yolks. **5.** Beat egg whites to stiff snow. Gently fold into sauce mixture with large metal spoon. **6.** Transfer to well-buttered 2 to 2½-pint soufflé dish (or similar straight-sided, heatproof dish). Put into centre of fairly hot oven (375°F. or Gas No. 5). **7.** Bake 45 minutes when Soufflé should be well-risen with a high, golden crown. **8.** Remove from oven and serve straight away with Red Jam Sauce (No. 158). **Serves 4.**

●*It is vital not to open the oven door while the Soufflé is baking or it will fall.*

26 ALMOND SOUFFLÉ

1. Follow recipe and method for Vanilla Soufflé (No.1225) but use almond essence instead of vanilla. **2.** Add 3 oz. ground almonds before beating in egg yolks. **3.** Serve with fresh single cream or Red Jam Sauce (No. 158). **Serves 4.**

27 APRICOT SOUFFLÉ

1. Follow recipe and method for Vanilla Soufflé (No.1225) but use ½ teaspoon almond essence instead of vanilla. **2.** Before beating in egg yolks add 4 tablespoons thick apricot purée (made from canned or fresh stewed apricots). **3.** Serve with fresh single cream. **Serves 4.**

BANANA SOUFFLÉ 1228

1. Follow recipe and method for Vanilla Soufflé (No.1225) but omit vanilla. **2.** Before beating in egg yolks add 2 small, finely-mashed bananas and 2 teaspoons lemon juice. **3.** Serve with fresh single cream. **Serves 4.**

CHOCOLATE SOUFFLÉ 1229

1. Follow recipe and method for Vanilla Soufflé (No.1225) but melt 2 oz. grated plain chocolate in the milk. **2.** Serve with fresh single cream. **Serves 4.**

COFFEE SOUFFLÉ 1230

1. Follow recipe and method for Vanilla Soufflé (No.1225) but omit vanilla. **2.** Add 2 to 3 level teaspoons instant coffee powder to warm milk. **3.** Serve with fresh single cream or Chocolate Sauce (No.177). **Serves 4.**

ORANGE OR LEMON SOUFFLÉ 1231

1. Follow recipe and method for Vanilla Soufflé (No.1225) but omit vanilla. **2.** Before beating in egg yolks add 2 level teaspoons finely-grated orange or lemon peel. **3.** Serve with fresh single cream. **Serves 4.**

WALNUT OR HAZELNUT SOUFFLÉ 1232

1. Follow recipe and method for Vanilla Soufflé (No. 1225) but before beating in egg yolks add 3 oz. very finely-chopped, shelled walnut halves or hazelnuts. **2.** Serve with fresh single cream or Chocolate Sauce (No. 177). **Serves 4.**

PINEAPPLE SOUFFLÉ 1233

1. Follow recipe and method for Vanilla Soufflé (No. 1225) but before beating in egg yolks add 4 level tablespoons finely-chopped canned pineapple (well drained). **2.** Serve with fresh single cream. **Serve 4.**

HOT SAVOURY SOUFFLÉS

1234 CHEESE SOUFFLÉ

2 oz. English or Welsh butter
2 oz. plain flour
$\frac{1}{2}$ pint lukewarm milk
$\frac{1}{4}$ lb. very finely-grated English Cheddar
cheese (stale for preference)
1 level teaspoon made mustard
$\frac{1}{2}$ level teaspoon salt
$\frac{1}{4}$ teaspoon Worcester sauce
Yolks of 3 large eggs
Whites of 3 or 4 large eggs

1. Melt butter in saucepan and add flour. Cook 2 minutes without browning, stirring all the time. **2.** Gradually whisk in warm milk (with a whisk, not a spoon). Continue whisking gently until sauce comes to boil and thickens. **3.** Simmer about 2 minutes. Sauce should be quite thick and leave sides of pan clean. **4.** Remove from heat and cool slightly. Beat in cheese, mustard, salt, Worcester sauce and egg yolks. **5.** Beat egg whites to stiff snow. Gently fold into sauce mixture with large metal spoon. **6.** Transfer to well-buttered 2 to $2\frac{1}{2}$-pint soufflé dish (or similar straight-sided, heatproof dish). Put into centre of fairly hot oven (375°F. or Gas No. 5). **7.** Bake 45 minutes. The Soufflé should be well-risen with a high, golden crown. **8.** Remove from oven and serve straight away. **Serves 4.**

●*It is vital not to open the oven door while the Soufflé is baking or it will fall*.

1235 BACON SOUFFLÉ

1. Follow recipe and method for Cheese Soufflé (No. 1234) but omit cheese. **2.** Before beating in egg yolks add $\frac{1}{4}$ lb. very finely-chopped, fried bacon. **Serves 4.**

1236 CRAB SOUFFLÉ

1. Follow recipe and method for Cheese Soufflé (No.1234) but omit cheese. **2.** Before beating in egg yolks add 1 teaspoon lemon juice, 2 teaspoons tomato ketchup, 1 level tablespoon finely-chopped parsley and 4 to 6 oz. finely-chopped crab meat. **Serves 4.**

HAM SOUFFLÉ 123

1. Follow recipe and method for Cheese Soufflé (No.1234) but omit cheese. **2.** Before beating in egg yolks add 4 to 6 oz. minced ham. **Serves 4.**

ASPARAGUS SOUFFLÉ 123

1. Follow recipe and method for Cheese Soufflé (No. 1234) but omit cheese and Worcester sauce. **2.** Before beating in egg yolks add $\frac{1}{4}$ lb. very finely-chopped asparagus. **Serves 4.**

MUSHROOM SOUFFLÉ 123

1. Follow recipe and method for Cheese Soufflé (No. 1234) but omit cheese and Worcester sauce. **2.** Before beating in egg yolks add $\frac{1}{4}$ lb. finely-chopped, fried mushrooms. **Serves 4.**

ONION SOUFFLÉ 124

1. Follow recipe and method for Cheese Soufflé (No. 1234) but omit cheese and Worcester sauce. **2.** Before beating in egg yolks add $\frac{1}{4}$ lb. very finely-chopped, boiled onions. **Serves 4.**

TONGUE SOUFFLÉ 124

1. Follow recipe and method for Cheese Soufflé (No. 1234) but omit cheese. **2.** Before beating in egg yolks add $\frac{1}{4}$ lb. minced tongue. **Serves 4.**

SMOKED HADDOCK SOUFFLÉ 124

1. Follow recipe and method for Cheese Soufflé (No.1234) but halve quantity of salt. **2.** Before beating in egg yolks add 4 to 6 oz. finely-flaked, cooked smoked haddock. **Serves 4.**

TURKEY SOUFFLÉ 124

1. Follow recipe and method for Cheese Soufflé (No. 1234) but omit cheese. **2.** Before beating in egg yolks add 1 level tablespoon very finely-chopped parsley and $\frac{1}{4}$ lb. cooked, minced turkey. **Serves 4.**

Omelettes

Spanish Omelette (No. 1265)

Ideally, omelettes should be made in a special omelette pan (kept only for omelette-making), or in a non-stick frying pan. If you have neither of these, and want to make omelettes in your ordinary frying pan, you can achieve better results by 'proving' the pan first. This will prevent the egg mixture from sticking and can be done very simply.

To 'prove' a pan quickly, first melt a knob of butter in the pan, then sprinkle the base liberally with cooking salt. Heat together slowly for a few minutes until hot, then rub clean with soft kitchen paper. You should **not** attempt to 'prove' non-stick pans.

If you are considering buying a special omelette pan, make sure it has a heavy base, curved sides, and is fairly shallow. It is important to 'prove' this pan well before use. After use just wipe the inside clean with soft kitchen paper. **Don't** wash, or it will need reproving.

One point to remember is that a 6-in. pan is ideal for a 2 large or 3 standard egg omelette and a 7-in. one ideal for a 3 large or 4 standard egg omelette.

SAVOURY OMELETTES

PLAIN OR FRENCH OMELETTE (UNFILLED)   1244

3 large or 4 standard eggs
4 teaspoons cold water
Seasoning to taste
1 oz. English or Welsh butter

GARNISH
Parsley

1. Beat eggs and water lightly together. Season to taste with salt and pepper. **2.** Put butter into omelette pan. Heat until sizzling but not brown. **3.** Pour in beaten eggs. **4.** After about 5 seconds, move edges of setting omelette to centre of pan with fork, knife or spatula. At same time tilt pan quickly in all directions with other hand so that uncooked egg flows to edges. **5.** Cook further $\frac{1}{2}$ to 1 minute (or until underneath is set and top is slightly moist). **6.** Remove from heat. Fold in half in pan and slide out on to a warm plate. **7.** Garnish with parsley and serve straight away. **Serves 2.**

1245 BACON, MUSHROOM & ONION OMELETTE

1. Fry gently in a little English or Welsh butter 1 level tablespoon *each* finely-chopped lean bacon, mushrooms and onion. **2.** Add to beaten eggs just before making Plain Omelette (No.1244). **Serves 2.**

1246 LEEK & MUSHROOM OMELETTE

1. Fry gently in a little English or Welsh butter 1 level tablespoon *each* finely-chopped leek, mushrooms and onion. **2.** Add to beaten eggs just before making Plain Omelette (No.1244). **Serves 2.**

1247 TARRAGON OMELETTE

Add 1 level teaspoon dried tarragon to beaten eggs just before making Plain Omelette (No.1244). **Serves 2.**

1248 CHEESE OMELETTE

Add $1\frac{1}{2}$ to 2 oz. very finely-grated English Cheddar cheese to beaten eggs just before making Plain Omelette (No.1244). **Serves 2.**

1249 CHIVE OMELETTE

Add 2 level tablespoons very finely-chopped chives to beaten eggs just before making Plain Omelette (No.1244). **Serves 2.**

1250 CROÛTON & PARSLEY OMELETTE

1. Fry 2 tablespoons $\frac{1}{4}$-in. bread cubes in a little English or Welsh butter until crisp and golden. **2.** Add, with 1 level tablespoon finely-chopped parsley, to beaten eggs just before making Plain Omelette (No.1244). **Serves 2.**

PARSLEY OMELETTE 1251

Add 1 level tablespoon finely-chopped fresh parsley to beaten eggs just before making Plain Omelette (No.1244). **Serves 2.**

HAM & POTATO OMELETTE 1252

1. Lightly fry 1 rounded tablespoon diced ham and 1 rounded tablespoon diced potatoes in a little English or Welsh butter. **2.** Add to beaten eggs just before making Plain Omelette (No.1244). **Serves 2.**

FRIED ONION OMELETTE 1253

1. Lightly fry about 1 level tablespoon finely-chopped onion in a little English or Welsh butter. **2.** Add to beaten eggs just before making Plain Omelette (No.1244). **Serves 2.**

WATERCRESS OMELETTE 1254

Add 1 level tablespoon very finely-chopped watercress to beaten eggs just before making Plain Omelette (No.1244). **Serves 2.**

FILLED FRENCH OR PLAIN OMELETTES

Cover half the made Plain Omelette (No.1244)— while still in the pan—with chosen filling. Fold other half over then slide Omelette on to plate.

ASPARAGUS OMELETTE 1255

Fill Plain Omelette (No.1244) with $\frac{1}{4}$ lb. cooked asparagus tips warmed through in a little English or Welsh butter. **Serves 2.**

BACON OMELETTE 1256

Fill Plain Omelette (No.1244) with $\frac{1}{4}$ lb. coarsely-chopped, lean bacon, lightly fried in a little English or Welsh butter. **Serves 2.**

257 CROÛTON OMELETTE

1. Fill Plain Omelette (No.1244) with 3 rounded tablespoons $\frac{1}{4}$-in. bread cubes fried until crisp and golden in a little English or Welsh butter. **2.** Sprinkle with onion, garlic or celery salt. **Serves 2.**

258 CHICKEN OMELETTE

Fill Plain Omelette (No.1244) with diced cooked chicken (about $\frac{1}{4}$ lb.) warmed through with a little Aurore Sauce (No. 119) or Mushroom Sauce (No.113). **Serves 2.**

259 TOMATO OMELETTE

Fill Plain Omelette (No.1244) with $\frac{1}{4}$ lb. skinned and coarsely-chopped tomatoes, fried gently in a little English or Welsh butter. **Serves 2.**

260 CRAB OMELETTE

Fill Plain Omelette (No.1244) with $\frac{1}{4}$ lb. flaked crab meat warmed through with a little Lemon Sauce (No. 111). **Serves 2.**

261 HAM OMELETTE

Fill Plain Omelette (No.1244) with $\frac{1}{4}$ lb. lean ham, lightly fried in a little English or Welsh butter. **Serves 2.**

262 KIDNEY OMELETTE

Fill Plain Omelette (No.1244) with $\frac{1}{4}$ lb. thinly-sliced kidneys, fried in a little English or Welsh butter. **Serves 2.**

263 MUSHROOM OMELETTE

Fill Plain Omelette (No.1244) with $\frac{1}{4}$ lb. sliced mushrooms lightly fried in a little English or Welsh butter. **Serves 2.**

ONION OMELETTE 1264

Fill Plain Omelette (No.1244) with $\frac{1}{4}$ lb. thinly-sliced onions, fried until pale gold in a little English or Welsh butter. **Serves 2.**

SPANISH OMELETTE 1265

1 large onion
1 large boiled potato
4 to 6 oz. tomatoes
2 oz. fresh red or green peppers or canned red peppers
1 oz. English or Welsh butter
2 teaspoons olive or corn oil
3 large or 4 standard eggs
2 teaspoons cold water
Seasoning to taste

1. Cut onion into very thin rings. **2.** Dice potato. Blanch, skin and chop tomatoes. Chop pepper. **3.** Put butter and oil into an 8 or 9-in. frying pan. When hot and sizzling, add onions and potato dice. **4.** Fry gently until both are pale gold, turning fairly often. Add tomatoes and peppers. Fry a further 2 to 3 minutes. **5.** Beat eggs lightly with water. Season to taste with salt and pepper then pour into pan over vegetables. **6.** Cook gently until base is firm. Stand below pre-heated hot grill. Leave 1 or 2 minutes (or until top is just set). **7.** Slide flat, unfolded Omelette on to warm platter. Cut into 2 portions. **8.** Serve straight away. **Serves 2.**

FLUFFY SAVOURY OMELETTE 1266

Yolks and whites of 3 large or 4 standard eggs
4 teaspoons water
Salt and pepper to taste
1 oz. English or Welsh butter

1. Beat egg yolks and water lightly together. Season to taste with salt and pepper. **2.** Beat egg whites to stiff, peaky snow. Gently fold egg yolks into them. **3.** Melt butter in large omelette pan. When hot and sizzling, pour in egg mixture. **4.** Cook, without moving, for 2 to $2\frac{1}{2}$ minutes or until base is set. Stand below pre-heated hot grill. Leave 2 to 3 minutes (or until top is well puffed and golden). **5.** Slide out on to warmed plate. Cut into 2 or 3 portions. Serve straight away. **Serves 2 to 3.**

SWEET OMELETTES

1267 SWEET SOUFFLÉ OMELETTE

Yolks and whites of 3 large or 4 standard eggs
1 oz. caster sugar
½ teaspoon vanilla essence
1 oz. English or Welsh butter
About 2 dessertspoons sifted icing sugar

1. Beat egg yolks with caster sugar and vanilla until very thick and pale in colour. **2.** Beat egg whites to stiff, peaky snow. Gently fold egg yolk mixture into them. **3.** Melt butter in large omelette pan. When hot and sizzling, pour in egg mixture. **4.** Cook without moving for 2 to 2½ minutes or until base is set. Stand below pre-heated hot grill. Leave 2 to 3 minutes (or until top is well puffed and golden). **5.** Remove from grill and turn out on to sheet of greaseproof paper dusted with icing sugar. **6.** Score line down centre, fold in half and serve at once. **Serves 4.**

1268 LEMON SOUFFLÉ OMELETTE

1. Follow recipe and method for Sweet Soufflé Omelette (No.1267). **2.** Add 1 level teaspoon finely-grated lemon peel to beaten yolks. **Serves 4.**

1269 ORANGE SOUFFLÉ OMELETTE

1. Follow recipe and method for Sweet Soufflé Omelette (No.1267). **2.** Add 1 level teaspoon finely-grated orange peel to beaten yolks. **Serves 4.**

1270 RASPBERRY SOUFFLÉ OMELETTE

1. Follow recipe and method for Sweet Soufflé Omelette (No.1267). **2.** After turning out on to sheet of greaseproof paper, score line down centre. **3.** Cover half with 3 level tablespoons warmed raspberry jam. **4.** Fold in half and serve at once. **Serves 4.**

APRICOT SOUFFLÉ OMELETTE 127

1. Follow recipe and method for Sweet Soufflé Omelette (No.1267). **2.** After turning out on to sheet of greaseproof paper, score line down centre. **3.** Cover half with 3 level tablespoons warmed apricot jam. **4.** Fold in half and serve at once. **Serves 4.**

STRAWBERRY SOUFFLÉ OMELETTE 127

1. Follow recipe and method for Sweet Soufflé Omelette (No.1267). **2.** After turning out on to sheet of greaseproof paper, score line down centre. **3.** Cover half with 2 to 3 oz. crushed strawberries mixed with a little orange juice or sweet sherry. **Serves 4.**

APPLE SOUFFLÉ OMELETTE 127

1. Follow recipe and method for Sweet Soufflé Omelette (No.1267). **2.** After turning out on to sheet of greaseproof paper, score line down centre. **3.** Cover half with 2 to 3 tablespoons warmed, sweetened apple purée flavoured with a little cinnamon. **Serves 4.**

●*For alternate method of serving, do not fold omelette but cut into 4 portions on sugared paper. Transfer to warm plates and spoon jam or fruit—where used—over each.*

Index

APPETISERS

Almonds, Buttered Savoury	5
Baby Burgers	42
Bacon & Mustard Puffs, Hot	11
Bacon & Prune Savouries	34
Brazils, Devilled	8
Cheese Aigrettes	17
Cheese & Caraway Seed Flakes	30
Cheese & Celery Balls	40
Cheese Fluffs, Hot	28
Cheese & Gherkin Balls	38
Cheese & Ham Balls	39
Cheese & Ham Puffs, Hot	10
Cheese & Olive Balls	37
Cheese Patties, Hot	1
Cheese & Pineapple Porcupine	36
Cheese & Poppy Seed Flakes	29
Cheese & Prawn Puffs	16
Cheese Savouries, Austrian	6
Cheese-Stuffed Celery	13
Cheese & Tomato Flakes	41
Cheese & Walnut Puffs	15
Chicken & Mushroom Puffs, Hot	9
Cream Cheese Sticks	2
Cucumbers, Stuffed	3
Cucumber Tartlets, Cold	33
Haddock & Parsley Puffs, Hot	12
Ham & Asparagus Rolls	18
Lancashire Rolls, Toasted	35
Mushroom Buttons	31
Mushroom Tartlets, Hot	32
Prawn-Stuffed Celery	14
Sausage Crisps, Hot	4
Walnuts, Curried	7

DIPS & DUNKS

Asparagus & Prawn	22
Cheddar Cheese & Celery	27
Cottage Cheese, Bacon & Onion	20
Cottage Cheese & Pineapple	26
Creamed Yogurt	21
Curried Cream Cheese	23
Leek	25
Mushroom & Ham	19
Onion	24

BATTERS

COATING & FRITTER BATTERS

Almond Fritter Batter	662
Curry Fritter Batter	667
Coating Batter	659
Cinnamon Fritter Batter	661
Mustard Fritter Batter	666
Orange or Lemon Fritter Batter	663
Savoury Fritter Batter	665
Spicy Fritter Batter	664
Sweet Fritter Batter	660

SAVOURY BATTER PUDDINGS

Bacon Batter Pudding	650
Corned Beef Batter Pudding	649
Meat Ball Batter Pudding	651
Toad-in-the-Hole	652

SWEET BATTER PUDDINGS

Apple Batter Pudding	653
Dried Fruit Batter Pudding	655
Fruit Popovers	658
Plum Batter Pudding	656
Popovers	657
Rhubarb Batter Pudding	654

PANCAKES

Pancake Batter	615
Pancakes	616

SAVOURY PANCAKES

American Pancakes	647
Bacon & Parsley Pancakes	645
Brittany Pancakes	634
Country Pancakes	635
Creamed Chicken Pancakes	637
Creamed Smoked Haddock Pancakes	636
Ham & Cheese Pancakes	644
Kidney Pancakes	638
Miniature Party Pancakes	639
Party Pancake Kebabs	640
Prawn & Lemon Pancakes	643
Small Yorkshire Pudding	642
Toreador Pancakes	648
Tuna & Cucumber Pancakes	646
Yorkshire Pudding	641

SWEET PANCAKES

Banana Cream Pancakes	619
Coconut & Apricot Pancakes	625
Cottage Cheese & Banana Blintzes	630
Cottage Cheese Blintzes	627
Cottage Cheese & Peach Blintzes	631
Cottage Cheese & Pineapple Pancakes	624
Cottage Cheese & Raisin Blintzes	628
Cottage Cheese & Strawberry Blintzes	629
Crêpes Suzettes	632
Golden Syrup & Orange Pancakes	622
Lemon & Apricot Pancakes	617
Lemon or Orange Pancakes	620
Mandarin Cream Pancakes	623
Mock Crêpes Suzettes	633
Party Layer Pancakes	626
Raspberry or Strawberry Pancakes	621
Spiced Apple Pancakes	618

BEEF

Beef Casserole	315
Beef Crumble	320
Beef Curry	331
Beef Stroganoff	332
Boiled Silverside & Carrots	321
Fried Steak & Onions	336
Grilled Steak	333
Grilled Steak Au Poivre	335
Grilled Tournedo Steak	334
Hamburgers	329
Meat Balls in Tomato Sauce	330
Meat & Vegetable Pasties	328
Pot Roasted Beef	313
Roast Beef	312
Sea Pie	316
Steak Pie, Deep Dish	326
Steak, Kidney & Oyster Pudding	323
Steak & Kidney Pie, Quick-Baking	325
Steak & Kidney Plate Pie	324
Steak & Kidney Pudding	322
Steak & Mushroom Pie, Deep Dish	327
Stewed Beef	314
Stewed Beef with Beer	318
Stewed Beef with Dumplings	317
Stewed Beef with Tomato	319

BISCUITS

Almond Biscuits	694
Almond Macaroons	724
Almond Shortbread Biscuits	706
Brandy Snaps	707
Butter Digestive Biscuits	726
Butter Whirls	717
Cherry Biscuits	697

Chocolate Cherry Cookies 722
Chocolate Drops 703
Chocolate Flake Biscuits 700
Chocolate Refrigerator
  Biscuits 710
Cinnamon or Spice Biscuits 698
Coconut Biscuits 699
Coconut Refrigerator
  Biscuits 714
Coffee Walnut Cookies 720
Currant Biscuits 696
Date Cookies 723
Flapjacks 718
Florentines 708
Ginger Nuts 721
Ginger Refrigerator Biscuits 713
Ginger Snaps 719
Jam Sandwich Biscuits 701
Nut Refrigerator Biscuits 711
Orange or Lemon Biscuits 695
Orange or Lemon Refrigerator
  Biscuits 715
Orange or Lemon
  Shortbread 705
Peanut Crisps 725
Plain Biscuits 692
Raisin Refrigerator Biscuits 716
Rich Shortbread 704
Spice or Cinnamon
  Biscuits 698
Spicy Refrigerator Biscuits 712
Sugar-Topped Biscuits 702
Treacle Bites 727
Vanilla Refrigerator Biscuits 709
Walnut Biscuits 693

CAKES, LARGE &
SMALL
Almond & Raisin Cake 768
Almond Slices 788
Butterfly Cakes 746
Cheese Cake 802
Cherry Cake 796
Cherry Cakes 784
Cherry & Ginger Cake 777
Chocolate Cakes 787
Chocolate Chip Cakes 737
Chocolate Cream Puffs 800
Christmas Cake, Iced 781
Coconut Cake 764
Coconut & Lemon Cake 778
Coffee Hazelnut Ring 794
Cream Horns 795
Cream Slices 801
Currant Cake 765
Date & Lemon Cakes 783
Date & Walnut Cake 774
Dundee Cake 762
Eccles Cakes 790

Éclairs
  Chocolate 798
  Coffee 799
Fairy Cakes 736
Family Fruit Cake 773
Farmhouse Cake 776
Gâteaux
  Caramel & Almond 757
  Chocolate Walnut 780
  Coffee Hazelnut 756
Genoa Cake 770
Genoese Cake 739
Genoese Pastries 772
Genoese Slab 769
Gingerbread 797
Ginger Cake 763
Layer Cakes
  Chocolate 740
  Lime & Chocolate 741
  Mocha 742
Lemon & Almond Ring 793
Madeira Cake 759
Madeleines 748
Marmalade Cake 791
Marmalade & Walnut Cake 792
Orange Cake 760
Parkin 789
Plain Family Cake 779
Rich Butter Cake 758
Rich Fruit Cake 771
Rock Cakes 782
Sandwiches
  Chocolate 735
  Fresh Fruit 743
  Genoese 738
  Jam 729
  Jam & Cream 730
  Lemon 731
  Mixed Fruit 744
  Orange 732
  Pineapple 733
  Victoria 728
  Walnut Coffee 734
Seed Cake 767
Small Iced Cakes 747
Small Seed Cakes 745
Spice & Raisin Cakes 786
Sponge Cake, Deep 750
Sponge Sandwich 749
Sponge Sandwich, Jam 751
Sponge Sandwich,
  Jam & Cream 752
Sultana Cake 766
Sultana & Orange Cake 775
Swiss Roll 753
Swiss Roll, Chocolate 754
Swiss Roll, Cream-Filled 755
Walnut Cake, Frosted 761
Walnut & Orange Cakes 785

CHICKEN
Blanquette of Chicken 39
Buttered Roast Chicken 38
Chicken With Almonds 39
Chicken Cacciatore 40
Chicken Maryland 39
Chicken & Parsley Casserole 39
Chicken Pie 39
Coq Au Vin 39
Curry of Chicken 40
Devilled Chicken 39
French-Style Roast Chicken 38
Fricassée of Chicken 39
Fried Chicken 39
Grilled Chicken 39
Roast Stuffed Chicken 38

CONFECTIONERY
Butterscotch 115
Chocolate Coconut Ice 115
Coconut Ice 114
Coffee Creams 114
Fudge
  Cherry 113
  Chocolate 113
  Coconut 113
  Fruit & Nut 113
  Marshmallow Almond 114
  Marshmallow Raisin 114
  Milk 113
  Uncooked Chocolate
    Cream 113
  Uncooked Mocha
    Cream 113
  Walnut 113
Honeycomb 115
Peppermint Wafers 114
Toffee
  Everton 115
  Nut 115
  Syrup 115
Truffles
  Chocolate Cream 114
  Chocolate Orange 114
  Chocolate Rum 114
  Chocolate Sherry 114
  Chocolate Whisky 114

DESSERTS, FROZEN
Baked Alaska (Omelette
  Soufflé Surprise) 101
Banana Splits 100
Cantaloupe Cups 102
Chocolate Cream Ice, Rich 100
Crunch Flan, Frozen 102
Crush Fruit Ice Cream 100
Dairy Cream Ice 98

airy Cream Ice
Almond	985
Apricot	1000
Chocolate	990
Chocolate Brandy	991
Chocolate Chip	988
Chocolate Hazelnut	992
Chocolate Rum	993
Coffee	986
Lemon	996
Maraschino	994
Orange	995
Peach	999
Pistachio	987
Praline	998
Preserved Ginger	989
Strawberry or Raspberry	1002
Tutti-Frutti	1001
rench Custard Dairy Ice	1004
rench Custard Ice Cream	1003
e Cream Gâteau	1009
alian Cream Ice	1006
emon Cream Snow	997
lidsummer Glories	1014
lousse, Raspberry, Frozen	1010
lousse, Strawberry,	
Frozen	1011
melette Soufflé Surprise	1019
(Baked Alaska)	1012
each Melba	1024
orbet, Tangy Fruit	1013
undaes	
Cherry Cream	1019
Chestnut Cream	1021
Coffee Cream	1018
Fruit Cocktail &	
Strawberry	1015
Mandarin & Lemon	1016
Pineapple & Coffee	1022
Pineapple & Lemon	1017
Pineapple & Strawberry	1020
Redcurrant	1023
utti-Frutti Basket	1027

DISHES FROM ABROAD
CANADA
aked Halibut Royal	1035

DENMARK
ornholm Herrings	1042

FRANCE
ipérade	1041
uiche Lorraine	1040

GERMANY
Sweet-Sour Red Cabbage	1034

GREECE
Moussaka	1037

HOLLAND
Buttercake	1036

ITALY
Gnocchi	1028
Pizza with Mushrooms	
& Ham	1033
Pizza Neapolitan	1032
Risotto Milanese	1029
Spaghetti Bolognese	1030
Spaghetti Neapolitan	1031

MEXICO
Chilli Con Carne	1039

SPAIN
Paella	1038

SWITZERLAND
Muselli or Swiss Breakfast	1043

DRINKS, HOT & COLD
COLD DRINKS
Apricot Crush	1160
Banana Rose Hip Shake	1171
Chocolate Cream, Chilled	1166
Chocolate Ginger Frappé	1163
Chocolate Peppermint	
Sizzlers	1162
Chocolate Shake	1168
Iced Coffee	1173
Malted Honey Whip	1165
Milk & Orange Nog	1164
Milk Shake Float	1175
Minted Orange Cups	1161
Mocha Cream, Chilled	1167
Mocha Shake	1169
Raspberry Crush	1158
Rose Hip Shake	1170
Silk on the Rocks	1176
Strawberry Crush	1159
Tropical Fruit Shake	1172
Viennese Coffee	1174
Yogurt Fruit Cup	1156
Yogurt Strawberry Cooler	1157

HOT DRINKS
Almond Flip	1184
Chocolate Cups, Dutch	1193
Chocolate, Jamaican	1185

Chocolate Marshmallow
Floats	1177
Coffee Foam	1195
Coffee	
French	1189
Irish	1186
Jamaican	1190
Russian	1188
Scotch	1187
Spanish	1191
Milk Posset	1192
Milk, Spiced	1194
Milk, Winter Punch	1183
Mocha Marshmallow	
Floats	1178
Nogs	
Brandy, Sherry or Rum	1180
Chocolate Cream	1182
Egg & Milk	1179
Orange or Lemon	1181

DUCKLING & GOOSE
Duck & Ham Loaf	410
Duckling & Apple Casserole	407
Duckling & Celery	
Casserole	408
Duckling or Goose with	
Apples & Prunes	404
Duckling or Goose	
Bigarrade	403
Duckling with Orange	
Sauce	405
Duckling with Pineapple	
& Cherries	406
Duckling Provençale-Style	409
Roast Duckling or Goose	402

FILLINGS & FROSTINGS
Almond Paste	832
Almond Butter Cream	811
American Boiled Frosting	818
Basic Butter Cream	809
Caramel Cream	814
Chocolate Butter Cream	816
Coffee Butter Cream	815
Coffee Cream	821
Coffee Fudge	817
Coffee Velvet	808
Grapefruit Velvet	807
Lemon Butter Cream	812
Lemon Velvet	804
Lime Velvet	805
Orange Butter Cream	813
Orange Velvet	803
Pineapple Velvet	806
Vanilla Butter Cream	810

Vanilla Cream	822
Whipped Cream	819
Whipped Cream with Nuts	820
Whipped Cream with Rum, Sherry or Brandy	823

Icings

Glacé Icing	824
Glacé Icing, Cocoa	831
Glacé Icing, Coffee	826
Glacé Icing, Chocolate	829
Glacé Icing, Mocha	830
Glacé Icing, Orange or Lemon	825
Royal Icing	827
Royal Icing for Piping	828

FISH

Cod Cutlets, Stuffed, Baked	259
Cod, Danish-Style	257
Cod with Orange & Walnuts	258
Fish Fritters	260
Fish Quenelles	256
Fried Fish	268
Haddock, Baked, with Cream	254
Haddock, Cheese-Baked	252
Haddock Fillet, Stuffed, Baked	255
Haddock, Savoury Casserole	251
Hake, Scalloped	267
Halibut au Gratin	264
Halibut, Creamed	266
Herring or Mackerel, Baked, Foil-Wrapped	244
Herrings, Fried	245
Herrings, Fried Scots-Style	247
Herrings, Soused	242
Herrings, Soused, with Cider	243
Kedgeree	248
Kippers, Jugged	249
Mackerel, Fried	246
Mackerel or Herring, Baked, Foil-Wrapped	244
Plaice, Buttered, with Bananas	272
Plaice, Grilled Whole	273
Plaice Portuguese	271
Plaice with Stilton Sauce	274
Salmon Fish Cakes	263
Skate, Lemon Buttered	261
Skate with Cider Sauce	262
Smoked Haddock Florentine	250
Sole, Grecian	269
Sole, Grilled	275
Sole with Cucumber Sauce	270
Trout with Almonds	253

Turbot au Gratin	265
Whiting, Crumbed, Meunière	276
Whiting, Normandy	277

GAME

Game, Curried	439
Game Pie, Raised	424
Grouse, Roast	435
Grouse, Salmi of	438
Hare, Jugged	432
Partridge, Roast	434
Partridge, Salmi of	437
Pheasant, Roast	433
Pheasant, Salmi of	436
Pigeons in Cream Sauce	426
Pigeons, Roast	427
Pigeons, Stewed	428
Rabbit Casserole, Milky	429
Rabbit, Fricassée of	431
Rabbit, Roast	430
Wild Duck, Grilled	425

HORS-D'ŒUVRES

Asparagus Mousse	232
Avocado Creams	239
Avocados, Cream-Filled	216
Avocados with Shellfish	218
Avocados with Yogurt	217
Buckling, Buttered	204
Cheese Cups, Hot	205
Crab Cocktail	234
Curried Egg & Shrimp Cocktail	208
Egg Mayonnaise	214
Egg & Smoked Salmon Mayonnaise	215
Eggs, Cream Cheese-Filled	209
Eggs, Stilton-Filled	206
Grapefruits, Grilled	223
Kipper Creams, Individual	207
Mushroom Cocktail	235
Mushrooms, Stuffed	241
Pâté	
Chicken & Bacon	231
French Country-Style	240
Liver Sausage	203
Pickled Mushrooms, Creamed	230
Potted Beef	213
Potted Ham	212
Potted Tongue	211
Prawn Cocktail	224
Salmon Mousse	233
Sole Fritters, Hot	210
Spaghetti Creams, Cold	238
Steak Tartare	237

Tomatoes, Stuffed	
Cheese	2?
Ham	2?
Lamb	2?
Onion	2?
Prawn	2?
Tuna Cocktail	2?
Vol-au-Vent, Large	2?
Vol-au-Vents	
Chicken & Mushroom	21
Ham & Mushroom	2?
Prawn	2?

LAMB & MUTTON

Blanquette of Lamb	3?
Boiled Mutton with Caper Sauce	3?
Braised Shoulder of Mutton or Lamb	3?
Cottage (or Shepherd's) Pie	3?
Crown Roast of Lamb	2?
Golden Creamed Lamb	3?
Grilled Lamb Chops	3?
Grilled Lamb Cutlets	3?
Irish Stew	3?
Lamb Curry	3?
Lamb Kebabs	3?
Lamb & Mushroom Hot Pot	2?
Lamb Stew	3?
Lancashire Hot Pot	2?
Mixed Grill	3?
Roast Lamb	2?
Roast Mutton	2?
Shepherd's (or Cottage) Pie	3?

LUNCH & SUPPER DISHES

Cheese & Crab Ramekins	111
Cheese, Egg & Noodle Ring	11?
Cheese & Ham Buns	10?
Cheese & Ham Pudding	10?
Cheese & Parsley Pudding	10?
Cheese & Prawn Buns	11?
Cheese & Raisin Buns	10?
Cheese Roll Puffs	11?
Cheese & Sausage Pie	10?
Cheese & Sultana Pie	10?
Cheese & Walnut Buns	10?
Corned Beef Pie	10?
Corned Beef & Vegetable Tarts	10?
Creamed Corn & Ham Scramble	11?
Creamed Roes on Toast	11?
Flaky Cheese & Onion Pasties	10?

acaroni Cheese 1107
acaroni Cheese with
 Bacon 1108
acaroni Cheese with
 Smoked Haddock 1109
Ichards Au Gratin 1096
arebit
 Bacon 1103
 Buck 1102
 Tomato 1104
 Welsh 1101
avoury Cheese & Onion
 Casserole 1088

MARINADES & SAVOURY BUTTERS
MARINADES
eer Marinade 182
hicken Marinade 185
ery Marinade 183
emon Marinade 179
pice Marinade 180
weet-Sour Marinade 181
Vine Marinade 184
ogurt Marinade 178

SAVOURY BUTTERS
nchovy Butter 194
hive Butter 196
urry Butter 195
evilled Butter 186
arlic Butter 187
reen Butter 188
am Butter 191
erring Roe Butter 192
orseradish Butter 198
emon Butter 197
Maître D'Hôtel Butter 190
Mustard Butter 199
aprika Butter 200
rawn Butter 201
moked Cod's Roe Butter 189
omato Butter 202
una Butter 193

MERINGUES
Almond Coffee Kisses 604
asic Meringues 601
Chocolate Cream Meringues 607
Coconut Pyramids 612
Coffee Meringues 602
Cream Meringues 606
ruit & Cream Pavlovas 611
Golden Coconut Pyramids 614
Hazelnut Meringues 603
Lemon or Orange
 Meringues 605

Meringue Basket 613
Meringue Topping 610
Raspberry or Strawberry
 Cream Meringues 608
Walnut Chocolate Fingers 609

OFFAL
Brain Sauté 381
Hearts, Stuffed, Baked 378
Kidneys, Devilled 373
Kidneys en Brochette 375
Kidneys Espagnole 374
Liver, Braised 385
Liver, Creamed 382
Liver, Fried, Creamed 384
Liver, Grilled 383
Oxtail, Stewed 386
Sweetbreads, Crumbed &
 Fried 380
Sweetbreads, Poached,
 in Cream Sauce 379
Tongue with Madeira Sauce 377
Tongue with Mustard Sauce 376
Tripe, Buttered, with Cheese 371
Tripe & Onions 370
Tripe, Savoury, Fried 372

OMELETTES
SAVOURY OMELETTES
Fluffy Savoury Omelette 1266
Spanish Omelette 1265

Unfilled Plain or French Omelettes
Plain or French Omelette 1244
Bacon, Mushroom & Onion
 Omelette 1245
Cheese Omelette 1248
Chive Omelette 1249
Croûton & Parsley
 Omelette 1250
Fried Onion Omelette 1253
Ham & Potato Omelette 1252
Leek & Mushroom
 Omelette 1246
Parsley Omelette 1251
Tarragon Omelette 1247
Watercress Omelette 1254

Filled French or Plain Omelettes
Asparagus Omelette 1255
Bacon Omelette 1256
Chicken Omelette 1258
Crab Omelette 1260
Croûton Omelette 1257

Ham Omelette 1261
Kidney Omelette 1262
Mushroom Omelette 1263
Onion Omelette 1264
Tomato Omelette 1259

SWEET OMELETTES
Apple Soufflé Omelette 1273
Apricot Soufflé Omelette 1271
Lemon Soufflé Omelette 1268
Orange Soufflé Omelette 1269
Raspberry Soufflé
 Omelette 1270
Strawberry Soufflé
 Omelette 1272
Sweet Soufflé Omelette 1267

PASTRY
Cheese Pastry 93
Choux Pastry 102
Cream Cheese Pastry 101
Flaky Pastry 99
Hot Water Crust Pastry 95
Lemon Pastry 92
Milk 'Puff' Pastry 100
Nut Pastry 90
Poppy Seed Pastry 91
Puff Pastry 96
Rich Short Crust Pastry 89
Rough Puff Pastry 94
Short Crust Pastry 88
Suet Crust Pastry 97
Sweet Flan Pastry 98

PORK
Baked Gammon Steak with
 Apples 346
Baked Pork Créole 353
Boiled Spare Ribs 354
Braised Pork Chops 352
Chinese-Style Fried Pork 341
Devilled Pork Sausages 349
Grilled Gammon Maryland 344
Grilled Gammon with Mustard
 or Devilled Butter 343
Grilled Gammon with
 Tomato Butter 342
Party Gammon 347
Pork with Cheese & Beer 345
Pork with Fried Peaches 339
Pork with Fried Pineapple 340
Pork Loaf 355
Pork Patties 351
Pork Pie 350
Pork & Pineapple Curry 338
Roast Pork 337
Steamed Bacon Pudding 348

PRESERVES (Jams, Marmalades & Curds)

Apple & Blackberry Jam	1209
Blackcurrant Jam	1196
Damson Jam	1198
Dried Apricot Jam	1200
Gooseberry Jam	1197
Gooseberry & Redcurrant Jam	1212
Grapefruit & Orange Marmalade	1216
Greengage Jam	1202
Lemon Curd	1207
Loganberry Jam	1204
Marrow & Ginger Jam	1206
Mixed Fruit Jam	1213
Orange Curd	1208
Orange Marmalade, Sweet	1215
Orange Marmalade, Thick	1214
Plum Jam	1201
Raspberry Jam	1203
Raspberry & Loganberry Jam	1205
Raspberry & Redcurrant Jam	1210
Raspberry & Rhubarb Jam	1211
Strawberry Jam	1199

PUDDINGS, COLD

Apple Whip, Spiced	866
Apricot Sherbet	871
Banana Snow	909
Blancmange	875
Blancmanges	
Coffee	878
Extra Creamy	880
Honey	879
Lemon	876
Orange	877
Charlotte Mocha	895
Chocolate Apricot Trifle	896
Crème Brulée (Burnt Cream)	890
Crème Café	885
Crème Caramel	891
Crème Monte Carlo	897
Crème Orange	886
Crèmes Caramel, Small	892
Flans	
Almond & Apricot	916
Berry	898
Chocolate Hazelnut	917
Fresh Grape	900
Glazed Apple	901
Peach or Apricot	899
Fruit Fools	
Custard	857
Custard Cream	856
Rich	855

Gâteau St. Honoré	918
Gooseberry Whip	854
Junket	881
Junkets	
Coffee	884
Fresh Lemon	882
Fresh Orange	883
Lemon Meringue Pie	905
Meringue Baskets	
Fruit Salad	904
Loganberry	902
Strawberry or Raspberry	903
Milk Jellies	
Chocolate	862
Coffee	863
Lemon	860
Orange	861
Vanilla	864
Moulds	
Basic Cream	910
Basic Fruit & Cream	914
Cherry Cream	913
Chocolate Cream	912
Coffee Cream	911
Frosted Fruit	859
Lemon Honeycomb	888
Orange Honeycomb	889
Vanilla Honeycomb	887
Mousse, Raspberry	920
Mousse, Strawberry	919
Oeufs à la Neige (Snow Eggs)	908
Orange Chiffon Pie	921
Orange Snow Creams	869
Orange & Strawberry Chantilly	853
Peach Condé	907
Peach Sherbet	870
Peaches Mistral	865
Pear Condé	906
Pineapple Romanoff	867
Pots-au-Chocolat	872
Pots-au-Chocolat with Coffee	873
Pots-au-Chocolat with Sherry, Brandy or Rum	874
Profiteroles	915
Raspberry Cream Ring	868
Strawberry Choux Ring	893
Summer Pudding	858
Syllabub	922
Trifle Alexandra	894

PUDDINGS, HOT

Apple Amber	983
Apple & Blackberry Turnovers	979

Apple Charlotte	94
Apple Dumplings, Baked	95
Apple Fritters	9
Apple (or Eve's) Pudding	96
Apple Turnovers	9
Apples Baked with Syrup & Lemon	9
Baked Jam Roll	98
Banana Sponge, Baked	96
Barley Pudding, Baked	93
Barley Pudding Variations: see Rice	
Bread & Butter Pudding	93
Cabinet Pudding	93
Chocolate Pudding	94
Chocolate Sponge Pudding	95
Christmas Pudding	96
Coconut Pudding	94
Coffee Fudge Cream Pie	95
College Pudding	96
Custard Tart	98
Date & Walnut Pudding	94
Egg Custards	
Baked	94
Coconut	94
Lemon	94
Orange	94
Eve's (or Apple) Pudding	96
Fair Lady Pudding	96
Four-Fruit Pudding	96
Fruit Crumble	95
Fruit (Fresh) Suet Pudding	95
Fruit Pie	95
Fruit Pie Double Crust	95
Fruit Sponge Pudding	95
Jam Sponge Pudding	95
Jam Tart	97
Macaroni Pudding, Baked	93
Macaroni Pudding Variations: see Rice	
Marmalade Pudding	96
Mince Pies	98
Mince Tart	97
Pineapple & Lemon Upside-Down Pudding	95
Plain Family Pudding	94
Queen of Puddings	97
Rice Pudding, Baked	93
Rice Puddings (or Barley, Tapioca or Macaroni)	
Chocolate	93
Fruit	93
Lemon	93
Orange	93
Vanilla	93
Roly-Poly Pudding	97
Sago Pudding	92
Sago Puddings	
Chocolate	92

Fruit 929
Lemon 926
Orange 927
molina Pudding 924
molina Pudding Variations:
see Sago
onge Pudding 949
otted Dick 966
et Pudding, Steamed 960
rup or Treacle Pudding 965
rup Tart 974
pioca Pudding, Baked 933
pioca Pudding Variations:
see Rice
eacle Tart 973

ALADS
AIN COURSE SALADS
eese Platter 536
ttage Cheese & Peach 547
ttage Cheese Summer
Salad 538
g & Sardine 540
glish Cheddar Cheese
& Apple 546
m, Cheese & Cabbage
Toss 544
rring 539
awn & Pineapple 543
inach & Cottage Cheese 541
edish Sausage Salad 545
eet Corn & Chicken 535
ngue & Cucumber 537
na & Bacon 542

DE SALADS
ple & Walnut 528
ssels Sprouts & Celery 530
eamed Avocado Salad
Slices 527
eamed Cabbage &
Caraway 526
cumber 523
essed Green Salad 519
een Bean 524
een Pepper & Onion 533
tato Cream Salad 522
ssian Salad 531
ffed Pepper 529
rian Salad 534
mato & Onion 520
mato & Parsley 521
picana Salad 532
nter Cole Slaw 525

SALAD DRESSINGS
Banana 572
Basic Cream Cheese
Dressing 562
Basic Soured Cream
Dressing 548
Basic Yogurt Dressing 566
Blue Stilton Dressing 599
Butter Dressing 594
Cottage Cheese & Mint 575
Cottage Cheese Salad
Dressing 574
Cream Cheese & Apricot 573
Cream Cheese & Celery 563
Cream Cheese & Garlic 564
Cream Cheese & Nut 561
Cream Cheese & Onion 565
Creamed Onion Dressing 593
Curry Yogurt Dressing 569
Dairy Salad Dressing 560
Egg, Anchovy & Yogurt 568
Fluffy Whipped Cream
Dressing 596
French Dressing 598
Fruity Yogurt Dressing 571
Mixed Cheese Dressing 576
Piquant Yogurt Dressing 570
Ravigotte 600
Soured Cream Dressings
With Chives 549
With Cucumber 553
With Dates 559
With Horseradish 552
With Lemon 555
With Mustard 551
With Nuts 557
With Paprika 556
With Parsley 550
With Stilton 558
With Tomato 554
Tomato Yogurt Dressing 592
Watercress & Yogurt
Dressing 567
Whipped Cream Dressing 595
Whipped Cream Horseradish
Dressing 597

MAYONNAISE
Aioli Mayonnaise 578
Camilla Mayonnaise 579
Chantilly Mayonnaise 581
Curry Mayonnaise 582
Green Dragon Mayonnaise 580
Louis Mayonnaise 583
Mayonnaise 577
Rémoulade Mayonnaise 584
Russian Mayonnaise 585
Spanish Mayonnaise 587
Swedish Mayonnaise 588

Tartare Mayonnaise 589
Thousand Island
Mayonnaise 586
Tivoli Mayonnaise 591
Verte Mayonnaise 590

SANDWICHES & SANDWICH FILLINGS
BASIC SANDWICHES
Afternoon Tea
Sandwiches 1058
Asparagus Rolls 1062
Avocado & Onion 1061
Bacon & Banana 1054
Cheese, Apple & Leek 1044
Cheese & Celery 1049
Cheese, Onion & Tomato 1052
Cream Cheese, Gherkin &
Tomato 1053
Cress, Cheese & Carrot 1045
Egg & Creamed Salad 1065
Fried Sandwiches 1064
Lettuce, Beef &
Horseradish 1046
Lettuce, Cheese & Walnut 1060
Lettuce, Cottage Cheese &
Pineapple 1048
Pin Wheel Sandwiches 1059
Pork & Apple 1051
Salmon & Lettuce 1057
Smoked Roe & Cucumber 1055
Stilton, Lettuce & Ham 1050
Tomato, Cress & Sardine 1056
Tongue & Cucumber 1063
Watercress & Creamed
Fish 1047

CLUB SANDWICHES
Egg & Cheese 1086
Ham 1087
Hawaiian 1084
Sausage & Chutney 1085

DANISH-STYLE OPEN SANDWICHES
Boiled Beef & Carrot 1068
Caviare, Egg Yolk & Onion 1074
Cheese & Date 1079
Cheese & Leek 1077
Cheese, Peach & Olive 1078
Egg & Tomato 1067
Ham, Cheese & Pineapple 1072
Lettuce & Tongue 1073
Liver Sausage & Potato
Salad 1070
Pork & Orange 1075
Prawn & Mayonnaise 1066

Rolimop & Yogurt 1069
Salami & Cheese 1076
Scrambled Egg & Salmon 1071

TOASTED SANDWICHES
Toasted Bacon &
  Mushroom 1081
Toasted Beef & Tomato 1080
Toasted Cheese & Pickle 1082
Toasted Egg & Haddock 1083

SAUCES
BARBECUE SAUCES
Meat Barbecue Sauce 152
Mild Barbecue Sauce 153
Poultry Barbecue Sauce 154

SAVOURY BUTTER SAUCES
Black Butter Sauce 149
Black Butter Sauce with
  Capers 150
Brown Butter Sauce 148
Lemon Butter Sauce 151

SAVOURY SAUCES
Basic White Coating Sauce 106
Basic White Pouring Sauce 105
Simple White Coating Sauce 104
Simple White Pouring
  Sauce 103
Allemande Sauce 129
Anchovy Sauce 114
Apple Sauce 146
Aurore Sauce 119
Béarnaise Sauce 126
Béchamel (or Rich White
  Sauce) 110
Bigarrade Sauce 133
Bread Sauce 139
Brown Onion Sauce 134
Brown (or Espagnole)
  Sauce 130
Caper Sauce 115
Chaud-Froid Sauce 120
Cheese Sauce 116
Cranberry Sauce 145
Cucumber Sauce 121
Cumberland Sauce 140
Curry Sauce 141
Egg Sauce 117
Espagnole (or Brown)
  Sauce 130
Hollandaise Sauce 131
Horseradish Sauce, Hot 122
Lemon Sauce 111
Madeira Sauce 135

Maître D'Hôtel Sauce 112
Meat or Poultry Gravy 147
Mint Sauce 143
Mock Hollandaise Sauce 124
Mornay Sauce 123
Mousseline Sauce 132
Mushroom Sauce 113
Mustard Sauce 118
Onion Sauce 108
Parsley Sauce 107
Pepper Sauce 136
Piquant Sauce 138
Prawn or Shrimp Sauce 109
Quick Cream Sauce 142
Réforme Sauce 137
Rich White Sauce
  (or Béchamel) 110
Suprème Sauce 128
Tartare Sauce, Hot 125
Tomato Sauce 144
Velouté Sauce 127

SWEET SAUCES
Apricot Jam Sauce 159
Brandy Hard Sauce 167
Brandy Sauce 163
Butterscotch Sauce 165
Butterscotch Sauce, Orange
  or Lemon 166
Chocolate Sauce 177
Chocolate Sauce, Quick 176
Chocolate Custard Sauce 173
Coffee Cream Sauce 169
Coffee Custard Sauce 172
Coffee Fudge Sauce 157
Custard Sauce 171
Fudge Sauce 155
Golden Syrup Sauce 164
Lemon Custard Sauce 174
Marmalade Sauce 160
Orange Custard Sauce 175
Red Jam Sauce 158
Rum or Brandy Fudge
  Sauce 156
Rum Hard Sauce 168
Sweet White Sauce 161
Vanilla Sauce 162
Whipped Sherry Sauce 170

SHELLFISH
CRABS
Crab Newburg 280
Crab Tartare 279
Devilled Crab 278

LOBSTERS
Lobster Newburg 281

Lobster Thermidor 2

MUSSELS
Moules Marinière 2

OYSTERS
Angels On Horseback 2
Butter-Fried Oysters 2
Oysters in Cream Sauce 2

SCALLOPS
Creamed Scallops 2
Crumbed & Fried Scallops 2
Fried Scallops 2

SCAMPI & PRAWNS
Creamed Scampi with
  Lemon 2
Creamed Scampi with Wine 2
Curried Prawns 2
Fried Scampi 2
Prawns in Soured Cream
  Sauce 2

SCONE MIXTURES
All-Purpose Scones 6
Buttermilk Scones 6
Cheese Scones 6
Cinnamon Scones 6
Currant Scones 6
Date & Walnut Scones 6
Dropped Scones 6
Dropped Scones with Ham 6
Dropped Scones with Spice 6
Ham & Parsley Scones 6
Lemon & Raisin Scones 6
Orange & Cherry Scones 6
Raspberry Shortcakes 6
Ring Doughnuts 6
Soured Cream Scones 6
Spice Scones 6
Strawberry Shortcakes 6
Sugar & Spice Rings 6
Sultana Scones 6
Syrup or Ginger Scones 6
Syrup or Honey Scones 6
Tea Scones 6
Wholemeal Scones 6
Yogurt Scones 6

SOUFFLÉS
COLD SWEET SOUFFLÉS
Chocolate 12
Coffee 12
Lemon 12
Loganberry 12

ocha 1221
ange 1218
spberry 1223
awberry 1222

T SAVOURY SOUFFLÉS
paragus 1238
con 1235
eese 1234
ab 1236
m 1237
shroom 1239
ion 1240
oked Haddock 1242
gue 1241
key 1243

T SWEET SOUFFLÉS
mond 1226
ricot 1227
nana 1228
ocolate 1229
ffee 1230
ange or Lemon 1231
eapple 1233
illa 1225
lnut or Hazelnut 1232

UPS & SOUP RNISHES
ichoke, Cream of 49
ef Broth 63
rtsch (Russian Beet
Soup), Cold 69
rtsch (Russian Beet
Soup), Hot 68
bage Soup 47
rot Soup, Creamy 61
uliflower, Cream of 50
eese & Onion Soup 51
eese & Tomato Soup 52
eese & Vegetable Soup 56
icken Soup 57
ck-a-Leekie Soup 58
cumber & Yogurt Soup,
ced 67
rried Chicken Soup 71
h Soup 45
til, Cream of 55
er and Bacon Soup 44
rrow, Cream of 54
nestrone 43
lligatawny Soup 59
ion Soup, French 46
ion Velouté Soup 64
ster Soup 73
prika Beef Soup 53
ato, Cream of 48

Scotch Broth, Creamed 60
Split Pea & Ham Soup 70
Tomato Consommé, Jellied 65
Tomato Soup, Clear 66
Vegetable Broth 62
Vichyssoise 72

STUFFINGS
Apple & Walnut 80
Bacon 76
Celery & Tomato 75
Chestnut Cream 82
Ham & Pineapple 86
Lemon, Parsley & Thyme 74
Liver & Onion 77
Mushroom & Lemon 78
Orange & Parsley 81
Pork Sausage 84
Prawn 85
Sage & Onion 79
Savoury Rice 87
Sweetcorn & Onion 83

TURKEY
Cheese & Turkey Flan 417
Creamed Turkey & Bacon
Toasts 423
Creamed Turkey &
Mushroom Toasts 412
Creamed Turkey Toasts 422
Roast Turkey 411
Turkey à la King 418
Turkey & Almond Loaf 421
Turkey Flan 416
Turkey Fritters 414
Turkey Loaf 420
Turkey in Paprika 413
Turkey Pilaf 419
Turkey & Walnut Fritters 415

VEAL
Blanquette of Veal 364
Escalopes in Lemon Sauce 369
Escalopes with Yogurt
Sauce 368
Fricassée of Veal 363
Italian Veal 358
Pot Roasted Veal Breast 362
Roast Veal 360
Swiss Veal 359
Veal Casserole with Cream 365
Veal & Egg Pie 366
Veal Goulash 367
Veal Marengo 361
Wiener Schnitzel 356
Wiener Schnitzel Holstein 357

VEGETABLES
Artichokes Mornay 481
Asparagus, Poached 467
Aubergine, Fried 472
Aubergines, Stuffed 473
Beans
  Broad, Creamed 479
  Green, Chinese-Style 480
  Green, Creamed 478
  Haricot, with Tomatoes 477
Beetroots in Yogurt 483
Broccoli Allemande 486
Brussels Sprouts, Crumbed 484
Brussels Sprouts with
  Chestnuts 485
Cabbage
  Baked, with Cream 471
  Crisp Boiled 468
  Savoury 469
  Sweet-Sour White 470
Carrots, Buttered, Baked 474
Carrots in Parsley Sauce 476
Carrots, Vichy 475
Cauliflower Sauté 488
Cauliflower with Cheese
  Sauce 487
Celery, Braised 492
Chicory au Beurre 489
Chicory Béchamel 490
Chicory with Cream 491
Corn Fritters 465
Corn on the Cob, Buttered 464
Corn with Almonds 466
Globe Artichokes, Cold 517
Globe Artichokes, Hot 518
Leeks Aurore 493
Leeks with White or
  Hollandaise Sauce 494
Marrow Provençale 512
Mushroom Fritters 496
Mushrooms
  Fried 498
  Grilled 499
  Stewed 497
  With Cream 495
Onion Rings, French-Fried 506
Onions
  Bacon-Stuffed 504
  Buttered Boiled 501
  Cheese and
    Parsley-Stuffed 505
  Fried 502
  Glazed & Sugared 503
  In Cheese Sauce 500
Parsnips, Baked 507
Peas
  Buttered 461
  French-Style 463
  Swiss, with Rice 462

Pease Pudding	460	Ratatouille	482	Potato Cheese & Onion	
Potatoes		Spinach with Cream Sauce	513	Pie	11
Anna	450	Swedes, Creamed	510	Potato Cheese & Parsley	
Casseroled	445	Tomatoes		Pie	11
Casseroled, with Cheese	447	Butter-Baked	514	Vegetable Curry with	
Casseroled, with Parsley	446	Fried, with Cream	516	Cheese	11
Creamed	440	Stewed	515		
Duchesse	442	Turnips, Creamed	511		
Jacket, with Butter	451				
Jacket, with Cream &				**YEAST RECIPES**	
Chives	452	**VEGETARIAN DISHES**		Babas	8
Lyonnaise	444			Bap, Scottish, or Flat Loaf	8
New Potatoes, Buttered &		Almond Rissoles	1119	Baps, Small, or Flat Loaves	8
Minted	459	Cashew Nut Rissoles	1121	Bath Buns	8
Roast, Buttered	458	Cheese & Noodle Hot Pot	1122	Bread	
Sauté	443	Cheese & Rice Hot Pot	1123	Brown, Quick	8
Snow (or Mousseline)	441	Cottage Cheese & Parsley		Currant	8
Stewed	448	Tart	1129	White	8
Stewed, with Cheese	449	Cottage Cheese & Walnut		Wholemeal	8
Stuffed Baked	453	Tart	1130	Bread Rolls, Crusty Brown	8
Stuffed with Bacon	454	Egg & Macaroni Curry	1126	Bread Rolls, White	8
Stuffed with Cheese &		Egg & Mushroom Savoury	1124	Brioches	8
Parsley	456	Gloucester Pie	1127	Cornish Splits	8
Stuffed with Ham &		Haricot Bean & Cheese		Doughnuts	8
Cheese	455	Curry	1117	Hot Cross Buns	8
Stuffed with Smoked		Hazelnut Rissoles	1120	Malt Loaves	8
Haddock	457	Marrow Cheese	1113	Milk Loaf	8
Peppers, Stuffed, with Rice		Nut & Macaroni Curry	1125	Muffins	8
& Cheese	509	Parsnip Cakes	1118	Poppy Seed Plaits	8
Peppers, Stuffed, with Rice		Parsnip Roast	1131	Savarin, Plain	8
& Meat	508	Peanut Mince	1128	Yorkshire Tea Cakes	8

PRINTED IN HOLLAND